Data-Driven **Security**

Analysis, Visualization and Dashboards

JAY JACOBS + BOB RUDIS

WILEY

Data-Driven Security: Analysis, Visualization and Dashboards

Published by
John Wiley & Sons, Inc.
10475 Crosspoint Boulevard
Indianapolis, IN 46256
www.wiley.com

Copyright © 2014 by John Wiley & Sons, Inc., Indianapolis, Indiana

Published by John Wiley & Sons, Inc., Indianapolis, Indiana

Published simultaneously in Canada

ISBN: 978-1-118-79372-5

ISBN: 978-1-118-79366-4 (ebk)

ISBN: 9789-1-118-79382-4 (ebk)

Manufactured in the United States of America

10 9 8 7 6 5 4 3 2 1

About the Authors

Jay Jacobs has over 15 years of experience within IT and information security with a focus on cryptography, risk, and data analysis. As a Senior Data Analyst on the Verizon RISK team, he is a co-author on their annual Data Breach Investigation Report and spends much of his time analyzing and visualizing security-related data. Jay is a co-founder of the Society of Information Risk Analysts and currently serves on the organization's board of directors. He is an active blogger, a frequent speaker, a co-host on the *Risk Science* podcast and was co-chair of the 2014 Metricon security metrics/analytics conference. Jay can be found on twitter as @jayjacobs. He holds a bachelor's degree in technology and management from Concordia University in Saint Paul, Minnesota, and a graduate certificate in Applied Statistics from Penn State.

Bob Rudis has over 20 years of experience using data to help defend global Fortune 100 companies. As Director of Enterprise Information Security & IT Risk Management at Liberty Mutual, he oversees their partnership with the regional, multi-sector Advanced Cyber Security Center on large scale security analytics initiatives. Bob is a serial tweeter (@hrbrmstr), avid blogger (rud.is), author, speaker, and regular contributor to the open source community (github.com/hrbrmstr). He currently serves on the board of directors for the Society of Information Risk Analysts (SIRA), is on the editorial board of the SANS Securing The Human program, and was co-chair of the 2014 Metricon security metrics/analytics conference. He holds a bachelor's degree in computer science from the University of Scranton.

About the Technical Editor

Russell Thomas is a Security Data Scientist at Zions Bancorporation and a PhD candidate in Computational Social Science at George Mason University. He has over 30 years of computer industry experience in technical, management, and consulting roles. Mr. Thomas is a long-time community member of Securitymetrics.org and a founding member of the Society of Information Risk Analysts (SIRA). He blogs at http://exploringpossibilityspace.blogspot.com/ and is @MrMeritology on Twitter.

Credits

Acknowledgments

While our names are on the cover, this book represents a good deal of work by a good number of (good) people. A huge thank you goes out to Russell Thomas, our technical editor. His meticulous attention to detail has not only made this book better, but it's also saved us from a few embarrassing mistakes. Thank you for those of you who have taken the time to prepare and share data for this project: Symantec, AlienVault, Stephen Patton, and David Severski. Thank you to Wade Baker for his contagious passion, Chris Porter for his contacts, and the RISK team at Verizon for their work and contribution of VERIS to the community. Thank you to the good folks at Wiley—especially Carol Long, Kevin Kent, and Kezia Endsley—who helped shape this work and kept us on track and motivated.

Thank you also to the many people who have contributed by responding to our emails, talking over ideas, and providing your feedback. Finally, thanks to the many vibrant and active communities around R, Python, data visualizations, and information security; hopefully, we can continue to blur the lines between those communities.

Jay Jacobs

First and foremost, I would like to thank my parents. My father gave me his passion for learning and the confidence to try everything. My mother gave me her unwavering support, even when I was busy discovering which paths not to take. Thank you for providing a good environment to grow and learn. I would also like to thank my wife, Ally. She is my best friend, loudest critic, and biggest fan. This work would not be possible without her love, support, and encouragement. And finally, I wish to thank my children for their patience: I'm ready for that game now.

Bob Rudis

This book would not have been possible without the love, support, and nigh-unending patience through many a lost weekend of my truly amazing wife, Mary, and our three still-at-home children, Victoria, Jarrod, and Ian.

Thank you to Alexandre Pinto, Thomas Nudd, and Bill Pelletier for well-timed (though you probably didn't know it) messages of encouragement and inspiration. A special thank you to the open source community and reproducible research and open data movements who are behind most of the tools and practices in this text. Thank you, as well, to Josh Corman who came up with the spiffy title for the tome.

And, a final thank you—in recipe form—to those that requested one with the book:

Pan Fried Gnocchi with Basil Pesto

- 2 C fresh Marseille basil
- 1/2 C fresh grated Romano cheese
- 1/2 C + 2 tbsp extra virgin olive oil
- 1/4 C pine nuts

- 4 garlic scapes

- Himalayan sea salt; cracked pepper

- 1 lb. gnocchi (fresh or pre-made/vacuum sealed; gnocchi should be slightly dried if fresh)

Pulse (add in order): nuts, scapes, basil, cheese. Stream in 1/2 cup of olive oil, pulsing and scraping as needed until creamy, adding salt and pepper to taste. Set aside.

Heat a heavy-bottomed pan over medium-high heat; add remaining olive oil. When hot, add gnocchi, but don't crowd the pan or go above one layer. Let brown and crisp on one side for 3–4 minutes then flip and do the same on the other side for 2–3 minutes. Remove gnocchi from pan, toss with pesto, drizzle with saba and serve. Makes enough for 3–4 people.

1

The Journey to Data-Driven Security

"It ain't so much the things we don't know that get us into trouble. It's the things we know that just ain't so."

Josh Billings, Humorist

This book isn't really about data analysis and visualization.

Yes, almost every section is focused on those topics, but being able to perform good data analysis and produce informative visualizations is just a means to an end. You never (okay, rarely) analyze data for the sheer joy of analyzing data. You analyze data and create visualizations to gain new perspectives, to find relationships you didn't know existed, or to simply discover new information. In short, you do data analysis and visualizations to learn, and that is what this book is about. You want to learn how your information systems are functioning, or more importantly how they are failing and what you can do to fix them.

The cyber world is just too large, has too many components, and has grown far too complex to simply rely on intuition. Only by augmenting and supporting your natural intuition with the science of data analysis will you be able to maintain and protect an ever-growing and increasingly complex infrastructure. We are not advocating replacing people with algorithms; we are advocating arming people with algorithms so that they can learn more and do a better job. The data contains information, and you can learn better with the information in the data than without it.

This book focuses on using real data—the types of data you have probably come across in your work. But rather than focus on huge discoveries in the data, this book focuses more on the process and less on the result. As a result of that decision, the use cases are intended to be exemplary and introductory rather than knock-your-socks-off cool. The goal here is to teach you new ways of looking at and learning from data. Therefore, the analysis is intended to be new ground in terms of technique, not necessarily in conclusion.

A Brief History of Learning from Data

One of the best ways of appreciating the power of statistical data analysis and visualization is to look back in history to a time when these methods were first put to use. The following cases provide a vivid picture of "before" versus "after," demonstrating the dramatic benefits of the then-new methods.

Nineteenth Century Data Analysis

Prior to the twentieth century, the use of data and statistics was still relatively undeveloped. Although great strides were made in the eighteenth century, much of the scientific research of the day used basic descriptive statistics as evidence for the validity of the hypothesis. The inability to draw clear conclusions from noisy data (and almost all real data is more or less noisy) made much of the scientific debates more about opinions of the data than the data itself. One such fierce debate[1] in the nineteenth century was between two medical professionals in which they debated (both with data) the cause of cholera, a bacterial infection that was often fatal.

The cholera outbreak in London in 1849 was especially brutal, claiming more than 14,000 lives in a single year. The cause of the illness was unknown at that time and two competing theories from two researchers emerged. Dr. William Farr, a well-respected and established epidemiologist, argued that cholera was caused by air pollution created by decomposing and unsanitary matter (officially called the *miasma* theory). Dr. John Snow, also a successful epidemiologist who was not as widely known as Farr, put forth the theory that cholera was spread by consuming water that was contaminated by a "special animal poison" (this was prior to the discovery of bacteria and germs). The two debated for years.

Farr published the "Report on the Mortality of Cholera in England 1848–49" in 1852, in which he included a table of data with eight possible explanatory variables collected from the 38 registration districts of London.

---

[1] And worthy of a bona fide Hollywood plot as well. See http://snowthemovie.com/

In the paper, Farr presented some relatively simple (by today's standards) statistics and established a relationship between the average elevation of the district and cholera deaths (lower areas had more deaths). Although there was also a relationship between cholera deaths and the source of drinking water (another one of the eight variables he gathered), he concluded that it was not nearly as significant as the elevation. Farr's theory had data and logic and was accepted by his peers. It was adopted as fact of the day.

Dr. John Snow was passionate and vocal about his disbelief in Farr's theory and relentless in proving his own. It's said he even collected data by going door to door during the cholera outbreak in the Soho district of 1854. It was from that outbreak and his collected data that he made his now famous map in Figure 1-1. The hand-drawn map of the Soho district included little tick marks at the addresses where cholera deaths were reported. Overlaying the location of water pumps where residents got their drinking water showed a rather obvious clustering around the water pump on Broad Street. With his map and his passionate pleas, the city did allow the pump handle to be removed and the epidemic in that region subsided. However, this wasn't enough to convince his critics. The cause of cholera was heavily debated even beyond John Snow's death in 1858.

The cholera debate included data and visualization techniques (long before computers), yet neither had been able to convince the opposition. The debate between Snow and Farr was re-examined in 2003 when statisticians in the UK evaluated the data Farr published in 1852 with modern methods. They found that the data Farr pointed to as proof of an airborne cause actually supported Snow's position. They concluded that if modern statistical methods were available to Farr, the data he collected would have changed his conclusion. The good news of course, is that these statistical methods are available today to you.

Twentieth Century Data Analysis

A few years before Farr and Snow debated cholera, an agricultural research station north of London at Rothamsted began conducting experiments on the effects of fertilizer on crop yield. They spent decades conducting experiments and collecting data on various aspects such as crop yield, soil measurements, and weather variables. Following a modern-day logging approach, they gathered the data and diligently stored it, but they were unable to extract the full value from it. In 1919 they hired a brilliant young statistician named Ronald Aylmer Fisher to pore through more than 70 years of data and help them understand it. Fisher quickly ran into a challenge with the data being confounded, and he found it difficult to isolate the effect of the fertilizer from other effects, such as weather or soil quality. This challenge would lead Fisher toward discoveries that would forever change not just the world of statistics, but almost every scientific field in the twentieth century.

What Fisher discovered (among many revolutionary contributions to statistics) is that if an experiment was designed correctly, the influence of various effects could not just be separated, but also could be measured and their influence calculated. With a properly designed experiment, he was able to isolate the effects of weather, soil quality, and other factors so he could compare the effects of various fertilizer mixtures. And this work was not limited to agriculture; the same techniques Fisher developed at Rothamsted are still used widely today in everything from medical trials to archaeology dig sites. Fisher's work, and the work of his peers, helped revolutionize science in the twentieth century. No longer could scientists simply collect and present their data as evidence of their claim as they had in the eighteenth century. They now had the tools to design robust experiments and the techniques to model how the variables affected their experiment and observations.

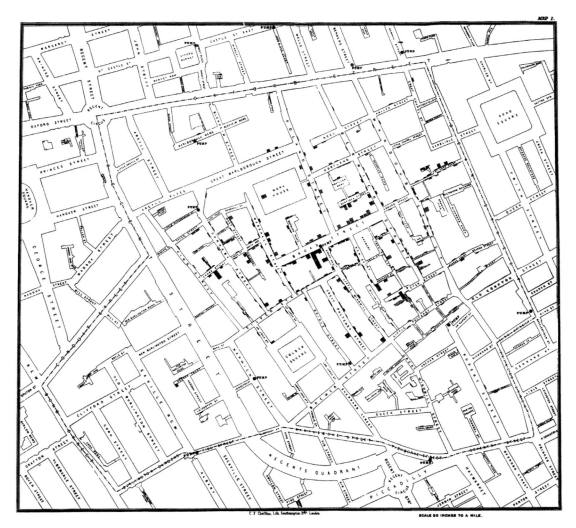

FIGURE 1-1 *Hand-drawn map of the areas affected by cholera*

At this point, the world of science included statistical models. Much of the statistical and science education focused on developing and testing these models and the assumptions behind them. Nearly every statistical problem started with the question—"What's the model?"—and ended with the model populated to allow description and even prediction using the model. This represented a huge leap forward and enabled research never before possible. If it weren't for computers, the world would probably still consider these techniques to be modern. But computers are ubiquitous and they have enabled a whole new approach to data analysis that was both impossible and unfathomable prior to their development.

Twenty-First Century Data Analysis

It's difficult to pull out any single person or event that captures where data analysis is today like Farr and Fisher captured the previous stages of data analysis. The first glimpse at what was on the horizon came from John Tukey, who wrote in 1962 that data analysis should be thought of as different from statistics (although analysis leveraged statistics). He stated that data analysis must draw from science more than mathematics (can you see the term "data science" in there?). Tukey was not only an accomplished statistician, having contributed numerous procedures and techniques to the field, but he was also an early proponent of visualization techniques for the purpose of describing and exploring the data. You will come back to some of Tukey's work later in this chapter.

Let's jump ahead to a paper written in 2001 by Leo Breiman, a statistician who focused on machine learning algorithms (which are discussed in Chapter 9). In the paper he describes a new culture of data analysis that does not focus on defining a data model *of nature* but instead derives an algorithmic model *from nature*. This new culture has evolved within computer science and engineering largely outside (or perhaps alongside) traditional statistics. New approaches are born from the practical problems created by the information age, which created large quantities of complex and noisy data. The revolutionary idea that Breiman outlined in this paper is that models should be judged on their predictive accuracy instead of validating the model with traditional statistical tests (which are not without value by the way).

At face value you may think of testing "predictive accuracy" by gathering data today and determining how it predicts the world of tomorrow, but that's not what the idea is about. The idea is about splitting the data of today into two data sets, using the first data set to generate (or "train") an algorithm and then validating (or "test") its predictive accuracy on the second data set. To increase the power of this approach, you can iterate through this process multiple times, splitting the data into various training and test sets, generating and validating as you go. This approach is not well suited to small data sets, but works remarkably well with modern data sets.

There are several main differences between data analysis in the modern information age and the agricultural fields of Rothamsted. First, there is a large difference in the available sample size. "Classic" statistical techniques were largely limited by what the computers of the day could handle ("computers" were the people hired to "compute" all day long). With generally smaller samples, generating a training and test was impractical. However, modern environments are recording hundreds of variables generated across thousands of systems. Large sample sizes are the norm, not the exception.

Second, for many environments and industries, a properly designed experiment is unlikely if not completely impossible. You cannot divide your networks into control and test groups, nor would you want to test the efficacy of a web application firewall by only protecting a portion of a critical application. One effect of these environmental limits is a much higher noise-to-signal ratio in the data. The techniques of machine learning (and the related field of data mining) have evolved with the challenges of modern data in mind.

Finally, knowledge of statistics is just one skill of many that contributes to successful data analysis in the twenty-first century. With that in mind, the next section spends some time looking at the various skills and attributes that support a good data analysis.

Gathering Data Analysis Skills

We know there is a natural allure to data science and everyone wants to achieve that sexy mystique surrounding security data analysis. Although we have focused on this concept of data analysis so far, it takes more than just analytic skills to create the mystique that everyone is seeking. You need to combine statistics and data analysis with visualization techniques, and then leverage the computing power and mix with a healthy dose of domain (information security) knowledge. All of this begins not with products or tools but with your own skills and abilities.

Before getting to the skills, there are a couple underlying personality traits we see in data analysts that we want to discuss: curiosity and communication. Working with data can at times be a bit like an archeological dig—spending hour after hour with small tools in the hope of uncovering even the tiniest of insights. So it is with data analysis—pearls of wisdom are nestled deep within data just waiting to be discovered and presented to an eagerly awaiting audience. It is only with that sense of wonder and curiosity that the hours spent cleaning and preparing data are not just tolerable, but somehow exciting and worth every moment. Because there is that moment, when you're able to turn a light on in an otherwise dark room, when you can describe some phenomenon or explain some pattern, when it all becomes worth it. That's what you're after. You are uncovering those tiny moments of enlightenment hidden in plain sight if you know where to look.

Once you turn that light on, you have to bring others into the room for the discovery; otherwise, you will have constructed a house that nobody lives in. It's not enough to point at your work and say, "see!" You have to step back and think of the best way to communicate your discovery. The complexity present in the systems and the analysis makes it difficult to convey the results in a way that everyone will understand what you have discovered. Often times it takes a combination of words, numbers, and pictures to communicate the data's insights. Even then, some people will take away nothing, and others will take away too much. But there is still a need to condense this complexity into a paragraph, table, or graphic.

Although we could spend an entire book creating an exhaustive list of skills needed to be a good security data scientist, this chapter covers the following skills/domains that a data scientist will benefit from knowing within information security:

- **Domain expertise**—Setting and maintaining a purpose to the analysis
- **Data management**—Being able to prepare, store, and maintain data
- **Programming**—The glue that connects data to analysis
- **Statistics**—To learn from the data
- **Visualization**—Communicating the results effectively

It might be easy to label any one of these skills as the most important, but in reality, the whole is greater than the sum of its parts. Each of these contributes a significant and important piece to the workings of security data science.

Domain Expertise

The fact that a data scientist needs domain expertise should go without saying and it may seem obvious, but data analysis is only meaningful when performed with a higher purpose in mind. It's your experience with information security that will guide the direction of the analysis, provide context to the data, and help apply meaning to the results. In other words, domain expertise is beneficial in the beginning, middle, and end of all your data analysis efforts.

And Why Expertise Shouldn't Get in the Way

We are probably preaching to the choir here. If you are reading this book, it is probably safe to assume that you have domain expertise and see value in moving toward a data-driven approach in information security. Therefore, rather than spend the effort discussing the benefits of domain expertise in data analysis, this section covers some objections you might encounter as other domain experts (or skeptical leadership) are brought into the data analysis effort.

People are smarter than models. There are those who hold the opinion that people will always outperform algorithms (or statistics, or models) and there is some truth to this. Teaching a machine, for example, to catch a fly ball is remarkably challenging. As Kahneman and Klein point out in their 2009 paper titled *Conditions for Intuitive Expertise: a Failure to Disagree,* however, determining when people will outperform algorithms is heavily dependent on the environment of the task. If the environment is complex and feedback is delayed or ambiguous, algorithms will generally and relatively consistently outperform human judgment. So, the question then becomes, how complex is the security of the information systems and how clear is the feedback? When you make a change or add a security control, how much feedback do you receive on how well it is actually protecting the information asset?

The result is that information security occurs in a very complex environment, but that doesn't mean you put all your eggs in the algorithm basket. What it does mean is that you should have some healthy skepticism about any approach that relies purely on human judgment, and you should seek ways to augment and support that expertise. That's not to compare algorithms to human judgment. It's not wise to set up an either-or choice. You do, however, want to compare human judgment combined with algorithms and data analysis against human judgment alone. You do not want to remove the human element, but you should be skeptical of unsupported opinion. In a complex environment, it is the combination of human intuition and data analysis that will produce the best results and create the best opportunity for learning and securing the infrastructure.

It's just lying with statistics. This expresses a general distrust in statistics and data analysis, which are often abused and misused (and in some cases flat out made up) for the sake of serving some ulterior motive. In a way, this distrust is grounded in a collective knowledge of just how easy it is to social-engineer people. However, you are in a different situation since your motive is to learn from the data. You are sitting on mounds of data that hold information and patterns just waiting to be discovered. Not leveraging data analysis because statistics are misused is like not driving a car because they are sometimes used as get-away vehicles. You need to be comfortable with adding statistics to your information security toolkit.

This is not to say that data analysis is infallible. There may be times when the analysis provides the wrong answer, perhaps through poor data collection, under-trained analysts, a mistake in the process, or simply using Excel (couldn't resist). But what you should see is simply fewer mistakes when you apply the rigor of data analysis combined with your expertise. Again, the key is combining data analysis and expertise.

This ain't rocket science. This statement has two insinuations. First, it says that whatever the problem is you're trying to solve, you should be able to solve it with common sense. But this concern goes back to the first point, which is thinking that people outperform algorithms consistently and a group of people around a conference table looking at a complex environment can solve the (complex) problem without the need for data analysis. But as we discussed, you should pull a chair up to the conference table for the data analysis because you are generally better off with it than without it.

The second implication of the statement is that data analysis is too complicated and will cost too much (in time, money, or resources). This view is simply misinformed and the objection is more likely to be a concern about an uncomfortable change in practices than a concern about time spent with data analysis. Many of the tools are open source (if the organization is averse to open source, there are plenty of commercial solutions out there as well) and the only real commitment is in the time to learn some of the basic techniques and methods in this book. The actual analysis itself can be fairly quick, and with the right combination of tools and experience, it can be done in real time.

We don't have the data. An alternate form of this objection is saying that we don't have actuarial-quality data (which is more prevalent when you start talking about risk analysis). Data detractors argue that anything less than perfect data is worthless and prevents you from creating well-designed experiments. This statement is untrue and quite harmful. If you were to wait around for perfect data, you would always be waiting and many learning opportunities would be missed. More importantly and to the heart of this objection, you don't *need* perfect data. You just need methods to learn from the messy data you do have. As Douglas Hubbard wrote in 2010 in his book *How to Measure Anything*, "The fact is that we often have more data than we think, we need less data than we think, and getting more data through observation is simpler than we think." So, generally speaking, data for security analysis absolutely exists; often times it is just waiting to be collected. You can, with a few alterations, collect and accurately analyze even sketchy data. Modern data analysis methods have evolved to work with the noisy, incomplete, and imperfect data you have.

But we will fall off the edge of the world. There is one last point to consider and it's not so much an objection to data analysis, but an obstacle in data analysis. When you are seen as a domain expert, you are expected to provide answers with confidence. The conflict arises when confidence is confused with certainty. Data analysis requires just enough self-awareness and humility to create space for doubt in the things you think you know. Even though you may confidently state that passwords should be so many characters long with a certain amount of complexity, the reality is you just don't know where the balance is between usability and security. Confidence needs to be balanced with humility and the ability to update your beliefs based on new evidence. This obstacle in data analysis is not just limited to the primary analyst. Other domain experts involved in the analysis will have to come face to face with their own humility. Not everyone will want to hear that his or her world isn't flat.

Programming Skills

As much as we'd like to portray data science as a glamorous pursuit of truth and knowledge, as we've said, it can get a little messy. Okay, that's an understatement. Working with data is a great deal more uncertain and unkempt than people think and, unfortunately, the mess usually appears early on when you're attempting to collect and prepare the data. This is something that many classes in statistics never prepare their students for. Professors hand out rather nice and neat data sets ready to be imported into the analysis tool *du jour*. Once you leave the comfort of the classroom, you quickly realize that the world is a disorganized and chaotic place and data (and its subsequent analyses) are a reflection of that fact.

This is a cold, hard lesson in data science: Data comes to you in a wide range of formats, states, and quality. It may be embedded in unstructured or semi-structured log files. It may need to be scraped from a website. Or, in extreme cases, data may come in an overly complex and thoroughly frustrating format known as XML. Somehow, you must find a way to collect, coax, combine, and massage what you're given into a format that supports further analysis. Although this could be done with a lot of patience, a text editor, and judicious use of summer interns, the ability to whip together a script to do the work will provide more functionality, flexibility, and efficiency in the long run. Learning even basic programming skills opens up a whole range of possibilities when you're working with data. It frees you to accept multiple forms of data and manipulate it into whatever formats work best with the analysis software you have. Although there is certainly a large collection of handy data conversion tools available, they cannot anticipate or handle everything you will come across. To be truly effective while working with data, you need to adapt to the data in your world, not vice versa.

AES-256-Bit Keys Are Twice as Good as AES-128, Right?

One natural assumption about AES-256-bit keys is that because they are twice as long as AES-128-bit keys, they are twice as secure. We've been around information security people when they force a project to use 256-bit keys because they are "twice as good." Well, let's look into the math. First, you are talking about bits here, and although 256 bits is twice as many bits as 128, 256-bit keys actually have 2^{128} *times* more keys. Break out your slide rules and work through an exercise to try to answer a simple question: If you had access to the world's fastest super-computer, how many 128-bit keys could you crack?

The world's fastest super computer (at the time of this writing) is the ***Tianhe-2*** in China, which does around 34 petaflops (34×10^{15} floating point operations) per second. If you assume it takes one operation to generate a key and one operation to test it (this is an absurd and conservative assumption), you can test an amazing 17×10^{15} keys per second. But a 128-bit key has 3.4×10^{38} possibilities, which means after a full year of cracking 128-bit keys, you will have exhausted 1.6×10^{-13} percent of the key space. Even if you run the super-computer for 1,000 years, you will only have searched 0.0000000000016 percent of all the possible keys (and spent a fortune on electricity).

To put this simply, ***the probability of brute-force cracking a 128-bit key is already so infinitesimally small that you could easily round off that probability to zero***. But let's be professional here and say, "Moving from a 128-bit key to a 256 is moving the probability from really-super-duper-infinitesimally-small to really-super-duper-infinitesimally-small x 2^{128}."

Any modern language will support basic data manipulation tasks, but scripting languages such as Python and R appear to be used slightly more often in data analysis than their compiled counterparts (Java and C). However, the programming language is somewhat irrelevant. The end results (and a happy analyst) are more important than picking any "best" language. Whatever gets the job done with the least amount of effort is the best language to use. We generally flip between Python (pandas) and R for cleaning and converting data (or perhaps some Perl if we're feeling nostalgic) and then R or pandas for the analysis and visualization. Learning web-centric languages like HTML, CSS, and JavaScript will help create interactive visualizations for the web, as you'll see in Chapter 11, but web languages are not typically involved in the preparation and analysis of data.

There is a tool worth mentioning in this section—the "gateway tool" between a text editor and programming—known as the ***spreadsheet*** (such as Microsoft Excel or OpenOffice Calc). Spreadsheets allow non-programmers to do some amazing things and get some quick and accessible results. Although spreadsheets have their own sets of challenges and drawbacks, they also have some benefits. If the data is not too large or complex and the task is not deciding the future of the world economy (see the following sidebar), Excel may be the best tool for the job. We strongly suggest seeing Excel as a temporary solution. It does well at quick one-shot tasks. But if you have a repeating analytic task or model that is used repeatedly, it's best to move to some type of structured programming language.

As a cleaning tool, spreadsheets seem like a very good solution at first (especially for those who have developed some skill with them). But spreadsheets are event-driven, meaning they work through clicking, typing, and dragging. If you want to apply a conversion to a row of data, you have to click to select the row and apply a conversion. This works for small data sets or quick tasks, but trust us, you will (more often than you think) have to go back to the source data and re-clean it. Another day of log files needs to be processed, or you realize you should have pulled another relationship from the source data, or (gasp) you identify an error in the cleaning process. Something, somewhere, and probably more than once, will cause you to go back to the source and repeat the data cleaning and conversion. Leveraging a spreadsheet means a lot more clicking. Writing a script, on the other hand, enables an easy, flexible, and consistent execution of the cleaning process each time it runs.

The Limits of Spreadsheets

On January 16th, 2013, J.P. Morgan issued a report to shareholders titled "Report of JPMorgan Chase & Co. Management Task Force Regarding 2012 CIO Losses" (full citation in Appendix B) in which they investigate the loss of $6 billion in trades. They perform a detailed examination of the breakdown and describe the spreadsheet as a contributory factor. "During the review process, additional operational issues became apparent. For example, the model operated through a series of Excel spreadsheets, which had to be completed manually, by a process of copying and pasting data from one spread-sheet to another." They uncovered a huge challenge with spreadsheets, which is the consistency and integrity of the computations made in the data. "Data were uploaded manually without suf-ficient quality control. Spreadsheet-based calculations were conducted with insufficient controls and frequent formula and code changes were made." They continue on and label the Excel-based model as "error prone" and "not easily scalable." As with any complex system, catastrophe requires multiple failures.[2] We cannot point to their use of an "error-prone" spreadsheet as the primary cause, but certainly it appears to have contributed in the loss of $6 billion.

---

[2] See Richard Cook's "How Complex Systems Fail" for a brief and wonderful discussion of this topic:
`http://www.ctlab.org/documents/How%20Complex%20Systems%20Fail.pdf`

After the data is ready for analysis, you can continue to benefit from understanding how to program. Many of the languages mentioned here have robust data analysis features built into (or onto) them. For example, statisticians developed the R language specifically for the purpose of performing data analysis. Python—with the addition of packages like NumPy, SciPy, and pandas—offers a rich and comparable data analysis environment. But, preparing and analyzing the data is not enough. You also need to communicate your results, and one of the most effective methods for that is data visualization (covered in several chapters of this book). Again, Excel can produce graphics. With judicial modification of the default settings, you can get good visualization with Excel. However, in our opinion, flexibility and detail in data visualization are best achieved through programming. Both Python and R have some feature-rich packages for generating and exporting data visualization. In many cases, however, you can combine all these steps and functions in the same script. You can write one script to grab the source data, manipulate/clean it, run the analysis on it, and then visualize the results.

Data Management

If there is one skill you can hold off on learning, it's data management, but you can put it off only for a while. Within information security (as well as most other disciplines), your data can quickly multiply. If you don't learn to manage it, the strain of ever-expanding data will take its toll on efficiency and effectiveness. As mentioned, you can leverage spreadsheets for the simple analyses. You will quickly outgrow that stage and should be resolved to expanding your repertoire to programming languages and simple formats like comma-separated value (CSV) files. At this point, you may see some benefits by moving your data into a database, but it still may not be necessary.

As the data repository grows, you reach a tipping point, either through the complexity of the data or the volume of data. Moving to a more robust data management solution becomes inevitable. There is a misconception that the large relational databases of yesteryear are reserved for the biggest projects, and that is not a helpful mindset. Many of the database systems discussed in Chapter 8 can be installed on a desktop and make the analysis more efficient and scalable. Once your data management skills become more natural, such skill can benefit even the smallest projects. We've installed a local database and imported the data even for some smaller one-time projects.

When discussing data management skills, we naturally focus on databases. You want to have enough knowledge to install a relational or NoSQL database to dump the data in and leverage it for analysis. However, data management is more than databases. Data management is also about managing the quality and integrity of the data. You want to be sure the data you are working with isn't inadvertently modified or corrupted. It doesn't hurt to have some checks that keep an eye on data quality and integrity, especially over long-term data analysis efforts (metrics). It's like the concept of unit tests in software development where the smallest piece of testable code in an application is isolated from the larger body of code and checked to determine whether it behaves exactly as expected. You may want to automate some data integrity checking after any new import or conversion, especially when the data analysis has sufficient efficacy to be performed regularly and used as a metric or control.

Finally, we work in information security, and we'd be negligent if we didn't talk about the security of the data for a bit here. Take a step back for some context first. There seems to be a pattern repeating: Some passionate need drives a handful of geniuses to work their tails off to produce an elegant solution, but the security of their system is not their primary concern; meeting the functional need is. As an example, when the UNIX platform was first developed it was intended to be a shared (but closed) platform for multiple users who use the platform for programs they would write. As a result, most of the authentication and permissions were constructed to protect the system from unintentional errors in their programs, and not from malicious users.[3] The point here is that "young" technology typically places an emphasis on functionality over security.

With the fast-paced and passionate push of the current data revolution, we are definitely seeing more emphasis on functionality and less on security. New data management platforms such as Hadoop and NoSQL environments were designed to solve a data problem and were not designed (initially) with many of the security policies or compliance requirements of most enterprise networks (though they are quickly learning). The result is a distributed computing platform with some difficult security challenges. The authentication and security features are far better than the early days of UNIX; they typically do not compare to the security and features of the more established relational databases. We won't focus too much on this point, but whatever data management platform is chosen, don't assume the security is built in.

---

[3] For an example of the focus on functionality and preventing error over stopping misuse, early authentication systems would store the user passwords in a clear text file. See Morris and Thompson, 1979 (full reference in Appendix B) for a discussion.

Statistics

Perhaps we are a little biased here, but picking up some statistics skills will improve almost every aspect of your life. Not only will it change the way to see and learn from the world around you, but it will also make you more interesting and probably even a bit more attractive to those around you. Seriously, though, statistics (we are discussing it as a single skill here) is a very broad topic and quite a deep well to drink from. We use the term to describe the varied collection of techniques and methods that have evolved (and continue to evolve) to attempt to learn from data. These skills include the classic statistical approaches as well as newer techniques like data mining and machine learning. Luckily, you can learn from the successes and mistakes of the generations of rather brilliant people who have worked with data very similar to ours, even if their calculations were performed with pencil and paper versus silicon circuits. Regardless of your personal belief in the utility of statistics and data analysis, when it comes to information security, there is a vast amount of evidence showing its significant influence and benefit to almost every other field of science.

Aside from the obvious "learning from data" approach, there are a few perhaps more subtle reasons to focus on improving your statistics skills:

- **Even though data never lies, it is far too easy to be tricked by it**—As heuristic beings, we are capable of pulling out patterns and meaning from the world around us. The ability to see subtle connections and patterns is usually helpful, and people use that skill on a daily basis. However, that skill can also mislead you, and you may think you see patterns and connections when none exist. A good understanding of statistics can raise awareness of this, and its tactics can help minimize incorrect conclusions.

- **Even though we just said that data never lies, the way it's generated and collected can create deceptive conclusions**—Consider that asking for the opinions of those around us may mistakenly confirm our own opinions, because we naturally surround ourselves with like-minded people. Data itself may not be deceptive, but it's quite easy to think the data means something it does not, as in the story of the 1936 election polling (see the following sidebar).

Statistics is not just a collection of tools; it is a collection of toolboxes each with their own set of tools. You can begin with descriptive statistics, which attempt to simplify the data into numbers that describe aspects of the data. For example, you can calculate the center of the data by calculating the mean, mode, or median; you can describe how spread out the data is with the standard deviation; you can explain the symmetry of the data with skew; and you can describe the width of peak with the kurtosis. However, any time you simplify the data, you lose some level of detail and this is where visualization can serve you well. With visualizations, you create a single representation, or message, that can contain and communicate every data point, without simplification. Think of this type of visualization as being a "descriptive visualization" since it is doing nothing more than simply describing the data to its viewers.

Aside from the challenge of oversimplifying, descriptive statistics is also limited to describing only the data that you collect. It is not correct to simply scan a few systems, calculate the mean number of vulnerabilities, and announce that the statistic describes all the systems in the environment. Inferential statistics helps you go beyond just describing the observations and enables you to make statements about a larger population given a smaller representative sample from that population. The key word there is "representative." Statistics teaches you about the "design of experiments" (thanks to Fisher and his peers) and this will help you gather data so that you reduce the probability of being misled by it. You want to have confidence that the samples you collect are representative of the whole. That lesson has been learned many times in the past by a good number of people.

When Data Deceives

The magazine *Literary Digest* ran a large public opinion poll in an attempt to predict the 1936 presidential race. They gathered names from a variety of sources, including the telephone directory, club memberships, and magazine subscriptions. They ended up with more than 2 million responses and predicted a clear winner: Alfred Landon (for those not up on their American history, the Democratic candidate, Theodore Roosevelt, won that election, carrying 46 states). The problem with the *Literary Digest* poll began long before a single response was collected or counted. Their trouble began with where they went looking for the data. Remember the year was 1936 and the great depression in the United States hadn't let up yet. Yet, they polled people with phones, club memberships, and magazine subscriptions. They systematically polled the middle and upper class, which generally leaned toward Landon, and arrived at an answer that was mathematically correct and yet completely wrong.

The data did not lie. If they wanted to know which presidential candidate would get the most votes among Americans with a phone, club membership, or magazine subscription, the data told an accurate story. However, they weren't looking for that story. They wanted to know about all registered voters in the United States, but through their selection of sources they introduced bias into their sample and drew meaning from the data that simply did not exist.

The fact that they had an unprecedented 2 million responses did not help improve the accuracy of their poll. Gathering more data with the same systemic flaw just generates a larger sample with the bias. To drive that point home, in the same 1936 election, a young man named George Gallup had gathered a relatively small sample of just 50,000 voters but he applied a much more representative sampling method and correctly predicted Franklin Roosevelt as the winner of the 1936 elections. The *Literary Digest* closed its doors a few years later, but Gallup, Inc. is now an international organization, still conducting surveys and gathering data.

You should always approach statistics with a healthy degree of respect and humility. As you slide more and more into the depths of applied mathematics, you'll realize how easy it is to find meaning where none exists (technically called a *type I error*). But what is more important to understand here is that this error can occur with or without data. Even before you fill a single cell in an Excel spreadsheet, you can make this mistake. The best tools in the toolbox are designed to limit the chance of these types of errors, but statistics alone is not enough. You need the combination of experience and data to decrease the chance of being misled. Errors can and will occur even with this combination, but you can reduce the frequency of these errors by applying the rigor and methods within statistics. Such rigor will place you in a much better position to learn from mistakes when they do occur.

Having built up the application of statistics on a pedestal, we should point out that you can learn a lot from data without advanced statistical techniques. Recall the "descriptive visualization" mentioned previously. Take some time to look around at many of visualizations out there; they are generally not built from statistical models, but describe some set of data and show the relationships therein. Snow's map of the areas around the water pump on Broad Street in Figure 1-1 did not involve logistic regression or machine learning; this map was just a visual description of the relationship between address and deaths. There is no doubt that you can improve your ability to secure your information assets with simple statistical methods and descriptive visualizations. All it takes is the patience to ask a question, gather the evidence, make sense of it, and communicate it to others.

Visualization (a.k.a. Communication)

The final skill is *visualization*, but really it is about communication. There are multiple ways to classify the types of visualizations out there, but for this discussion we want to talk about two general types of visualization, which are separated by who you want to read and interpret the visualization. The distinction we make here is quite simple: 1) visualizing for ourselves, or 2) everyone else.

For example, Figure 1-2 shows four common plots, which are automatically generated by R's `lm()` function (for linear regression) and they are used to diagnose the fit of a linear regression model (which you'll run in Chapter 5). Let's face it; these plots are quite ugly and confusing unless you've learned how to read them. We would not include these in our next presentation to the Board of Directors. This type of visualization serves to provide information to the analyst while working with the data, or in this case about a data model.

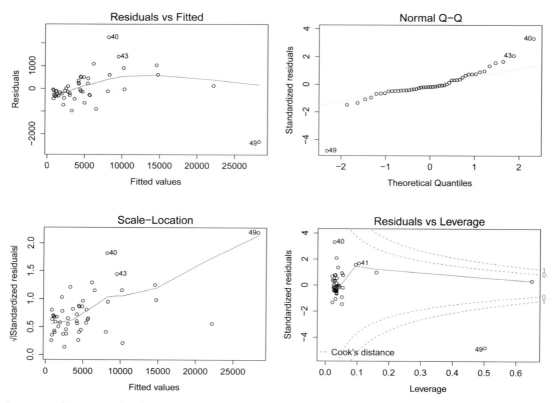

FIGURE 1-2 *Diagnostic plots for regression model of bot infections*

These graphs are generated as a way to understand certain relationships and attributes of the model. They communicate from the data to the analyst and are used to visually inspect for anomalies, strength of relationships, or other aspects of the data for the purpose of understanding it better. Very little effort is spent on making these attractive or presentable since they are part of the analysis, not the result.

The other type of visualization exists to communicate from the analyst to others and serves to explain the story (or the lack of a story) the analyst uncovered in the data. These are typically intended to be attractive and carry a clear message, as it is a communication tool for non-analysts. Figure 1-3 (which you'll learn to generate in Chapter 5) is derived from the same data as Figure 1-2 but is intended for a completely different audience. Therefore, it is cleaner and you can pull a message for each of the 48 continental states from this one picture.

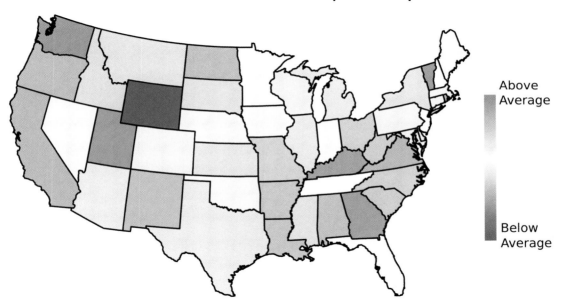

FIGURE 1-3 *Visualization for communicating density of ZeroAccess bot infections*

Combining the Skills

You need some combination of skills covered in this chapter in order to make the analysis run smoother and improve what you can learn from the data. Although we may have portrayed these skills as belonging to a single person, that is not required. As the data grow and the demands for analysis become more embedded into the culture, spreading the load among multiple individuals will help lighten the load. Moreover, if you are just beginning to build your security data science team, you may be setting yourself up for an impossible task if you try to find even one individual with all these skills. Take the time to talk through each of these points with candidates to ensure there is at least some element of each of the skills discussed here.

Centering on a Question

While we consider data analysis to be quite fun, it is never performed for its own sake. Data analysis is always performed within a larger context and understanding that context is the key to successful data analysis. Losing sight of that context is like running a race without paying attention to where the finish line is. You want to have a good concept of what you're trying to learn from the data. Therefore, every good data analysis project begins by setting a goal and creating one or more *research questions*. Perhaps you have come across a visualization or research and thought, "Yeah, but so what?" That reaction is probably caused by the lack of a well-prepared research question in the analysis. Remember, the purpose of data analysis is to learn from the environment; learning can be done with or without data (with varying degrees of success). Creating and following a good research question is a component of *good learning*, not just of good data analysis. Without a well-formed question guiding the analysis, you may waste time and energy seeking convenient answers in the data, or worse, *you may end up answering a question that nobody was asking in the first place*.

For example, Figure 1-4 shows the amount and categories of spam blocked at an organization during a given month. Thanks to the logs generated by an email filtering system, it is entirely possible to collect and show this information. However, the questions this data answers (and whatever subsequent actions it may drive) are of little interest to the typical organization. It's hard to imagine someone looking at this graphic and thinking, "Let's understand why travel spam was up in December." Outcomes like those shown in Figure 1-4 are the result of poor question selection or skipping a question altogether—data analysis for the sake of analyzing data, which does not help to inform anyone about the environment in any meaningful way.

A good research question around spam might be, "How much time do employees spend on spam that is not blocked by the spam filter?" Just counting how much spam is blocked has little value since it will have no contextual meaning (nobody can internalize the effective difference between 1,000 and 5,000 spam emails). What you want to know is the impact spam has on employee productivity. Although "productivity" may be a challenge to measure directly, you can flip that around and just assume it is impossible to be productive when employees are reading and deleting spam. Therefore, what you really want to measure is the time employees spend dealing with unfiltered spam.

Now that you've framed the question like this, it's clear that you can't look to the spam filter logs to answer this spam-related question. You really don't care that thousands of emails were blocked at the perimeter or even what proportion of spam is blocked. With a research question in hand, you now know to collect a measurement of employee time. Perhaps you can look for logs from the email clients of events when users select the "mark as spam" option. Or perhaps, it's important enough to warrant running a short survey in which you select a sample of users and ask them to record the amount of spam and time spent going through it for some limited period of time. Either way, the context and purpose of the analysis is being set by the research question, not by the availability of data.

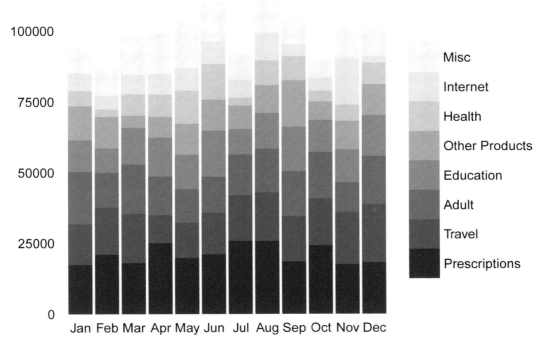

FIGURE 1-4 *Amount of spam by category—the result of a poor research question*

Creating a Good Research Question

Creating a good research question is relatively straightforward but requires a bit of practice, critical thinking, and discipline. Most research questions will serve as pivot points for a decision or action (or inaction).
Knowing the context of the result may also help determine what to collect. Going back to the spam example,
maybe you learn there is some tolerance for wasted time. If so, maybe you don't need to how much time is
wasted, but just whether the time spent dealing with spam is simply above or below that tolerance. Planning
the analysis with that information could change how data is sought or simplify data storage and analysis.

You usually begin with some topic already in mind. Perhaps you are measuring the possible benefit from
a technical change or you are trying to protect a specific asset or data type, or simply trying to increase your
visibility into a network segment. Even if you just have a general sense of direction, you can begin by coming
up with a series of questions or things you'd like to know about it. Once you have a good list of questions,
you can whittle those down to one or just a few related questions. Now the fun really begins—you have
to make those questions objective.

Consider this simple example. The Human Resources department submits a proposal to post a searchable lunch menu from the company's cafeteria to the Internet. Although this may raise all sorts of questions around controls, processes, and procedures, suppose the core security-oriented decision of the proposal is limited to either allowing authentication with the corporate username and password, or investing in a more expensive two-factor authentication mechanism. You may brainstorm a question like "How much risk does single factor authentication represent?" Or perhaps, "How effective is two-factor authentication?" These types of questions are really nice and squishy for the initial phase of forming a research question, but not well suited to serious analysis. You would struggle to collect evidence of "risk" or "effectiveness" in these questions. So, you must transform them to be more specific and measurable as an approach to inform the decisions or actions in context. Perhaps you start by asking how many services require single-factor versus dual-factor authentication. You might also like to know how many of those services have been attacked, and with what success, and so on. Perhaps you have access to a honey pot and can research and create a profile of Internet-based brute force attempts. Perhaps you can look at the corporate instance of Microsoft Outlook Web Access and create a profile of authentication-based attacks on that asset. These are all good questions that are very answerable with data analysis. They can produce outcomes that can help support a decision.

Exploratory Data Analysis

Now that we've explained how a good data analysis should begin, we want to talk about how things will generally occur in the real world. It'd be great to start each day with a hot, caffeinated beverage, a clear research question, and a bucket of clean data, but in reality you'll usually have to settle for just the hot, caffeinated beverage. Often times, you do start off with data and a vague question like, "Is there anything useful in this data?" This brings us back to John Tukey (remember him from earlier in this chapter?). He pioneered a process he called *exploratory data analysis*, or EDA. It's the process of walking around barefoot in the data, perhaps even rolling around a bit in it. You do this to learn about the variables in the data, their significance, and their relationships to other variables. Tukey developed a whole range of techniques to increase your visibility into and understanding of the data, including the elegantly simple *stem and leaf plot*, the *five-number summary*, and the helpful *box plot* diagram. Each of these techniques is explained or used later in this book.

Once you get comfortable with the data, you'll naturally start to ask some question of it. However, and this is important, you always want to circle back and form a proper research question. As Tukey said in his 1977 book, "Exploratory data analysis can never be the whole story." He refers to EDA as the foundation stone and the first step in data analysis. He also said that, "Exploratory data analysis is an attitude, a state of flexibility, a willingness to look for those things that we believe are not there, as well as those we believe to be there." With that in mind, most of the use cases in this book use exploratory analysis. We will take an iterative approach, and you'll learn as you walk around in the data. In the end though, you need to remember that data analysis is performed to find an answer to a question that's worthy of asking.

Summary

The cyber world is just too large, has too many components, and has grown far too complex to simply rely on intuition. Generations of people before us have paved the way; and with a mixture of domain expertise, programing experience and statistics combined with data management and visualization skills, we can improve on our ability to learn from this complex environment through the data it produces.

In the next chapter we will walk you through setting up your data analysis environment, and then proceed into Chapter 3, where you will be guided through a gentle introduction to data analysis techniques.

Recommended Reading

The following are some recommended readings that can further your understanding on some of the topics we touch on in this chapter. For full information on these recommendations and for the sources we cite in the chapter, please see Appendix B.

"Conditions for Intuitive Expertise: A Failure to Disagree" by Daniel Kahneman and Gary Klein—This dense article covers a lot of ground but gets at the heart of when and why you should look for help in complex environments and when your expertise is enough. The references in this paper also provide a good jumping point to answer questions about how people learn.

"How Complex Systems Fail" by Richard Cook—If you are wondering whether or not you are dealing with complexity, this short and brilliant paper looks at qualities of complex systems and how they fail.

Naked Statistics: Stripping the Dread from Data **by Charles Wheelan**—This is a great introductory book to statistical concepts and approaches, written in an easy-to-consume style and written so that the math is not required (but it is included).

2

Building Your Analytics Toolbox: A Primer on Using R and Python for Security Analysis

"If you add a little to a little and do this often, soon the little will become great."

Hesiod

Before you jump right into the various use cases in the book, it's important to ensure you at least have a basic familiarity with the two most prominent languages featured in nearly all of the scenarios: Python (`www.python.org/`) and R (`www.r-project.org/`). Although there are an abundance of tools available for data analysis, we feel these two provide virtually all the features necessary to help you go from data to discovery with the least amount impedance.

A sub-theme throughout the book, and the distilled process at the heart of security data science, is *idea*, *exploration*, *trial* (and *error*) and *iteration*. It is ineffective at best to attempt to shoehorn this process into the *edit/compile/run* workflow found in most traditional languages and development environments. The acts of performing data analyses and creating informative visualizations are highly interactive and iterative endeavors. Despite all of their positive features, even standalone Python and R do not truly enable rich, dynamic interaction with code and data. However, when they are coupled with IPython (`http://ipython.org/`) and RStudio (`www.rstudio.com/`), respectively, they are transformed into powerful exploration tools, enabling rapid development and testing of everything from gnarly data munging to generating sophisticated visualizations.

This chapter provides pointers to installation resources for each tool, introduces core features of each language and development environment, and explains the structure of the examples you will find in the remaining chapters of the book. Each chapter will have the following "setup" code (Listing 2-0) at the beginning to ensure you have the proper environment in place to run the code examples. There are example scripts at the end of this chapter that will help you create structured directories if you are typing as you go.

LISTING 2-0

```
# This is for the R code in the chapter
# set working directory to chapter location
# (change for where you set up files in ch 2)
setwd("~/book/ch02")
# This is for the Python code in the chapter
# loads the necessary Python library for chdir
import os
# set working directory to chapter location
os.chdir(os.path.expanduser("~") + "/book/ch02")
```

Why Python? Why R? And Why Both?

A discussion of which programming language is better than another for a certain set of tasks often turns (quickly) into a religious war of words that rarely wins converts and never becomes fully resolved. As a security data scientist, you will find that you do not have the luxury of language bias. There will be times when one language shines in one area while a different one shines in another, and you need the skills of a diplomat to bring them both together to solve real problems.

We've honed in on both R/RStudio and Python/IPython/pandas in this book, as they are the two leading data analysis languages/environments with broad similarities but also with unique elements that make them work well for some tasks and not others. As you read about the rationale behind each choice and as you become proficient in one or both environments, do not lull yourself into a sense of complacency.

For readers with an existing programming background, getting up to speed with Python should be pretty straightforward and you can expect to be fairly proficient within 3–6 months, especially if you convert some of your existing scripts over to it as a learning exercise. Your code may not be "pythonic" (that is, utilizing the features, capabilities, and the syntax of the language in the most effective way), but you will be able to "get useful stuff done." For those who are new to statistical languages, becoming proficient in R may pose more of a challenge. Statisticians created R, and that lineage becomes fairly obvious as you delve into the language. If you can commit to suffering through R syntax and package nuances, plus commit to transitioning some of your existing Excel workflows into R, you too should be able to hang with the cool kids on the `#rstats` Twitter stream in 3–6 months.

Note

A hallmark of a good data scientist is adaptability and you should be continually scouring the digital landscape for emerging tools that will help you solve problems. We introduce you to some of these upstarts in Appendix A.

Why Python?

Guido van Rossum created the Python programming language in December of 1989 to solve a problem. He and his colleagues needed a common way to orchestrate system administration tasks that could take advantage of specific features in the operating systems they were using at that time. Although there were existing interpreted, administrator-friendly tools and languages available, none were designed (from Guido van Rossum's point of view) with either the flexibility or extensibility features baked into the design principles of Python.

Python's flexibility and extensibility (and the fact that it was free as in both "speech" and "beer") were especially appealing to the scientific, academic, and industrial communities starting in the early 2000s. Innovators in these fields quickly adapted this general-purpose programming language to their own disciplines to solve problems easier than—ostensibly—the domain-specific languages available at that time.

You have to search long and hard to find a file-type Python cannot read, a database Python cannot access, and an algorithm Python cannot execute. As you familiarize yourself with the language, Python's ability to acquire, clean, and transform source data will quickly amaze you, but those tasks are just the early steps in your analysis and visualization process. It wasn't until 2008 that the pandas (`http://pandas.pydata.org/`) module was created by AQR Capital Management to provide "Pythonic" counterparts to the analytical foundations of languages like R, SAS, or MATLAB, which is where the "real fun" begins.

Although Python's interpreter provides an interactive execution shell, aficionados recognized the need to extend this basic functionality and developed an even more dynamic and robust interactive environment—IPython—to fill the need. When coupled with the pandas module, budding data analysts now have a mature and data-centric toolset available to drive their quest for knowledge.

Why R?

Unlike Python, R's history is inexorably tied to its domain specific predecessors and cousins, as it is 100 percent focused and built for statistical data analysis and visualization. Although it too can access and manipulate various file types and databases (and was also designed for flexibility and extensibility), R's lisp- and S-like syntax plus extreme focus on foundational analytics-oriented data types has kept it, mostly, in the hands of the "data crunchers."

Base R makes it remarkably simple to run extensive statistical analyses on your data and then generate informative and appealing visualizations with just a few lines of code. More modern R libraries such as `plyr` and `ggplot2` extend and enhance these base capabilities and are the foundations of many of mind- and eye-catching examples of cutting-edge data analysis and visualization you have no doubt come across on the Internet.

Like Python, R also provides an interactive execution shell that has enough basic functionality for general needs. Yet, the desire for even more interactivity sparked the development of RStudio, which is a combination of integrated development environment (IDE), data exploration tool, and iterative experimentation environment that exponentially enhances R's default capabilities.

Why Both?

If all you have is a hammer, everything starts looking like a nail. There are times when the flexibility of a general-purpose programming language comes in very handy, which is when you use Python. There are other times when three lines of R code will do something that may take 30 or more lines of Python code (even with pandas) to accomplish. Since your ultimate goal is to provide insightful and accurate analyses as quickly and as visually appealing as possible, knowing which tool to use for which job is a critical insight you must develop to be as effective and efficient as possible.

We would be a bit dishonest, though, if we did not concede that there are some things that Python can do (easily or at all) that R cannot, and vice-versa. We touch upon some of these in the use cases throughout the book, but many of the—ah—"learning opportunities" will only come from performing your own analyses, getting frustrated (which is the polite way of saying "stuck"), and finding resolution by jumping to another tool to "get stuff done." This situation comes up frequently enough that there is even an `rJython` package for R that lets you call Python code from R scripts, and `rpy` and `rpy2` modules for Python that let you call R code from Python scripts.

By having both tools in your toolbox, you should be able to tackle most, if not all, of the tasks that come your way. If you do find yourself in a situation where you need functionality you don't have, both R and Python have vibrant communities that are eager to provide assistance and even help in the development of new functions or modules to fit emerging needs.

Jumpstarting Your Python Analytics with Canopy

It *is* possible to set up an effective and efficient installation of Python, IPython, and pandas from the links we've provided, especially if you are already familiar or proficient with Python; however, we don't recommend it. For those new to Python, the base installation leaves you with the core interpreter and extensive set of built-in, standard libraries. You can think of it as a having an inexpensive blank canvas and introductory set of paints and brushes. You'll need better materials to create a work of art, and that's where the enhanced statistics, computational and graphing libraries come in. Even the most stalwart Python aficionado can find it challenging to manage dependencies and updates for the numerous necessary components. This can waste hours of your time. This is especially true if you have to manage analytics processes across multiple operating systems and environments.

To facilitate both ease of installation and maintenance, we highly recommend using the freely available Enthought Canopy Python data analysis environment (`www.enthought.com/products/canopy/`). Canopy works on Linux, Microsoft Windows, and Mac OS X; has a built-in Python integrated development environment (IDE); incorporates a meta-package manager that will help you keep current with changes in every dependent package and module; and also comes with an IPython console. For those working in organizations that shy away from open source solutions, Enthought also offers commercially supported options for Canopy.

Given that there is a comprehensive installation, setup, and update guide available (`http://docs.enthought.com/canopy/quick-start.html`), we will not go over step-by-step instructions on how to install Canopy for each platform, but we strongly recommend reviewing the documentation before attempting any of the Python examples in the book. Once the base installation is complete, getting started should be as straightforward as opening up the Canopy application, which will display the welcome screen (see Figure 2-1).

One of the first steps you should perform is to instruct Canopy to display all images *inline* within the IPython console. This is an optional step, but it will help keep all output self-contained within the Canopy environment. You can change this setting once you have an open Canopy editor session by going into the Preferences window, finding the Python tab, and selecting the Inline (SVG) option for the PyLab Backend preference (see Figure 2-2).

To validate that your environment is set up properly, run the following code in the IPython console area in the editor:

```
import pandas as pd
import numpy as np
np.random.seed(1492)
test_df = pd.DataFrame({ "var1": np.random.randn(5000) })
test_df.hist()
```

and verify that it produces the output shown in Figure 2-3. If it does, you have the basic environment installed and are ready to start working through the data analysis examples. If the bar chart is not displayed, you may need to check your installation steps or verify that you have the proper graphics display options mentioned earlier.

Once everything is working properly, you should carve out 10 minutes to read through "Learn Python in 10 Minutes" (`www.stavros.io/tutorials/python/`) by Stavros Korokithakis, if you are not familiar with Python, and then spend 10 additional minutes to go through the "10 Minutes to Pandas" tutorial (`http://pandas.pydata.org/pandas-docs/dev/10min.html`) to learn a bit more about the pandas data analysis module.

Understanding the Python Data Analysis and Visualization Ecosystem

Although there are scores of libraries available for Python, a few stand out when it comes to crunching data. We call these libraries an "ecosystem" because each library is developed and supported by a different organization, community, or individual. They coordinate with each other, but the coordination is loose.

FIGURE 2-1 *Canopy welcome screen*

Here are some libraries that you will find yourself using in nearly every project:

- **NumPy** (`www.numpy.org/`)—A library providing foundational capabilities for creating multi-dimensional containers of generic data, performing a wide range of operations on data and generating random numbers. It also implements the capability to "broadcast" operations to Python objects, which can make for succinct and highly efficient code.

- **SciPy library** (`www.scipy.org/scipylib/index.html`)—Built on top of NumPy, this library makes quick work of array-oriented operations and provides a facility to expand NumPy's "broadcast" operations to other types of data elements in Python; it also provides additional statistical operations.

- **Matplotlib** (`http://matplotlib.org/`)—The most powerful and commonly used library to turn your data into production-quality images in Python.

- **pandas** (`http://pandas.pydata.org`)—A library providing high-performance, easy-to-use data structures and data analysis tools; pandas introduces the `Data.Frame` type into the Python namespace, which we discuss in more detail in the "Introducing Data Frames" section later in the chapter. Although this may cause some die-hard Python folks to cringe, pandas, in essence, makes Python more like R and should make it easier for you to jump between languages.

These modules, combined with IPython, are sometimes referred to the core components of the SciPy *stack* (which is confusing, since it contains the SciPy *library*). You can read more about the stack at `www.scipy.org/`.

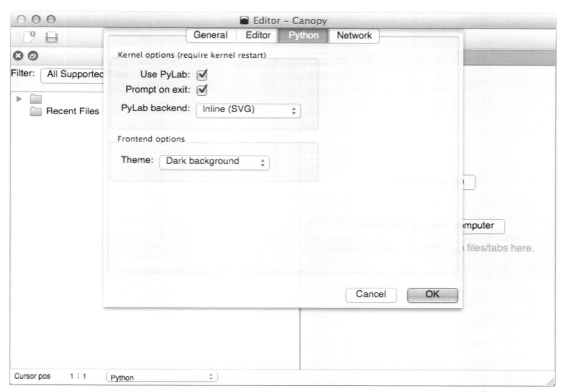

FIGURE 2-2 *Canopy IDE with preferences open*

As you make your way through this ecosystem, you will notice the following code pattern emerge:

```
import numpy as np
import scipy as sp
import matplotlib as mpl
import matplotlib.pyplot as plt
import pandas as pd
```

```
In [1]: import pandas as pd
   ...: import numpy as np
   ...: np.random.seed(1492)
   ...: test_df = pd.DataFrame({ "var1": np.random.randn(5000) })
   ...: test_df.hist()
   ...:
Out[1]: array([[<matplotlib.axes.AxesSubplot object at 0x7e0cbb0>]],
dtype=object)
```

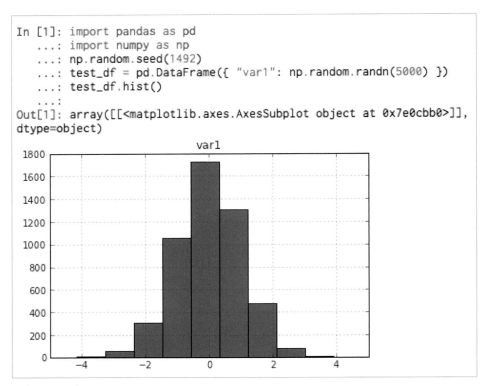

FIGURE 2-3 Test IPython console output

The import statement loads the functions and variables of the Python code in those libraries and makes their names and overall functionality available in the current Python working session. The as component of the statement provides an abbreviated reference for the functions, objects, and variables in the module.

Since you'll be using many of the components of each of the modules in the SciPy stack on a regular basis, you will save time and typing if you create a text file to use as a basic template and include these imports and other (future) much reused code built into it.

You will, of course, use other packages for connecting to databases, reading from files, and performing other functions and you can burn countless hours perusing all the nifty modules at the Python Package Index (PyPI), https://pypi.python.org/pypi, but the ones associated with the SciPy stack will become familiar and regular companions on your data science journey.

Python "Gotchas"

There are two features of Python that are liable to both frustrate and perhaps become problematic for new users. The first "gotcha" is whitespace. Spaces are significant in Python code. There are no { } braces or `begin`/`end` pairs to signify a block of code. You must use consistent indentation to identify groups of statements that will execute together. Inconsistency will result either in error messages from the interpreter or cause your code to fail or just not work as expected. Most modern text editors or IDE can be configured to take care of this for you.

The second "gotcha" is the lack of a requirement to declare variables before using them. Initializing a variable named **breaches** to some value then inadvertently referring to it later as **breached** may not throw an error in the interpreter, but will most assuredly generate unexpected output.

Canopy's package manager (`http://docs.enthought.com/canopy/quick-start/package_manager.html`) makes it very easy to keep the core Python installation and all associated packages updated and current. If you've chosen the manual installation route, you should rely on the package manager of your operating system for the base Python interpreter installation. Updating the individual add-on modules can be accomplished with the following short Python script:

```
import pip from subprocess
import call
for distributions in pip.get_installed_distributions():
    call("pip install --upgrade " +
    distributions.project_name, shell=True)
```

A Word about Python Versions

The Python examples in this book were created under Python 2.7. At the time of this writing, Canopy also uses Python 2.7. There are currently two major production versions of Python, 2.7.x and 3.3.x. Python 3 introduced numerous changes into the default behavior of Python 2.7, and a good number of packages have updated to be compatible with the newer version. However, many packages are still compatible only with Python 2.7. The stability and ubiquity of Python 2.7 make it a good choice to begin exploring Python for data analysis.

For more information on the changes between Python 2.7 and Python 3.3 refer to "What's New In Python 3.0" (`http://docs.python.org/3/whatsnew/3.0.html`).

Setting Up Your R Environment

To build your R/RStudio environment, you will need to download and install R (`http://cran.rstudio.com/`), and then do the same for RStudio (`www.rstudio.com/ide/download/`).

Both links provide full installation details for Linux, Windows, and Mac OS X systems, so we won't delve into the minutiae in this section. You do, however, need to make a choice when you install RStudio, as it comes in two flavors: Desktop and Server. Both provide the same core features:

- Built-in IDE
- Data structure and workspace exploration tools
- Quick access to the R console
- R help viewer
- Graphics panel viewer
- File system explorer
- Package manager
- Integration with version control systems

The primary difference is that one runs as a standalone, single-user application (RStudio Desktop) and the other (RStudio Server) is installed on a server, accessed via browser, and enables multiple users to take advantage of the compute infrastructure. If you are not familiar with R or RStudio, begin by downloading and installing RStudio Desktop. (All examples in this book involving RStudio assume you are working in the Desktop version.)

Note

For those of you limited to working with commercially supported tools, Revolution Analytics (`www.revolutionanalytics.com/support/`) *provides commercial offerings and technical support for R.*

Once everything is installed, open RStudio and verify that you see the default workspace, which should look similar to Figure 2-4.

If all is working correctly, you should take some time to walk through "A (Very) Short Introduction to R" by Paul Torfs and Claudia Brauer (`http://cran.r-project.org/doc/contrib/Torfs%2BBrauer-Short-R-Intro.pdf`). It will run through just enough of the basics of the R language and RStudio environment to make you dangerous.

Although you can use the built-in package manager with RStudio to install packages, you will eventually come to the realization that using the console method is much more convenient. To get familiar with this process right away, you should install the `ggplot2` package, which is the primary graphics library used in the book's examples. Installation is as straightforward as entering the following into the RStudio console pane:

```
> install.packages("ggplot2")
Installing package(s) into '/Library/Frameworks/R.framework/
```

```
Versions/3.0.0/Resources/library'
(as 'lib' is unspecified)
trying URL 'http://cran.mirrors.hoobly.com/bin/macosx/leopard/
contrib/3.0.0/ggplot2_0.9.3.1.tgz'
Content type 'application/x-gzip' length 2659920 bytes (2.5 Mb)
opened URL
==================================================
downloaded 2.5 Mb


The downloaded binary packages are in
/var/folders/qg/vmtfcv1j7vjfq_p5zw86mk7mxkhymk/T/
/RtmpiZ5FD3/downloaded_packages
```

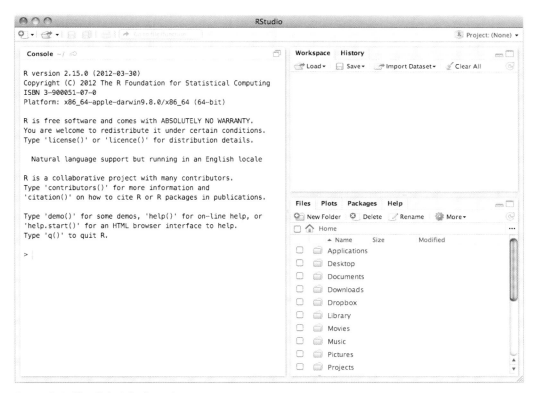

FIGURE 2-4 *RStudio's default workspace*

Run the following code to verify that `ggplot2` has been installed correctly and to ensure your R/RStudio environment is functional:

```
library(ggplot2)
set.seed(1492)
test.df = data.frame(var1=rnorm(5000))
ggplot(data=test.df) + geom_histogram(aes(x=var1))
```

If there are no errors and you see the bar chart in Figure 2-5, your environment is ready to run through the examples in the book. If you do encounter errors, try starting the standalone R (not RStudio) application, re-install the `ggplot2` package in that R console, and execute the bar chart code in that environment. If that works, try uninstalling and re-installing RStudio to fix the errors.

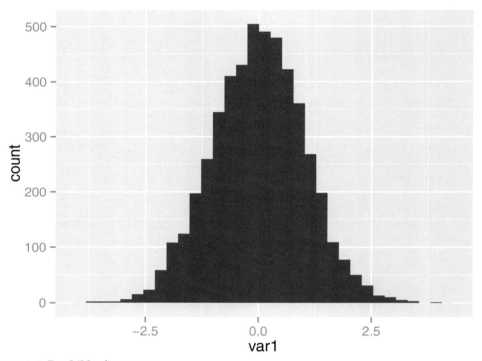

FIGURE 2-5 *Test R/RStudio output*

Like Python, R has a vast repository of useful modules that can simplify many tasks. We will introduce a few of them in the coming chapters, but you should also peruse the Comprehensive R Archive Network (CRAN) (`http://cran.r-project.org/web/packages/`) to see the breadth and depth covered by a host of contributors.

A Word about R Versions

The R examples in this book were created under R version 3.0. Some package managers may still have R version 2.15 as the default version. It is recommended that you install R from the sources identified in this chapter to ensure maximum compatibility with the packages we use in later chapters.

Introducing Data Frames

If you are coming from another programming language you should have a basic understanding of general data types such as strings, integers, and arrays. R and Python offer the standard set of data types, but both have one data type in common—the *data frame*—which truly gives them power. On the surface, a data frame is just a way to hold tabular data (the type of data you see organized in a typical Excel spreadsheet) and may feel like a two-dimensional (2D) array. If you dig a bit deeper, though, you will find that these data frames are really an all-in-one combination of a database table, matrix, 2D array, and pivot table with many additional time-saving features.

Much like a database table, each column in a data frame has a column name and holds elements of the same *type* of data. You can perform operations on whole columns, rows, or subsets of each. Adding, merging, flattening, expanding, changing, deleting, and searching for data are all—usually—one-line operations in both languages, as are methods to read and write the contents of data frames to and from files. In essence, Python and R achieve this expressive power by putting intelligence into the data structure and the functions that operate on them. In contrast, other programming languages have less sophisticated data structures, meaning you need to write your own code and create your own data structures to achieve similar results.

The following code (Listings 2-1 and 2-2) provides a compact overview of data frame operations on both R and Python, respectively, but it is still highly recommended that you check out the aforementioned introductory resources before moving into Chapter 3. As indicated in the Introduction, you can find all code on the book's companion website at www.wiley.com/go/datadrivensecurity.

LISTING 2-1

```
# Listing 2-1
# R Data Frame Example
# create a new data frame of hosts & high vuln counts
assets.df <- data.frame(
    name=c("danube","gander","ganges","mekong","orinoco"),
    os=c("W2K8","RHEL5","W2K8","RHEL5","RHEL5"),
    highvulns=c(1,0,2,0,0))

# take a look at the data frame structure & contents
str(assets.df)
## 'data.frame':    5 obs. of  3 variables:
##$ name     : Factor w/ 5 levels "danube","gander",..: 1 2 3 4 5
## $ os       : Factor w/ 2 levels "RHEL5","W2K8": 2 1 2 1 1
```

(continues)

LISTING 2-1   *(continued)*

```
## $ highvulns: num  1 0 2 0 0

head(assets.df)
##        name     os highvulns
## 1   danube   W2K8         1
## 2   gander  RHEL5         0
## 3   ganges   W2K8         2
## 4   mekong  RHEL5         0
## 5  orinoco  RHEL5         0

# show a "slice" just the operating systems
# by default R creates "factors" for categorical data so
# we use as.character() to expand the factors out
head(assets.df$os)
## [1] W2K8   RHEL5 W2K8   RHEL5 RHEL5
## Levels: RHEL5 W2K8

# add a new column
assets.df$ip <- c("192.168.1.5","10.2.7.5","192.168.1.7",
                  "10.2.7.6", "10.2.7.7")
# extract only nodes with more than one high vulnerability
head(assets.df[assets.df$highvulns>1,])
##     name   os highvulns          ip
## 3 ganges W2K8         2 192.168.1.7

# create a 'zones' column based on prefix IP value
assets.df$zones <-
    ifelse(grepl("^192",assets.df$ip),"Zone1","Zone2")

# take a final look at the dataframe
head(assets.df)
##        name     os highvulns          ip zones
## 1   danube   W2K8         1 192.168.1.5 Zone1
## 2   gander  RHEL5         0    10.2.7.5 Zone2
## 3   ganges   W2K8         2 192.168.1.7 Zone1
## 4   mekong  RHEL5         0    10.2.7.6 Zone2
## 5  orinoco  RHEL5         0    10.2.7.7 Zone2
```

LISTING 2-2

```
# Listing 2-2
# Python (pandas) DataFrame Example
import numpy as np
import pandas as pd
# create a new data frame of hosts & high vuln counts
assets_df = pd.DataFrame( {
    "name" : ["danube","gander","ganges","mekong","orinoco" ],
    "os" : [ "W2K8","RHEL5","W2K8","RHEL5","RHEL5" ],
```

LISTING 2-2   *(continued)*

```
    "highvulns" : [ 1,0,2,0,0 ]
    } )

# take a look at the data frame structure & contents
print(assets_df.dtypes)
## highvulns      int64
## name          object
## os            object
## dtype: object


assets_df.head()
##    highvulns      name     os
## 0          1    danube   W2K8
## 1          0    gander  RHEL5
## 2          2    ganges   W2K8
## 3          0    mekong  RHEL5
## 4          0   orinoco  RHEL5


# show a "slice" just the operating systems
assets_df.os.head()
## 0     W2K8
## 1    RHEL5
## 2     W2K8
## 3    RHEL5
## 4    RHEL5
## Name: os, dtype: object


# add a new column
assets_df['ip'] = [ "192.168.1.5","10.2.7.5","192.168.1.7",
                    "10.2.7.6", "10.2.7.7" ]


# show only nodes with more than one high vulnerability
assets_df[assets_df.highvulns>1].head()
##    highvulns    name    os           ip
## 2          2  ganges  W2K8  192.168.1.7


# divide nodes into network 'zones' based on IP address
assets_df['zones'] = np.where(
    assets_df.ip.str.startswith("192"), "Zone1", "Zone2")


# get one final view
assets_df.head()
##    highvulns      name     os           ip  zones
## 0          1    danube   W2K8  192.168.1.5  Zone1
## 1          0    gander  RHEL5     10.2.7.5  Zone2
## 2          2    ganges   W2K8  192.168.1.7  Zone1
## 3          0    mekong  RHEL5     10.2.7.6  Zone2
## 4          0   orinoco  RHEL5     10.2.7.7  Zone2
```

The data frame is the core data structure you will find yourself using in either language for most analytics projects. It lets you focus on *what* you want to do with the data versus *how* to do it. This is one of the core differences between domain-specific and general-purpose programming languages. If you were still on the fence about switching to R or Python for performing data analysis, hopefully this brief introduction to the power of each language has helped convince you of their efficacy.

Organizing Analyses

Finally, as you prepare to jump into data-analysis projects, it's a good idea to set up an area where you organize input data, analysis scripts, output (visualizations, reports, and/or data), and any supporting documentation. For the purposes of the examples in this book, we use the following directory structure:

```
/book/ch02
    |-R
    |-data
    |-docs
    |-output
    |-python
    |-support
    |-tmp
```

Like most elements of programming, there is no single best way to set up this structure, but you should strive to find one that works for you and stick with it. A great way to do that is to take a lesson from modern web framework builders and use a simple setup shell script that builds the structure for you. We've provided example shell scripts in Bourne shell for Mac OS X/Linux and in the Windows CMD shell (Listings 2-3 and 2-4):

LISTING 2-3

```
# Listing 2-3
# Sample Analysis Preparation Script (Bourne Shell Script)
#!/bin/sh
#
# prep: prep analytics directory structure
#
# usage: prep DIRNAME
#

if [ "$#" == "0" ]; then
    echo "ERROR: Please specify a directory name"
    echo
    echo "USAGE: prep DIRNAME"
fi


DIR=$1

if [ ! -d "${DIR}" ]; then
```

(continues)

LISTING 2-3   *(continued)*

```
    mkdir -p ${DIR}/R \
             ${DIR}/data \
             ${DIR}/docs \
             ${DIR}/output \
             ${DIR}/python \
             ${DIR}/support \
             ${DIR}/tmp
    > ${DIR}/readme.md
    ls -lR ${DIR}
else
    echo "Directory "${DIR}" already exists"
fi
```

LISTING 2-4

```
REM Listing 2-4
REM Sample Analysis Preparation Script (Windows Shell Script)
SET PDIR=%1
IF EXIST %%PDIR GOTO HAVEPDIR
MKDIR %%PDIR
MKDIR %%PDIR\R
MKDIR %%PDIR\data
MKDIR %%PDIR\docs
MKDIR %%PDIR\output
MKDIR %%PDIR\python
MKDIR %%PDIR\support
MKDIR %%PDIR\tmp
<NUL (SET/P Z=) >%%PDIR\readme.md
DIR %%PDIR
:HAVEPDIR
ECHO "Directory exists"
```

You now only need to type `prep` **NAME** whenver you want to start a new project (so, for this project, you type `prep ch02`). As you develop your own styles and patterns, you can expand this script to include the generation of various templates and even initialization of source code repositories. Once the structure is in place, it's time to retrieve, explore, and analyze some data!

Summary

Python and R are key components of a security data scientist's toolbox. Python's similarity to existing scripting languages; its large and supportive community; its diverse data manipulation capabilities; and recent additions of robust statistics, graphics, and computational packages make it an excellent choice for many kinds of analytics work. R's statistical foundations, equally large and supportive contributor base, robust library of packages, and growing popularity within the analytics community make it one of the "must learn/use" languages for data science tasks. While it's possible to work with standard/base installations of each language, using specialized development environments will enable you to focus on your analysis work instead of system administration tasks.

The "data frame" is an "intelligent data structure" that is behind much of the power of both R and Python's data crunching capabilities. It combines the capabilities of a database, pivot table, matrix, and spreadsheet, and we'll be introducing more features of data frames in the next chapter as we walk you through the basic framework of a security data analysis project.

Recommended Reading

The following are some recommended readings that can further your understanding on some of the topics we touch on in this chapter. For full information on these recommendations and for the sources we cite in the chapter, please see Appendix B.

The R Book **by Michael J. Crawley**—One of the most comprehensive R texts that provides examples but also serves as a complete R reference book.

Learning R **by Richard Cotton**—This provides an excellent conversational introduction to the R programming language through numerous step-by-step examples.

Learn Python the Hard Way **by Zed A. Shaw**—Pressure makes diamonds out of coal, and the disciplined nature of the text and exercises requiring actual typing to complete will have you going from "0" to "Python" in short order if you can stick with it.

Learning Python **by Mark Lutz**—If the brutal nature of *Learn Python the Hard Way* is a bit much for you, this text offers a more traditional approach to getting acclimated to the Python ecosystem.

3

Learning the "Hello World" of Security Data Analysis

"From one thing, know ten thousand things."

Miyamoto Musashi, *The Book of Five Rings*

If you've ever tried to learn a new programming language there's a good chance you started off with a "Hello World" example that quickly introduces basic language structure and code execution. The immediate sense of accomplishment as the syntax is verified by the compiler/interpreter and the familiar two-word output is displayed becomes a catalyst for the notion that, soon, you shall have the ability to bend this new language to your will.

This chapter takes the "Hello World" concept and expands it to a walk-through of a self-contained, introductory security data analysis use case that you will be able to follow along with, execute, and take concepts from as you start to perform your own analyses. There are parallel examples in Python and R to provide a somewhat agnostic view of the similarities, strengths, and differences between both languages in a real-life data analysis context. If you're not familiar with one or both of those languages, you should read Chapter 2 and at least skim some of the external resources referenced there.

This is a good place to reinforce the recommendation to use IPython Notebooks or RStudio for your analyses and exploration because they provide very robust and forgiving environments, which means you will be much more productive compared to the alternative of writing, saving, and executing scripts within the bare interpreter shells. Remember, all the source code, sample data, and visualizations are on the book's website (www.wiley.com/go/datadrivensecurity), so there's no need for transcription. You can just cut/paste and focus on the flow and concepts presented in the examples. Listings 3-0 and 3-1 provide you with the setup code for this chapter.

LISTING 3-0

```
# This is for the R code in the chapter
# set working directory to chapter location
# (change for where you set up files in ch 2)
setwd("~/book/ch03")
# make sure the packages for this chapter
# are installed, install if necessary
pkg <- c("ggplot2", "scales", "maptools",
         "sp", "maps", "grid", "car" )
new.pkg <- pkg[!(pkg %in% installed.packages())]
if (length(new.pkg)) {
  install.packages(new.pkg)
}
```

LISTING 3-1

```
# This is for the Python code in the chapter
# loads the necessary Python library for chdir
import os
# set working directory to chapter location
# (change for where you set up files in ch 2)
os.chdir(os.path.expanduser("~") + "/book/ch03")
```

Solving a Problem

Chapter 1 emphasized the criticality of developing a solid research question before going off and "playing with data." For this "Hello World" example, you are working on a problem given to you by the manager of the Security Operations Center (SOC). It seems the SOC analysts are becoming inundated with "trivial" alerts ever since a new data set of indicators was introduced into the Security Information and Event Management (SIEM) system. They have asked for your help in reducing the number of "trivial" alerts without sacrificing visibility.

This is a good problem to tackle through data analysis, and we should be able to form a solid, practical question to ask after we perform some exploratory data analysis and hopefully arrive at an answer that helps out the SOC.

Getting Data

We are entering the age of data in information security. The challenge is no longer where to get data from, but what to do with it. And, the kind of information in each data set will drive the type of research you perform.

For this example, the SOC chose to integrate AlienVault's IP Reputation database (`http://labs.alienvault.com/labs/index.php/projects/open-source-ip-reputation-portal/download-ip-reputation-database/`) into the SIEM. AlienVault itself develops OSSIM—an open source security information manager—and a proprietary unified security management (USM) product, both of which make use of this freely available data set that contains information on various types of "badness" across the Internet. AlienVault provides this data in numerous formats free of charge. The version you work with is the OSSIM Format (`http://reputation.alienvault.com/reputation.data`) since it provides the richest information of all the available formats.

Note

AlienVault updates their IP reputation data set hourly and produces a companion "revision" file (`http://reputation.alienvault.com/reputation.rev`), enabling you to ensure you are working with the latest data set or keep a history of data sets. If you plan on performing a long term analysis of this data set—often referred to as a longitudinal study—it's a good idea to script some code to perform this check to see if it's time to download a new one, even in scheduled jobs.

When performing an exploratory analysis or getting a first look at a data set, you might find it helpful to perform an initial download via browser (or use `wget/curl` if you are handy on the command line). The AlienVault database hovers near 16MB, so it may take a minute or two to download on slower connections. When you download the AlienVault IP Reputation database and examine the first few data elements, you can get an idea of the contents and format, which will come in handy when you start to read in and work with the data. In the following code, you use some simple Linux/UNIX commands to inspect the download:

```
$ head -10 reputation.data # look at the first few lines in the file
222.76.212.189#4#2#Scanning Host#CN#Xiamen#24.479799270,118.08190155#11
222.76.212.185#4#2#Scanning Host#CN#Xiamen#24.479799270,118.08190155#11
222.76.212.186#4#2#Scanning Host#CN#Xiamen#24.479799270,118.08190155#11
5.34.246.67#6#3#Spamming#US##38.0,-97.0#12
```

```
178.94.97.176#4#5#Scanning Host#UA#Merefa#49.823001861,36.0507011414#11
66.2.49.232#4#2#Scanning Host#US#Union City#37.59629821,-122.0656966#11
222.76.212.173#4#2#Scanning Host#CN#Xiamen#24.479799270,118.08190155#11
222.76.212.172#4#2#Scanning Host#CN#Xiamen#24.479799270,118.08190155#11
222.76.212.171#4#2#Scanning Host#CN#Xiamen#24.479799270,118.08190155#11
174.142.46.19#6#3#Spamming###24.4797992706,118.08190155#12

$ wc -l reputation.data # see how many total records there are
  258626 reputation.data
```

For most projects, it's better to get into the habit of retrieving the data source directly from your analysis scripts. If you still prefer to download files manually you should provide some type of comment in your programs that provides details about where the source data comes from and when you retrieved the data for your current analysis. These comments make it easier to repeat the analyses at a later date, and trust us, you'll revisit your code and analyses more often than you think.

The following examples (Listings 3-2 and 3-3) show how to perform the data retrieval in both R and Python. If you are following along with RStudio or IPython, all the code examples assume a working directory of the top level of the project structure (such as executing in the book/ch03 directory that was suggested in Chapter 2, which you either manually created or created using the prep script we provided). Code blocks are, for the most part, self-contained, but each block expects this first snippet and the snippet in the next section on "Reading in Data" to have been executed in the running RStudio or IPython session.

LISTING 3-2

```
# URL for the AlienVault IP Reputation Database (OSSIM format)
# storing the URL in a variable makes it easier to modify later
# if it changes. NOTE: we are using a specific version of the data
# in these examples, so we are pulling it from an alternate
# book-specific location.
avURL <-
  "http://datadrivensecurity.info/book/ch03/data/reputation.data"

# use relative path for the downloaded data
avRep <- "data/reputation.data"

# using an if{}-wrapped test with download.file() vs read.xxx()
# directly avoids having to re-download a 16MB file every time
# we run the script
if (file.access(avRep)) {
  download.file(avURL, avRep)
}
## trying URL 'http://datadrivensecurity…/ch03/data/reputation.data'
## Content type 'application/octet-stream' length 17668227 bytes
## opened URL
## ==================================================
## downloaded 16.8 Mb
```

LISTING 3-3

```
# URL for the AlienVault IP Reputation Database (OSSIM format)
# storing the URL in a variable makes it easier to modify later
# if it changes. NOTE: we are using a specific version of the data
# in these examples, so we are pulling it from an alternate
# book-specific location.
import urllib
import os.path

avURL = "http://datadrivensecurity.info/book/ch03/data/reputation.data"

# relative path for the downloaded data
avRep = "data/reputation.data"

# using an if-wrapped test with urllib.urlretrieve() vs direct read
# via panads avoids having to re-download a 16MB file every time we
# run the script
if not os.path.isfile(avRep):
    urllib.urlretrieve(avURL, filename=avRep)
```

The R and Python code looks very similar and follow the same basic structure: using variables whenever possible for URL and filenames plus testing for the existence of the data file before downloading it again. These are good habits to get into and we'll be underscoring other suggested good practices throughout the rest of the book.

With the IP reputation data in hand, it's now time to read in the data so you can begin to work with it.

Reading In Data

R and Python (especially with pandas) abstract quite a bit of complexity when it comes to reading and parsing data into structures for processing. R's `read.table()`, `read.csv()`, and `read.delim()` functions and pandas' `read_csv()` function cover nearly all your delimited file-reading needs and provide robust configuration options for even the most gnarly input file. Both tools, as you learn in later chapters, also provide ways to retrieve data from SQL and NoSQL databases, HDFS "big data" setups, and even handle unstructured data quite well.

The Revolution Will Be Properly Delimited!

Base R and Python's pandas package both excel at reading in delimited files. Although they are also both agnostic when it comes to what that delimiter is, there is a general acceptance in the data science community that it should be either a comma-separated value (CSV) or a tab-separated value (TSV), and the majority of the sample data sets available to practice with come in one of those two flavors. The CSV format is thoroughly defined in RFC 4180 (`http://www.rfc-editor.org/rfc/rfc4180.txt`) and has the following high-level attributes:

- There should only be one record per line.
- Data files can include an optional header line.

(continues)

(continued)

- Header and data rows have fields separated by commas (or tabs).
- Each line should have the same number of fields.
- Spaces in fields should be treated as significant.

Though RFC 4180 explicitly specifies the comma as the separator, the same rules apply when using tabs (there is no corresponding RFC for tab-separated files).

Many tools in the security domain can import and export CSV-formatted files. If you intend to do any work in environments like Hadoop, you have to become familiar with CSV/TSV.

Another established format is JSON (JavaScript Object Notation), which has grown to become the preferred way to transport data between servers and browsers. As you'll see in Chapter 8, it is also the foundational data format behind many NoSQL database environments/tools. The JSON format is defined in RFC 4627 (`http://www.rfc-editor.org/rfc/rfc4627.txt`) and has two primary structures:

- A collection of name/value pairs (a "dictionary")
- An ordered list of values (an "array")

JSON enables richer and more complex data representation than CSV/TSV and is rapidly superseding another popular, structured format—the Extensible Markup Language (XML)—as the preferred *data exchange* representation. This is because it's syntactically less verbose, much easier to parse, and (usually) more readable. XML has and will continue to excel at document representation, but you should strongly consider using JSON for your structured data-processing needs.

From a cursory examination of the downloaded file, you can see the AlienVault data has a fairly straightforward record format with eight primary fields using a # as the field separator/delimiter.

```
222.76.212.189#4#2#Scanning Host#CN#Xiamen#24.479799270,118.08190155#11
```

Notice also that the reputation data file lacks the optional header, so the example code segment assigns more meaningful column names manually. This is a completely optional step, but it helps avoid confusion as you expand your analyses and, as you see in later chapters, helps build consistency across data frames if you bring in additional data sets.

The consistency in the record format makes the consumption of the data equally as straightforward in each language. In each language/environment, we follow a typical pattern of:

- Reading in data
- Assigning meaningful column names (if necessary)
- Using built-in functions to get an overview of the structure of the data
- Taking a look at the first few rows of data, typically with the `head()` function

that we'll cover in more detail in Chapter 4.

The code that follows (Listings 3-4 and 3-5) builds on the code from the previous section. It won't work correctly otherwise. This is the pattern we will follow in the book, so you should load and run the code in each chapter sequentially.

LISTING 3-4

```r
# read in the IP reputation db into a data frame
# this data file has no header, so set header=FALSE
av <- read.csv(avRep,sep="#", header=FALSE)

# assign more readable column names since we didn't pick
# any up from the header
colnames(av) <- c("IP", "Reliability", "Risk", "Type",
                  "Country", "Locale", "Coords", "x")

str(av) # get an overview of the data frame
## 'data.frame': 258626 obs. of  8 variables:
## $ IP : Factor w/ 258626 levels "1.0.232.167",..: 154069 154065
##    154066 171110 64223 197880 154052 154051 154050 56741 ...
## $ Reliability: int 4 4 4 6 4 4 4 4 4 6 ...
## $ Risk : int 2 2 2 3 5 2 2 2 2 3 ...
## $ Type : Factor w/ 34 levels "APT;Malware Domain",..: 25 25 25 31 25
##    25 25 25 25 31 ...
## $ Country : Factor w/ 153 levels "","A1","A2","AE",..: 34 34 34 143
##    141 143 34 34 34 1 ...
## $ Locale : Factor w/ 2573 levels "","Aachen","Aarhus",..: 2506 2506
##    2506 1 1374 2342 2506 2506 2506 1 ...
## $ Coords : Factor w/ 3140 levels "-0.139500007033,98.1859970093",..:
##    489 489 489 1426 2676 1384 489 489 489 489 ...
## $ x : Factor w/ 34 levels "11","11;12","11;2",..: 1 1 1 7 1 1 1 1 1
##    7 ...

head(av) # take a quick look at the first few rows of data
##             IP Reliability Risk          Type Country     Locale
## 1 222.76.212.189           4    2 Scanning Host      CN     Xiamen
## 2 222.76.212.185           4    2 Scanning Host      CN     Xiamen
## 3 222.76.212.186           4    2 Scanning Host      CN     Xiamen
## 4    5.34.246.67           6    3      Spamming      US
## 5 178.94.97.176           4    5 Scanning Host      UA     Merefa
## 6   66.2.49.232           4    2 Scanning Host      US Union City
##                          Coords  x
## 1    24.4797992706,118.08190155 11
## 2    24.4797992706,118.08190155 11
## 3    24.4797992706,118.08190155 11
## 4                    38.0,-97.0 12
## 5   49.8230018616,36.0507011414 11
## 6 37.5962982178,-122.065696716 11
```

LISTING 3-5

```
# first time using the pandas library so we need to import it
import pandas as pd
# read in the data into a pandas data frame
av = pd.read_csv(avRep,sep="#")
# make smarter column names
av.columns = ["IP","Reliability","Risk","Type","Country",
              "Locale","Coords","x"]
print(av) # take a quick look at the data structure
## <class 'pandas.core.frame.DataFrame'>
## Int64Index: 258626 entries, 0 to 258625
## Data columns (total 8 columns):
## IP            258626  non-null values
## Reliability   258626  non-null values
## Risk          258626  non-null values
## Type          258626  non-null values
## Country       248571  non-null values
## Locale        184556  non-null values
## Coords        258626  non-null values
## x             258626  non-null values
## dtypes: int64(2), object(6)

# take a look at the first 10 rows
av.head().to_csv(sys.stdout)
## ,IP,Reliability,Risk,Type,Country,Locale,Coords,x
## 0,222.76.212.189,4,2,Scanning Host,CN,Xiamen,"24.4797992706,
## 118.08190155",11
## 1,222.76.212.185,4,2,Scanning Host,CN,Xiamen,"24.4797992706,
## 118.08190155",11
## 2,222.76.212.186,4,2,Scanning Host,CN,Xiamen,"24.4797992706,
## 118.08190155",11
## 3,5.34.246.67,6,3,Spamming,US,,"38.0,-97.0",12
## 4,178.94.97.176,4,5,Scanning Host,UA,Merefa,"49.8230018616,
## 36.0507011414",11
```

Within Canopy, IPython has a set of functions to output data to a more viewer-friendly HTML format (see Listing 3-6) that can be used to make the head() output in Listing 3-5 much easier to read (see Figure 3-1).

LISTING 3-6

```
# require object: av (3-5)
# See corresponding output in Figure 3-1
# import the capability to display Python objects as formatted HTML
from IPython.display import HTML
# display the first 10 lines of the dataframe as formatted HTML
HTML(av.head(10).to_html())
```

	IP	Reliability	Risk	Type	Country	Locale	Coords	x
0	222.76.212.189	4	2	Scanning Host	CN	Xiamen	24.4797992706,118.08190155	11
1	222.76.212.185	4	2	Scanning Host	CN	Xiamen	24.4797992706,118.08190155	11
2	222.76.212.186	4	2	Scanning Host	CN	Xiamen	24.4797992706,118.08190155	11
3	5.34.246.67	6	3	Spamming	US	NaN	38.0,-97.0	12
4	178.94.97.176	4	5	Scanning Host	UA	Merefa	49.8230018616,36.0507011414	11
5	66.2.49.232	4	2	Scanning Host	US	Union City	37.5962982178,-122.065696716	11
6	222.76.212.173	4	2	Scanning Host	CN	Xiamen	24.4797992706,118.08190155	11
7	222.76.212.172	4	2	Scanning Host	CN	Xiamen	24.4797992706,118.08190155	11
8	222.76.212.171	4	2	Scanning Host	CN	Xiamen	24.4797992706,118.08190155	11
9	174.142.46.19	6	3	Spamming	NaN	NaN	24.4797992706,118.08190155	12

FIGURE 3-1 *IPython HTML head() output*

Exploring Data

Now that you have a general idea of the variables and how they look, it's time to bring your security domain expertise into the mix to explore and discover what is interesting about the data. This will enable you to form good questions to ask and answer. Despite having almost 260,000 records, you have many tools at your disposal to help get a feel for what it contains.

Before going any deeper into the data, however, there are some tidbits of information you know about the data, so we will summarize them here:

- Reliability, Risk, and x are *integers*.

- IP, Type, Country, Locale, and Coords are *character strings*.

- The IP address is stored in the dotted-quad notation, not in hostnames or decimal format.

- Each record is associated with a unique IP address, so there are 258,626 IP addresses (in this download).

- Each IP address has been geo-located into the latitude and longitude pair in the Coords field, but they are in a single field separated by a comma. You will have to parse that further if you want to use that field.

When you have quantitative variables (which is a fancy way to say "numbers representing a quantity"), a good first exploratory step is to look at the basic *descriptive statistics* on the variables. These are comprised of the following:

- *Minimum* and *maximum* values; taking the difference of these will give you the *range* (*range = max - min*)

- *Median* (the value at the middle of the data set)

- *First* and *third quartiles* (the 25th and 75th percentiles, or you could think of it as the median value of the first and last halves of the data, respectively)

- *Mean* (sum of all values divided by the number of count)

You may see the min, max, median, and quartiles referred to as the *five number summary* of a data set (as developed by Tukey), and both languages have built-in functions to calculate them—summary() in R and describe() in Python—along with the mean. Take a look at the summary on the two primary numeric columns: Reliability and Risk (Listings 3-7 and 3-8).

LISTING 3-7

```
# require object: av (3-4)
summary(av$Reliability)
## Min. 1st Qu.  Median    Mean 3rd Qu.    Max.
## 1.000   2.000   2.000   2.798   4.000  10.000

summary(av$Risk)
## Min. 1st Qu.  Median    Mean 3rd Qu.    Max.
## 1.000   2.000   2.000   2.221   2.000   7.000
```

LISTING 3-8

```
# require object: av (3-5)
av['Reliability'].describe()
## count     258626.000000
## mean           2.798040
## std            1.130419
## min            1.000000
## 25%            2.000000
## 50%            2.000000
## 75%            4.000000
## max           10.000000
## Length: 8, dtype: float64

av['Risk'].describe()
## count     258626.000000
## mean           2.221362
## std            0.531571
## min            1.000000
## 25%            2.000000
## 50%            2.000000
## 75%            2.000000
## max            7.000000
## Length: 8, dtype: float64
```

As you look at these results, note that the Reliability column spreads across the *documented* potential range of [1...10] (Slide 10 of http://www.slideshare.net/alienvault/building-an-ip-reputation-engine-tracking-the-miscreants), but the Risk column—which AlienVault says has a documented potential range of [1...10]—only has a spread of [1...7]. You can also see that both Risk and Reliability appear to center on a value of 2.

You can now dig a bit deeper and use the fact that the Reliability, Risk, Type, and Country fields can be used together to define data set categories. Even though we just treated Reliability and `Risk` as numbers, they actually are ordinal, meaning each entry is assigned an integer, and a value of 4 is not necessarily twice the Reliability or Risk of 2. It only means that Reliability or Risk that is scored 4 is higher than that scored 2. In other words, the number has more meaning as a label than a measurement. Categorical data may also be referred to as *nominal values*, *factors*, or in some cases, *qualitative variables*.

Isn't "Data" Just "Data"?

You may be used to treating data holistically, thinking that the contents of a log file or database extract is just, well, *data*. If you're used to working with data in spreadsheet form (like Microsoft Excel), you aren't really encouraged to think of it any other way. Individual data elements can, however, be broken down into two broad categories: *quantitative* and *qualitative*. Quantitative data elements represent actual quantities whereas qualitative (or *categorical*) data elements are more descriptive in nature.

TCP or UDP port numbers may be numeric, but they don't actually represent a quantity; they are just parts of a category, in this case numerically named entities. Port "22" is not truly greater or less port "7070." Conversely, "number of bytes transferred" or "number of infected hosts" represents actual quantities that can be compared numerically.

Categorical data is easily manipulated in R as `factors` and in Python as a pandas `Categorical` class. In fact, both R and Python have extensive functions that allow you to group, split, extract, and perform analysis on and with factors. You can see in Listing 3-4 that R made a correct educated guess that `IP`, `Type`, `Country`, and `Locale` were all categorical in nature as it scanned through the AlienVault IP reputation data file. Country names and malware types are easily identified as just classifications (*nominal* data in statistics terms). You can also see that R did *not* properly recognize that `Reliability` and `Risk` were both qualitative in nature. Even though there is a meaningful sequence to them—risk level "5" is greater than "1"—the numeric, *ordinal* arrangement is not expressing quantity (that is, you should not try to calculate the mean of the `Risk` values or subtract one `Risk` value from another).

Within R, the difference between the two is automatically handled by the `summary()` function (Listing 3-9), and it displays the count for each category. This doesn't work on the quantitative variables though. In order to get a count of those, you can use the `table()` function if there are not too many unique values in the variable. Within Python, you can create a short function that leverages pandas to convert a data frame column (which is just an array) into a very appropriately named `Categorical` object (Listing 3-10), which you can tweak a bit to give you similar helpful output.

LISTING 3-9
```
# require object: av (3-4)
table(av$Reliability)
##  1       2       3       4       5       6       7       8       9
## 5612 149117  10892   87040       7    4758     297      21     686
##  10
```

(continues)

LISTING 3-9   *(continued)*
```
## 196

table(av$Risk)
## 1         2        3       4       5       6        7
## 39  213852   33719    9588    1328     90       10

# summary sorts by the counts by default
# maxsum sets how many factors to display
summary(av$Type, maxsum=10)
##                 Scanning Host              Malware Domain
##                        234180                        9274
##                    Malware IP               Malicious Host
##                          6470                        3770
##                      Spamming                         C&C
##                          3487                         610
## Scanning Host;Malicious Host    Malware Domain;Malware IP
##                           215                         173
## Malicious Host;Scanning Host                     (Other)
##                           163                         284

summary(av$Country, maxsum=40)
##      CN       US       TR              DE      NL      RU       GB
##   68583    50387    13958    10055    9953    7931    6346     6293
##      IN       FR       TW      BR      UA      RO      KR       CA
##    5480     5449     4399    3811    3443    3274    3101     3051
##      AR       MX       TH      IT      HK      ES      CL       AE
##    3046     3039     2572    2448    2361    1929    1896     1827
##      JP       HU       PL      VE      EG      ID      RS       PK
##    1811     1636     1610    1589    1452    1378    1323     1309
##      VN       LV       NO      CZ      BG      SG      IR  (Other)
##    1203     1056      958     928     871     868     866    15136
```

LISTING 3-10
```
# require object: av (3-5)
# factor_col(col)
#
# helper function to mimic R's "summary()" function
# for pandas "columns" (which are really just Python arrays)

def factor_col(col):
    factor = pd.Categorical.from_array(col)
    return pd.value_counts(factor,sort=True).reindex(factor.levels)

rel_ct = pd.value_counts(av['Reliability'])
risk_ct = pd.value_counts(av['Risk'])
type_ct = pd.value_counts(av['Type'])
country_ct = pd.value_counts(av['Country'])
```

(continues)

Listing 3-10   *(continued)*

```
print factor_col(av['Reliability'])
## 1        5612
## 2      149117
## 3       10892
## 4       87040
## 5           7
## 6        4758
## 7         297
## 8          21
## 9         686
## 10        196
## Length: 10, dtype: int64

print factor_col(av['Risk'])
## 1          39
## 2      213852
## 3       33719
## 4        9588
## 5        1328
## 6          90
## 7          10
## Length: 7, dtype: int64

print factor_col(av['Type']).head(n=10)
## APT;Malware Domain                  1
## C&C                               610
## C&C;Malware Domain                 31
## C&C;Malware IP                     20
## C&C;Scanning Host                   7
## Malicious Host                   3770
## Malicious Host;Malware Domain       4
## Malicious Host;Malware IP           2
## Malicious Host;Scanning Host      163
## Malware Domain                   9274
## Length: 10, dtype: int64

print factor_col(av['Country']).head(n=10)
## A1    267
## A2      2
## AE   1827
## AL      4
## AM      6
## AN      3
## AO    256
## AR   3046
## AT     51
## AU    155
## Length: 10, dtype: int64
```

These numerical tables help you get a general view of the data, but a graph of the distribution of the data has the potential to provide a whole new perspective, oftentimes giving insights that numbers alone cannot reveal. We start with a simple bar chart to get a very quick visual overview of the `Country`, `Risk` and `Reliability` factors (see Figures 3-2 through 3-4, respectively). You'll need to execute each R code listing individually (Listings 3-11, 3-12, and 3-13) to see each graph.

LISTING 3-11

```
# require object: av (3-4)
# We need to load the ggplot2 library to make the graphs
# See corresponding output in Figure 3-2
# NOTE: Graphing the data shows there are a number of entries without
#       a corresponding country code, hence the blank entry
library(ggplot2)

# Bar graph of counts (sorted) by Country (top 20)
# get the top 20 countries' names
country.top20 <- names(summary(av$Country))[1:20]
# give ggplot a subset of our data (the top 20 countries)
# map the x value to a sorted count of country
gg <- ggplot(data=subset(av,Country %in% country.top20),
             aes(x=reorder(Country, Country, length)))
# tell ggplot we want a bar chart
gg <- gg + geom_bar(fill="#000099")
# ensure we have decent labels
gg <- gg + labs(title="Country Counts", x="Country", y="Count")
# rotate the chart to make this one more readable
gg <- gg + coord_flip()
# remove "chart junk"
gg <- gg + theme(panel.grid=element_blank(),
                 panel.background=element_blank())
# display the image
print(gg)
```

LISTING 3-12

```
# requires packages: ggplot2
# require object: av (3-4)
# See corresponding output in Figure 3-3
# Bar graph of counts by Risk
gg <- ggplot(data=av, aes(x=Risk))
gg <- gg + geom_bar(fill="#000099")
# force an X scale to be just the limits of the data
# and to be discrete vs continuous
gg <- gg + scale_x_discrete(limits=seq(max(av$Risk)))
gg <- gg + labs(title="'Risk' Counts", x="Risk Score", y="Count")
gg <- gg + theme(panel.grid=element_blank(),
                 panel.background=element_blank())
print(gg)
```

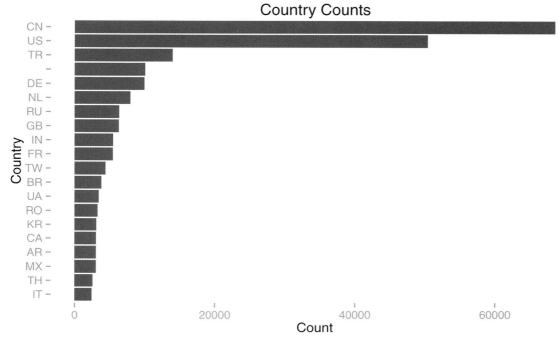

LISTING 3-13

```
# requires packages: ggplot2
# require object: av (3-4)
# See corresponding output in Figure 3-4
# Bar graph of counts by Reliability
gg <- ggplot(data=av, aes(x=Reliability))
gg <- gg + geom_bar(fill="#000099")
gg <- gg + scale_x_discrete(limits=seq(max(av$Reliability)))
gg <- gg + labs(title="'Reliabiity' Counts", x="Reliability Score",
                y="Count")
gg <- gg + theme(panel.grid=element_blank(),
                 panel.background=element_blank())
print(gg)
```

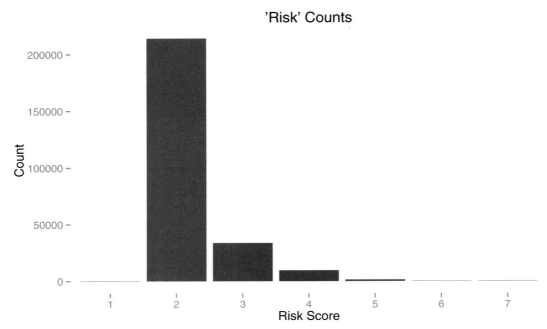

FIGURE 3-3 *Risk factor bar chart (R)*

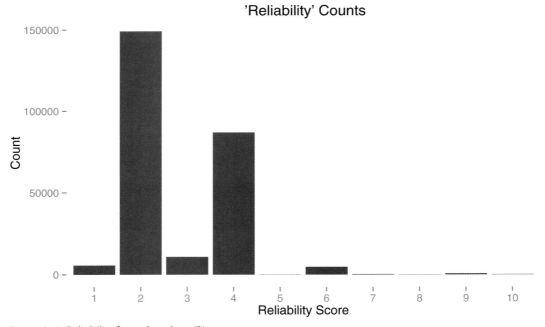

FIGURE 3-4 *Reliability factor bar chart (R)*

The Python versions of these visualizations are offered in Listings 3-14, 3-15, and 3-16.

LISTING 3-14
```
# require object: av (3-5), factor_col (3-10)
# See corresponding output in Figure 3-5
# NOTE: Notice the significant differnce in the Python graph in that the
#       blank/empty country code entries are not in the graph
# need some functions from matplotlib to help reduce 'chart junk'
import matplotlib.pyplot as plt
# sort by country
country_ct = pd.value_counts(av['Country'])

# plot the data
plt.axes(frameon=0) # reduce chart junk
country_ct[:20].plot(kind='bar',
    rot=0, title="Summary By Country", figsize=(8,5)).grid(False)
```

LISTING 3-15
```
# require object: av (3-5), factor_col (3-10)
# See corresponding output in Figure 3-6
plt.axes(frameon=0) # reduce chart junk
factor_col(av['Reliability']).plot(kind='bar', rot=0,
          title="Summary By 'Reliability'", figsize=(8,5)).grid(False)
```

LISTING 3-16
```
# require object: av (3-5), factor_col (3-10)
# See corresponding output in Figure 3-7
plt.axes(frameon=0) # reduce chart junk
factor_col(av['Risk']).plot(kind='bar', rot=0,
          title="Summary By 'Risk'", figsize=(8,5)).grid(False)
```

The Country chart, as shown in Figure 3-5, shows there are definitely some countries that are contributing more significantly to the number of malicious nodes, and you can go back to numbers for a moment to look at the percentages for the top ten in the list (Listings 3-17 and 3-18):

LISTING 3-17
```
# require object: av (3-4)
country10 <- summary(av$Country, maxsum=10)
# now convert to a percentage by dividing by number of rows
country.perc10 <- country10/nrow(av)
# and print it
print(country.perc10)
##         CN         US         TR                    DE         NL
## 0.26518215 0.19482573 0.05396983 0.03887854 0.03848414 0.03066590
##         RU         GB         IN    (Other)
## 0.02453736 0.02433243 0.02118890 0.30793501
```

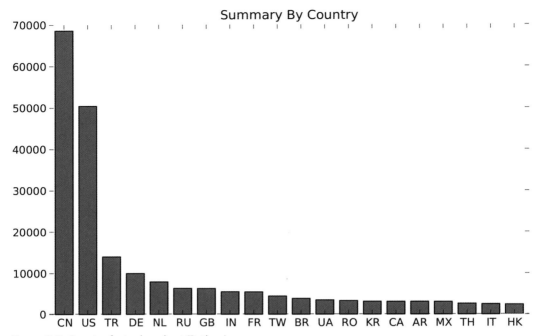

FIGURE 3-5 *Country factor bar chart (Python)*

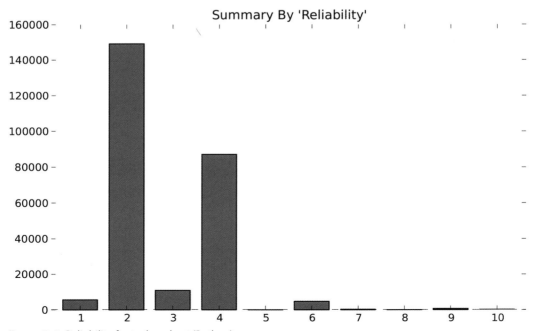

FIGURE 3-6 *Reliability factor bar chart (Python)*

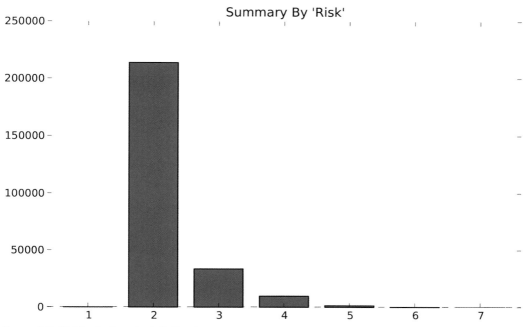

FIGURE 3-7 *Risk factor bar chart (Python)*

LISTING 3-18

```
# require object: av (3-5)
# extract the top 10 most prevalent countries
top10 = pd.value_counts(av['Country'])[0:9]
# calculate the % for each of the top 10
top10.astype(float) / len(av['Country'])
## CN    0.265182
## US    0.194826
## TR    0.053970
## DE    0.038484
## NL    0.030666
## RU    0.024537
## GB    0.024332
## IN    0.021189
## FR    0.021069
## Length: 9, dtype: float64
```

These quick calculations show that China and the United States together account for almost 46 percent of the malicious nodes in the list, and Russia accounts for just 2.4 percent. One avenue to explore here is to see how this compares with various industry reports since you would expect many of these countries to be in the top ten. However, the amount that some countries contribute suggest that there might be some bias in the data set. You can also see that 3 percent of the nodes cannot be geo-located (in the R output, [Other] category).

> **Note**
>
> Chapter 5 covers the challenges and pitfalls of IP address geolocation, so we'll refrain from exploring that further here.

Looking at the `Risk` variable, you can see that the level of risk of most of the nodes is *negligible* (that is, so low that they can be disregarded). There are other elements that stand out with this data though, foremost being that practically no endpoints are in categories 1, 5, 6, or 7, and none in the rest of the defined possible range [8–10]. This anomaly is a sign to you that it is worth digging a bit deeper, but the anomaly is significant evidence of bias in the data set.

Finally, the `Reliability` rating of the nodes also appears to be a bit skewed (that is, the distribution is extended to one side of the mean or central tendency). The values are mostly clustered in levels 2 and 4, with not many ratings above level 4. The fact that it completely skips a reliability rating of 3 should raise some questions in your mind. It could indicate a systemic flaw in the assignment of the rating, or it could be that you have at least two distinct data sets. Either way, that large quantity of 2s and 4s and low quantity of 3s is a clear sign that you should investigate further, because it's just a little odd and surprising.

You now have some leads to pursue and a much better idea of the makeup of the key components of the data. This preliminary analysis gives you enough information to formulate a research question.

Homing In on a Question

Consider both the problem and the primary use case for the AlienVault reputation data: importing it into a SEIM or Intrusion Detection System/Intrusion Prevention System (IDS/IPS) to alert incident response team members or to log/block malicious activity. How can this quick overview of the reputation data influence the configuration of the SIEM in this setting to ensure that the least number of "trivial" alerts are generated?

Let's take a slightly more practical view of those questions by asking, "Which nodes from the Reputation database represent a potentially real threat?"

There *is* a reason AlienVault included both `Risk` and `Reliability` fields, and you should be able to use these attributes to classify nodes into two categories: 1) the nodes you really care about, and 2) everything else. The definition of "really care about" can be somewhat subjective, but it is unrealistic to believe you would want to generate an alert on all detected activity by one of these 258,626 nodes. Some form of prioritization triage and prioritization *must* occur, and it is a far better approach to base the triage and prioritization on statistical analysis of data and evidence rather than a "gut call" or solely on "expert opinion" alone.

It's possible to see which nodes should get your attention by comparing the `Risk` and `Reliability` factors. To do this, you use a *contingency table*, which is a tabular view of the multivariate frequency distribution of specific variables. In other words, a contingency table helps show relationships between two variables. After building a contingency table, you can take both a numeric and graphical look at the results to see where the AlienVault nodes "cluster."

The output from the R code in Listing 3-19 is Figure 3-8, which shows the output of the contingency table as a level plot and uses size and color to show quantity, whereas the Python code in Listing 3-20 is used to generate a standard heatmap (Figure 3-9) that relies on color alone to show quantity. (A *heatmap* is a graphical representation of data where the individual values contained in a matrix are represented as colors. See `http://en.wikipedia.org/wiki/Heat_map` for more information.) With both factors combined, it is very apparent that the values in this data set bias are concentrated around [2, 2], which might be a sign of bias.

LISTING 3-19

```
# require object: av (3-4)
# See corresponding output in Figure 3-8
# compute contingency table for Risk/Reliability factors which
# produces a matrix of counts of rows that have attributes at
# each (x, y) location
rr.tab <- xtabs(~Risk+Reliability, data=av)
ftable(rr.tab) # print table
## virtually identical output to pandas (See Listing 3-20)

# graphical view of levelplot
# need to use levelplot function from lattice package
library(lattice)
# cast the table into a data frame
rr.df = data.frame(table(av$Risk, av$Reliability))
# set the column names since table uses "Var1" and "Var2"
colnames(rr.df) <- c("Risk", "Reliability", "Freq")
# now create a level plot with readable labels
levelplot(Freq~Risk*Reliability, data=rr.df, main="Risk ~ Reliabilty",
          ylab="Reliability", xlab = "Risk", shrink = c(0.5, 1),
          col.regions = colorRampPalette(c("#F5F5F5", "#01665E"))(20))
```

LISTING 3-20

```
# require object: av (3-5)
# See corresponding output in Figure 3-9
# compute contingency table for Risk/Reliability factors which
# produces a matrix of counts of rows that have attributes at
# each (x, y) location
# need cm for basic colors
# need arange to modify axes display
from matplotlib import cm
from numpy import arange

pd.crosstab(av['Risk'], av['Reliability'])

## Reliability    1       2       3       4    5     6     7    8    9    10
## Risk
## 1              0       0      16       7    0     8     8    0    0     0
## 2            804  149114    3670   57653    4  2084    85   11  345    82
## 3           2225       3    6668   22168    2  2151   156    7  260    79
## 4           2129       0     481    6447    0   404    43    2   58    24
## 5            432       0      55     700    1   103     5    1   20    11
```

(continues)

LISTING 3-20   *(continued)*

```
## 6              19     0    2   60   0    8   0   0   1   0
## 7               3     0    0    5   0    0   0   0   2   0
```

```
# graphical view of contingency table (swapping risk/reliability)
xtab = pd.crosstab(av['Reliability'], av['Risk'])
plt.pcolor(xtab,cmap=cm.Greens)
plt.yticks(arange(0.5,len(xtab.index), 1),xtab.index)
plt.xticks(arange(0.5,len(xtab.columns), 1),xtab.columns)
plt.colorbar()
```

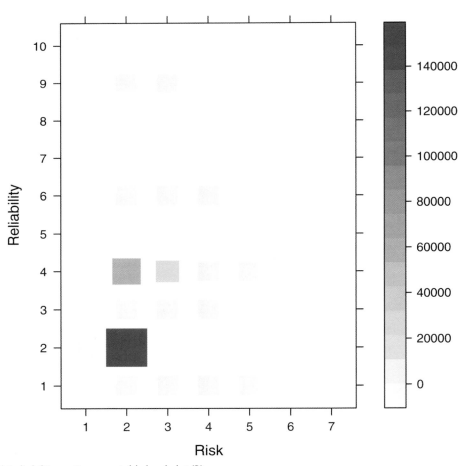

FIGURE 3-8 *Risk/reliability contingency table level plot (R)*

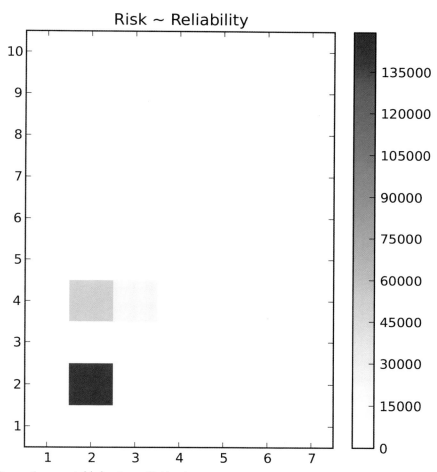

FIGURE 3-9 Risk/reliability contingency table heatmap (Python)

As a fun aside, you can determine whether the patterns you're seeing are occurring by chance, or whether there is some underlying meaning to them. Although you could do some fancy-pants statistics here and maybe apply Fisher's exact test, you don't need to get crazy. What if you assumed that every value of Risk and Reliability had an equal chance of occurring? What would the level plot look like? You should expect some amount of natural variation—both in the systems and the data collection process—so some combinations would naturally occur more often than others. But how different would it look from the current data?

You can use the sample() function to generate random samples from a Uniform distribution [1, 7] and [1, 10] and then build a contingency table from those random samples. Running this multiple times should produce a different set of random tables each time. Each run is called a *realization* of the random processes.

The R code in Listing 3-21 produces the levelplot in Figure 3-10 and shows two things. First, you can make some pretty and colorful random boxes with a few lines of code. Second, there is definitely something pulling nodes into the lower `Risk` and `Reliability` categories (that is, toward zero for each). It could be because the world just has low risk and reliability or the sampling method or scoring system is introducing the skew.

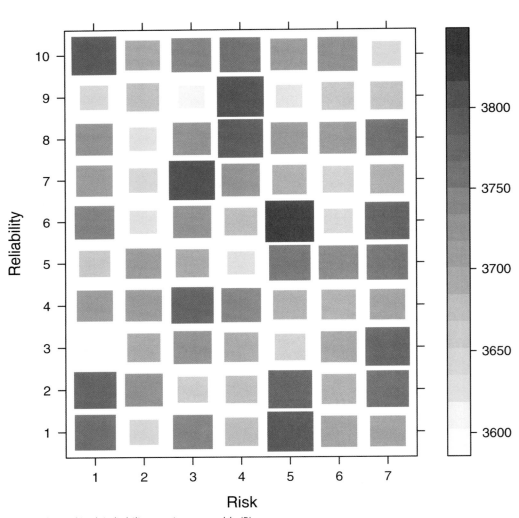

FIGURE 3-10 *"Unbiased" risk/reliability contingency table (R)*

LISTING **3-21**

```
# require object: av (3-4), lattice (3-19)
# See corresponding output in Figure 3-10
# generate random samples for risk & reliability and re-run xtab
# starting PRNG from reproducable point
set.seed(1492) # as it leads to discovery
# generate 260,000 random samples
rel=sample(1:7, 260000, replace=T)
rsk=sample(1:10, 260000, replace=T)
# cast table into data frame
tmp.df = data.frame(table(factor(rsk), factor(rel)))
colnames(tmp.df) <- c("Risk", "Reliability", "Freq")
levelplot(Freq~Reliability*Risk, data=tmp.df, main="Risk ~ Reliabilty",
          ylab="Reliability", xlab = "Risk", shrink = c(0.5, 1),
             col.regions = colorRampPalette(c("#F5F5F5", "#01665E"))(20))
```

Now turn your attention to the `Type` variable to see if you can't establish a relationship with the `Risk` and `Reliability` ratings. Looking closely at the `Type` variable, you notice that some entries have more than type assigned to them, and they are separated by a semicolon (there are 215 `Scanning Host;Malicious Host` values, for example). Since you want to see how those types compare, those with a combination of types shouldn't be mixed with other types. So, rather than try to parse out the nodes with multiple types, you can just reassign all of them into a category of `Multiples` to show that they were assigned more than one type. Then you can create a three-way contingency table and see how that looks. Pull in the `Type` column and see how that impacts the view.

The R code in Listing 3-22 produces the three-way contingency table lattice graph in Figure 3-11, enabling you to visually compare the amount of impact `Type` has on the `Risk` and `Reliability` classifications. The Python code in Listing 3-23 also computes the three-way contingency table, but shows an alternate output representation in a simple bar chart (Figure 3-12).

LISTING **3-22**

```
# require object: av (3-4), lattice (3-19)
# See corresponding output in Figure 3-11
# Create a new varible called "simpletype"
# replacing mutiple categories with label of "Multiples"
av$simpletype <- as.character(av$Type)
# Group all nodes with mutiple categories into a new category
av$simpletype[grep(';', av$simpletype)] <- "Multiples"
# Turn it into a factor again
av$simpletype <- factor(av$simpletype)

rrt.df = data.frame(table(av$Risk, av$Reliability, av$simpletype))
colnames(rrt.df) <- c("Risk", "Reliability", "simpletype", "Freq")
levelplot(Freq ~ Reliability*Risk|simpletype, data =rrt.df,
          main="Risk ~ Reliabilty | Type", ylab = "Risk",
          xlab = "Reliability", shrink = c(0.5, 1),
             col.regions = colorRampPalette(c("#F5F5F5","#01665E"))(20))
```

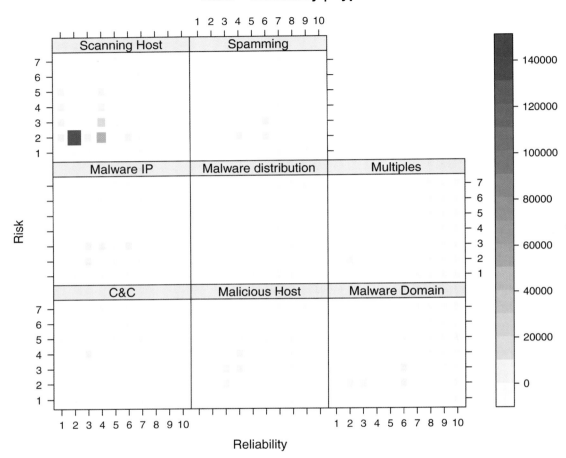

FIGURE 3-11 *Three-way risk/reliability/type contingency table (R)*

LISTING 3-23

```
# require object: av (3-5)
# See corresponding output in Figure 3-12
# compute contingency table for Risk/Reliability factors which
# produces a matrix of counts of rows that have attributes at

# create new column as a copy of Type column
av['newtype'] = av['Type']

# replace multi-Type entries with Multiples
```

(continues)

LISTING 3-23   *(continued)*

```
av[av['newtype'].str.contains(";")] = "Multiples"

# setup new crosstab structures
typ = av['newtype']
rel = av['Reliability']
rsk = av['Risk']

# compute crosstab making it split on the
# new type column
xtab = pd.crosstab(typ, [ rel, rsk ],
          rownames=['typ'], colnames=['rel', 'rsk'])

# the following print statement will show a huge text
# representation of the contingency table. The output
# is too large for the book, but is worth looking at
# as you run through the exercise to see how useful
# visualizations can be over raw text/numeric output
print xtab.to_string() #output not shown

xtab.plot(kind='bar',legend=False,
   title="Risk ~ Reliabilty | Type").grid(False)
```

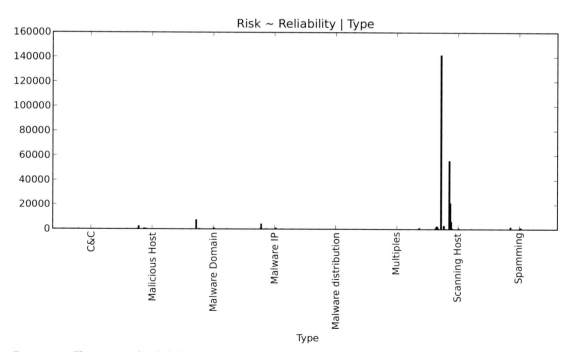

FIGURE 3-12 *Three-way risk/reliability/type contingency table bar chart (Python)*

They say a picture is worth a thousand words, but in this case it's worth about 234,000 data points in the `Scanning Hosts` category (about 90 percent of the entries are classified as scanning hosts). That category is so large and generally low risk that it is overshadowing the rest of the categories. Remove it from the `Type` factors and regenerate the image. This isn't to say the `Scanning Hosts` category isn't important, but remember you are trying to understand which of these entries you really care about. Nodes with low risk and reliability ratings are things you don't want to be woken up from your nap for. You want to peel those away and look at the relationships that exist underneath the scanning hosts. We continue the examples from Listings 3-22 and 3-23 and generate new corresponding Figures 3-13 (R lattice) and 3-14 (Python bar chart) in Listings 3-24 and 3-25.

LISTING 3-24

```
# require object: av (3-4), lattice (3-19)
# See corresponding output in Figure 3-13
# from the existing rrt.df, filter out 'Scanning Host'
rrt.df <- subset(rrt.df, simpletype != "Scanning Host")
levelplot(Freq ~ Reliability*Risk|simpletype, data =rrt.df,
        main="Risk ~ Reliabilty | Type", ylab = "Risk",
        xlab = "Reliability", shrink = c(0.5, 1),
        col.regions = colorRampPalette(c("#F5F5F5","#01665E"))(20))
```

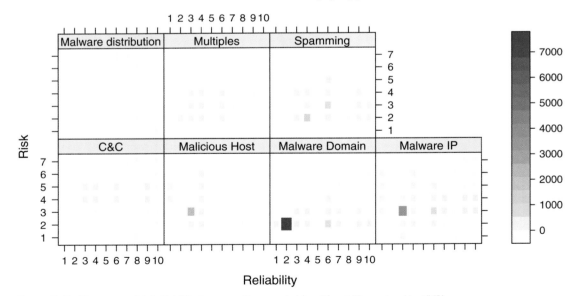

FIGURE 3-13 *Three-way risk/reliability/type contingency table without "Scanning Host" (R)*

LISTING 3-25

```
# require object: av (3-5)
# See corresponding output in Figure 3-14
# filter out all "Scanning Hosts"
rrt_df = av[av['newtype'] != "Scanning Host"]
typ = rrt_df['newtype']
rel = rrt_df['Reliability']
rsk = rrt_df['Risk']
xtab = pd.crosstab(typ, [ rel, rsk ],
     rownames=['typ'], colnames=['rel', 'rsk'])
xtab.plot(kind='bar',legend=False,
   title="Risk ~ Reliabilty | Type").grid(False)
```

Now you are getting somewhere. In Figure 3-13, you can see the Malware domain type has risk ratings limited to 2s and 3s, and the reliability is focused around 2, but spreads the range of values. You can also start to see the patterns in the other categories as well even in Figure 3-14, but it's time to regenerate the graphics once more after you remove the Malware domain. Also, it looks like Malware distribution does not seem to be contributing any risk, so you can filter that factor out of the remaining types as well (in Listings 3-26 and 3-27) to get the final results in Figure 3-15 (R lattice plot) and Figure 3-16 (Python bar chart).

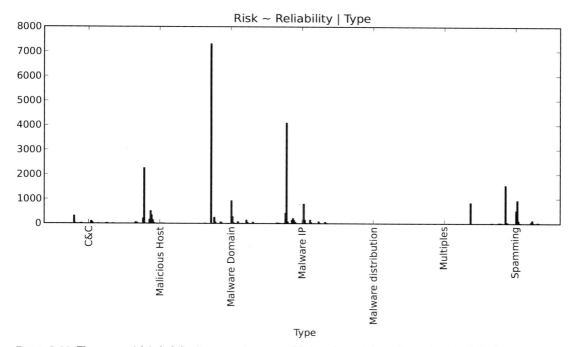

FIGURE 3-14 *Three-way risk/reliability/type contingency table bar chart without "Scanning Host" (Python)*

LISTING 3-26

```
# require object: av (3-4), lattice (3-19), rrt.df (3-24)
# See corresponding output in Figure 3-15
rrt.df = subset(rrt.df,
            !(simpletype %in% c("Malware distribution",
                                 "Malware Domain")))
sprintf("Count: %d; Percent: %2.1f%%",
        sum(rrt.df$Freq),
        100*sum(rrt.df$Freq)/nrow(av))
## [1] Count: 15171; Percent: 5.9%

levelplot(Freq ~ Reliability*Risk|simpletype, data =rrt.df,
        main="Risk ~ Reliabilty | Type", ylab = "Risk",
        xlab = "Reliability", shrink = c(0.5, 1),
        col.regions = colorRampPalette(c("#F5F5F5","#01665E"))(20))
```

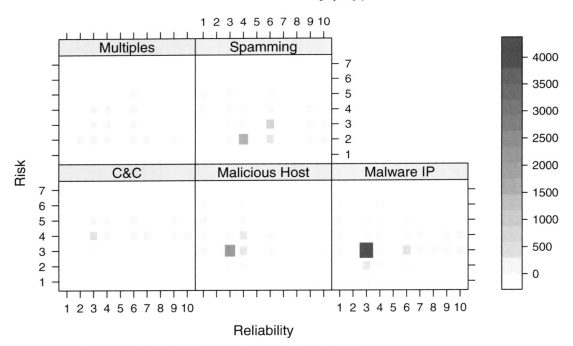

FIGURE 3-15 *Three-way risk/reliability/type contingency table—final (R)*

LISTING 3-27

```
# require object: av (3-5), rrt_df (3-25)
# See corresponding output in Figure 3-16
rrt_df = rrt_df[rrt_df['newtype'] != "Malware distribution" ]
rrt_df = rrt_df[rrt_df['newtype'] != "Malware Domain" ]
typ = rrt_df['newtype']
rel = rrt_df['Reliability']
rsk = rrt_df['Risk']
xtab = pd.crosstab(typ, [ rel, rsk ],
        rownames=['typ'], colnames=['rel', 'rsk'])

print "Count: %d; Percent: %2.1f%%" % (len(rrt_df), (float(len(rrt_df))
    / len(av)) * 100)
## Count: 15171; Percent: 5.9%

xtab.plot(kind='bar',legend=False)
```

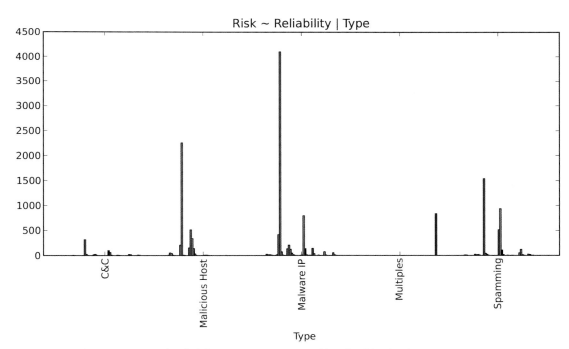

FIGURE 3-16 *Three-way-Way risk/reliability/type contingency table—final (Python)*

With this final bit of filtering, you've reduced the list to less than 6 percent of the original and have honed in fairly well on the nodes representing the ones you really should care about. If you wanted to further reduce the scope, you could filter by various combinations of `Reliability` and/or `Risk`. Perhaps you want to go back to the categories you filtered out and bring a subset of those back in.

The rather simple parsing and slicing done here doesn't show which variables are most important; it simply helps you understand the relationships and the frequency with which they occur. Just because 90 percent of the data was Scanning Hosts, perhaps you only want to filter those hosts with a risk of 2 or below. This analysis has merely helped you identify a set of nodes on which you can generate higher priority alerts. You can still capture the other types into a lower priority or into an informational log.

Since AlienVault updates this list hourly, you can create a script to do this filtering before importing new revisions into your security tools. You can then keep track of the percentage of nodes filtered out as a flag for the need to potentially readjust the rules. Furthermore, you should strongly consider performing this exploratory analysis on a semi-frequent basis. This will help you determine whether you need to re-think your perspective on what constitutes non-trivial nodes.

Summary

This chapter introduced the core structure and concepts of data analyses in Python and R. It incorporated basic statistics, foundational scripting/analysis patterns, and introductory visualizations to help you ask and answer a pertinent question. In addition, each example demonstrated the similarity of Python (with pandas) and R coding techniques and generated output. The steps presented are just one direction this particular analysis could lead. Every situation is different and will require you to pull in different tools and techniques as needed.

Future chapters focus mainly on R code, with some Python sprinkled in on occasion. If you are familiar with Python/pandas, the previous examples should help you translate between the two languages. If you are new to both R and Python, the standardization of future examples in one language should help you follow along with less confusion and help you learn R a bit better.

Recommended Reading

The following are some recommended readings that can further your understanding on some of the topics we touch on in this chapter. For full information on these recommendations and for the sources we cite in the chapter, please see Appendix B.

Statistics and Data with R: An Applied Approach Through Examples **by Yosef Cohen and Jeremiah Y. Cohen**

Python for Data Analysis **by Wes McKinney**

4

Performing Exploratory
Security Data Analysis

"Sometimes, bad is bad."

Huey Lewis and the News, *Sports*, Chrysalis Records, 1983

What constitutes "security data" is often in the eye of the beholder. Malware analysts gravitate toward process, memory and system binary dumps. Vulnerability researchers dissect new patch releases, and network security professionals tap wired and wireless networks to see what secrets can be sifted from the packets as they make their way from node to node.

This chapter focuses on exploring IP addresses by starting with further analyses on the AlienVault IP Reputation database first seen in Chapter 3. You'll examine aspects of the ZeuS botnet (a fairly nasty bit of malware) from an IP address perspective and then perform some basic analyses on real firewall data. To fully understand the examples in this chapter, you should be familiar with the description of the AlienVault data set and have at least followed along with all previous, preliminary analyses. The other major goal of the chapter is to help you get more proficient in R by walking you through a diversity of examples that bring into play many core programming idioms of the language.

IP addresses—along with domain names and routing concepts—are the building blocks of the Internet. They are defined in RFC 791, the "Internet Protocol / DARPA Internet Program / Protocol Specification" (`http://tools.ietf.org/html/rfc791`), which has an elegant and succinct way of describing them:

> **A name** *indicates what we seek.* **An address** *indicates where it is.* **A route** *indicates how to get there.*

Global entities slice and dice IP address space for public and private use; devices, systems, and applications log IP addresses for reference; network management systems test, group, display, and report on IP addresses; and security tools often make critical decisions based on IP addresses. But, what—exactly—*is* an IP address? What can you learn from them and what part do they play in the quest for finding and mitigating malicious activity?

> ### Note
>
> *We make no attempt to incorporate consideration of or conduct analyses on Internet Protocol (IP) version 6 (IPv6) addresses. Likewise, all the examples in this chapter are based on IPv4. Given the slow adoption and migration to IPv6, the plethora of malicious activity still found on IPv4 networks, and the fact that it's fairly straightforward to extrapolate IPv4 concepts to IPv6, this should not be a practical limitation.*

If you plan on typing the code from the chapter versus executing each snippet from the `ch04.R` source file, you will need to download the data files in the `ch04/data` directory from the repository on the book's website (`www.wiley.com/go/datadrivensecurity`) for many of the listings to work correctly. You will also need to run the code in Listing 4-0 to set up your R environment for the code examples in this chapter.

LISTING 4-0

```
# Listing 4-0
# This code sets up the R environemnt for the chapter
# set working directory to chapter location
```

(continues)

Listing **4-0**   *(continued)*
```
# (change for where you set up files in ch 2)
setwd("~/book/ch04")
# make sure the packages for this chapter
# are installed, install if necessary
pkg <- c("bitops","ggplot2", "maps", "maptools",
         "sp", "maps", "grid", "car" )
new.pkg <- pkg[!(pkg %in% installed.packages())]
if (length(new.pkg)) {
  install.packages(new.pkg)
}
```

Dissecting the IP Address

Some information security practitioners may think of IP addresses as simply the strings used with a `ping`, `nessus`, `nmap`, or other commands. But to perform security-oriented analyses of your system and network data, you must fully understand as much as you can about security domain data elements, just as those who perform data analyses in financial, agricultural, or bio-medial disciplines must understand the underpinnings of the data elements in those fields. IP addresses are, perhaps, the most fundamental of security domain data elements. In this section you'll dig a bit deeper into them so you can fully integrate them into your own analytics endeavors.

Representing IP Addresses

IPv4 addresses comprise four bytes, which are known as *octets*, and you'll usually come across them in a form called *dotted-decimal notation* (such as 192.168.1.1). Practically everyone reading this book understands this representation, if only by sight. This method of representation was briefly introduced in the IETF RFC 1123 in 1989 when they denoted it as # . # . # . #, but it was more clearly defined in the IETF's uniform resource identifier (URI) generic syntax draft (RFC 3986, `http://tools.ietf.org /html/rfc3986`) in 2005.

> ## Note
>
> *When you come across other security domain elements, you'll want to do plenty of similar digging to ensure you have all the information you need to process them or create complete regular expressions to locate them in unstructured data.*

Since you know an 8-bit byte can range in value from 0 to 255, you also know the dotted-decimal range is 0.0.0.0 through 255.255.255.255, which is 32 bits. If you count the possible address space, you have a total of 4,294,967,296 possible addresses (the maximum value of a 32-bit integer). This brings up another point of storing and handling IP addresses: *Any IP address can be converted to/from a 32-bit integer value*. This is important because the integer representation saves both space and time and you can calculate some things a bit easier with that representation than with the dotted-decimal form. If you are writing or using a tool that perceives an IP address only as a character string or as a set of character strings, you are potentially wasting space by trading a 4-byte, 32-bit representation for a 15-byte, 120-bit representation (worst case). Furthermore, you are also choosing to use less efficient string comparison code versus integer arithmetic and comparison plus bitwise operations to accomplish the same tasks. Although this may have little to no impact in some scenarios, the repercussions grow significant when you're dealing with large volumes of IP addresses (and become worse in the IPv6 world) and repeated operations.

Converting IPv4 Addresses to/from 32-Bit Integers

To take advantage of integer operations for IPv4 addresses, you need to have some method of converting them to and from dotted-decimal notation. IEEE Standard 1003.1 defines the common low-level (for example, C) method of performing this conversion via the `inet_addr()` and `inet_ntoa()` functions (`http://pubs.opengroup.org/onlinepubs/009695399/functions/inet_addr.html`). However, these functions are not exposed to R. Although it would be possible to write a C library and corresponding R glue module, it's easier to write the functions in pure R with some help from the ***bitops*** package. In Listing 4-1 you will find R functions that convert IPv4 address strings to/from 32-bit integer format.

LISTING 4-1

```
# Listing 4-1
# requires packages: bitops

library(bitops) # load the bitops functions

# Define functions for converting IP addresses to/from integers
# take an IP address string in dotted octets (e.g.
#"192.168.0.1")
# take an IP address string in dotted octets (e.g.
#"192.168.0.1")
# and convert it to a 32-bit long integer (e.g. 3232235521)
ip2long <- function(ip) {
  # convert string into vector of characters
  ips <- unlist(strsplit(ip, '.', fixed=TRUE))
  # set up a function to bit-shift, then "OR" the octets
  octet <- function(x,y) bitOr(bitShiftL(x, 8), y)
  # Reduce applys a function cumulatively left to right
  Reduce(octet, as.integer(ips))
}

# take an 32-bit integer IP address (e.g. 3232235521)
# and convert it to a (e.g. "192.168.0.1").
long2ip <- function(longip) {
  # set up reversing bit manipulation
  octet <- function(nbits) bitAnd(bitShiftR(longip, nbits),
0xFF)
```

(continues)

(continued)

```
# Map applys a function to each element of the argument
# paste converts arguments to character and concatenates them
paste(Map(octet, c(24,16,8,0)), sep="", collapse=".")
}
```

You can test the functionality by reviewing the output from the following test code:

```
long2ip(ip2long("192.168.0.0"))
## [1] "192.168.0.0"
long2ip(ip2long("192.168.100.6"))
## [1] "192.168.100.6"
```

Note: Python coders can use the preexisting *ipaddr* package (`https://code.google.com/p/ipaddr-py/`), which has been incorporated into the Python 3 code base as the *ipaddress* module.

Segmenting and Grouping IP Addresses

There are a few different reasons you'd want to divide and group IP addresses. Internally, you might separate hosts by functionality or sensitivity, which means the routing tables would be overwhelmed if they needed to track each individual IP address. Due to the way TCP/IP was designed and how IPv4 networks are implemented, there are numerous ways to segment or group them so that it's easier to manage individual networks (subnets) and interoperate in the global Internet. The original specification identified top-level *classes* (`A` through `E`), which were nothing more than a list of corresponding bitmasks for consuming consecutive octets. This limited the usable range of addresses in each class and put some structure around the suggested use of each class.

A more generalized, *classless* method of segmentation was established in RFC 4632 (`http://tools.ietf.org/html/rfc4632`). Rather than segment on whole octets, you can now specify address ranges in the CIDR (Classless Inter-Domain Routing) prefix format by appending the number of bits in the mask to a specified IP address. So, `172.16.0.0` (which has a mask of `255.255.0.0`) now becomes `172.16.0.0/16`. These CIDR *blocks* themselves can be used to look for "bad neighborhoods" (that is, identifying network packets coming from or going to groups of malicious nodes).

It's important to understand these points because you'll want to leverage the groupings to dig into the data and relationships to pull out meaning. Once you understand the CIDR prefix format, you can see how those prefixes are grouped and defined as an autonomous system (AS) that are all assigned a numerical identifier known as the autonomous system number (ASN). ASNs have many uses (and associated data); for example, they are used by the border gateway protocol (BGP) for efficient routing of packets across the Internet. Because of the relationship between ASN and BGP, it's also possible to know the adjacent "neighbors" of each ASN. If one ASN "neighborhood" is rife with malicious nodes, it might be a leading indicator that ASNs around it are also harboring malicious traffic. You'll use this relationship later in the chapter to get an ASN view of malicious activity.

There are many more details regarding autonomous systems that you should investigate even if you only occasionally work with IP addresses in your analyses. To get a feel for the global make-up of autonomous systems, you can explore public ASN information at the CIDR Report (`http://www.cidr-report.org/as2.0/`). But keep reading, as you'll be looking at malicious traffic through an ASN lens later in the chapter.

Testing IPv4 Address Membership in a CIDR Block

When you're performing ASN- and CIDR-based analyses, one task that comes up regularly is the need to determine whether an address falls within a given CIDR range. To do this in R, you just expand on the previously defined IPv4 address operations, convert both the IP address in question and the network block address to integers, and then perform the necessary bitwise operations to see if they do, indeed, line up. Listing 4-2 defines a new R function for testing membership of an IPv4 address in a specified CIDR block.

LISTING 4-2

```
# Listing 4-2
# requires packages: bitops
# requires all objects from 4-1
# Define function to test for IP CIDR membership
# take an IP address (string) and a CIDR (string) and
# return whether the given IP address is in the CIDR range
ip.is.in.cidr <- function(ip, cidr) {
  long.ip <- ip2long(ip)
  cidr.parts <- unlist(strsplit(cidr, "/"))
  cidr.range <- ip2long(cidr.parts[1])
  cidr.mask <- bitShiftL(bitFlip(0),
(32-as.integer(cidr.parts[2])))
  return(bitAnd(long.ip, cidr.mask) == bitAnd(cidr.range,
cidr.mask))
}

ip.is.in.cidr("10.0.1.15","10.0.1.3/24")
## TRUE
ip.is.in.cidr("10.0.1.15","10.0.2.255/24")
## FALSE
```

Your organization most likely uses CIDRs and ASNs internally as well, but these are not the only logical grouping mechanisms of sets of IP addresses. For example, you might have "workstations" as a high-level grouping that covers all the user-endpoint DHCP-assigned address space or "printers" to logically associate all statically assigned single- or multi-function output devices. Servers can be grouped according to function or operating system type (or both). The concept of "internal" and "external" groupings for nodes may apply even if you use publicly routable addresses across your entire network. When looking for malicious activity, do not discount the power of these logical groupings, since you may be able to tie characteristics of them (data!) to various indicators you may be looking for. For example, it's reasonable to expect the typical end-user workstation to make attempts to access nodes on the Internet. However, the same is probably not true for printers. Therefore, one of the keys to learning about malicious activity is this type of metadata and relationships.

Locating IP Addresses

Going down in detail, IP addresses map to individual devices that (usually) have unique media access control (MAC) addresses. It's a fairly straightforward process to identify the switch and port of a node on your local network. With the proper metadata, you can create logical groupings based on this physical information and tie additional attributes to it, such as where the node lives—organizationally-geographically speaking. By tying this information to an IP address, you won't have to wait until a barrage of help desk calls come in to discover that there is something amiss in a particular department.

On a broader scale, there are also ways to tie an IP address that lives on the Internet to a geographical location, with varying degrees of accuracy. One of the most popular ways to do so is with the Maxmind GeoIP database and APIs (`http://dev.maxmind.com/geoip/`), which are also used by the freegeoip project (`http://freegeoip.net/`). The Maxmind data has varying degrees of precision depending on whether you use the free databases or their commercial offerings. For country-level identification, using the freely available databases should provide sufficient precision for most organizations. The freegeoip project provides an online query interface to the free Maxmind data set, but it also provides all the code for the service that you can then clone and set up internally to avoid working directly with Maxmind's low-level APIs and avoid rate-limiting and other restrictions from the free service. Chapter 5 goes into more detail on working with geolocated data.

Once you know where a malicious node physically is, it's a fairly straightforward process to visualize it on a map. The AlienVault data provides over 250,000 pre-geolocated addresses, but you'll need to extract the pairs from the ***coords*** field first. You'll find example code for performing this extraction in Listing 4-3. Note that if you have a slightly slower machine, it may take 30–60 seconds to read and parse the data.

LISTING **4-3**

```
# Listing 4-3
# R code to extract longitude/latitude pairs from AlienVault data
# read in the AlienVault reputation data (see Chapter 3)
avRep <- "data/reputation.data"
av.df <- read.csv(avRep, sep="#", header=FALSE)
colnames(av.df) <- c("IP", "Reliability", "Risk", "Type",
                     "Country", "Locale", "Coords", "x")

# create a vector of lat/long data by splitting on ","
av.coords.vec <- unlist(strsplit(as.character(av.df$Coords), ","))
# convert the vector in a 2-column matrix
av.coords.mat <- matrix(av.coords.vec, ncol=2, byrow=TRUE)
# project into a data frame
av.coords.df <- as.data.frame(av.coords.mat)
# name the columns
colnames(av.coords.df) <- c("lat","long")
# convert the characters to numeric values
av.coords.df$long <- as.double(as.character(av.coords.df$long))
av.coords.df$lat <- as.double(as.character(av.coords.df$lat))
```

With the latitude and longitude coordinates in hand, you could avoid R or Python code altogether and use Google Maps to visualize the locations—if you felt like grabbing a caffeinated beverage while it uploads to Google Fusion Tables (`http://tables.googlelabs.com/`) and renders. Even though Google has considerably sped up their online mapping API, the resultant—albeit, handsome—map would end up being partially obscured with map markers. For example, mapping the AlienVault data set with Google Maps (see Figure 4-1) produces a result that makes it seem like malicious hosts have consumed Japan. Rather than rely solely on Google, you can use the mapping functions in R (see Listing 4-4) to accomplish a similar task (see Figure 4-2) with far greater precision.

Note

There are more examples of geographical mapping and analysis in Chapter 5.

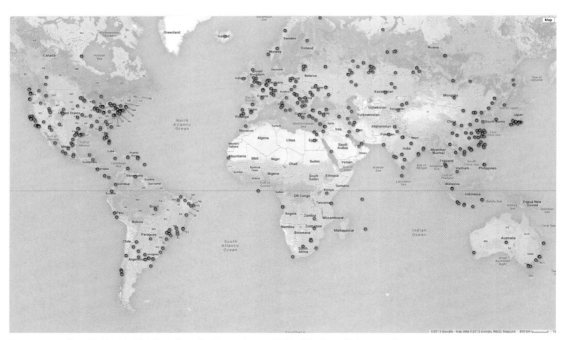

FIGURE 4-1 *Google Fusion Table + Google Maps chart of AlienVault malicious nodes*

LISTING 4-4

```
# Listing 4-4
# requires packages: ggplot2, maps, RColorBrewer
# requires object: av.coords.df (4-3)
# generates Figure 4-2
# R code to extract longitude/latitude pairs from AlienVault data
# need plotting and mapping functions
library(ggplot2)
```

```
library(maps)
library(RColorBrewer)
library(scales)

# extract a color pallete from the RColorBrewer package
set2 <- brewer.pal(8,"Set2")

# extract the polygon information for the world map, minus Antarctica
world <- map_data('world')
world <- subset(world, region != "Antarctica")

# plot the map with the points marking lat/lon of the geocoded entries
# Chapter 5 examples explain mapping in greater detail
gg <- ggplot()
gg <- gg + geom_polygon(data=world, aes(long, lat, group=group),
                        fill="white")
gg <- gg + geom_point(data=av.coords.df, aes(x=long, y=lat),
                       color=set2[2], size=1, alpha=0.1)
gg <- gg + labs(x="", y="")
gg <- gg + theme(panel.background=element_rect(fill=alpha(set2[3],0.2),
                                               colour='white')))

gg
```

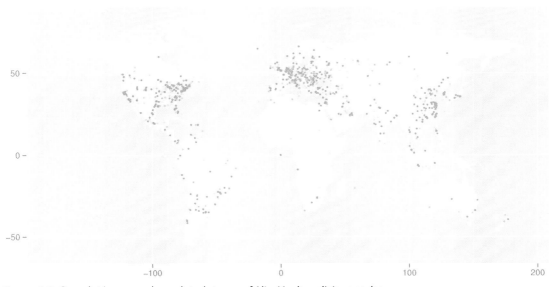

Figure 4-2 *R ggplot/maps package dot-plot map of AlienVault malicious nodes*

The ability to associate an IP address with a physical location and display it on a map has inherent utility (which will become even more apparent in Chapter 5). It's one thing to read the destinations of your Internet users and quite another to "see" them on a map, especially when you're trying to communicate the groupings versus just analyze them. Yet, you do not necessarily need to generate a pretty picture to looking at malicious activities geographically.

Augmenting IP Address Data

In an analyst's dream world, every data set you are asked to crunch through would be error-free and have all the attributes necessary for thorough and robust analyses. Sadly, information security is no different from other disciplines when it comes to imperfect data sets and highly distributed referential data or just a plethora of potential metadata sources. This less than perfect data *can* pose challenges to effective data analyses, but it is usually possible to find and use the data you need.

Even though you have geographic information in the AlienVault data set, the Internet has, as indicated, physical and logical groupings. It might be interesting to see how this data looks through a different lens. For this example, the data set (see Listing 4-3) is augmented with additional data from the IANA IPv4 Address Space Registry (`https://www.iana.org/assignments/ipv4-address-space/ipv4-address-space.xml`). This data represents a very high-level grouping of IPv4 address space registry allocations, and it should be emphasized that most of the registrants are not responsible for the malicious activity of individual nodes. So, although you cannot use this information to cast blame, it will give you one view of where malicious nodes are clustered, setting up possible, additional investigations.

> ### Note
>
> On their web page under the heading "Alternative Formats," the IANA provides a handy link to the CSV version of the IPv4 address space allocations as well as a link to the traditional annotated text file. If you run the example code, you may see some strange behavior at times due to the CSV file being incomplete. It seems there is an automated process that converts a source of the IP table into the various formats and stops processing when the first octet hits three digits. You can either practice your data-munging skills and convert the fixed-width version in the text file to CSV or use the version of the CSV that's on the companion website if you encounter any issues.

The data frame foundational data structure in R and pandas makes it very straightforward to reference and incorporate new data into your analyses, and your own projects will follow something close to this basic data-analysis workflow pattern:

1. Downloading (if necessary) new data
2. Parsing/munging and converting the new data into a data frame
3. Validating the contents and structure of the new data
4. Extracting or computing relevant information from the new data source
5. Creating one or more new columns in the existing data frame
6. Running new analyses

For the example Listing 4-5, you'll process the IANA data to see which registry allocations have the most malicious nodes. Note that the `sapply()` function call may take some time to execute depending on the speed of your machine.

LISTING **4-5**

```
# Listing 4-5
# requires object: av.df (4-3)
# R code to incporporate IANA IPv4 allocations
# retrieve IANA prefix list
ianaURL <- "http://www.iana.org/assignments/ipv4-address-space/ipv4-
address-space.csv"
ianaData <- "data/ipv4-address-space.csv"
if (file.access(ianaData)) {
  download.file(ianaURL, ianaData)
}

# read in the IANA table
iana <- read.csv(ianaData)

# clean up the iana prefix since it uses the old/BSD-
# number formatting (i.e. allows leading zeroes and
# we do not need to know the CIDR component.
iana$Prefix <- sub("^(00|0)", "", iana$Prefix, perl=TRUE)
iana$Prefix <- sub("/8$", "", iana$Prefix, perl=TRUE)

# define function to strip 'n' characters from a string
# (character vector) and return the shortened string.
# note that this function is 'vectorized' (you can pass it a single
# string or a vector of them)
rstrip <- function(x, n){
  substr(x, 1, nchar(x)-n)
}

# extract just the prefix from the AlienVault list
av.IP.prefix <- rstrip(str_extract(as.character(av.df$IP),
                       "^([0-9]+)\\."), 1)

# there are faster ways than 'sapply()' but we wanted you to
# see the general "apply" pattern in action as you will use it
# quite a bit throughout your work in R
av.df$Designation <- sapply(av.IP.prefix, function(ip) {
  iana[iana$Prefix == ip, ]$Designation
})

##      Administered by AFRINIC       Administered by APNIC
##                          322                        2615
##        Administered by ARIN    Administered by RIPE NCC
##                        17974                        5893
##                      AFRINIC                       APNIC
##                         1896                       93776
##                         ARIN   AT&T Bell Laboratories
##                        42358                          24
## Digital Equipment Corporation    Hewlett-Packard Company
```

(continues)

LISTING 4-5   *(continued)*

```
##                              1                        3
##               LACNIC  Level 3 Communications, Inc.
##               18914                        31
##          PSINet, Inc.                  RIPE NCC
##               30                        74789
```

You can do a quick check against the main IANA allocation table to see if this matches overall block assignments. The code in Listing 4-6 makes a data frame from the `table()` summary of the `iana$Designation` column and merges that data with the AlienVault data.

LISTING 4-6

```
# Listing 4-6
# requires packages: ggplot2, maps, RColorBrewer
# requires object: av.coords.df (4-3), iana (4-5)
# Code to extract IANA block assignments & compare w/AlienVault groups
# create a new data frame from the iana designation factors
iana.df <- data.frame(table(iana$Designation))
colnames(iana.df) <- c("Registry", "IANA.Block.Count")

# make a data frame of the counts of the av iana
# designation factor
tmp.df <- data.frame(table(factor(av.df$Designation)))
colnames(tmp.df) <- c("Registry", "AlienVault.IANA.Count")

# merge (join) the data frames on the "reg" column
combined.df <- merge(iana.df, tmp.df)
print(combined.df[with(combined.df, order(-IANA.Block.Count)),],
      row.names=FALSE)
##                        Registry IANA.Block.Count AlienVault.IANA.Count
##                           APNIC               45                 93776
##             Administered by ARIN              44                 17974
##                            ARIN               36                 42358
##                        RIPE NCC               35                 74789
##                          LACNIC                9                 18914
##            Administered by APNIC               6                  2615
##         Administered by RIPE NCC              4                  5893
##                          AFRINIC               4                  1896
##          Administered by AFRINIC              2                   322
##      Level 3 Communications, Inc.             2                    31
##             AT&T Bell Laboratories            1                    24
##      Digital Equipment Corporation            1                     1
##          Hewlett-Packard Company              1                     3
##                     PSINet, Inc.               1                    30
```

Then you plot the data (see Listing 4-7) to generate the chart in Figure 4-3.

LISTING 4-7

```
# Listing 4-7
# requires packages: reshape, grid, gridExtra, ggplot2, RColorBrewer
# requires object: combined.df (4-6), set2 (4-4)
# generates Figure 4-3
# plot charts from IANA data
# flatten the data frame by making one entry per "count" type
# versus having the counts in individual columns
# need the 'melt()' function from the reshape package
# to transform the data frame shape
library(reshape)
library(grid)
library(gridExtra)

# normalize the IANA and AV values to % so bar chart scales
# match and make it easier to compare
combined.df$IANA.pct <- 100 * (combined.df$IANA.Block.Count /
                              sum(combined.df$IANA.Block.Count))
combined.df$AV.pct <- 100 * (combined.df$AlienVault.IANA.Count /
                            sum(combined.df$AlienVault.IANA.Count))

combined.df$IANA.vs.AV.pct <- combined.df$IANA.pct - combined.df$AV.pct

melted.df <- melt(combined.df)
# plot the new melted data frame values
gg1 <- ggplot(data=melted.df[melted.df$variable=="IANA.pct",],
              aes(x=reorder(Registry, -value), y=value))
# set min/max for axis so scale is same for both charts
gg1 <- gg1 + ylim(0,40)
gg1 <- gg1 + geom_bar(stat="identity", fill=set2[3]) # using bars
# make a better label for the y axis
gg1 <- gg1 + labs(x="Registry", y="%", title="IANA %")
# make bar chart horizontal
gg1 <- gg1 + coord_flip()
# rotate the x-axis labels and remove the legend
gg1 <- gg1 + theme(axis.text.x = element_text(angle = 90, hjust = 1),
                   panel.background = element_blank(),
                   legend.position = "none")

gg2 <- ggplot(data=melted.df[melted.df$variable=="AV.pct",],
              aes(x=reorder(Registry,-value), y=value))
gg2 <- gg2 + ylim(0,40)
gg2 <- gg2 + geom_bar(stat="identity", fill=set2[4]) # using bars
gg2 <- gg2 + labs(x="Registry", y="%", title="AlienVault IANA %")
gg2 <- gg2 + coord_flip()
gg2 <- gg2 + theme(axis.text.x = element_text(angle = 90, hjust = 1),
                   panel.background = element_blank(),
                   legend.position = "none")
```

(continues)

LISTING 4-7   *(continued)*

```
# grid.arrange makes it possible to do very precise placement of
# multiple ggplot objects
grid.arrange(gg1, gg2, ncol=1, nrow=2)
```

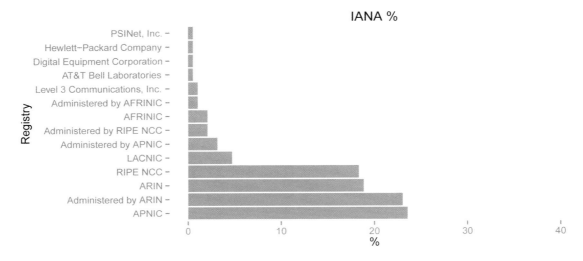

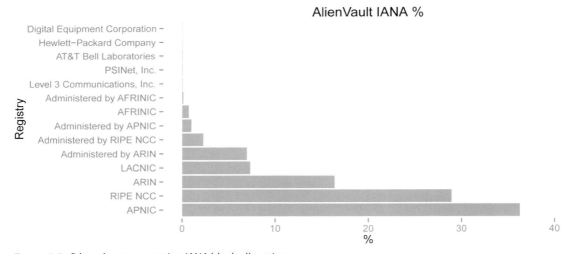

FIGURE 4-3   *R bar charts comparing IANA block allocations*

There is some variation, but overall the larger blocks contribute the majority of malicious hosts. We've highlighted RIPE NCC, Administered by ARIN, and LACNIC in the text/console output in Listing 4-6 since RIPE NCC has a significantly larger number of malicious hosts than its allocation block count might imply (nearly double that of its very close neighbor ARIN). LACNIC and Administered by ARIN both have a similar number of malicious hosts yet have different allocation block counts. Even with these discrepancies, can you make a more confident statement regarding the comparison between the number of malicious hosts in the /8s managed by a registrar and the number of /8s managed by a registrar? You can if you do one more visualization (see Listing 4-8), displaying the number of AlienVault malicious nodes per IANA block, sorted by IANA block (lowest to highest), as seen in Figure 4-4.

LISTING 4-8

```
# Listing 4-8
# requires packages: ggplot2
# requires object: combined.df (4-7), set2 (4-4)
gg <- ggplot(data=combined.df,
              aes(x=reorder(Registry, -IANA.Block.Count), y=AV.pct ))
gg <- gg + geom_bar(stat="identity", fill=set2[2])
gg <- gg + labs(x="Registry", y="Count",
              title="AlienVault/IANA sorted by IANA (low-to-high")
gg <- gg + coord_flip()
gg <- gg + theme(axis.text.x = element_text(angle = 90, hjust = 1),
              panel.background = element_blank(),
              legend.position = "none")
gg
```

The AlienVault population does gravitate toward the IANA blocks with the most allocations, but we can do better by introducing some basic statistics into the mix in the next section.

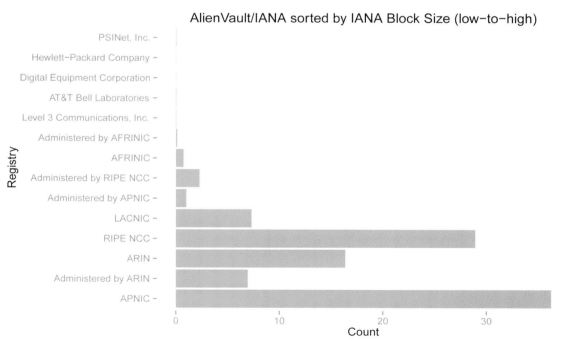

FIGURE 4-4 *Plotting AlienVault population per IANA block sorted by IANA block size*

Association/Correlation, Causation, and Security Operations Center Analysts Gone Rogue

Since this chapter contains the first examples where you group data elements (variables) and compare them to other variables, this is a good place to mention the concept of *association* or, as you'll see it referred to more often, *correlation*. Correlation is simply a measurement of the linear relationship between two or more variables.

- A *positive* correlation is a relationship between two or more variables whereby their values increase or decrease together.

- Similarly, a *negative* correlation is a negative relationship, whereby when one variable increases, the other will decrease, and vice versa.

If there is no consistent linear pattern in the change between variables, they are said to be uncorrelated. When you calculate the correlation value (stats nerds call it the *r* value or correlation coefficient), you get a value between 1 (perfect positive correlation) and -1 (perfect negative correlation). As *r* gets closer to zero, the linear correlation decreases. At zero, you say there is no correlation between the two values.

It's important to remember that a simple correlation like this is a *linear* comparison. By contrast, look at the scatterplot in Figure 4-5 that has the parabola (upside down U shape). Obviously there is a pattern and some type of relationship, but it's not a linear correlation, so the calculated *r* value is very close to zero. Like most elements of statistics (or any complex discipline), there are many methods available to perform various tasks. This is also true when calculating correlation between two variables. Chapter 5 looks at a topic called *linear regression*, which provides more detailed insight into correlation. Linear regression is also the basis for one type of predictive modeling. For the purposes of this chapter, you'll use a basic form of correlation. The code to generate the scatterplots in Figure 4-5 is in the ch04/R/ch04.R file on the book's web site.

Correlation Caveats

Believe it or not, there are parallels between statistics and information security. Statisticians use strange symbols and tools to perform their dark art much like malware researchers and network security specialists stare at rows of hexadecimal, octal, and binary data to derive meaning. Security researchers also understand which tool to use for the job at hand (you wouldn't use NetFlow data to try to understand detailed payload information in a communication session between two nodes). The same holds true for data scientists. There are, unfortunately, further considerations to take into account when working with even basic correlation techniques.

This chapter describes the *Pearson* correlation method, which is widely used given that it can work with data on an interval or ratio scale, with no restrictions placed on both variables being the same type. If you have ordinal or ranked data, you should use two other algorithms—Spearman or Kendall's Tau—instead. We aren't delving into the correlation algorithm subtleties in this book, but you should have a solid understanding of the uses and limits of each before applying correlation in your own analyses. You can find out more details about these correlation coefficients at http://www.statisticssolutions.com/academic-solutions/resources/directory-of-statistical-analyses/correlation-pearson-kendall-spearman/.

Finally, correlation is a descriptive statistical measure versus an inferential one, meaning that you can only describe the population you are studying and cannot use the outcome to generalize a statement about a larger group or make predictions based on the outcome.

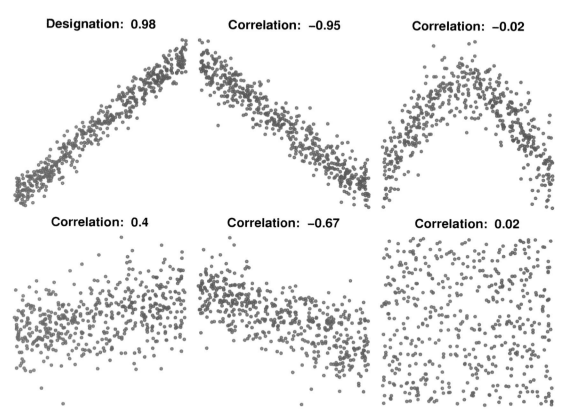

Designation: 0.98   **Correlation: –0.95**   **Correlation: –0.02**

Correlation: 0.4   **Correlation: –0.67**   **Correlation: 0.02**

FIGURE 4-5 *Scatterplots showing correlations*

It's also important to remember that correlation is just showing some existence of a relationship between variables, with no implication of **causation**. For example, imagine that a hypothetical analyst looked at the relationship between security incidents and the number of security operations staff, and reported, "There is a strong positive correlation between the number of SOC analysts in an organization and the number of incidents reported." This could be misunderstood to imply that SOC analysts cause security incidents. In reality, the patterns of data have similar trends with nothing else implied. Perhaps organizations with more incidents hire more SOC analysts, or after hiring more analysts, organizations discover more incidents. Perhaps the two are both a product of something else completely, such as larger organizations are targeted more and have both more incidents and analysts. When you calculate relationships like correlation, you have to be careful to keep it in context. People (and especially those looking for a headline) put a lot of faith in mathematically derived answers and in "having a number." That overconfidence may cause an analyst to take the results out of context and into some really weird places, such as "Researchers suggest we fire SOC analysts to reduce breaches!" You have to be careful of how you position your work and be sure to present the results with an appropriate communication of confidence in the techniques.

For the IANA data, it makes sense that there would be more malicious nodes in larger groups of assigned network blocks. This is an expert opinion that's based on a cursory observation of data and an intuitive feel for the "right" answer. To make a more statistically backed statement, use the code in Listing 4-9 to generate the plot in Figure 4-6 of the relationship between the two variables `IANA.Block.Count` and `AlienVault.IANA.Count`.

LISTING 4-9

```
# Listing 4-9
# requires packages: ggplot2
# requires object: combined.df (4-7), set2 (4-4)
# generates figure 4-6
gg <- ggplot(data=combined.df)
gg <- gg + geom_point(aes(x=IANA.Block.Count,
                          y=AlienVault.IANA.Count),
                      color=set2[1], size=4)
gg <- gg + labs(x="IANA Block Count", y="AlienVault IANA Count",
                title="IANA ~ AlienVault")
gg <- gg + theme(axis.text.x = element_text(angle = 90, hjust = 1),
                 panel.background = element_blank(),
                 legend.position = "none")
gg
```

The scatterplot in Figure 4-6 appears to show a positive correlation, but to be sure, you should move from eyeballs to keyboards to run a statistical comparison. There are a number of methods available to perform basic pairwise correlation. R provides access to three fundamental algorithms via the built-in `cor()` function:

```
cor(combined.df$IANA.Block.Count,
    combined.df$AlienVault.IANA.Count, method="spearman")
## [1] 0.9488598
```

The value returned by `cor()` is known as the ***correlation coefficient*** and, as pointed out earlier, if it falls close to +1, this indicates there is a strong positive linear relationship between the two variables. As previously noted, R's built-in `cor()` function offers three methods of correlation:

- `pearson` (which is the default if no parameter is specified) refers to the Pearson product moment correlation function and was designed to be most effective when run on continuous data sets with a normal distribution (see later in this chapter) that is free of outliers;

- `spearman` refers to the Spearman rank-order correlation coefficient and—as the name implies—works on rank-ordered data, in other words, if you have two columns in an R data frame that have either pre-ranked data (for example, ordered "top 10" elements) or can be put into rank order (especially to avoid the outlier problems that reduce the efficacy of the Pearson algorithm). Algorithmically, the Spearman calculation is actually the Pearson correlation coefficient calculated from ranked variables;

- `kendall` refers to Kendall's ***tau*** scorrelation coefficient and was specifically designed to work on ranked, ordinal variables. It represents the difference between the probabilities of the outcome variable increasing and decreasing with respect to an input variable.

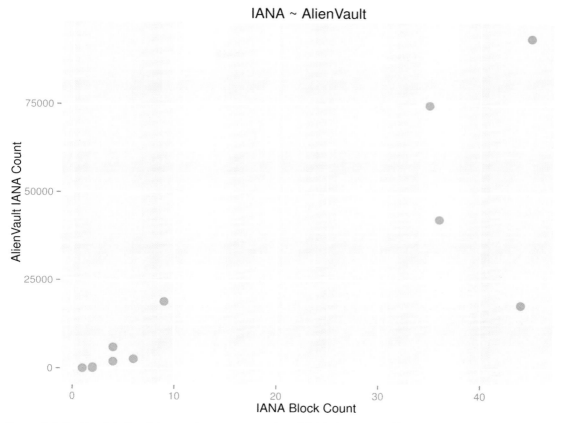

IANA ~ AlienVault

FIGURE 4-6 *Scatterplot of malicious node counts to number of /8 blocks managed by a registrar*

For this example, we applied the Spearman correlation, as it produces a rank correlation coefficient and is generally more suited to variables that do not have a normal distribution (you can execute the `hist()` function on each list to see how far removed each data set is from the normal distribution) and are better compared by rank. For readers who are unfamiliar with what a normal distribution is, a simplified explanation is that a data set is normally distributed if:

- It has an equal mean and median.
- 68 percent of the values lie within one standard deviation of the mean.
- 95 percent of the values lie within two standard deviations of the mean.
- 99.7 percent (or more) lie within three standard deviations of the mean.

You now have some statistical backing to help validate the visual pattern and logical (common sense) view that larger blocks of networks will contain more malicious hosts. You could run a similar analysis of your own internal data and, say, determine if there's a relationship between the number of employees in a department and the number of viruses detected.

> **Note**
>
> Chapter 5 goes into more detailed methods for determining relationships between variables.

Mapping Outside the Continents

Calculating and graphing information about malicious nodes is highly useful and vital to the operation of most, if not all, security technologies deployed in today's organizations. However, as a security data scientist, it's a good idea to get into the habit of visualizing data to pick up structures or patterns you might not see otherwise. The classic example of this is Anscombe's quartet, illustrated in Figure 4-7.

Here (Listing 4-10) are the (x,y) pairs that make up the plots in Figure 4-7:

LISTING 4-10

```
# Listing 4-10
# anscombe is a data set that comes with R
# Use the column indexing feature of the
# data frame to show them as pairs
anscombe[,c(1,5,2,6,3,7,4,8)]
##     x1    y1  x2    y2  x3     y3  x4     y4
## 1   10  8.04  10  9.14  10   7.46   8   6.58
## 2    8  6.95   8  8.14   8   6.77   8   5.76
## 3   13  7.58  13  8.74  13  12.74   8   7.71
## 4    9  8.81   9  8.77   9   7.11   8   8.84
## 5   11  8.33  11  9.26  11   7.81   8   8.47
## 6   14  9.96  14  8.10  14   8.84   8   7.04
## 7    6  7.24   6  6.13   6   6.08   8   5.25
## 8    4  4.26   4  3.10   4   5.39  19  12.50
## 9   12 10.84  12  9.13  12   8.15   8   5.56
## 10   7  4.82   7  7.26   7   6.42   8   7.91
## 11   5  5.68   5  4.74   5   5.73   8   6.89

# calculate mean and standard deviation for each column
sapply(anscombe,mean)
## x1        x2        x3        x4        y1        y2        y3
## 9.000000  9.000000  9.000000  9.000000  7.500909  7.500909  7.500000
## y4
## 7.500909
sapply(anscombe,sd)
## x1        x2        x3        x4        y1        y2        y3
## 3.316625  3.316625  3.316625  3.316625  2.031568  2.031657  2.030424
## y4
## 2.030579
sapply(anscombe,var)
##        x1        x2        x3        x4        y1        y2
```

```
## 11.000000 11.000000 11.000000 11.000000  4.127269  4.127629
##          y3            y4
## 4.122620  4.123249
for (i in 1:4) cat(cor(anscombe[,i], anscombe[,i+4]), "\n")
## 0.8164205
## 0.8162365
## 0.8162867
## 0.8165214
```

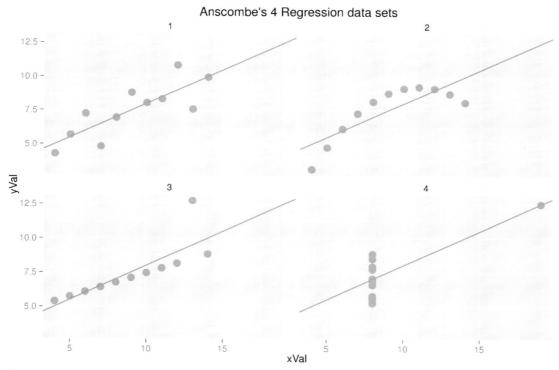

FIGURE 4-7 *Anscombe's quartet*

All four data sets have the same statistical description (mean, standard deviation, variance, correlation), and they even fit the same linear regression—the blue diagonal line—in the charts in Figure 4-7. Yet, when visualized, patterns emerge. Panel 1 in Figure 4-7 shows a basic linear relationship of a data set that is distributed fairly normally. Panel 2 is definitely not exhibiting a linear relationship, but there is clearly *some* relationship between them. Panel 3 has a mostly linear relationship but with an obvious outlier. Finally, Panel 4 shows the power outliers hold, as the extreme point in the upper right is strong enough to have the data still show a strong correlation despite the lack of a linear relationship. Visualizations like this are often key to gaining a much better understanding of the data.

As you learned earlier in the chapter, maps can also be powerful tools for communicating information visually. However, there are other logical and physical visual representations of IP addresses available, especially when you want to see the interconnectedness of nodes. One very versatile representation is the *graph* structure since it provides statistical data and has a myriad of options for visual presentation. Do not confuse the term "graph structure" here with producing a graphic or chart. A *graph structure* is nothing more than a collection of nodes (vertices) and links between nodes (edges). Nodes and edges have inherent attributes, such as a name/label, but also have attributes that are calculated, such as the number of links going into and coming from the node (the degree). In a traditional graph structure, the direction of an edge (in or out) can be specified as well. In fact, as you'll see in Chapter 8, graphs are becoming so generally useful that there are extremely popular, custom databases that make it very straightforward to store, modify, and analyze large graph structures.

Visualizing the ZeuS Botnet

In this section, you combine the metadata you can pull from IP addresses and apply the graph structure to that data to visualize relationships in IP addresses that have been affiliated with malicious behavior. You'll mostly be focusing on building and visualizing graph structures and touching on graph-based analytics for the remainder of this chapter. Previous examples have worked with the AlienVault IP Reputation database, but it's time to switch things up a bit and look at one particularly pervasive bit of maliciousness on the Internet: the ZeuS botnet. Most security professionals have heard of ZeuS before, but just in case, here's the description from the abuse.ch ZeuS tracker site (https://zeustracker.abuse.ch/):

> *ZeuS (also known as Zbot/WSNPoem) is a crimeware kit that steals credentials from various online services like social networks, online banking accounts, FTP accounts, email accounts, and other (phishing).*

Despite some prominent attempts at taking down this botnet, it continues to hum along siphoning credentials. The abuse.ch site provides a handy blocklist (https://zeustracker.abuse.ch/blocklist.php?download=badips) of IP addresses that organizations can use to both identify ZeuS infected nodes and prevent infected systems from communicating with ZeuS command and control (C&C) servers, which orchestrate all operations within the botnet. To work with the blocklist, you need to use the code in Listing 4-11 to get the data file into R (a task you're hopefully getting very familiar with by now).

LISTING 4-11

```
# Listing 4-11
# Retrieve and read ZeuS blocklist data into R
zeusURL <- "https://zeustracker.abuse.ch/blocklist.php?\
download=ipblocklist"
zeusData <- "data/zeus.csv"
if (file.access(zeusData)) {
  # need to change download method for universal "https" compatibility
  download.file(zeusURL, zeusData, method="curl")
}
# read in the ZeuS table; skip junk; no header; assign colnames
zeus <- read.table(zeusData, skip=5, header=FALSE, col.names=c("IP"))
```

We've switched to `read.table()` (`read.csv()` is a variant of that function) in Listing 4-11 since there's only one column. This particular data file has no header but it does have five lines at the beginning of the file that are comments and of no use to you programmatically. We also use some short-hand by avoiding a separate call to `colnames()` and embedding the column names right in the `read.table()` function call.

Let's start by determining which countries host ZeuS bots. You could use a geolocation service to get this data, but we'll take a different approach here since you will also require some additional information for the next part of your analysis. The Team Cymru firm provides a number of IP-based lookup services (`http://www.team-cymru.org/Services/ip-to-asn.html`), including an IP to ASN mapping service that supports bulk queries over port 43 and returns quite a bit of handy information:

- AS number
- BGP prefix
- Country code
- Registry
- When it was allocated
- AS organization name

The Team Cymru site clearly states that the country code data is only as accurate as the regional registry databases, but we've run some comparisons against geolocation databases and for the purposes of the examples in this chapter the data is accurate enough. To use this data, you need some helper functions that can be found in the `ch04.R` file in `ch04/R` directory provided on the book's website (`www.wiley.com/go/datadrivensecurity`):

- `trim(c)` —Takes a character string and returns the same string with leading and trailing spaces removed
- `BulkOrigin(ips)` —Takes a list of IPv4 addresses and returns a detailed list of ASN origins
- `BulkPeer(ips)` —Takes a list of IPv4 addresses and returns a detailed list of ASN peers

To build the graph structure, you'll perform the following steps:

1. Look up the ASN data.
2. Turn the IP addresses into graph vertices.
3. Turn the AS origin countries into graph vertices.
4. Create edges from each IP address to its corresponding AS origin country.

Surprisingly, it's simple R code, as shown in Listing 4-12.

LISTING 4-12

```
# Listing 4-12
# Building ZeuS blocklist in a graph structure by country
# requires packages: igraph, plyr, RColorBrewer, colorspace
# requires object: set2 (4-4)
```

(continues)

LISTING 4-12 *(continued)*

```r
library(igraph)
library(plyr)
library(colorspace)
# load the zeus botnet data used to perform the
# remainder of the analyses in the chapter
zeus <- read.table("data/zeus-book.csv", skip=5, header=FALSE,
                   col.names=c("IP"))
ips <- as.character(zeus$IP)
# get BGP origin data & peer data;
origin <- BulkOrigin(ips)
g <- graph.empty() # start graphing
# Make IP vertices; IP endpoints are red
g <- g + vertices(ips, size=4, color=set2[4], group=1)
# Make BGP vertices
g <- g + vertices(origin$CC, size=4, color=set2[2], group=2)
# for each IP address, get the origin AS CC and return
# them as a pair to create the IP->CC edge list
ip.cc.edges <- lapply(ips, function(x) {
  iCC <- origin[origin$IP==x, ]$CC
  lapply(iCC, function(y){
    c(x, y)
  })
})
g <- g + edges(unlist(ip.cc.edges)) # build CC->IP edges
# simplify the graph by combining commmon edges
g <- simplify(g, edge.attr.comb=list(weight="sum"))
# delete any standalone vertices (lone wolf ASNs). In "graph" terms
# delete any vertex with a degree of 0
g <- delete.vertices(g, which(degree(g) < 1))
E(g)$arrow.size <- 0 # we hate arrows
# blank out all the IP addresses to focus on ASNs
V(g)[grep("\\.", V(g)$name)]$name <- ""
```

Now that you have a graph structure, it's equally as straightforward to make the graph visualization in Figure 4-8 just by passing the graph structure to the `plot()` function with some layout and label parameters as seen in Listing 4-13.

LISTING 4-13

```r
# Listing 4-13
# Visualizing the ZeuS blocklist country cluster graph
# requires packages: igraph, plyr
# requires all objects from Listing 4-11
# this is a great layout for moderately sized networks. you can
# tweak the "n=10000" if this runs too slowly for you. The more
# iterations, the cleaner the graph will look
```

```
L <- layout.fruchterman.reingold(g, niter=10000, area=30*vcount(g)^2)
# plot the graph
par(bg = 'white', mfrow=c(1,1))
plot(g, margin=0, layout=L, vertex.label.dist=0.5,
     vertex.label.cex=0.75,
     vertex.label.color="black",
     vertex.label.family="sans",
     vertex.label.font=2,
     main="ZeuS botnet nodes clustered by country")
```

If your country code memory is a bit rusty, you can use the R code in Listing 4-14 to provide a lookup table.

Listing **4-14**

```
# Listing 4-14
# require package: igraph (4-11)
# requires object: V() (4-11), g (4-11)
# read in country code to name translation table
zeus.cc <- grep("[A-Z]", V(g)$name, value=TRUE)
zeus.cc <- zeus.cc[order(zeus.cc)]
# read in the country codes data frame
cc.df <- read.csv("data/countrycode_data.csv")
# display cc & name for just the ones from our data set
print(head(cc.df[cc.df$iso2c %in% zeus.cc, c(7,1)], n=10),
      row.names=FALSE)
## iso2c    country.name
##    AR        ARGENTINA
##    AU        AUSTRALIA
##    AT          AUSTRIA
##    AZ       AZERBAIJAN
##    BG         BULGARIA
##    CA           CANADA
##    CL            CHILE
##    CN            CHINA
##    CZ CZECH REPUBLIC
##    DE          GERMANY
```

As stated earlier, simple bar charts and tables make it easier to understand quantities, but the graph tends to add a visual impact that traditional presentation techniques lack. Therefore, depending on the consumers, it may be useful/helpful to put them both together when presenting your output.

From your previous work with ASNs, you know that IPs live in both physical and logical space. Now that you have a graph view of the physical world, you can use the code in Listing 4-15 to create the graph network in Figure 4-9 and take look at the ZeuS IP addresses in relation to their ASNs of origin and include ASN peers to truly start to see it as a network.

LISTING 4-15

```
# Listing 4-15
# requires objects: BulkOrigin() & BulkPeer() from book's web site
# require package: igraph (4-11)
# create connected network of ZeuS IPs, ASNs, and ASN peers
# generates Figure 4-9
g <- graph.empty()
g <- g + vertices(ips, size=3, color=set2[4], group=1)
origin <- BulkOrigin(ips)
peers <- BulkPeer(ips)
# add ASN origin & peer vertices
g <- g + vertices(unique(c(peers$Peer.AS, origin$AS)),
                  size=3, color=set2[2], group=2)
# build IP->BGP edge list
ip.edges <- lapply(ips, function(x) {
  iAS <- origin[origin$IP==x, ]$AS
  lapply(iAS,function(y) {
    c(x, y)
  })
})

bgp.edges <- lapply(
  grep("NA",unique(origin$BGP.Prefix),value=TRUE,invert=TRUE),
  function(x) {
    startAS <- unique(origin[origin$BGP.Prefix==x,]$AS)
    lapply(startAS,function(z) {
      pAS <- peers[peers$BGP.Prefix==x,]$Peer.AS
      lapply(pAS,function(y) {
        c(z,y)
      })
    })
  })
g <- g + edges(unlist(ip.edges))
g <- g + edges(unlist(bgp.edges))
g <- delete.vertices(g, which(degree(g) < 1))
g <- simplify(g, edge.attr.comb=list(weight="sum"))
E(g)$arrow.size <- 0
V(g)[grep("\\.", V(g)$name)]$name = ""
L <- layout.fruchterman.reingold(g, niter=10000, area=30*vcount(g)^2)
par(bg = 'white')
plot(g, margin=0, layout=L, vertex.label.dist=0.5,
     vertex.label=NA,
     main="ZeuS botnet ASN+Peer Network")
```

By expanding the network with the ASN peers, you can see a cluster of interconnected ASNs that might be worth exploring further, but you'll need to reference the resources in the "Recommended Reading" section to take that next step.

ZeuS botnet nodes clustered by country

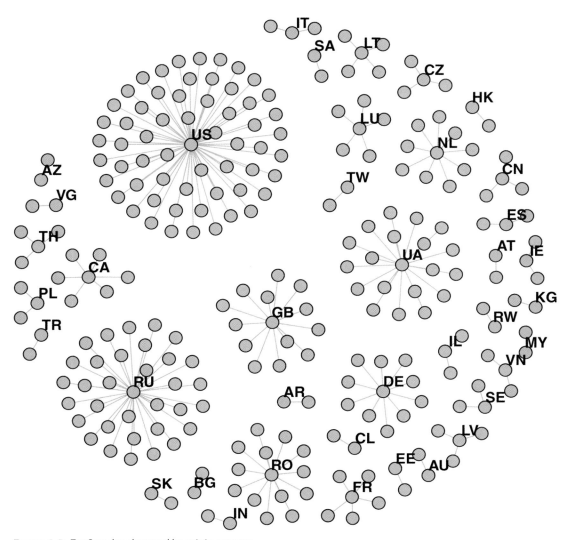

FIGURE 4-8 *ZeuS nodes clustered by origin country*

With basic graph network concepts well in hand, you can turn your attention to a more practical application of these functions—visualizing malicious activity on *your* network using actual data from a real environment and attempting to *visualize* the answer to the question, "What potentially malicious nodes are attempting to come into/get out of my network?"

ZeuS botnet ASN+Peer Network

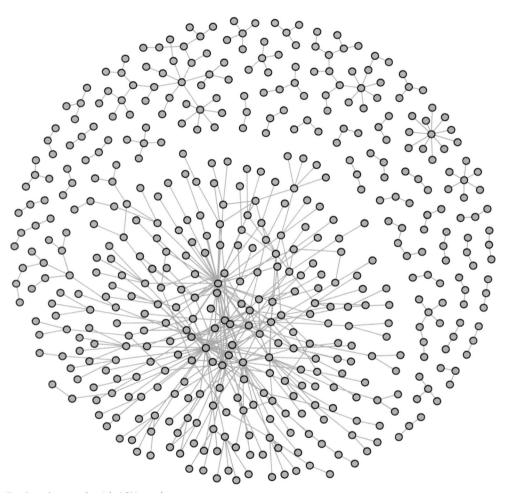

FIGURE 4-9 *ZeuS nodes graph with ASNs and peers*

Visualizing Your Firewall Data

Examining generic data about malicious nodes has some merit, but it's more helpful to apply these analysis and visualization techniques to your own organization. To that end, this last example provides a way to use both the AlienVault IP Reputation database and the graphing techniques presented in this chapter to examine what's happening on a perimeter firewall. Rather than generate some artificial data, we obtained 24 hours' worth of Internet-bound IP addresses from volunteers, which can be found in the file `dest.ips` in the `ch04/data` directory on the book's website (`www.wiley.com/go/datadrivensecurity`).

This example has also created two new functions, which can be found on the website in the `ch04.R` file in the `ch04/R` directory:

- `graph.cc(ips,av.df)` —Takes in a list of IPv4 addresses and an AlienVault data frame and returns a complete graph network structure of nodes clustered by country code. It also (optionally) plots the graph with a summary of malicious traffic types.

- `graph.asn(ips,av.df)` —Takes in a list of IPv4 addresses and an AlienVault data frame and returns a complete graph network structure of nodes clustered by ASN. It also (optionally) plots the graph with a summary of malicious traffic types.

You can start by loading the destination IP addresses and filtering out everything that isn't in the AlienVault database. You then assess the result and try to get a feel for what type of malicious activity to hone in on. Even with the potential bias in the data (as described in Chapter 3), a higher reliability rating should still mean there is a better chance the node is actually "bad." Therefore, you can focus on entries with reliability greater than 6, which will give you 127 nodes to send to `graph.cc()` to process and plot. See Listing 4-16.

LISTING **4-16**

```
# Listing 4-16
# requires objects: BulkOrigin() & BulkPeer(), graph.cc(), graph.asn()
#    from book's web site & set2 (4-4)
# working with Real Data
# create connected network of ZeuS IPs, ASNs, and ASN peers
# generates Figure 4-10
# require package: igraph, RColorBrewer
avRep <- "data/reputation.data"
av.df <- read.csv(avRep, sep="#", header=FALSE)
colnames(av.df) <- c("IP", "Reliability", "Risk", "Type",
                     "Country", "Locale", "Coords", "x")

# read in list of destination IP addresses siphoned from firewall logs
dest.ips <- read.csv("data/dest.ips", col.names= c("IP"))

# take a look at the reliability of the IP address entries
# (you could also plot a histogram)
table(av.df[av.df$IP %in% dest.ips$IP, ]$Reliability)
##  1   2   3   4   5   6   7   8   9  10
## 16 828 831 170   1 266  92   2  23  24

# extract only the "bad" ones, designated by presence in alienvault
# database with a reliability greater than 6 since there seems to
# be a trailing off at that point
ips <- as.character(av.df[(av.df$IP %in% dest.ips$IP) &
                          (av.df$Reliability > 6), ]$IP)
# graph it
g.cc <- graph.cc(ips, av.df)
```

The bar chart on the right serves as a legend for the colors of the graph nodes and also provides a summary of the totals of each classification type. In Figure 4-10, you can see there is some potential C&C traffic and that the United States has the highest number of possible malicious destinations. With `graph .cc()`'s ASN cousin and the slicing and dicing example in Listing 4-16, you should have enough tools to generate your own views in order to look at different aspects of the malicious traffic.

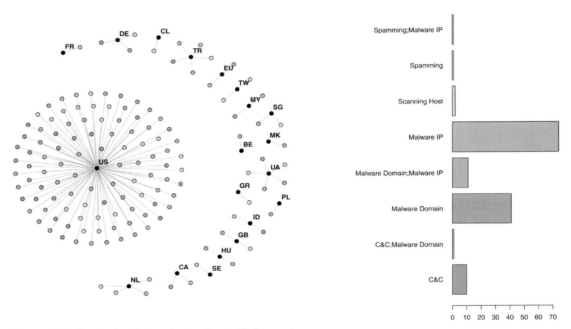

FIGURE 4-10 *Graph of malicious destination traffic by country*

Summary

The goal of this chapter was to show you the importance of fully understanding the data elements you want to analyze and visualize, as well as the need to start with a question and iterate through computations and visualizations to work toward an answer. There are plenty of other similar data sets available on the Internet to substitute for the ones provided in most of the examples. Hunting those down (or just using your own firewall data in the last example), working through the sample analyses, and formulating your own questions will help to ingrain the pattern of the data analysis workflow in your mind.

There are many ways to look at IP-based malicious activity and this chapter was by no means comprehensive. Furthermore, R was not entirely necessary for anything but the visualizations and statistical analyses. Much of the sorting, slicing, and dicing could have been performed in a database and—as you'll see in Chapter 8—that is definitely the place to start when working with larger data sets.

The next chapter expands on these analyses and should give you a new "out of this world" perspective on botnet data.

Recommended Reading

The following are some recommended readings that can further your understanding on some of the topics we touch on in this chapter. For full information on these recommendations and for the sources we cite in the chapter, please see Appendix B.

Mining Graph Data by Diane J. Cook and Lawrence B. Holder

Graphical Models with R by Søren Højsgaard, David Edwards, and Steffen Lauritzen

5

From Maps to Regression

"Even before you understand them, your brain is drawn to maps."

Ken Jennings, author and *Jeopardy!* champ

You have been learning some basics about security data and how to pull meaning from IP addresses. As briefly discussed in Chapter 4, IP addresses can be associated with geographic data if you look them up using a geolocation service. But what is the value in doing that? How much can you learn by associating a longitude and latitude with your data? The answer to that is dependent on what the IP represents and how deep you are willing to go. In order to describe the value of mapping the virtual world into the physical, this chapter begins with a list of over 800,000 latitude/longitude pairs shared by our friends at Symantec. The location data is from client IP addresses infected with the ZeroAccess rootkit, collected over a 24-hour period during the month of July in 2013.

Now that you know these are locations of hosts with ZeroAccess, you could ask a series of questions:

- How is ZeroAccess distributed across geographic areas and is there any significance to this distribution?

- What types of clients are more likely to be infected with ZeroAccess? Do things like education and income affect the rate of infection?

- Are ZeroAccess infections the result of alien visitors?

Obviously, this chapter hones in on that last question. It is the most important and worthy of some serious research (anyone have some spare grant money?). But seriously, our purpose is to explore the benefits (and pitfalls!) you'll get from tying secondary data points, like alien visitors, to the primary data. Oftentimes, more can be learned through the combination and merging of related data, than just the original data in isolation. Therefore, as you bring the lessons from this chapter back to your own work, realize that insight may not just be in the primary data you collect, but in how it relates to other data you can collect from your environment. For example, we could ask the following questions that will combine two or more sources of data:

- Is there a relation between phishing victims and their HR data (education, pay grade, etc.)?

- Is there a relation between netflow (network) patterns and the software and services running on hosts?

- Is there a relationship between surfing habits and productivity or performance review scores of employees?

This is where you are heading in this chapter. You'll begin with one single data point (location data for systems infected with ZeroAccess) and explore the relationships within the data. Then you'll combine the location data with other geographic observations and apply a statistical technique known as *linear regression* to test the relationships of the various data points and look for significant (and perhaps even spurious) relationships. Prepare for the examples in this chapter by setting the directory to the working directory for this chapter and make sure the R libraries are installed (Listing 5-0).

Listing 5-0

```
# set working directory to chapter location
# (change for where you set up files in ch 2)
setwd("~/book/ch05")
```

(continues)

Listing 5-0   *(continued)*

```
# make sure the packages for this chapter
# are installed, install if necessary
pkg <- c("ggplot2", "scales", "maptools",
         "sp", "maps", "grid", "car" )
new.pkg <- pkg[!(pkg %in% installed.packages())]
if (length(new.pkg)) {
  install.packages(new.pkg)
}
```

Simplifying Maps

It's easy to get all wrapped up thinking that visualizing spatial data (maps) is special, complicated, or will somehow take a lot more effort. But with the right tools (and there are plenty available), working with spatial data can not only be relatively simple, but also quite fun. In order to take some of the mystique out of maps, we want to start by loading the latitude and longitude points from Symantec and treating them as x,y coordinates to create a simple scatterplot (Listing 5-1).

Listing 5-1

```
# Load ggplot2 to create graphics
library(ggplot2)
# read the CSV with headers
za <- read.csv("data/zeroaccess.csv", header=T)

# create a ggplot instance with zeroaccess data
gg <- ggplot(data=za, aes(x=long, y=lat))
# add the points, set transparency to 1/40th
gg <- gg + geom_point(size=1, color="#000099", alpha=1/40)
# add axes labels
gg <- gg + xlab("Longitude") + ylab("Latitude")
# simplify the theme for aesthetics
gg <- gg + theme_bw()
# this may take a while, over 800,000 points plotted
print(gg)
```

Figure 5-1 looks remarkably like a world map without placing borders or loading any map specific tasks. This works with this data because there are over 800,000 coordinate pairs and one point is covering more than a large city. We made the points a little less overwhelming by setting the alpha (transparency of the color) to be 1/40 of a full color. With the alpha at 1/40, it will take 40 points on top of one another to create a non-transparent color. With 20 points, for example, on top of one another, you see 50 percent transparency.

From this basic scatterplot, you can see the density in the Eastern half and West coast of the United States and most of Europe is covered. You see some concentration in Brazil, and India is outlined quite well. One interesting thing to note here is that China has almost no density and Japan is clearly visible. But at this point, you can only make guesses as to what's going on with what looks like a significant difference in Asian countries.

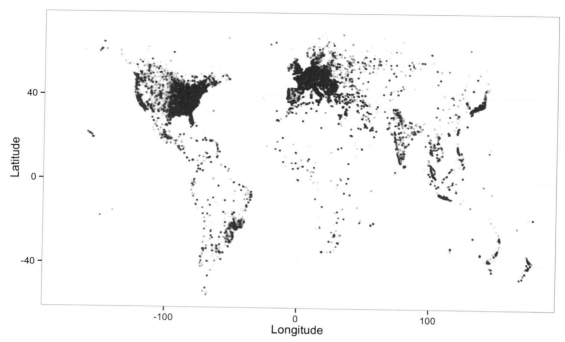

FIGURE 5-1 *Basic scatterplot using latitude and longitude*

There is something unique about maps, because you need to "project" the three-dimensional spherical world onto a two-dimensional flat canvas. When you do that, aspects of the map are distorted—shapes will be distorted, land areas will shrink or be over-represented, or distances will be skewed. But for most applications within information security, you are simply trying to represent some attribute of, or difference between, geographic areas. So the choice of map projections is more about personal preference and aesthetics rather than communicating a specific geographic message. Figure 5-2 shows a few different map projections.

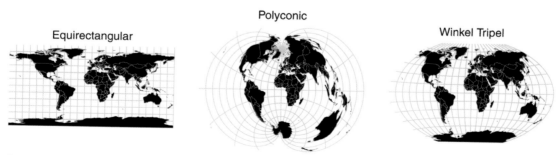

FIGURE 5-2 *Map projections*

If you take another look at Figure 5-1, it's a little hard to know where all those points land unless you were among the few who didn't fall asleep during world geography in high school. Let's recreate that image, build a map with a specific projection of the landmasses, and **then** add the points on top of it. Luckily, within R, most of the basic map data is already available with a few packages installed. The ggplot2 package has a function called map_data() that wraps the maps package to return a ggplot2-compatible data frame.

Calling map_data() with one character string of "world" will load just over 25 thousand rows of map data into a data frame, which means, as you've seen in Chapter 3, you can explore any and all of this data with commands like str(), head(), and summary(). You can plot the countries by tracing a path along the latitude and longitude pairs in the map data, which has the effect of drawing the country borders. Paths are grouped by the column labeled **group** (in this data, groups are the country), and the data frame must be sorted in order (an important detail, as you'll see later). To create the final map (see Listing 5-2), you call coord_map() to create the map projections (you will use the Mercator projection for this example), and you'll use a simple black and white theme on it with the theme_bw() function. Once you have the countries traced, you then add the points from the ZeroAccess data on the map as if you are creating a scatterplot like you did before (see Figure 5-3).

LISTING 5-2

```
# requires package : ggplot2
# requires object: za (5-1)
# the "maps" and "mapproj" packages are used by ggplot2
# load map data of the world
world <- map_data("world")
# nothing personal penguins, but strip out Antarctica
world <- subset(world, world$region!="Antarctica")
# load world data into ggplot object
gg <- ggplot(data=world, aes(x=long, y=lat))
# trace along the lat/long coords by group (countries)
gg <- gg + geom_path(aes(group=group), colour="gray70")
# now project using the mercator projection
# try different projections with ?mapproject
gg <- gg + coord_map("mercator", xlim=c(-200, 200))
# load up the ZeroAccess points, overiding the default data set
gg <- gg + geom_point(data=za, aes(long, lat),
                      colour="#000099", alpha=1/40, size=1)
# remove text, axes ticks, grid lines and do gray border on white
gg <- gg + theme(text=element_blank(),
              axis.ticks=element_blank(),
              panel.grid=element_blank(),
              panel.background=element_rect(color="gray50",
                                          fill="white"))
print(gg)
```

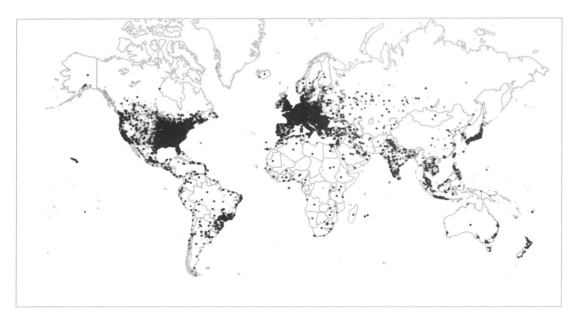

FIGURE 5-3 *Worldwide ZeroAccess infections*

Now, ***that's*** a real map; but, what can you learn from it? The answer is not much. This map communicates very little beside the fact that the ZeroAccess botnet is an international traveler, and that should surprise nobody. It's time to probe a bit deeper and see whether you can use maps to help you visualize the data a bit better.

How Many ZeroAccess Infections per Country?

It's very difficult to look at Figure 5-3 and determine which countries have the most infections. You can't expect anyone to look at a map like this and extract the proportion of bot infections in countries. It looks like the United States and Europe are blanketed in bots; so, let's try a different type of map. You need to count how many infections you have in each country and then you can visualize the results with a *choropleth*. A choropleth is a map in which the country is shaded or filled with color that is then associated with the data. For your first choropleth, you will have to figure out which country the latitude/longitude points are in and then you will use a single continuous color scale to represent that quantity (see Listing 5-3). To convert latitude and longitude to a country, you will adapt a function from Ryan Weald and call the function `latlong2map()`. That function will accept a data frame of longitude and latitude pairs along with the name of a map to translate onto.

LISTING 5-3
```
# require packages: maps, maptools
# packages are not required to create function
```

(continues)

LISTING 5-3   *(continued)*

```
# but it cannot be executed without these loaded
library(maps)
library(maptools)
# slightly modified verison of Ryan Weald's (@rweald) function
# https://gist.github.com/rweald/4720788
latlong2map <- function(pointsDF, mapping) {
  # load up the map data
  local.map <- map(mapping, fill=TRUE, col="transparent", plot=FALSE)
  # pull out the IDs from the name
  IDs <- sapply(strsplit(local.map$names, ":"), function(x) x[1])
  # Prepare SpatialPolygons object
  maps_sp <- map2SpatialPolygons(local.map, IDs=IDs,
            proj4string=CRS("+proj=longlat +datum=wgs84"))
  # Convert pointsDF to a SpatialPoints object
  pointsSP <- SpatialPoints(pointsDF,
              proj4string=CRS("+proj=longlat +datum=wgs84"))
  # Use 'over' to get _indices_ of the Polygons object containing each
point
  indices <- over(pointsSP, maps_sp)
  # Return the names of the Polygons object containing each point
  mapNames <- sapply(maps_sp@polygons, function(x) x@ID)
  # now return a vector of names that match the points
  mapNames[indices]
}
```

The function returns a vector of names (country names in this case), and you can count how many times the country appears with the `table()` command. Next in Listing 5-4, you'll want to `merge()` the count of countries with the map data and reorder it for the plotting. By merging the data directly into the map data, you can associate the shading of the country with an attribute in the data, specifically the count of infections in that country. You will use the `scale_fill_gradient2()` function within `ggplot2` to get the color gradient associated with the quantity of infections. See the result in Figure 5-4.

LISTING 5-4

```
# requires packages: ggplot2, maps and maptools
# requires objects: za (5-1), world (5-2), latlong2map (5-3)
# convert ZeroAccess long/lat into country names from world map
zworld <- latlong2map(data.frame(x=za$long, y=za$lat), "world")
# count up points in the country and conver to data frame
wct <- data.frame(table(zworld))
# label the country as "region" to match map data
colnames(wct) <- c("region", "count")
# merge will match on "region" in each and add "count" to "world"
za.choro <- merge(world, wct)
```

(continues)

LISTING 5-4 *(continued)*

```
# now we sort the map data to original sequence
# otherwise the map is disasterous
za.choro <- za.choro[with(za.choro, order(group, order)), ]
# and plot
gg <- ggplot(za.choro, aes(x=long, y=lat, group=group, fill=count))
gg <- gg + geom_path(colour="#666666") + geom_polygon()
gg <- gg + coord_map("mercator", xlim=c(-200, 200), ylim=c(-60,200))
gg <- gg + scale_fill_gradient2(low="#FFFFFF", high="#4086AA",
                                    midpoint=median(za.choro$count),
                                    name="Infections")
# remove text, axes ticks, grid lines and do gray border on white
gg <- gg + theme(axis.title=element_blank(),
                axis.text=element_blank(),
                axis.ticks=element_blank(),
                panel.grid=element_blank(),
                panel.background=element_rect(color="gray50",
                                            fill="white"))
print(gg)
```

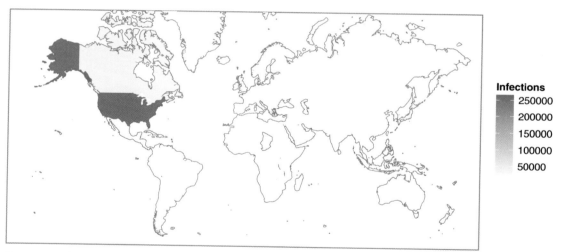

FIGURE 5-4 *Choropleth of ZeroAccess infections*

Voila! You have a rather good-looking (some might say, "spiffy") map and it looks like the United States has cornered the market on ZeroAccess infections. There would be no way you could learn that from the points in Figure 5-3. However, it's very difficult to tell the specific quantity by color density (Chapter 6 discusses visualization techniques in more detail); all you can tell from this type of map is that the United States has more infections. To learn just how much more, you can look into the wct variable and then calculate the proportion of infections in the United States (Listing 5-5).

<small>LISTING 5-5</small>

```
# requires object: wct (5-4)
head(wct)
##          region count
## 1 Afghanistan     53
## 2      Albania   1166
## 3      Algeria   3014
## 4      Andorra      4
## 5       Angola    160
## 6    Argentina   6016

# for each wct$count, divide by sum, gives us proportion of the whole
perc <- wct$count/sum(wct$count)
# covert to a readable format, round it and create percent
wct$perc <- round(perc, 4)*100
# now order the highest percentages on top
wct <- wct[with(wct, order(perc, decreasing=T)), ]
# look at the top few entries.
head(wct)
##        region  count   perc
## 148      USA 261627 35.23
## 24    Canada  35607  4.79
## 74     Japan  33590  4.52
## 145       UK  31813  4.28
## 50   Germany  27336  3.68
## 71     Italy  25717  3.46
```

You could have just created this table in the beginning to answer the question, "How is ZeroAccess distributed across geographic areas?" The map visually highlights the gap between the United States and the rest of the world. Also keep in mind that these are just total counts and not normalized for population or anything. So at this point, the 35 percent represents a proportion solely within the ZeroAccess data, and you should not infer more without further analysis.

Changing the Scope of Your Data

You can't lose sight of the goal here, which is to find a way to correlate Zero Access infections with other data points like alien visits. To get closer to answering this, you can simplify the data set to the U.S. infections. We chose to do this not just because working with over 800,000 data points can be a bit slow on some systems, but also because it will be much easier to focus in on the United States because of our knowledge of the geography and accessibility of data (especially around alien visitors).

However, as you change the scope within the data like this, you need to consider how this may change the question you're able to answer. You can no longer generalize about every infection everywhere because you cannot readily transfer what you learn from infections in the United States to other countries and/or cultures. Another way to state this is that you cannot be sure that the factors that contribute to infections in the United States will match the factors elsewhere. Those considerations go beyond and outside the data you are looking at now, so be sure to avoid making any broad assumptions as you continue your analysis and present your results.

If you attempt to plot a U.S. map and then project all the points on it, the auto-scaling feature in ggplot will create a rather funny picture. It will show all of the world points in the data set, but will trace out only the U.S. map. You need to reduce the data size and remove data that are not in the United States. You can reuse the latlong2map() function, this time mapping the points to the United States by specifying "state" as the second argument. From an R-perspective, this means anything that does not get mapped to a U.S. state will be retuned as the *NA* value, which can then be filtered out of the data.

Once all that processing is done, you can make a nice map of the continental United States showing all the ZeroAccess infections in the country (Figure 5-5). Notice that for this plot and the last few you have been removing all the extra ***chartjunk*** (a term coined by Edward Tufte) on the map. This is done with the theme() function at the end and removing graphical features by assigning them to element_blank(). See Listing 5-6.

LISTING 5-6

```
# requires package: ggplot2, maps, maptools
# requires objects: za (5-1), latlong2map (5-3)
zstate <- latlong2map(data.frame(x=za$long, y=za$lat), "state")
# select rows from za where the zstate is not NA
za.state <- za[which(!is.na(zstate)), ]
# load map data of the U.S.
state <- map_data("state")

gg <- ggplot(data=state, aes(x=long, y=lat))
gg <- gg + geom_path(aes(group=group), colour="gray80")
gg <- gg + coord_map("mercator")
gg <- gg + geom_point(data=za.state, aes(long, lat),
                      colour="#000099", alpha=1/40, size=1)
# stripping off the "chart junk"
gg <- gg + theme(axis.title=element_blank(),
               axis.text=element_blank(),
               axis.ticks=element_blank(),
               panel.grid=element_blank(),
               panel.background=element_blank())
print(gg)
```

Consider Figure 5-5 for a moment. Does it look…*strange*? This is where you really have to be careful because after working with spatial data, we can tell you *this looks like a reflection of population density* and *not* infections. Therefore, after reviewing Figure 5-5, you might find yourself asking a slightly different question: *Could ZeroAccess infections just be a reflection of the population*? You *could* stop and apply a statistical technique called regression analysis (you will later), but for now stick with pictures and create another choropleth. This time you'll break up the data and perform counts based on the U.S. states.

FIGURE 5-5 *ZeroAccess infections in the United States*

The Potwin Effect

As you dig deeper than just country, you have to account for something we call the "Potwin Effect" after the town by that name in Kansas with a population of 449. The population is important because if you examine the data, you'll see that there are 12,643 reported ZeroAccess infections in the town of Potwin, Kansas. We first stumbled across this "anomaly" in a different (and more subtle) analysis and spent days trying to understand why Potwin was so odd. We realized that these couldn't be valid entries after we had some crazy ideas about Potwin trying to justify the data. Finally, we remembered that there were several data points that were strangely rounded off to integers and they were all 38,-97.

Then, it dawned on us. IP geolocation services should always know what country an IP address is in because the IANA records are clear about that. But if the geolocation service cannot get any more granular than identifying the country, they return a rounded-off integer location near the geographic center of the country. In the United States, the geographic center is just outside of Potwin, Kansas. For this purpose, they are "unknown U.S. locations" and not really in Kansas, so you are going to remove these data points from the next bit of code to avoid unfairly assigning infections to Kansas.

In this map, you want to again use color to show quantity. Rather than just using a single hue (a fancy term for color), you'll use a ***diverging color scheme*** (two opposite colors) and assign the mid-point of the range to the mean count per state (see Listing 5-7). This will allow you to show states with above average infection counts with one hue and the below average states with another. As a side note, let's also change the projection from the Mercator projection to the Polyconic. That projection looks odd at the world level (as you can see in Figure 5-2), but it puts a nice slope and curve in a U.S. map. It's good (and dare we say fun!) to play around with different projections.

LISTING 5-7

```
# requires package: ggplot2, maps, maptools
# requires objects: za (5-1), latlong2map (5-3)
# create a choropleth of the U.S. states
# because all of these vectors are from the same source (za),
# we can cross the indexes of the vectors
zstate <- latlong2map(data.frame(x=za$long, y=za$lat), "state")
# pull out those that are not NA, and take care of Potwin effect
state.index <- which(!is.na(zstate) & za$lat!=38 & za$long!=-97)
# now create a count of states and filter on those indexes
sct <- data.frame(table(zstate[state.index]))
colnames(sct) <- c("region", "count")
# merge with state map data
za.sct <- merge(state, sct)
# Now plot a choropleth using a diverging color
colors <- c("#A6611A", "#DFC27D", "#F5F5F5", "#80CDC1", "#018571")
gg <- ggplot(za.sct, aes(x=long, y=lat, group=group, fill=count))
gg <- gg + geom_polygon(colour="black")
gg <- gg + coord_map("polyconic")
gg <- gg + scale_fill_gradient2(low=colors[5], mid=colors[3],
                                high=colors[1],
                                midpoint=mean(za.sct$count),
                                name="Infections")
gg <- gg + theme(axis.title=element_blank(),
                 axis.text=element_blank(),
                 axis.ticks=element_blank(),
                 panel.grid=element_blank(),
                 panel.background=element_blank())
print(gg)
```

Figure 5-6 shows another handsome but *relatively useless* map. You can easily see that California, Texas, Florida, and New York are above average, but it's also good to have the wherewithal to realize that the four most populated states are California, Texas, New York, and Florida, in that order.

In other words, you are just seeing a reflection of population in this map, so you have to *normalize* this data to the population. In order to normalize you can take multiple approaches. The simplest ways to normalize involve answering one of these questions:

- How many people per one infection?
- What proportion of the people are infected?
- How many infections per 1,000 people?

FIGURE 5-6 *Choropleth of U.S. states with ZeroAccess*

The differences between these questions are subtle, and in this case you will do the first method because you will get whole numbers, and it will be a little easier to conceptualize for your reader. In order to determine the number of people per infection, you divide the population in a state by the number of infections in that state (Listing 5-8). In this case, we have already scraped population data from `http://www.internetworldstats.com/stats26.htm` and made it available in an easy format on the book's website (`state-internets.csv` in the Chapter 5 download materials at `www.wiley.com/go/datadrivensecurity`).

LISTING 5-8

```
# requires package: ggplot2, maps, maptools
# requires objects: sct (5-7), colors (5-7), latlong2map (5-3)
# read in state population and internet users
# data scraped from http://www.internetworldstats.com/stats26.htm
users <- read.csv("data/state-internets.csv", header=T)
# all the state names are lower case in map data, so convert
users$state <- tolower(users$state)
# now merge with the sct data from previous example
# merge by sct$region and users$state
za.users <- merge(sct, users, by.x="region", by.y="state")
# calculate people to infection
# change this to internet users if you would like to try that
za.users$pop2inf <- round(za.users$population/za.users$count, 0)
```

(continues)

LISTING 5-8   *(continued)*

```
# and create a simple data frame and merge
za.norm <- data.frame(region=za.users$region,
                      count=za.users$pop2inf)
za.norm.map <- merge(state, za.norm)
# now create the choropleth
gg <- ggplot(za.norm.map, aes(x=long, y=lat, group=group, fill=count))
gg <- gg + geom_polygon(colour="black")
gg <- gg + coord_map("polyconic")
gg <- gg + scale_fill_gradient2(low=colors[5], mid=colors[3],
                                high=colors[1],
                                midpoint=mean(za.norm.map$count),
                                name="People per\nInfection")
gg <- gg + theme(axis.title=element_blank(),
                 axis.text=element_blank(),
                 axis.ticks=element_blank(),
                 panel.grid=element_blank(),
                 panel.background=element_blank())
print(gg)
```

Remember California, Texas, Florida, and New York having the highest infection counts? Using the `za.norm` data generated in Listing 5-8, you can view the exact counts. When you normalize to population, California and New York drop to below average with one infection per 1,440 and 1,287 people on average, respectively (see Figure 5-7). Wyoming now sticks out as the most infected state since one in 724 people in Wyoming appear to have ZeroAccess infections.

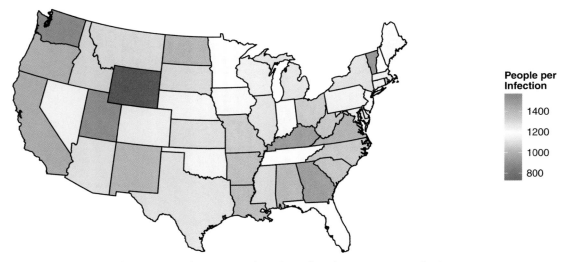

FIGURE 5-7 *Normalized ZeroAccess infections: Number of people in the state per one infection*

Note

In the `state-internets.csv` *data, we also included the count of Internet users if you want to try to create a choropleth normalized on estimated Internet users per state (it is a prettier picture).*

Is This Weird?

Let's stop for a moment and look at the current results. You have a range of normalized values from 1 in 724 people with an infection in Wyoming to 1 in 1,550 people in Washington state. Does this mean that the citizens in Wyoming are much more careless than those in Washington? Perhaps more Washingtonians run Linux? Or—and this is an important concept—is the range of observations simply from *natural variation in the measuring accuracy* and the world? Is Wyoming the most infected state because someone had to be in last place and in this data it just so happened to be Wyoming? You need to understand if the extreme values are *outliers* or if they are within expectations. There are two key methods to test for outliers:

- Using a boxplot (the "IQR" method)
- Calculating a z-score

Using a Boxplot to Find Outliers

The boxplot was developed by John Tukey (you met him briefly in Chapter 1) and was designed to show a distribution of values visually. It does this by plotting a box from the 25th percentile to the 75th percentile in the distribution. This distance is called the *inter-quartile range* (IQR). Then lines are extended from the box for a distance one and half times the length of the IQR. Anything beyond the length of these lines is a good candidate to be labeled as an outlier, and is represented by point. The further these points are, the more likely they an outlier. In order to create a boxplot, you will use the default R graphics `boxplot()` function. You'll save the results returned into a variable called `popbox` (see Listing 5-9) for exploring in Listing 5-10. While there are multiple ways to create a boxplot, the default function just accepts in a vector of values for the distribution, and then it works its magic (see Figure 5-8).

LISTING 5-9

```
# requires objects: za.norm (5-8)
# create a box plot of the count
popbox <- boxplot(za.norm$count)
```

Looks like you may have a few outliers, which are represented by individual points. There are clearly three points above the plot and two points below. Although you could sort the data in `za.norm` and look for the top three and bottom two, you saved the output from `boxplot()`, which has various data points about the boxplot, into the `popbox` variable, so you can look up the values in the `popbox$out` (the outliers) vector in the original data (Listing 5-10).

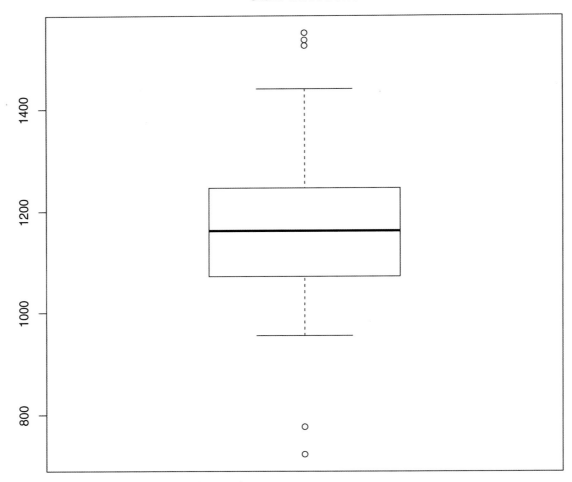

FIGURE 5-8 *Distribution of normalized state infections*

LISTING 5-10

```
# requires objects: za.norm (5-8), popbox (5-9)
# the values that are considered outliers
print(popbox$out)
## [1]   777 1536 1525 1550   724

# pull the rows from za.norm that have those values
za.norm[za.norm$count %in% popbox$out, ]
```

(continues)

LISTING 5-10   *(continued)*
```
##                      region count
## 8   district of columbia   777
## 43                   utah  1536
## 44                vermont  1525
## 46             washington  1550
## 49                wyoming   724
```

According to the method employed by Tukey in the boxplot, you could consider these five states as being odd (outliers).

Calculating a Z-Score to Find Outliers

There's another measure of determining oddballs; you can calculate what's known as a **z-score**. It will help you get a feel for just how much of an outlier a point is by showing how many **standard deviations** from the **mean** it is. A z-score is most often used to compare distributions from completely different scales, a method sometimes labeled "standardizing" the data. In order to do this calculation, you need to know the standard deviation and mean of the distribution. Then, for each value in the distribution, you calculate how many standard deviations from the mean the observation is. That is, you subtract the mean from each value and divide by the standard deviation. (See Listing 5-11.)

If your eyes started to glaze over from the z-score description, don't worry—every time we calculate one, we have to look up how it's done. You'll want to compare what you see in the distribution to something known as the "empirical rule" of a standard normal distribution. In a normal distribution (the familiar bell curve, which is also known as the **Gaussian distribution**), you expect that roughly 68 percent of the distribution will fall within one standard deviation (above or below) of the mean, and 95 percent of the data will fall within two standard deviations, and then 99.7 percent should be within three standard deviations.

One point to note—this method doesn't work well if the data is skewed, so you should probably check a quick histogram (pass za.norm$count into the `hist()` function) to be sure it's not obviously skewed.

When using this approach, anything outside of three standard deviations is typically labeled as an outlier, and you might even consider anything more than two standard deviations as a possible outlier.

LISTING 5-11
```
# requires objects: za.norm (5-8)
# get the standard deviation
za.sd <- sd(za.norm$count)
# get the mean
za.mean <- mean(za.norm$count)
# now calculate the z-score and round to 1 decimal
za.norm$z <- round((za.norm$count-za.mean)/za.sd, 1)
# we can inspect the "z" variable for the specific z-scores
# pull out values where absolute value of z-score is > 2
za.norm[which(abs(za.norm$z)>2), ]
##                      region count    z
## 8   district of columbia   777 -2.4
## 43                   utah  1536  2.2
```

(continues)

Listing 5-11   *(continued)*

```
## 44           vermont  1525   2.1
## 46        washington  1550   2.2
## 49           wyoming   724  -2.7
```

It appears those same five entries fall within three standard deviations. This knowledge calls into question the use of population in the normalization process (perhaps "Internet users" would be a better measure—hint, hint).

Rather than focus on solving things at the state level, you could bring this data down to the county level within the states. Doing so will supply more data points and allow a finer separation of the population, which will open up more possibility.

> ### Note
>
> *Overall, it'd be okay to consider these values within expectations given they are within three standard deviations, but if you had time, it would be a good practice to look into these more and be sure the measurements are valid. The takeaway is that you must answer the question, "Is this weird?" with either a squishy "probably not" or a non-committal "not so sure."*

What's the P-Value?

Trying to identify *weird* versus *normal* is a core concept within statistics, and, depending on the circumstances, there is usually more than one way to identify it. At the heart of "statistically significant" is knowing whether something is weird or just the result of natural variations. One very common and widespread approach is the p-value. Don't mistake its widespread use with a widespread understanding or even consistent use. The p-value has a very specific (and difficult to remember) meaning. In order to define and calculate a p-value, you begin with a statement (technically called a *null hypothesis*) and calculate the probability of the data being generated by chance if the statement is true—this is the p-value. Now the subtlety of the p-value is often lost, and people jump to convenient (and wrong) assumptions, like it's the probability of the statement being true (it's not).

To complicate this concept even more, somehow it became generally accepted that a p-value of 0.05 (1/20th) or less was "statistically significant," creating what is essentially an arbitrary cut-off point. You will be revisiting the value of p-values when you read about regression analysis later in this chapter. Just tuck the term "p-value" away in your memory bank as a measure of significance or, in this case, of "weirdness."

Counting in Counties

It is difficult to generalize at the state level because, well, it is a very generalized population. You would be obscuring a wide range of diversity among people behind a single label. You would be hard-pressed to calculate the influence of something like income or—more importantly—alien visits on ZeroAccess infections at the state level. You can get more granular by repeating `latlong2map()` again, but at the county level.

There are a few additional items to consider as you get into a more detailed breakdown of geolocation of IP addresses. Most of the popular IP geolocation services publish estimations of their accuracy beyond country. For example, the service used on this data claims that just over four out of five entries are accurate to about 25 miles and about one out of seven are resolved to an incorrect city. Does that mean you should be very wary of this data? In order to answer that question, you need to understand a statistical concept—natural variations will cancel out more often than stack up, especially as you get more data (and over 3,000 U.S. counties do represent *more* data).

Does Variation Stack or Cancel?

Within statistics, natural variations generally cancel each other out, but this is counterintuitive to fields in engineering (like computer science) where people are taught that if they add components that all have a slight variation, the effect will compound itself and they should expect a wide range of results. What's the difference? Which viewpoint is right?

This is kind of a tricky concept, so consider an example. Say you are manufacturing a physical part and you want it to be 100 millimeters (mm) long. Natural variation in the quality of materials and manufacturing process produces parts that range equally between 98 and 102 millimeters. Engineers are taught that if they stack up 100 of those parts, they can expect something equally likely between plus or minus two times the number of parts (100). Meaning, it is possible that all 100 parts will be 98 millimeters, or it's possible that all the parts will be 102 millimeters, so they can expect a wide range in the output. The more they stack, the wider the range of output.

In statistics, if you can assume that each part has an equal chance of being any length within the range (and you'll want to validate that assumption in the real world), the differences in lengths will begin to cancel each other out. Thanks to a basic understanding of programming, you can model this and see how variation occurs across multiple parts.

The example generates 100 parts and uniformly "manufactures" them between 98 and 102 millimeters. It then averages the length (it could also be the sum or some other measurement, but the mean works here). The engineering brains out there will guess that this will appear between 98 and 102, but let's see (Listing 5-12).

LISTING 5-12

```
#setting seed for reproducibility
set.seed(1492)
# run 100 times, getting random values between 98 and 102
mean(runif(100, min=98, max=102))
## [1] 100.0141
```

After one run, you get 100.0141. Let's manufacture 10,000 sets of 100 stacked parts and see how many get to the edge of the range (Listing 5-13). Surely if it's possible, you should see at least a few sets in 10,000 push toward the edge, right?

(continues)

(continued)

LISTING 5-13

```
#setting seed for reproducibility
set.seed(1492)
# iterate seq(10000) times, generate a set of 100 parts and calc mean
parts <- sapply(seq(10000), function(x) mean(runif(100, min=98, max=102)))
# result is a vector of 10,000 sets
# show the min and max of these parts
range(parts)
## [1]  99.57977 100.47559
```

What is up with this? Even with 10,000 iterations of 100 random parts, none of them get close to the ranges of 98 or 102. You can visualize all of the parts in a quick histogram by running hist (***parts***). You see a nice symmetric distribution centering around 100. Even though the parts could all be 98 or 102, the variation will cancel out, especially as the sets increase (rather than 100 in a set, try 1,000 or 10,000 in the runif function). As you add more parts within the range, the results are more likely to cluster even closer around the mean.

There are a couple of takeaways from this tangent. First, it's really fun to geek out a bit and generate data to answer questions with "what if" scenarios. Second, ***you shouldn't toss out less-than-perfect data***. If the variations are caused by natural or random variations, you can assume the variation has more of a cancelling effect than a stacking effect. Now, this doesn't mean you should ignore variations like this, but instead it means that the variation will have less of an impact on throwing the analysis off than you think. You should still account for this variation in your work.

Relating this back to the analyses, you have all sorts of items in the spatial data that may be throwing off the calculations. All of the geolocation lookups have a 25-mile radius of accuracy (so, some points that are supposed to be, say, in Southern Maine, end up in New Hampshire). Several of the data points will be farther off than that. But these might cancel out if the variation is random (meaning points in New Hampshire could also just as easily end up in Maine). This doesn't mean the data is worthless. Until you can learn some more advanced techniques, you can just take the error introduced as a grain a salt. In other words, you can use this data to estimate how much of an effect alien visits have, but you wouldn't want to balance the fate of a company on this analysis—at least not without a lot more rigor and investigation of the data.

Moving Down to Counties

To transition the data down to the county level, you'll begin by calling the same latlong2map() function on the same ZeroAccess data, but ask it to translate to the county names (Listing 5-14). Keep in mind, there are over 3,000 counties in the United States and over 800,000 latitude/longitude pairs to go through, so depending on the system, this could take a few seconds or so to run. Like last time, you want to ignore anything that doesn't resolve in the United States (is set to NA in the data) and account for the Potwin Effect (anything below country should account for it). But rather than count things with table() and toss them into a data frame, you have to do some transformation on the returned names. The county names come back from latlong2map() as a single text string in the "state, county" format. You can use the `strsplit()` function to split the county names. It returns a list object, so you convert it to a vector with the `unlist()` function. The result will be one long vector with the values alternating state and county, which is okay because you'll transform this into a matrix with two columns (state and county) with the `ncol=2` argument and tell it to go row by row (rather than column by column). The result is then converted into a data frame, along with the count of infections in each county. And now you're beginning to see how fun this data-munging thing can be, right?

LISTING 5-14

```
# requires package: maps, maptools
# requires objects: za (5-1), latlong2map (5-3)
## now mapping lat/long down to county
county <- latlong2map(data.frame(x=za$long, y=za$lat), "county")
za.county <- county[which(!is.na(county) & za$lat!=38 & za$long!=-97)]
# count the occurances
county.count <- table(za.county)
# need to convert "county, state" into a data frame
# so we split it out by comma
temp.list <- strsplit(names(county.count), ",")
# convert the list into a vector
temp.list <- unlist(temp.list)
# force the vector into a 2 column matrix, filling row by row
temp.matrix <- matrix(temp.list, ncol=2, byrow=T)
# and now create the data frame with the count of county infections
za.county <- data.frame(temp.matrix, as.vector(county.count))
# finally assign names to the fields
# names match the field names in the county map_data
colnames(za.county) <- c("region", "subregion", "infections")
head(za.county)
##      region subregion infections
## 1 alabama    autauga         44
## 2 alabama    baldwin        184
## 3 alabama    barbour         13
## 4 alabama       bibb         13
## 5 alabama     blount         26
## 6 alabama    bullock         11
```

You now have a data frame with three columns—the state, county, and count of infections—and you need to label the columns accordingly. There is a lingering "so what?" you need to answer before proceeding. Aside from the initial "wow" factor of generating a cool-looking map, there is not much to learn from a raw count being displayed on a map. You may see some hot spots and you may be able to compare different areas on the map, but you can't really learn much from this amount of detailed data on a map. Moving forward, you'll switch from creating maps with this data to performing some *real* analysis to see whether you can find an explanation for the infections.

You'll need to pull in other data here (also split out by the county), just as you did at the state level with population. Then you may be able to understand a bit more about these malware infections. Perhaps there is some foreign (some would say alien) data that would either help explain variations in the malware infections or help support the techniques we want to cover.

We scoured the Internet, pulled together a collection of rather interesting data points, and did the data-munging to produce the data you'll use here. For the purposes of creating a tutorial, we've extracted a few statistics by county from various places and made it available on the book's website (`county-data .csv` on `www.wiley.com/go/datadrivensecurity` as part of Chapter 5's download materials).

- `region` and `subregion` are the state and county, respectively.
- `pop` is the estimated county population.
- `income` is the median income for the county.
- `ufo2010` is the number of UFO sightings in the county during 2010 (as recorded on the national UFO reporting center: `nuforc.org`).
- `ipaddr` is the number of IP addresses that translate to the county (pulled from the open `freegeoip.net` package).

As luck would have it (for you), the data is in a perfect state so it can be read in and simply merged with the ZeroAccess county data you just created. There is one special note with the `merge()` function: By default, it will drop any rows that are not in both data sets. In this case, you have 160 counties not represented in the ZeroAccess data. This could be for a variety of reasons; perhaps the IP geolocation services are especially inaccurate in those counties or they are just sparsely populated counties and not having infections isn't weird.

Feel free to dig into the values, but sure enough, 90 percent of the uninfected counties have a population of less than 10,000. By specifying `all.x=T` in the `merge()` command, you are telling it not to drop any rows from the x data, which is the first argument passed into the `merge()` function, or **county.data** in the command (see Listing 5-15). To help illustrate we are including the argument labels when we call `merge()`.

LISTING 5-15

```
# requires objects: za.county (5-14)
# read up census data per county
county.data <- read.csv("data/county-data.csv", header=T)
# notice the all.x option here
za.county <- merge(x=county.data, y=za.county, all.x=T)
# replace all NA's with 0
za.county$infections[is.na(za.county$infections)] <- 0
summary(za.county)
##       subregion           region          pop              income
## washington: 32    texas   : 254   Min.   :      71   Min.   : 19344
## jefferson :  26   georgia : 159   1st Qu.:  11215   1st Qu.: 37793
## franklin  :  25   kentucky: 120   Median :  26047   Median : 43332
## jackson   :  24   missouri: 115   Mean   : 101009   Mean   : 45075
## lincoln   :  24   kansas  : 105   3rd Qu.:  67921   3rd Qu.: 50010
## madison   :  20   illinois: 102   Max.   :9962789   Max.   :120096
```

(continues)

Listing 5-15   *(continued)*

```
## (Other)   :2921   (Other) :2217
##      ipaddr              ufo2010            infections
## Min.   :         0  Min.   :  0.000  Min.   :   0.00
## 1st Qu.:      5367  1st Qu.:  0.000  1st Qu.:   6.00
## Median :     15289  Median :  2.000  Median :  17.00
## Mean   :    387973  Mean   :  7.943  Mean   :  83.33
## 3rd Qu.:     62594  3rd Qu.:  6.000  3rd Qu.:  55.25
## Max.   : 223441040  Max.   :815.000  Max.   :7692.00
```

Running `summary(za.county)` on the data, you can get a good feel for what things look like in there (and you learn that people who name counties have an affinity for the founding fathers).

Now that you've looked at the data, can you pick out the relationship with UFO visits? Not yet? How can you begin to pick apart the relationships in this data? Thanks to the work of statisticians, you have a technique known as *linear regression* that is extremely powerful and yet extremely dangerous.

Introducing Linear Regression

This section discusses a collection of techniques loosely called *linear regression*, but it's important to know that college courses focus on nothing but linear regression for a semester and still don't cover all aspects of it. Books such as *Applied Linear Statistical Models by John Neter, William Wasserman, and Michael H. Kutner* are over 1,300 pages and packed with statistical notation (it's a page-turner!). This is all to say that regression analysis is an incredibly rich and deep topic and we will barely scratch the surface here. What we hope to do here is clear up some of the mystery around regression analysis and put the technique in context, while at the same time introduce enough warnings and common pitfalls so that you don't end up shooting yourself in the foot with this powerful and flexible technique.

Note

This section applies some techniques that you should not take lightly. This section focuses more on walking through the concepts and techniques rather than attempting to perform insightful research. Using statistical methods without fully understanding them is akin to an unlicensed teenager taking a car out for a spin.

Regression analysis is a workhorse, and it is behind many of the scientific findings you hear about. Works that say, "Scientists find a link between something and something else" are almost always based on regression analysis. Researchers use regression analysis for two general purposes.

- **First, it can be used to estimate how different observable inputs contribute to an observable output**. In this case, you want to estimate how alien visits to U.S. counties (observable inputs) contribute to the rate of ZeroAccess infections in that county (observable output). With regression analysis, not only can you estimate the significance (or lack thereof) of each variable, you can also estimate how strong that contribution is. Don't worry if it is a bit confusing now; we will cover this more as you get into the data. Regression analysis is a powerful tool to describe relationships between observations.

● **The second purpose for regression analysis is *prediction*.** The output of regression analysis is a formula. Given specific inputs, you can make an estimate, or ***predict*** what the output will be. A classic example with this is the relationship between height and weight. It's relatively intuitive that taller people weigh more, but if you add other variables such as male and female, age, and so on, you can determine an expected value, and establish an expected range of a person's weight. This is the method doctors use to tell patients they are above or below their expected weight, height, and so on. Regression analysis is a powerful tool for estimating and comparing observed outputs.

To demonstrate these two purposes, you'll create fictitious (and rather simple) data. You'll start with a single input variable and generate random data points from a normal distribution (any distribution will work, the normal is just pretty). You'll use the `rnorm()` command and create 200 points with a mean of 10 and a standard deviation of 1 (the default). See Listing 5-16.

LISTING 5-16
```
# for reproducability
set.seed(1)
# generate 200 random numbers around 10
input <- rnorm(200, mean=10)
summary(input)
##  Min. 1st Qu.  Median    Mean 3rd Qu.    Max.
## 7.785   9.386   9.951  10.040  10.610  12.400
```

If you look at the summary in Listing 5-16, you see the result is data that ranges from 7.2 to 12.9. You now need to generate the output data. You want to create a linear relationship between the input and the output, so you'll pass the mean in as double the input variables. By using `rnorm()` you are introducing more random variations so you don't have perfectly linear relationship, but by centering the randomness (mean) on the input variable you are creating enough of a linear relationship to model. You then create a data frame out of the input and output for easy handling and plotting.

With the input and output created, you can pass all of this into `ggplot` (Listing 5-17) and create a scatterplot to visualize the relationship. Let's add something special by including the `geom_smooth()` function and telling it to use a linear model, `"lm"`. This will overlay a single straight line that best describes the relationship between the input and output data (see Figure 5-9).

LISTING 5-17
```
# generate output around a mean of 2 x input
output <- rnorm(200, mean=input*2)
# put into data frame to plot it
our.data <- data.frame(input, output)
gg <- ggplot(our.data, aes(input, output))
gg <- gg + geom_point()
gg <- gg + geom_smooth(method = "lm", se=F, color="red")
gg <- gg + theme_bw()
print(gg)
```

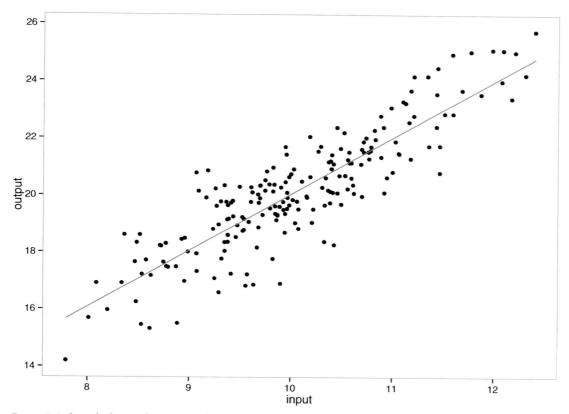

FIGURE 5-9 *Sample data with regression line*

You can see from Figure 5-9 that the data isn't exactly nice and neat (this is rnorm() introducing some random variation), but there is a definite trend. As the input variable increases, the output variable also increases, and the data flows from the lower left to the upper right. It sure looks like there is a relationship from this data (of course), but it's difficult to describe it beyond simple descriptions . . . enter regression analysis.

In order to run a linear regression on the data, you call one very simple command (Listing 5-18):

LISTING 5-18
```
# requires objects: input (5-16), output (5-17)
model <- lm(output ~ input)
```

Congratulations! You have just run your first linear regression. Take a look at the output with the summary() function, and we'll walk through it.
```
summary(model)
## Call:
## lm(formula = output ~ input)
##
```

(continues)

LISTING 5-18   *(continued)*

```
## Residuals:
##      Min       1Q    Median      3Q      Max
## -2.93275 -0.54273 -0.02523  0.66833  2.58615
##
## Coefficients:
##              Estimate Std. Error t value Pr(>|t|)
## (Intercept)  0.27224    0.77896   0.349   0.727
## input        1.97692    0.07729  25.577   <2e-16 ***
##    ---
##    Signif. codes:  0 '***' 0.001 '**' 0.01 '*' 0.05 '.' 0.1 ' ' 1
##
## Residual standard error: 1.013 on 198 degrees of freedom
## Multiple R-squared:  0.7677,  Adjusted R-squared:  0.7665
## F-statistic: 654.2 on 1 and 198 DF,  p-value: < 2.2e-16
```

There are many, many things to look at here. It starts with the function you used ("Call") and a summary of the *residuals*. The residuals are the difference between what the model predicts and what you observed in the output. The line is specifically calculated so the mean of the residuals is zero (making it the "best fit" for the data). Oftentimes, we'll skip over this residuals section, as there are better methods for interpreting the residuals.

The next section talks about the coefficients. In this model there are two—the *intercept*, which is always present, and the *input variable*. If you had more observed inputs, they would be listed here, one per line. The first column is the estimated value for the coefficient. For most linear models, the intercept has little to no meaning. The intercept coefficient signifies that if the input is at zero, you could estimate the output to be around 0.27 (which doesn't make sense if you were talking about a person's height for example). We didn't set this when we created this data (which made it zero), so 0.27 is pretty close.

Looking at the coefficients, you can construct the model:

$$output = 0.27224 + 1.97692 \times input$$

You would use this model to estimate new output values given an observed input (or just use the predict.lm() command passing in your model and new input variables to predict with). But remember that you generated the data by multiplying the input by 2? The linear model here thinks you multiplied by 1.97692, which is pretty close. This coefficient for the input variable (or variables) is where you can begin to see the power of regression analysis when used for inference about the input variables. You can interpret it like this:

If all the other input variables are held constant, a one-unit change in this input variable is associated with an average change of 1.97 in the output.

Since you have only one input variable, you have nothing else to hold constant. Even if you have dozens of variables, you can isolate the effect of the individual variables with regression analysis. In the next section you'll go back to the ZeroAccess infection data and use this approach to make inferences about the effects of alien visits on infections.

The next column in the coefficients represents the standard error. You can use this along with the estimated coefficient to generate a confidence interval for the coefficient. Or you can do this by passing the output of the `lm()` command to the `confint()` function (Listing 5-19) and the confidence interval is calculated for you:

LISTING **5-19**

```
# requires objects: model (5-18)
confint(model)
##                    2.5 %     97.5 %
## (Intercept) -1.263895  1.808368
## input         1.824502  2.129343
```

The output tells you that, with 95 percent confidence, the input coefficient is between 1.82 and 2.13 (the value of 2 is well within that range).

The next two columns are measurements of how much the variable contributes to the model. The last column is called the p-value, which was introduced earlier in this chapter. As a simplification, smaller p-values contribute more significantly to the overall model and larger p-values mean the relationship between this input variable and the output is more likely to be chance. When you have a high p-value, you might want to look for other explanatory variables and remove any variables with a high p-value.

Most people settle on 0.05 as the threshold for significance. This means that if the p-value is less than 0.05 (and your p-value is well beneath it), the variable is significant and should stay in the model. When you have a p-value that is above 0.05, you should consider tossing it to the curb. Although, it's slowly becoming a common practice to evaluate p-values using at least three different thresholds of significance: 0.1, 0.05, and 0.01, which allows some flexibility to enter into the model and reduces an arbitrary cutoff point that was traditional in academic publications. You can see in the output of the model in Listing 5-18 that it denotes which level of significance our p-value is rated at (0.001 in this case).

There are two other points to consider with linear regression output. Look at the *Adjusted R-squared* value in the second-to-last line in Listing 5-18. The adjusted R^2 (or technically the *adjusted coefficient of determination*) signifies the amount of variation explained by the model. Values ranges from 0, meaning the model is no better than using the output mean, to 1, meaning the model describes the output perfectly. In this model it was calculated as 0.76, which means the linear model can reasonably explain 76 percent of the variation in the output data. There is no magic number you want the R^2 to be because it's relative. If you are starting from a place where you are simply guessing at the output (that is, you can't explain any of the variation in the output), then an R^2 of 0.05 is a little helpful. But if you have an existing model at 0.76, then 0.05 is a large step backward.

Note

When people want a quick understanding of a model, they focus on the R^2 value.

The last thing to consider is the p-value on the bottom line in Listing 5-18. This is the p-value of the entire model. At this point, you probably have a feel as to whether this is a good model or not, but keep an eye on this p-value. In this example, the p-value is tiny, so you should have confidence in this model.

Understanding Common Pitfalls in Regression Analysis

We hesitated even discussing regression analysis in this book. There are so many ways things can go wrong and so many ways to screw up, not to mention all the assumptions within the process that must be kept in check. However, we did include it and so we must also include some of the common pitfalls.

You Cannot Extrapolate Beyond the Data

Your data represents the entire range of your knowledge. You can verify that there is a linear relationship in the data you have, but you cannot extend that belief beyond the input values. As an example, say you've developed a simple model to estimate the cost of a data breach (output) from a count of records lost (input). If you look only at breaches that have lost 1,000 to 100,000 records, you cannot extend this to breaches with more than 100,000 or less than 1,000 records lost. You have no confidence that the relationship holds beyond the data you have. (Although if you did develop such a blatantly ridiculous model, you'd be sure to discuss the small R^2 value so people may have a fair shot at dismissing such a simple model.)

Outliers Have a Lot of Influence

Before regression analysis is performed, it's worthwhile to validate the data and identify any outliers that are the result of mistakes or errors. Outliers will have a large influence in the output of the model and will greatly influence the model selection. This doesn't mean that you remove all of the oddball observations (even though this was a common practice many years ago). For every observation that appears to be an outlier, it is good practice to verify its validity before continuing. Sometimes outliers are valid, and you must include them and account for them in the model. Other times, they may just be a result of mistyping or recording something in different units of measurement. Those types of outliers should be fixed or removed.

Hidden Relationships Hide Well

It's easy to gather a whole bunch of variables and toss them into a linear regression and have many of them turn out to be significant. But you have to approach these relationships with some element of common sense. It's standard practice to keep the number of variables to a minimum (see the next pitfall). But internal relationships in the data can be misleading and you want to be careful of something called *multicollinearity*. If you have two or more input variables that are highly correlated to each other, you may be incorrectly assigning meaning where none exits. You will see an example of this when you get back to the ZeroAccess data later in this chapter.

Too Many Variables

If you gather enough variables and toss them into regression analysis, it is inevitable that something in there will be significantly correlated. This actually applies to many concepts beyond regression analysis. These misleading findings occur because as more and more variables are added to the model, the likelihood of a spurious relationship (statistically significant correlation caused by pure chance) increases and is exacerbated if the analysis is complex or done without the common sense of domain expertise. It's common and a good practice with linear regression to seek out the smallest set of input variables, and not uncommon to exclude variables that only marginally improve the model for the sake of simplicity (even if the variable has a tiny p-value). This is also leading to a discussion of overfitting, which is when the model works really well on the initial data, but performs quite poorly when applied to real data.

Note

We'll be discussing challenges with overfitting in Chapter 9 and methods to reduce overfitting.

Visualize and Apply the Sniff Test

It's a good idea to visually inspect the data before jumping into regression analysis. In the example here, you created a simple scatterplot and added the regression line. This gets a little more complicated as you add multiple variables, but it's a good habit to get into. But even beyond that, you want to apply a healthy dose of logic to the variables and make sure that they have at least some reason to be included. This will help reduce the overall number of variables and hopefully help the analyst get to know the data if they didn't before.

Regression on ZeroAccess Infections

If you made it through the previous section, you should have a basic understanding of a regression model and some of the ways you can screw up when using it. Now you can start to pull more meaning from the spatial data than maps would allow.

Let's do a simple regression on the real data and see how well "visits from aliens" describes ZeroAccess infections. Although this may be silly to non-believers, we should be open to the possibility as researchers. We couldn't find any hard data related to alien visits, but the good folks at the National UFO Reporting Center have collected sightings of the visitors. You will be using that data as a proxy, and it's in the `ufo2010` variable in the prepared data. In order to run the linear regression, you again call the built-in `lm()` function and specify the output variable (`infections` in the `za.county` data frame), and then the tilde character, followed by, the variable with alien sightings (see Listing 5-20). If you wanted to add more variables you could add them—literally—with the plus (+) symbol. If you wrap the whole command in the `summary()` call, you get the output immediately. The output is trimmed to the relevant information.

LISTING 5-20
```
# requires object: za.county (5-14 and 5-15)
summary(lm(infections ~ ufo2010, data=za.county))
## Coefficients:
##              Estimate Std. Error t value Pr(>|t|)
## (Intercept) 17.97998    2.63775   6.816 1.12e-11 ***
## ufo2010      8.22677    0.08843  93.029  < 2e-16 ***
## ---
```

(continues)

Listing 5-20 *(continued)*
```
## Signif. codes:  0 '***' 0.001 '**' 0.01 '*' 0.05 '.' 0.1 ' ' 1
##
## Residual standard error: 140.9 on 3070 degrees of freedom
## Multiple R-squared:  0.7382,  Adjusted R-squared:  0.7381
## F-statistic:  8654 on 1 and 3070 DF,  p-value: < 2.2e-16
```

Using your new skills, you can see the p-value of the UFO variable is really tiny at < 2e-16, indicating the connection is significant and the R^2 value is 0.74. That's quite impressive. The coefficient on UFO sightings (8.31867) tells you that for every UFO sighting, you should expect about eight more ZeroAccess infections. This is an incredibly strong model, and there is enough to submit to a hoity-toity peer-reviewed journal explaining how you have scientifically proven that UFOs are causing the spread of ZeroAccess malware! We can see the headlines already:

Researchers Link ZeroAccess Infections to Alien Visitors

Before you get ahead of yourself, maybe you should looks at some of these other variables. Even though we cautioned about adding in too many variables, you'll need to explore these relationships and various models. Chapter 9 will discuss some techniques for variable selection. For now, run another regression with all of these variables and see what happens (Listing 5-21).

Listing 5-21
```
# requires object: za.county (5-14 and 5-15)
summary(lm(infections ~ pop + income + ipaddr + ufo2010,
           data=za.county))
## Coefficients:
##               Estimate Std. Error t value Pr(>|t|)
## (Intercept)  1.091e+01  5.543e+00   1.968   0.0492 *
## pop          7.700e-04  9.072e-06  84.876  < 2e-16 ***
## income      -2.353e-04  1.215e-04  -1.937   0.0528 .
## ipaddr       2.281e-06  3.027e-07   7.534 6.41e-14 ***
## ufo2010      5.495e-01  9.943e-02   5.526 3.54e-08 ***
## ---
## Signif. codes:  0 '***' 0.001 '**' 0.01 '*' 0.05 '.' 0.1 ' ' 1
##
## Residual standard error: 74.9 on 3067 degrees of freedom
## Multiple R-squared:  0.9261,  Adjusted R-squared:  0.926
## F-statistic:  9610 on 4 and 3067 DF,  p-value: < 2.2e-16
```

Scanning down the p-values, it looks like all of these are quite tiny with the exception of income, which looks like it may be suspect, and you could try re-running this with income removed. However, the influence of IP address and UFO visits still appear strong. Notice that as you've added more variables, the influence of UFO visits has dropped (the coefficient is smaller and the p-value increased) and is accounted for in other variables.

Although you have all of these variables in this model, you should check for something we discussed in the "Understanding Common Pitfalls in Regression Analysis" section earlier in this chapter called *multicollinear variables*. This is when two or more of the input variables are correlated and that relationship is masking the [in]significance of a variable. You check for this by looking at something called the *variance inflation*. R has a nice `vif()` function in the Companion to Applied Regression (`car`) package (see Listing 5-22). As a general rule, if the square root of the variance inflation is greater than 2 (something I have to look up every time I do this), the variables are correlated and you shouldn't trust that both are significantly contributing to the model.

LISTING **5-22**

```
# requires object: za.county (5-14 and 5-15)
library(car) # for the vif() function
model <- lm(infections ~ pop + income + ipaddr + ufo2010,
            data=za.county)
sqrt(vif(model))
##      pop   income   ipaddr  ufo2010
## 2.165458 1.038467 1.046051 2.115512
```

You can see that the population and `ufo2010` are collinear. Oh no! Is it possible that UFO sightings are just a function of population? In order to test that, you normalize the population. To do so, you just divide both values by the population, making them infections and sighting per capita, and rerun the single regression (Listing 5-23).

LISTING **5-23**

```
# requires object: za.county (5-14 and 5-15)
za.county$za.by.pop <- za.county$infections/za.county$pop
za.county$ufo.by.pop <- za.county$ufo2010/za.county$pop
summary(lm(za.by.pop ~ ufo.by.pop, data=za.county))
## Coefficients:
##               Estimate Std. Error t value Pr(>|t|)
## (Intercept) 7.050e-04  1.213e-05  58.106  < 2e-16 ***
## ufo.by.pop  2.679e-01  6.956e-02   3.852  0.00012 ***
## ---
## Signif. codes:  0 '***' 0.001 '**' 0.01 '*' 0.05 '.' 0.1 ' ' 1
##
## Residual standard error: 0.0005793 on 3070 degrees of freedom
## Multiple R-squared:  0.004809,  Adjusted R-squared:  0.004485
## F-statistic: 14.84 on 1 and 3070 DF,  p-value: 0.0001197
```

Great! The p-value is still under 0.05! But . . . oh . . . wait a second, the R^2 value is telling you that this model is quite useless, as it describes 0.4 percent of the data (R^2 is 0.004). At this point, it might be safe to listen to that little voice of logic and conclude that UFO visits and ZeroAccess infections are not related (so much for the grant money).

Let's run one more analysis, but keep in mind that all of this data is available for download from the book's website along with the code in this chapter. There is plenty of room for exploration here.

What Is Correlated to ZeroAccess Infections?

Say you have a strong suspicion (or you've applied some of the variable selection techniques discussed in Chapter 9) that the population of a county is the best overall *predictor* of how many infections occur in that county (see Listing 5-24).

LISTING 5-24

```
# requires object: za.county (5-14 and 5-15)
summary(lm(infections ~ pop, data=za.county))
## Coefficients:
##               Estimate Std. Error t value Pr(>|t|)
## (Intercept) 4.545e-01  1.435e+00   0.317   0.752
## pop         8.204e-04  4.247e-06 193.199   <2e-16 ***
## ---
## Signif. codes:  0 '***' 0.001 '**' 0.01 '*' 0.05 '.' 0.1 ' ' 1
##
## Residual standard error: 75.92 on 3070 degrees of freedom
## Multiple R-squared:  0.924,  Adjusted R-squared:  0.924
## F-statistic: 3.733e+04 on 1 and 3070 DF,  p-value: < 2.2e-16
```

With an R^2 value of 0.94, you're going to be hard pressed to add more variables in here that mean much. Sure enough, when you cycle through the other variables, you'll find that income and the number of IP addresses in that county do not add much to the overall model. What you can draw from the output of the regression on population is in the coefficient of 8.313e-04, which is engineering notation for 0.0008313. If you invert that number (1/0.0008313), you can determine that for about every 1,200 people a county has, you can expect one more infection of ZeroAccess.

Go back to the maps to see whether you can't visualize what this looks like at the county level. You can generate a choropleth map at the county level for the number of infections and the population. If the regression analysis is accurate, you should see a very clear relationship between the two (see Figure 5-10).

ZeroAccess Infections

U.S. Population

FIGURE 5-10 *Visual relationship between ZeroAccess infections and population*

Summary

You created quite a few maps in this chapter, with points and with choropleths. Although you can pick out variations across the map quite rapidly with the visual representation, you shouldn't rely solely on visualizations with spatial data. Even though the maps showed variation, the data showed through linear regression that *population largely explains the variation*. That's something to consider when you're creating maps (or any other visualization for that matter). Be sure to take a step back and ask the ever-popular question of "So what?!" If you can't answer that question, maybe you don't need the map at all and the analysis needs to go in a different direction.

Recommended Reading

The following are some recommended readings that can further your understanding on some of the topics we touch on in this chapter. For full information on these recommendations and for the sources we cite in the chapter, please see Appendix B.

Data Points: Visualization That Means Something by **Nathan Yau**—Yau provides several beautiful geospatial visualizations and discusses the design principles behind them. There is no example code, but plenty of inspiration among the pages, plus he included a map of UFO sightings.

R Graphics Cookbook by **Winston Chang**—If you will be doing any visualizations with R, you should have this book. Winston Chang goes into more depth on map creation than we do here and includes hands-on examples and explanations for R.

Naked Statistics: Stripping the Dread from the Data by **Charles Wheelan**—When it comes to introductory material on statistics, nothing beats this book. Wheelan presents the statistical concepts without heavy math and builds up to a chapter on linear regression, covering many of the assumptions and pitfalls of the technique.

6

Visualizing Security Data

"The human visual system is a pattern seeker of enormous power and subtlety. The eye and the visual cortex of the brain form a massively parallel processor that provides the highest bandwidth channel into human cognitive centers."

Colin Ware, *Information Visualization*

Chapter 1 briefly mentioned that data analysis is similar to how archeology might be: spending hour after hour with small tools in the hope of uncovering even the tiniest of insights in the earth. That analogy can be extended into the shared desire to create a narrative. Archeologists attempt to recreate the stories of history by digging up parts of a story; it's the same with data analysts. There are stories buried in the data; and it's up to the data analyst to uncover that narrative, piece it back together, and communicate that story to others. When it comes to data, with its unique blend of complexity and subtlety, nothing can tell a good story—a *data story*—like a well-crafted visualization.

A data story is built from several attributes, the two most important of which are **truth** and **relevance**. Although you can have a good story without truth, you cannot have a good *data story* without truth. You cannot affect meaningful and successful change if your stories are built on lies or half-truths. Therefore, you need all the skills to uncover the truth within the data, and then you need the visualization skills to be sure the story the reader perceives matches the story you uncovered. The visual language should be a wrapper around the truth; thus, it needs to be clear and unambiguous. Every point, line, color, and shape you place into a visualization should carry some piece of information supporting the truth in the data and in the data story.

A good story is good only when it is relevant and actionable to the reader. You wouldn't want to show a board-level executive the Security Incident & Event Management (SIEM) dashboard any more than you'd want to force market reports on the SIEM operator. Stories fail to communicate if the readers don't feel they apply to them. Therefore you have to know the audience for your visualizations. Are you trying to elicit a budget change or firewall change? As you create your message, a good question to ask yourself is "so what?" and if you struggle to answer that question for the reader, rethink the approach. Another good mental exercise is to run through a few other possible outcomes of the story. If the result of the visualization is the same (from the reader's perspective), you should be rethinking the visualizations. For example, if you're showing a line graph with an obvious upward slant, imagine if that line went down. Would the reader have a different reaction? If it went up much more than it does, *so what*?

We aren't suggesting that all data should be visualized. If the story in the data is best summarized with a sentence in an email, so be it. If the data can be expressed in a simple lookup table, so be it. The goal here is communicating the data. If you can communicate better, more succinctly, or simpler in any other way, you should go with that method. We also aren't suggesting that visualizations be the center of the story. All data exists within a context, and all our stories need to have a beginning, middle, and end. Visualizations can play an important and supporting role in the entire communication process, but it should not be the only means of communication. Your focus is on the successful communication of the narrative and the method of communication is just a means to that end.

Why Visualize?

By far, the most efficient path to human understanding is through the visual sense. Like a good hacker, you need to learn about the system, understand how it functions (or why it doesn't function), and then exploit this cognitive system to achieve your goal. In this case, the goal is to effectively and efficiently communicate the stories you find in the data. There are many advantages to using data visualization as a communication tool compared to other methods. To paraphrase Colin Ware (who we quoted to open this chapter), data visualization has the following advantages:

- **Data visualizations communicate complexity quickly.** Descriptive statistics (mean, median, variance, and so on) exist to describe and simplify data but tend to remove subtleties that exist. It's possible to communicate millions of data points in seconds while minimizing the loss of detail and resolution through visualization.

- **Data visualizations enable recognition of latent patterns.** Patterns that would never be apparent using statistical methods or scanning the data may be revealed through visualization. When data is visually presented, patterns in a single variable or relationships across many variables may leap off the screen.

- **Data visualizations enable quality control on the data.** Mistakes and errors in data collection or preparation can often be revealed through visualization. Data visualizations can serve as a good and quick sanity check on your work.

- **Data visualizations can serve as a muse.** It's been said that most breakthroughs in science didn't start with a "Eureka!" but instead with a "Huh, that's odd." Laying out the data visually can give you a new perspective and help facilitate your thinking and discovery processes.

Unraveling Visual Perception

The human system for processing visual information is incredibly complex and much of our knowledge around it is still evolving. There are a few key (and hopefully easy) concepts that you should understand since knowing how the brain visually processes information will help you create great visuals. Equally as important, knowing this information will also help you avoid creating visuals that aren't effective or helpful.

Our eyes convert visual stimulus in the form of light into electrical signals for our brains. This information passes through stages of our *visual memory*, each with a specific set of strengths, limitations, and functions. Before we are consciously aware of it, our brains rapidly scan the visual field, which is called *preattentive processing*. Finally, the brain will instruct the eyes to focus elsewhere, and through a series of *saccadic movements*, our eyes will focus on various features to help build the image in our mind. The goal is to use three concepts from our visual processing system to create a solid foundation for good visuals and dashboards.

Visual Thinking

This section steps through the various stages of memory within our visual perception: iconic memory, working memory, and long-term memory.

- **Iconic memory** is the first stop for the visual information. It is a very brief stop, lasting around half a second or until new information comes in. What happens in this tiny window is critical to creating good visualizations and dashboards. Using the information stored in iconic memory, the brain preprocesses the image prior to giving it any conscious attention. From an evolutionary perspective, this is quite helpful; this preattentive processing can help you quickly identify possible threats in your environment. For example, anyone who has been driving when an animal dashes in front of the car has probably felt that urgent message from the brain when it recognizes a possible threat. We begin to react immediately even before we can process the full extent of the threat. Even though you don't want your visualizations to be treated like a threat, through the use of colors, shapes and other cues, you can leverage this visual searching and preattentive processing in order to draw attention and communicate some basic attributes of your data. This will make processing much easier when viewers begin to consciously process it, and we will discuss preattentive processing in detail later in this chapter.

- **Working memory** is the next stop and things get a little more complicated here. First the brain groups visual aspects into meaningful objects and holds these in working memory. There is a lot of flexibility within working memory. We can rapidly replace or drop objects as we take in more information, but this flexibility comes at a cost in capacity. We can hold only three to five objects in working memory depending on the task and objects. This limit is important when you are designing visualizations and dashboards. If you create a visualization with a legend that has 10 different attributes, viewers will have to continually reference the legend in order to understand what they're looking at. Therefore, as you communicate the stories in your data, limit each visual to no more than five objects (or four to be safe).

- **Long-term memory** is not directly involved in the visual processing but instead affects visual communication through the expectations and norms built up in long-term memory. In order for something to move into long-term memory, the viewer needs to visually "rehearse" the information to transition it from working memory into long-term memory. If the reader has seen visualizations before (and chances are very good they have), they have a certain level of expectation for what they are looking at. For example, if you create a scatterplot, the reader expects the origin of the graph to be in the lower left corner, with positive values of each axis extended up and to the right. If multiple colors are used, the reader will expect meaning to the color and will seek it out. It's very important to know what those norms and expectations might be, and if you deviate from them, do so for a very good reason and give visual queues to help people understand those deviations.

Tracking Eye Movements

When people focus on something like a dashboard or graphics on a computer screen, they do not simply fix their gaze on it and take in the image as a whole. Their eyes actually dash around the screen, focusing on very small portions for very short periods of time in order to build the image in their mind. These rapid eye movements are called *saccades*, and overall they are called saccadic movements. They are anything but random. The brain has a set of rules (guidelines really) for how the next fixation point is prioritized. As an example, when another person greets you, your eyes perform scanning saccades over their entire face, bouncing from the distinct features of the face (eyes, nose, and mouth) and establishing the edges. The scanning saccades help you recognize not only the person, but also cues to allow you to judge their emotions.

The same applies to visualizations and dashboards. The eyes will fixate on an obvious feature and bounce around and between the points it considers important. Viewers build up the entire picture over a series of these movements and over time. Understanding these movements can help you build a visualization flow that seems natural (or at least not strained).

The saccadic motion is largely unconscious and is thought to be a *ballistic* movement. Once the brain initiates a saccadic movement, the muscles take over and handle the rapid acceleration and deceleration from beginning to end. This is important for two reasons—once it is initiated it cannot be changed or stopped and during the motion we suppress much of the visual input. We will want to limit the distance of these motions by creating compact dashboards and visualizations.

We can pull together a few important learning points from saccadic eye movements. Knowing that the eyes will bounce around from feature to feature and understanding the ballistic nature of the movement, you should keep several points in mind as you create dashboards and graphics:

- **Don't overload the dashboard with visual features.** Keep the number of attention-grabbing features under control because if everything is important visually, nothing will be important visually, and the reader will have to put more effort into understanding the visual.

- **Make the important messages obvious visual features.** Just as we scan the important parts of a human face, we look for the similar attention-grabbing features on the screen. Make sure that those features are clear and important to the viewer.

- **Limit time wasted on saccadic movements.** Saccadic movements that jump longer distances take longer to execute. Do not push the visual features into the corners or toward the edges. Forcing the viewer to bounce across large distances will decrease the amount of time they are actually seeing the features (and increase the time spent in saccadic movements).

The role of saccadic movements is more significant in the design of dashboards than with static data visualizations. A static visualization will typically have one, perhaps two, visual features we want to draw attention to, and the eye movements are contained in a relatively compact space. A dashboard may be designed to communicate several independent messages simultaneously with varying degrees of urgency. Good dashboard design, as you'll see in Chapter 10, limits the time viewers spend in a saccadic movement and exploits eye movements for efficiency.

Preattentive Processing

The best way to describe preattentive processing is through pictures. Take a look at Figure 6-1 and try to count how many capital Xs there are in this completely random mix of letters and numbers.

V3JpdGIuZyBhIGJvb2sgaXMgaGFyZCB3b3JkLCBidXXgb25lIHNpZGUgcGVyYXyBp
cyB3ZSBnZXQgdG8gaW5qZXd0IGVhc3RlciBpZ2dzIGxpa2UgdGhpcy4gIEVtIHIIv
dSd2ZSBmb3VuZCBCB0aGlzIGNCZW55ISHVzIGEgbWVzc2FnZSBvbiB0d2l0dGVyICHA
aHJici cm1zdHIgYW5kIEBqYXIgYWNvYnYnMp IHNheW4g uZyA iSGFwcHkgRWF zdGVyISiE=

FIGURE 6-1 *Count the number of "X" characters*

Because all of the letters are the same color and contain the same relative space, nothing about any of the characters really stands out. The brain simply sees a collection of shapes. In order to count the Xs, you have to scan through each letter across the four rows. While you're doing that you also have to remember how many you've found so far. In contrast, look at a completely random mix of letters and numbers with the X characters emphasized (see Figure 6-2).

You can immediately see the Xs and count four of them. When you first look at this, your brain sees a background of gray symbols with four completely different objects that are similar to each other. Your preattentive processing mentally creates two groups: one of all the gray symbols and a second with the dark red Xs. A split-second later, you will consciously recognize the second group as what you're interested in (the Xs). It becomes trivial to visually exclude the gray characters and now you can scan just through this group. Counting the Xs becomes a simple and quick task.

V3JpdGIuZyBhIGJvb2sga**X**MgaGFyZCB3b3JrLCBid**X**Qgb25IIHNpZGUgcGVyayBp
cyB3ZSBnZ**X**QgdG8gaW5qZWN0IGVhc3RIciBIZ2dzIGxpa2UgdGhpcy4gIEImIHIv
dSd2ZSB mb3VuZCB0aGGIzLCBzZW5kIHVzIGEgbWVzc2FnZSBvbiB0d2I0dGVyIChA
aHJicm1zdHIgYW55kIEBqY**X**IqYWNvYnMpIHNheWIuZyAiSGFwcHkgRWF zdGVyIIiE=

FIGURE 6-2 *Now, count the number of "X" characters*

That mental grouping and ease of focus is what you're after. You want to enable your preattentive processing to effortlessly group similar objects and highlight where you want attention to be focused. But you have to keep in mind that the preattentive processing is not all that smart. It cannot project meaning, interpret the objects, or make meaningful associations (beyond simple visual grouping).

Through hundreds of studies, researchers have been able to differentiate between visual attributes based on those that can be identified preattentively and those that can't. Some of these studies seem a little silly or abstract (for example, how easy is *parallel* detected?), but by looking at them as a whole, we can create some basic visual attribute categories that can be preattentively processed.

These categories are:

- **Form** (line, shape, and size)
- **Color** (hue and intensity)
- **Spatial position** (two-dimensional, stereoscopic)
- **Motion** (blink, direction)

The list of specifics within those categories can get quite long, but, thankfully, you can experiment with your graphics to find what works. If one version doesn't highlight the data, try something different. If it's easy for you to pick out what's important, chances are that it'll be easy for others. Of course, it's always a good idea to run things by others as a sanity check. Figure 6-3 shows some ways to differentiate based on preattentive attributes.

Not all preattentive attributes are created equal. Look at Figure 6-3 again. Although they all highlight the three data points, some make the three points slightly easier to see than others. In Figure 6-3(e) for example, if you used pink and red, it would be slightly more difficult to pick out the subtle difference in colors. The amount of "pop" for preattenttive attributes depends on how different the attributes are. The shapes in the example in Figure 6-3(a) are more different from each other than the circles and squares in Figure 6-3(b) and slightly easier to see. It's still possible to distinguish the difference in Figure 6-3(b), but it's just not as obvious.

This concept of preattentive processing should be treated as just that—a concept. The line between our preattentive processing and conscious processing is blurry. When looking at a visualization, you can slip between the two quickly and quietly. With repeated exposure, you can actually train our preattentive processing. Meaning, over time, no matter how poorly designed a dashboard is, analysts will eventually pick up skills to quickly identify important features depending on environment and culture. But the point remains—if you want to direct the viewer's focus and attention, you should leverage some basic elements like form and color to highlight the point you need to make in the data.

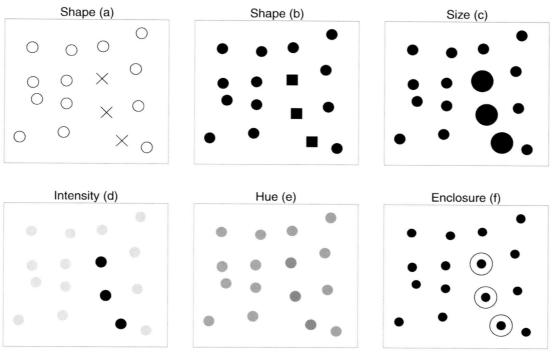

F<small>IGURE</small> 6-3 *Examples of preattentive attributes*

Finally, one last word of caution about preattentive processing: It's possible to overload this process and negate any benefit. Take a look at Figure 6-4.

- In Figure 6-4(a), we have separated the data into three groups and then coded them by color. It's easy to tell them apart. Not only are they spatially grouped, but color highlights their differences.

- In Figure 6-4(b), we separated the data into two groups—*different* from the groups in Figure 6-4(a)—and then coded them by shape. It's a little harder to tell them apart, but you can still pick out the two groups.

- When we combine the methods in Figure 6-4(c), things get a bit more complicated. To separate them based on shape, you have to actively inspect individual elements and separate them consciously.

The lesson here is that you have to be careful to keep the visuals as simple as possible to exploit the viewer's preattentive processing for their benefit.

Note

This chapter has a lot of visualizations and not a lot of source code. If you are interested in how we created the figures in this chapter, the accompanying source code for the chapter is on the book's website (www.wiley.com/go/datadrivensecurity).

Color (a)	Shape (b)	Shape and Color (c)
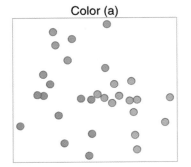	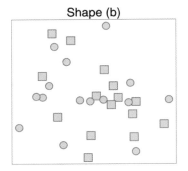	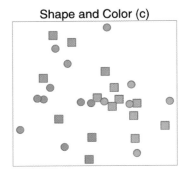

FIGURE 6-4 *Too many attributes*

Understanding the Components of Visual Communications

The chapter began by looking at how the brain visually processes information, including how you can leverage your preattentive processing and saccadic movements to increase the viewer's visual perception. This section focuses on the visual building blocks and material that you have to work with. You need to begin with the data and encode the values through various attributes like position, shape, length, and size. Perhaps you'll want to encode changes over time with slopes or angles and separate categories by color hue, saturation, or lightness. If you combine elements, you can communicate relationships and groupings. Every choice you make in creating a visualization will affect how well others will decode the data.

Avoiding the Third Dimension

First and foremost, unless you are creating a physical data sculpture, or are working with special software that allows you to model in three dimensions, you are dealing in two dimensions. The screens you look at, the reports you print, and the slides you project on the wall are all limited to width and height. Of course, you can simulate a third dimension of depth, but this is a challenge. Simulating a third dimension will always be just that, a simulation.

In order to simulate depth, you need to change the very attributes you are using to convey the meaning of your data. Elements that are closer in the simulation will need to be bigger and those further away will be smaller. The effect from the simulated perspective will modify the viewer's ability to compare and consume the data accurately. For this reason, we strongly recommend staying away from plotting in three dimensions. Plus, two dimensions offer a tremendous amount of flexibility. Even though readily available desktop tools like Excel make 3D charts incredibly easy, you should fight the urge if your goal is to communicate your data to others.

Don't think of working with two dimensions as a limiting factor any more than just 12 notes in a chromatic scale is limiting to Western music. Much research has been conducted into communicating in two dimensions; we will highlight two seminal papers published in the mid-1980s by two statisticians—William S. Cleveland and Robert McGill. They open the first paper, "Graphical Perception: Theory, Experimentation, and Application to the Development of Graphical Methods" with, "The subject of graphical methods for data analysis and for data presentation needs a scientific foundation." And, they did just that. They conducted

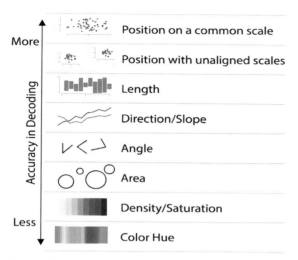

FIGURE 6-5   *Accuracy of decoding*

experiments where subjects were shown various graphics and measured how accurately they were able to visually decode the quantitative information in them. In their second paper, "Graphical Perception and Graphical Methods for Analyzing Scientific Data," they updated their results and offered an ordered list of visual encodings and the relative accuracy in their decoding. See Figure 6-5.

These are not mutually exclusive and the distinctions between these methods can get a little blurry. For example to decode a simple bar chart, you might use position on a common scale to determine the quantity, but then use length to compare two bars within the same chart. In a pie chart, you might primarily use angles, but the area of the slice and arc length may also factor into your perception. The findings from this research should serve as a guideline. If your goal is communicating quantitative data accurately, a bar chart is always better than a pie chart and a grouped bar chart is better than a stacked bar chart.

As with all guidelines, you can deviate from this advice. Sometimes your goal is not to convey specific quantitative data, and the lack of accuracy in decoding is desired. As an example, look at Figure 6-6. When looking at the pie chart on the left, it is relatively difficult to gauge the specific difference between the five slices. Looking at just the pie chart, you'd probably conclude that they are all about equal. However, if you look at the bar chart on the right, it's relatively trivial to see the differences because you are using position on a common scale. Obviously, if you had confidence in the accuracy of the data, the bar chart on the right is far easier to interpret. But what if the data you have is from a small opinion survey? Although you can calculate precise values, the differences in the values could easily be explained with sample error. In this case, you could justify using a less accurate method to communicate the data.

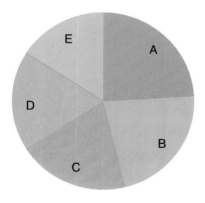

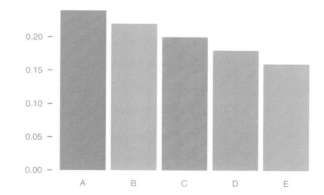

FIGURE 6-6   *Comparing pie and bar charts*

Save the Pies for Dessert

If you are new to data visualization, there are essentially two distinct (and sometimes very passionate) opinions when it comes to visualizations that use techniques lower on Cleveland's accuracy list. Pie charts are often at the center of debate since they are used (and abused) more often than others. The core argument against pie charts is that the data can always be represented better and more accurately with other methods. As Stephen Few said in his 2007 paper "Save the Pies for Dessert," "Of all the graphs that play major roles in the lexicon of quantitative communication, the pie chart is by far the least effective. Its colorful voice is often heard, but rarely understood. It mumbles when it talks." On the other side is the point we made here—that the goal of communication may not be precision. There are other less convincing arguments in the defense of pie charts, but there is one piece of common ground: Choose the visualization method deliberately and be sure it communicates the message you want to send.

Using Color

If you've not been tasked with selecting colors for a project, this brief introduction may make color selection seem easy. There are a few guidelines about which types of color palettes go with which types of variables, and a deep well of knowledge from color research has created a handful of easy rules for palette creation. However, it won't be until you're trying yet another set of colors in your visualization that you will truly appreciate the words of Edward Tufte from his book *Envisioning Information*: "Avoiding catastrophe becomes the first principle in bringing color to information: Above all, do no harm."

There are many websites and tools that apply color theory to make palette selection relatively painless (see Appendix A for a complete list of resources, but ColorBrewer [`http://colorbrewer2.org/`] and HCL Picker [`http://tristen.ca/hcl-picker/`] are our favorites). With some understanding of your data, picking pertinent colors is the easy part. Colors also have to support and hopefully even highlight the message and be pleasing to the eye, which has a large element of subjectivity and is unique to each and every visual story. This creates the challenge with color: You have to balance function, aesthetics, and theory across just a handful of colors.

Color Is Relative

The first and perhaps most important aspect of color selection is that colors are always interpreted relative to the surrounding environment. For example, Figure 6-7 shows two rows of gray boxes on a gradient background. Even if you know each row has a consistent shade of gray, you will still see different shades on the same row as you scan from side to side. And to some, the upper-left box looks to be the same color as the lower-right box. That's because you see the shade in the boxes relative to the surrounding background. The boxes appear darker on a white background and lighter on a dark background. You can use this fact to your benefit. If you want to emphasize one variable above all else, you can choose a contrasting color from the rest. For example, red shapes will stand out among shades of light blue shapes, but will blend in with pink and orange shapes.

FIGURE 6-7 *Visual signal and noise detection illusion*

We Are the ~~99 Percent~~ 10 Percent

Nearly 10 percent of males and about 1 percent of the females are color blind. This means that at some point (probably sooner than you think) your visualizations and dashboards will be viewed by someone incapable of seeing the entire spectrum of the rainbow. Having some understanding of the types of color blindness can help you choose colors that everyone can see. The largest portion of color blind people have either protanomaly (red blindness) or deuteranomaly (green blindness), making red and green a poor choice to include in the same graphic. Some color-selection tools (like ColorBrewer) factor in color blindness and have an option to select colorblind safe palettes. Whatever your color tools are, keep in mind the 10 percent.

Palettes Depend on Data

We briefly discussed data types in a sidebar in Chapter 3 titled, "Isn't 'data' just 'data'?" There are only a handful of high-level data types that you'll need to be aware of and most of them fall into either categorical or quantitative values.

- **Categorical data** are represented as groups with category names, such as operating systems by type or lists of programming languages. Categorical data sometimes has a natural order. Rankings such as "first," "second," "third," or "high," "medium," and "low" are treated like categorical values but have an added sense of order.

- **Quantitative data** are numerical values, which are things you count or measure such as bytes, packets, sessions, number of servers, and so on.

The difference between categorical and quantitative can sometimes be tricky. For example, TCP/UDP port numbers appear quantitative since they are sequential numbers going up to 65,535. But you have to treat them as categories: You would never add `echo` and two `telnet` ports to get `DNS` because the sum would make no sense in terms of port numbers. Another confusing data type is date/time. Most of the time you'll treat it as an ordered categorical variable (such as the year, month, day of week, and so on), but other times you'll store it as a quantity (seconds since the epoch) to enable calculations on time and time series data.

You have to be careful when using colors to represent a quantity. Consumers are relatively inaccurate when decoding quantity from a color scale. But color can be used in circumstances where rough comparisons are enough. For example, back in Figure 5-7 in Chapter 5, you don't need to see that exactly 1 in 724 people in Wyoming were infected with ZeroAccess. The color is simply communicating that Wyoming had more infections per person than any other state.

Figure 6-8 shows three types of color palettes—sequential, divergent, and qualitative—from the ColorBrewer website.

- You select a palette of **sequential colors** to represent quantity or perhaps ordered categorical data. Sequential color palettes are built using a single hue (blue, for example) and then adjust the lightness or saturation of that color to cover the range of the quantitative data.

- **Divergent colors** are also used on quantitative or ordered data, but help communicate above or below some middle value. Typically, the middle value is white and two divergent hues are used on either end. Divergent color scales may be used to convey two directions in the data such as above or below average (as it was used in Figure 5-7).

- Finally, you have **qualitative colors**, which are intended to simply be distinct from one another. This makes them well suited for visualizing categorical data.

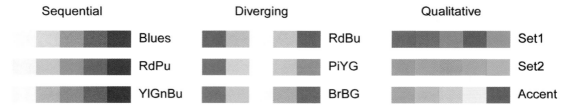

FIGURE 6-8 *Sample color palettes from ColorBrewer*

Putting It All Together

We've laid some good groundwork here, so it's time to look at how these things come together to help communicate your data. This section spends less time talking about how to create these and more time on *why* we create these as we do. All of the source data and code needed to create these visualizations in this chapter are on the book's website. Creating the basic types of plots is relatively easy using the R language and ggplot2. Most of these plots are available as options in more familiar tools such as Excel.

Using Points

The easiest method to communicate and compare two quantitative variables is the basic scatterplot. Scatterplots position points along a common scale (both x and y scales) and allow the viewer to very accurately determine the value of each variable for each data point and to make comparisons between points. It is insanely simple to create scatterplots in R (plot(x, y)). You can do this often just to "see" the data you are working with. For example, Figure 6-9 shows 8 hours of firewall traffic. Each dot represents total number of packets (x-axis) and total number of bytes transferred (y-axis) processed by the firewall over 5 minutes.

This is a good example of a pattern quickly jumping out of a plot. You can see that the firewall traffic for the day ranges from 7 to 19 gigabytes, and packets range from 12 to 27 million. The linear relationship is very apparent here: As you see more packets, you see more bytes. Now this isn't exactly a news flash or all that informative, but a simple scatterplot can show patterns when you're not sure whether they exist. Figure 6-10 shows an example of a scatterplot that reveals something you didn't know. The time of day is along the x-axis and the number of sessions is on the y-axis.

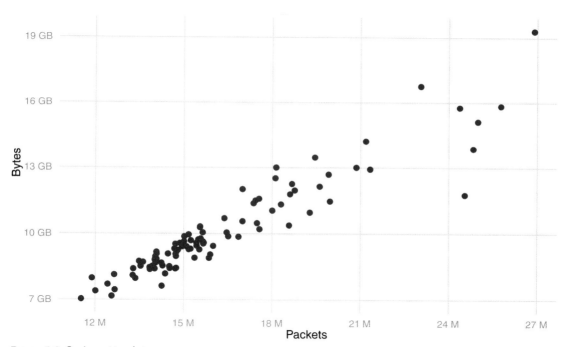

FIGURE 6-9 Basic scatterplot

The scatterplot in Figure 6-10 has a few extra features. Note the faint lines down from the points; they give just a hint of a bar chart and visually tie the points (which are rather bunched up) back to the x-axis. To highlight the repeating element of time, the line at the top of the hour is thickened (and falls on the grid lines); the points also change to red every 30 minutes. There is a noticeable dip at the top of the hour and not much change at the half-hour marks, and it's important to emphasize those times for easier comparison (remember the preattentive processing?). What is the cause of this dip? Perhaps this organization has a meeting-heavy culture, and network activity drops as people head to their next meeting? You can't know the cause from this data, but the dip pattern really jumps out with a simple scatterplot.

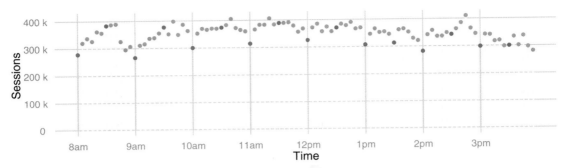

FIGURE 6-10 *Dot plot: packets over time*

Creating Directions with Lines

You may have heard at some point that "lines are just points in motion," and that's true—you generally see lines having a sense of direction. In this section, you'll take the same firewall traffic and separate the types of devices on the network:

- Desktops

- Servers

- Printers

- Networking equipment

You'll see two plots: first, the same type of scatterplot as the time series and then a line plot (see Figure 6-11).

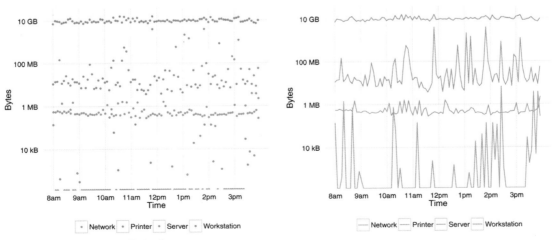

FIGURE 6-11 *Line plot: traffic by device*

It's rather clear what's going on with the line plot and it's easy to follow the traffic over time for each of the four devices. The scatterplot on the left is a little difficult to follow, although you can see trends and differences between the categories. Line plots are quite good at accurately communicating data; they compare points on the line along a common scale and use the slope of the line as a sign of change. For example, notice the steep slopes in the data series for printers. Most commonly, line plots have an ordered variable on the horizontal axis (often "time") and one or more quantitative variables on the vertical axis. (It's possible to flip the orientation depending on the presentation circumstances.) In this case, you are plotting number of packets (quantitative) on the y-axis against successive five-minute periods (ordered) with each line representing a category of device.

Log Scales for Logs

In Figure 6-11 the y-axis is plotted on a logarithmic scale. Notice how the values on the axis increase by powers of ten for a given physical distance on the plot. If this plot was plotted on a linear scale, you'd see the workstation traffic at the top and the other three lines would be reduced to almost zero. We chose a log scale because we needed to show these data series on the same chart, even though they differed by three orders of magnitude. . You have to be careful when you use a log scale. Most people in business are used to seeing linear scales, and they are conditioned to do comparisons assuming a linear scale. For example, the viewers might come to the conclusion that the networking equipment has about half the traffic of the workstations because it's visually about half the distance from the axis. But, in reality, workstations are generating about 10,000 times more traffic than network devices. If the logarithmic scale isn't clear to the viewers, they could draw incorrect conclusions.

Building Bar Charts

Bar charts are one of the most effective ways to communicate when one variable is quantitative and the other variable is categorical. There are a few variations on the basic bar chart. Figure 6-12 shows three different ways of displaying vulnerability counts and severity classification per device. On the far left, you have a typical bar chart with vertical bars. One simple modification (not shown) would be to flip the orientation so that the bars are horizontal. The difference between vertical and horizontal orientation is largely aesthetic and depends on where the chart will appear. The vertical bar chart is simple: The length of each bar is proportional to the total number of vulnerabilities for each device type. You can easily see that workstations have the most vulnerabilities, and servers are close, with 20 percent less or so. In comparison, it is obvious that the number of vulnerabilities in networking devices and printers are quite small.

The other two bar charts have an additional categorical variable for the severity of the vulnerability —High, Medium, or Low. The stacked and group bar charts use sequential color scheme severity levels. With the stacked bar charts, you are still able to compare totals. It's still clear that workstations have more vulnerabilities than all others. But comparing across severity is difficult as you lose the common scale. As an example, attempt to visually compare the high vulnerabilities of workstations to servers. Since they are not aligned you judge them purely by length on a non-aligned scale and are therefore less accurate.

Now look at the grouped bar chart and it quickly becomes clear that workstations have more high-severity vulnerabilities than servers. The one drawback to the grouped bar chart is that you lose the overall count comparison. When the overall totals are close, it's more difficult to tell that workstations have more vulnerabilities overall from the grouped bar chart. The type of bar chart you choose is largely dependent on the message you are trying to send.

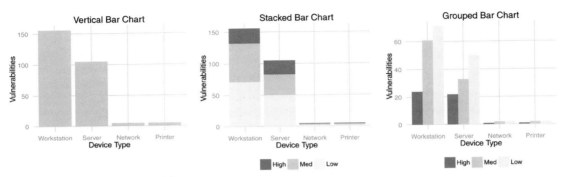

FIGURE 6-12 *Bar charts: vulnerability counts*

Leveraging Opacity

Another technique for communicating differences in variable values is the opacity or transparency of colors within graphs. If the data is overlapping or dense and you plot it with a solid opaque color, you have no way of knowing just how many points are stacked up underneath that. Luckily, you can simply make the color semi-transparent. This will allow any points beneath to show through a given point. Within R there are two methods for doing this. First within `ggplot2` most (perhaps all) of the chart types allow for an alpha setting between 0 and 1 (*alpha* is the term used in color specifications to define opacity). Or you can code the alpha right into the color with a 4th byte, meaning a red value of `#FF0000` is the same as `#FF0000FF` (with the last `FF` setting opacity to maximum). If you want to set opacity to 50 percent, $255/2 = 128 = 0x80$, so you can set the color to `#FF000080`. The red color is now 50 percent opaque. The benefit of adjusting the alpha (opacity) is demonstrated in Figure 6-13.

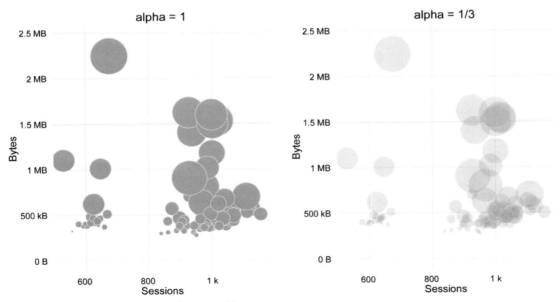

FIGURE 6-13 *Bubble chart: opacity shows stacking*

These two charts show the same data: 8 hours of firewall data for networking devices split into 5-minute totals. The number of network sessions is plotted along the x-axis and the number of bytes is on the y-axis. The size of each point ("bubble") is proportional to the packet count. One challenge in this visualization is that many points overlap. By setting the alpha value to 1/3 in the chart on the right, you can see through any bubble to bubbles that lie underneath it.

It's handy for you to set the alpha as a fraction (such as 1/3 instead of 0.33) because it makes it obvious how many points or bubbles will stack up to equal the maximum color value (solid). This allows you to tweak the alpha for how many layers you have. If you have 50 layers (some of the maps in Chapter 5 have code that use small alpha values like this), you can set the alpha to 1/50 (as opposed to converting to 0.02 and typing that in).

Size Encoding

Figure 6-13 is encoding another quantitative variable by mapping the size (*area*) of the circle ("bubble") to the number of packets in a 5-minute period. Looking back at the accuracy chart in Figure 6-5, you can see that *area* is relatively low on the list. This difficulty is compounded in Figure 6-13 because there is no legend for bubble size (an intentional oversight on our part). But for the purposes of this chapter, note the relative values here—the relatively large versus relatively small number of packets. In a more formal setting, you'd want to add a description to the title or use some other annotation to indicate the significance of the "bubble" size. For the purposes of this exercise, you are simply looking for any obvious patterns and this type of graphic shows relative sizes. Bubble charts like this are good for crude estimates, and are thus similar in communication capability to pie charts.

Another visualization method with similar traits is the *treemap*. A treemap uses *area* and *color* to encode two *quantitative* variables (see Figure 6-14). The treemap visualization method relies on area, and thus is relatively low in visual accuracy.

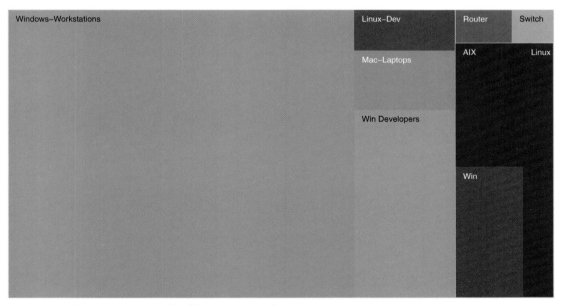

FIGURE 6-14 *Treemap: devices and traffic on the network*

Figure 6-14 portrays the number of devices on a network and the traffic volume for each type. It uses the size of rectangles to communicate a quantity and the color of the rectangle to communicate a different quantitative variable. Often times the rectangles are visually grouped to depict categorical relationships. In Figure 6-14, the size of each rectangle is proportional to the quantity of devices on the network by type (workstations, servers, and networking devices), and the lightness of color of each rectangle is proportional to the volume of traffic they produce (normalized).

We should reiterate—a treemap combines two relatively inaccurate methods of encoding quantities. This makes treemaps difficult to execute well and often confusing to viewers. The same rule applies to treemaps as to pie charts and bubble plots—there are usually better visualization methods to communicate the data.

Communicating Distributions

Sometimes you'll just want to show the values within a single variable and how they are distributed. Within classical statistics, you have descriptive statistics that attempt to reduce a distribution to a set of descriptive values. For example, if you go back to the 8 hours of firewall data shown in Figures 6-9 and 6-10, you could describe the distribution of total sessions within each 5-minute window like this:

Description	Statistic
Min	265,800
Median	356,500
Mean	350,500
Standard Dev.	32,093
Max	410,700
Skew	−0.5
Kurtosis	−0.457

Most people can't look at these numbers and understand what the data is telling them. Nor will they be able to see any subtle patterns; descriptive statistics are about reducing a distribution of values to a set of individual numbers. This is where visualizations can help out considerably.

Histograms and Density Plots

Rather than reduce a distribution to a few descriptive statistics, you can represent every value in the variable. Figure 6-15 shows a basic histogram on the left and a density plot on the right, both for the same data set.

A histogram uses a simple process called *binning*. It works by creating equally spaced "bins" and then counting how many of the measurements are in each bin. In this example, we created bins that are 12,000 sessions wide. You can see that at the peak—around 350,000 sessions—we had about 18 sessions within

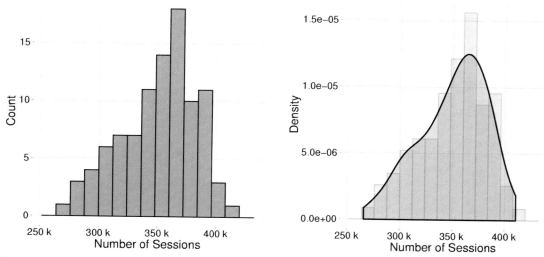

FIGURE 6-15 *Histogram and density plot of the firewall sessions*

that bin. Part of the criticism of histograms is that you can affect how histograms appear by adjusting the size and position of the bins. But these plots are indispensable when you want to get a feel for a distribution and they are quite effective in communicating the basic shape.

The plot on the right in Figure 6-15 is a density plot. It uses the same approach as the histogram, but the bins are quite small and a smoothing process is applied over it. By projecting the original histogram behind it, you can see how it flattens the peaks and diminishes the valleys. There's no right or wrong between the two—both involve some approximations. When you are exploring your data, it's quite easy to pass in data to hist() and get an immediate (although maybe not pretty) histogram.

Boxing in Boxplots

Another method, which was developed by John Tukey (remember him from Chapter 1?), is the boxplot, which we touched on in Chapter 5 when discussing outliers. This is not something your viewers will intuitively understand if they haven't seen one before, so it may require a little more supporting material than other methods need. In the fall of 2012, one of the authors (Jay) set up a simple honey pot to record the packets it saw on the Internet. How often is a host scanned when it's on the Internet? You can get a feel for the answer in the boxplot in Figure 6-16.

The boxplot begins with the median (middle) value of the distribution and it places the center bar there. Then it computes the 25th and 75th percentiles. This means that 25 percent of the data is below the 25th percentile, 25 percent of the data is above the 75th percentile, and 50 percent of the data is between the two. These two points form the length of the box and represent the *inter-quartile range* or IQR.

There are a few different methods used to represent the length of the lines. The most common method places the lines one and a half times the IQR away from the box. Other methods place the end of the line at the minimum and maximum of the data. Figure 6-17 attempts to convey a large number of distributions within one chart with boxplots.

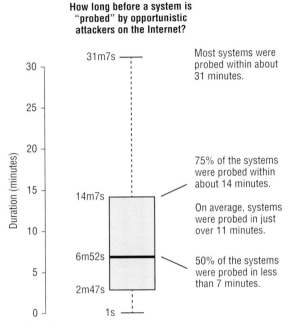

FIGURE 6-16   *Honey pot traffic: boxplot*

What's interesting about Figure 6-17 is that it was generated with over 100 million values. It not only conveys a large quantity of data, but it's also able to represent a certain amount of confidence in the data. In this case, just stating the mean or median would have been a disservice, since some of these have a very wide range of possible observations. How well could you have explained these values and the variations with anything other than a visualization of the distributions?

Visualizing Time Series

This chapter has glossed over time series data even though you've been working with it in most of the visualizations. Time series data are data collected over the same and repeated time intervals. For most of the firewall figures in this chapter, we parsed the log files and counted up the bytes, sessions, and packets within a sequence of 5-minute time windows. This allows aggregation of individual entries into more manageable data points. But depending on how you slice up time and aggregate the data, you can get and see different types of things.

Figure 6-18 is looking at 21 days of firewall traffic sliced into 5-minute chunks. This is quite a bit of data for a small line graph (over 6,000 data points in a few inches), and when you try to represent that data with a line plot, the lines crisscross over one another so much that they look like one thick and jittery line. If you try to reduce the mess by simplifying the underlying data with an hourly average (the middle plot in

Figure 6-18), you lose the extremes and the details, which is not generally good in a field like information security where extremes matter. In the bottom plot, we replaced the lines in the first plot with points. This

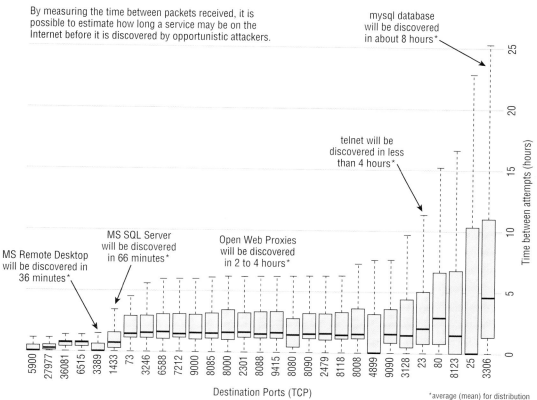

FIGURE 6-17 *Boxplots: opportunistic packets*

removes much of the mess and allows you to see the general trends and the extreme points.

Time series data can get very dense to visualize when you are talking about data from logs. We even made it easier by looking at 5-minute slices instead of 1-minute slices. How you prepare and visualize the data is dependent on what you are looking for in the data. If you are looking for specific spikes or gaps in traffic, you should avoid using a rolling average. However, if you want to understand general patterns, averages are usually good enough.

Experiment on Your Own

We've covered quite a few techniques so far in this chapter. Feel free to get creative and try one or more techniques on your time series data. What if you tried showing each hour with a boxplot? What if you used larger points and varied color based on size and turned down the alpha? Creating good visualizations is generally an iterative process, so take this as a license to experiment! Remember that you aren't limited to static visualizations. You can create interactive visualizations (as you'll see Chapter 11) or turn the time series into a video fit for YouTube, as you will see in the next section.

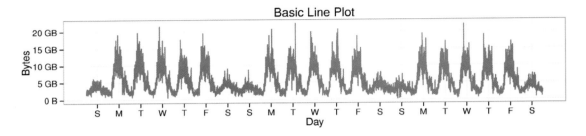

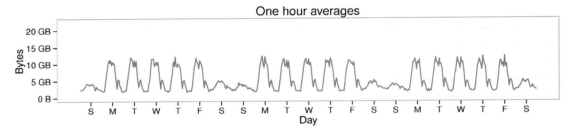

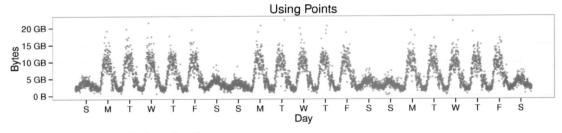

FIGURE 6-18 *Time series: 21 days of traffic*

Turning Your Data into a Movie Star

This chapter has focused primarily on foundational components of data visualizations. These apply to static or interactive graphics, dashboards, and as you'll now see, to videos as well. One of the more fun "tricks" we've learned is how to turn data into a video. In order to do this, you combine two techniques: automated sequential graphics and stop-motion software.

If you aren't familiar with stop-motion by name, you're certainly familiar with it by sight. It's the Claymation technology of setting up a scene, taking a picture, and then changing it slightly, taking another picture, and so on. When you string all of those pictures together you get the appearance of motion and you have a video. Same concept with data animation, but instead of taking a picture, you want to generate a graphic and save it as a picture. Then you can use any number of stop-motion software packages (mencoder, avconv, FFmpeg, iMovie, and so on) to create a movie from the pictures. If you want to get fancy, you can include music or voice-overs so you can explain the data as it's progressing.

To see how this looks, try Listing 6-1 in an open R session.

LISTING 6-1

```
# random walk
set.seed(1)
# set up nine directions
dirs <- matrix(c(rep(seq(-1, 1), 3),
rep(seq(-1, 1), each=3)), ncol=2, byrow=T)
# start in the center
cpos <- matrix(c(0, 0), ncol=2)
# set full screen
par(mar=c(0,0,0,0))
# take 200 steps
for(i in seq(200)) {
  plot(cpos, type="p", col="gray80", xlim=c(-20, 20), ylim=c(-20,20),
yaxt="n", ann=FALSE, xaxt="n", bty="n")
  cpos <- rbind(cpos, cpos[nrow(cpos), ] + dirs[sample(1:9, 1), ])
  points(cpos[nrow(cpos), 1], cpos[nrow(cpos), 2],
type="p", pch=16, col="red")
  Sys.sleep(0.1)
}
# reset screen back to default
par(mar=c(5.1,4.1,4.1,2.1))
```

This code will set up a matrix of nine directions. It will loop 200 times, adjusting the point in some random direction and drawing the new plot for it. It then will sleep for a tenth of a second so you can view the plot. On all but the slowest machines this looks like a random walking point on the screen. If you want a challenge, modify this script to write each of the images (hint, take a look at help(png)) and then create a video of it. We've done this and it's available at http://datadrivensecurity.info/book/ch06/movie/chapter6-movie.mov (or as part of the Chapter 6 materials on the book's website at www.wiley.com/go/datadrivensecurity) if you'd like to see this random walk in action!

Summary

Communicating data visually allows you to communicate complex data and relationships quickly, enable pattern recognition, spot anomalies, and gain new perspectives. Understanding how the brain processes and stores information allows you to create visuals that leverage preattentive cues and minimize saccadic movements for efficiency. Through the work of Cleveland and McGill, you've learned that some visual methods are better for communicating quantity (in contrast, some methods "mumble"). You should combine these lessons into colors, points, lines, and shapes to communicate the stories you uncover in the data.

Recommended Reading

The following are some recommended readings that can further your understanding on some of the topics we touch on in this chapter. For full information on these recommendations and for the sources we cite in the chapter, please see Appendix B. Resources for visualization are plentiful and we had a hard time keeping this list as short as we did.

Data Points: *Visualization That Means Something* **by Nathan Yau**—This is Nathan Yau's second book on visualization, and it offers a gentle introduction to the topic of visualization. His first book, *Visualize This*, offers examples and source code if you'd like that more. But both books are good places to start exploring visualizations.

Show Me the Numbers: *Designing Tables and Graphs to Enlighten* **by Stephen Few**—Stephen Few is known for his many technical contributions to the visualization field. His books lean toward the technical side, yet carry coherent and valuable lessons for communicating through data visualizations.

Envisioning Information **by Edward R. Tufte**—Another well-known name in the field, but with a much more design-centric approach with a little more emphasis on aesthetics and function. Any one of Tufte's books is worth their price, and if you can catch his touring seminar, his books are usually included in the price of the registration.

Information Visualization **by Colin Ware**—This is a hardcore book on the mechanics and cognitive science behind visualization. If you are really curious how humans interpret data visually, this is the book to read.

7

Learning from Security Breaches

"In times like these when unemployment rates are up to 13 percent,
income has fallen by 5 percent, and suicide rates are climbing, I get so angry
that the government is wasting money on things like the collection of statistics!"

Hans Rosling, quoting a caller on a radio talk show, *The Joy of Stats*

When organizations experience a security event, their natural reaction is to focus on getting back to normal as fast as possible. They see the event as a sign of failure or an embarrassment and everything they do centers on minimizing the impact and putting the event behind them. In that environment, they often overlook one important task and miss the silver lining.

During such an event, a rich set of a data is generated and just waiting to be collected and analyzed. Think of it—If you could somehow gather that data, make sense of it, and perhaps even compare and contrast it with other security events, you could learn how to prevent the next attack. Maybe even better, you could identify trends and patterns so that you could prevent multiple common attacks with a single preventative control. Achieving such a benefit is the goal of this chapter. You'll learn how to determine what data to collect and how to manage it. The chapter also discusses how to analyze and share this data.

In order to tackle the challenge of learning from breach data, this chapter leverages the Vocabulary for Event Recording and Incident Sharing (VERIS) framework. One of the authors of this book (Jay) and the RISK team at Verizon have been developing and evolving VERIS in order to produce the Data Breach Investigation Report (DBIR). In an effort to promote adoption and use, Verizon has opened VERIS. Details about its use and implementation are hosted at `http://veriscommunity.net`. Because it is open, any organization can adopt the framework and start collecting data from their own internal events. When it comes to information sharing, the data will be ready to pass around and exchange.

> **Note**
>
> *The Verizon Data Breach Investigations Report (DBIR) leverages the VERIS framework for its data collection and data analysis and may help you get a context for this chapter. The most recent report can be found at* `www.verizonenterprise.com/DBIR/`

Besides being an open framework, VERIS has another benefit. There is a relatively new project called the VERIS Community Database (VCDB) that offers a free and downloadable data set of publicly disclosed security events, which are all recorded using the VERIS format. This means you have thousands of VERIS records you can download and analyze throughout this chapter. At the time of this writing, the VCDB data is being housed at GitHub (`https://github.com/vz-risk/VCDB`).

Setting Up the Research

First and foremost, you should approach this breach analysis as a research project. If you think of this as a "metrics program" or a "security project," you might fool yourself into thinking this is somehow unique to information security, but it isn't. This is all about data collection and analysis, something that has been done countless times before across many disciplines and generations. Approaching this as if it were a unique project and trying to reinvent the (data analysis) wheel is not only wasteful of time and resources, but you'd be laughed at and ridiculed by all the grown-up data scientists. Let's avoid all that and call this what it is—a research project.

Most of the work in this book has been of an exploratory nature. You worked with data to see what it contained and then formed the questions you wanted to answer with the data and went back into the data.

This effort is different because you are starting with no data. If you jumped right in and started to collect the breach data, you'd waste countless resources, capture data that you'd discover later to be meaningless, and end up wishing you had data you didn't collect. Therefore, it's better to set a frame for this effort and think of a handful of questions you'd like to explore. From that, you can determine which data points you want to collect.

VERIS was developed to support the strategic decision process. In other words, where can you focus your limited resources to get the biggest benefit for your security spending? Given a list of audit findings or remediation projects, how can you prioritize those so you fix the most critical first? Perhaps even more importantly, you also want to answer the opposite questions. Can you identify areas and tasks where you do **not** want to spend your time and money? Supporting these questions is the goal of this chapter and can be summarized as follows:

The goal in collecting and analyzing breach data is to support the decision-making process within security leadership.

Notice the word **support** in there. This research will exist to **support** a decision process. It is not intended to be or replace the decision process. You need to have the wherewithal to recognize that security prioritization is a complex issue, and those working in the industry are just beginning to scrape away at it. At this point in that scraping, where you have very little data, you should not make the assumption that you'll get the research perfect right out of the gate. You want to focus on how much uncertainty you have now and strive to reduce that uncertainty as much as you can through this work. The decisions have been made for far too long without data analysis. You need to support that decision process so it uses every bit of information you can gather.

Breach Data Reduces Uncertainty

Although it would be great to collect breach data to create a perfect and prescriptive list of priorities, it just won't happen. The data will simply help you know more than you currently do, but it can't definitively show you the path forward. This raises the question for some whether it's worth it to collect this data. Is it worth spending the time and resources to create information that doesn't tell you exactly what to do?

The answer is an emphatic yes.

Uncertainty exists in the gap between what you know and what you need to know to make the best decision. Although it's tempting to toss out imperfect information because it contains uncertainty, the value of the information should be assessed by comparison. Not between the perfect information you'd want and the information you'll get, but instead between the information you **currently have** and the information **you will have**. This is where you see the value of this type of data analysis. Data will help you reduce your uncertainty by reducing the gap between what you know and what you need to know. It will help you work from a better place than you were working from before. You will be making progress and setting a foundation for reducing even more uncertainty next time. This is how scientific knowledge has evolved: a series of small steps, each reducing uncertainty a little more. Therefore, the goal is not to aim for perfect information and give up when you miss that. You should aim to simply learn more than you know now. That is where you will find value.

Considerations in a Data Collection Framework

Generating data manually from a process has several pitfalls, and if that process isn't approached carefully, it can produce shaky data and probably several big headaches. Since we have an inside view of how VERIS has developed (and some of those headaches), we have gathered the following set of guidelines for manual data collection. These are not limited to the collection of security event data, though. Any type of manual data collection can benefit from these guidelines.

Aiming for Objective Answers

First and foremost the questions you ask should *aim for objective answers*. If a question asks for an opinion, the answers will have a whole lot of variety and be influenced by strange things like the weather or what the analyst had for lunch. In some cases this may be okay, because inconsistent answers might be better than no answers at all, and sometimes you do want to solicit the opinion of an expert with some restrictions. Most of the time, however, the questions should be focused on asking about facts that are observable or deducible from observations.

For example, it's far better to ask whether malware was involved in the attack and which functions it performed instead of asking how advanced the malware was. The investigator during the breach can answer yes or no as to whether malware was used. If the investigator has the resources to analyze the malware (or the malware is identifiable), there isn't a lot of guesswork about what it's capable of. These are things you either know or don't know.

Limiting Possible Answers

Next, constrain the possible answers to a short set of options. If the question asks for a sentence or description, it won't be useful directly in the data analysis without a lot more effort. Most of the time, free text fields are helpful to record unique aspects or to set context if you ever want to understand why these data points look like they do. With this in mind, manual data collection should make judicious use of Notes fields and a field for the overall Summary of the event. But remember, all of the data analysis will use the data found in the constrained lists or numbers. Having the data limited to a set of values will make that analysis easier in the long run.

Allowing "Other," and "Unknown" Options

Most every constrained list of answers must allow "Unknown" and "Other" answers. Even though a question may seem so easy that everyone should know the answer, the world will always create a circumstance to prove that assumption wrong. Including an "Unknown" option allows you to differentiate between when you really don't know and when the question isn't applicable. This is a subtle distinction, but one that can really mess up the analysis. There are a few rare questions that don't need an "Unknown" option, but they are rare, and you'll know them when you see them.

For example, if you'd like to know if a server is virtualized or not, it may be tempting to create a simple checkbox if it was virtualized. But that doesn't account for the circumstances when the information isn't available (and there will *always* be a circumstance when it won't be available). Now you've set up the response as "yes" and "everything else," where "everything else" represents both "no" and "I don't know."

The result is you would not be able to create a percentage of hosts that were virtualized or look at non-virtualized systems because you can't tell a "no" answer from an "I don't know" answer.

The second field you need to add is "Other" or, depending on the question, "Not Applicable." Avoid trying to capture all the options in an exhaustive list. Exhaustive lists become unmanageable (which slows down data entry), and you need to capture only *most* of the answers. You'll find that a handful of common answers, especially within security events, will be used most of the time. The common answers create the trends and statistics, whereas the uncommon answers do little more than create interesting stories. Therefore, you want to capture the common things for data analysis and relegate the uncommon to the "Other" category and the Notes field. Keep an eye on anything marked "Other," but if you create a good list of options, they should show up few and far between.

Note

It's okay to be lazy when creating lists of selection options by seeking out standards to reference and leverage. For example, don't create your own list of industries to gather. Leverage the good work of the U.S. Census Bureau and its North American Industry Classification System (NAICS). The Census Bureau has already figured out that industries are nested has and created a system to capture both the general industry and an organization's specific function within that industry. They assign a six-digit code where each digit adds a level of detail about the industry of the organization. Details about the NAICS classification can be found at `http://www.census.gov/eos/www/naics/`.

Avoiding Conflation and Merging the Minutiae

The last two points may seem subtle, but you want to avoid conflation and merge the minutiae where possible. These two concepts are opposites, and you have to find the middle ground between them. Conflation occurs when a question (and its answers) combines more than one concept.

For example, the breach types used by DataLossDB (`http://datalossdb.org/analysis`) conflate the actor, actions, and assets into the type. Their framework lists a type of "Hack" for a "computer based intrusion" (no asset or actor defined), or "snooping," which is an "employee . . . accessing confidential records" (conflating the actor and action). You can specify "stolen media" or "stolen drive" or "stolen tape," which are all unique options that conflate and repeat the action (physical loss) with the asset.

The assignment of a single conflating "breach type" should not be thought of as wrong or bad, it just represents a different goal within the research. Just be aware that conflation of terms like this will create a challenge during data analysis. You have the most flexibility and see the most benefit when you can compare and contrast across specific categories, but with conflated terms you'll find it challenging to clearly separate the categories. The result is that the data analysis may not be able to do anything more than simply count the frequency of the conflated breach types.

Where conflation combines more than one concept into a single variable, you have to be careful of the opposite, whereby you split a single concept into too many details. You want to get just enough detail and separation in the list to support your goal.

An example of collecting too much detail is when you try to collect how incidents are discovered and want to classify the discovery method. Although it may be interesting to know if it was an external security researcher, and perhaps amusing to know what color hat they wore (white, black, or even grey), creating several options based on details wouldn't help you achieve your goals. You have to split one concept (an external security researcher) across multiple selections (such as Researcher-white hat, Researcher-gray hat). In this case, maybe you'll just want to drop the distinction of an external security researcher altogether and merge everything into one broad field of "an external unrelated party."

Having said this, don't be afraid to go into detail when necessary. As an example, the list of possible assets within VERIS is split into several categories and dozens of detailed assets under each category. There are times you'll want to split details and times you can combine them—the trick is getting that balance right.

Luckily, all these issues have been in consideration as VERIS has been evolving. One of the biggest challenges is saying no to new questions. We've found there is always more we'd like to know, but we know that each data point we try to collect has a cost. And it's sometimes proven to be a higher cost than imagined.

Consider the Cost per Datum

During a manual data-collection effort, it is very tempting to dream up all sorts of questions you'd like answered. Creating such a list isn't bad, and it may even be helpful to lay out all the questions to answer. But choose the questions you are going to ask very carefully because every question adds exponential cost across the lifetime of the data. Even before the question is answered, you have to build a method to collect it, so every question must be built into the data-collection methodology. When the analyst is entering an incident, each question will require some thought and perhaps even some research before it can be answered, again adding time and effort. That data point may require processing and cleanup, and will need to be stored and managed. Anytime you want to parse the data (and you'll want to parse it in many different ways), you might have to consider this field, or worse, consider all the interactions of all the fields. Beyond that, there are dozens of other subtle interactions with the data that will increase the cost of each data point beyond what you can imagine, as the questions and data points are selected.

It's helpful to pretend you are about to take a long journey to a wise sage who lives on top of a mountain. You will have a limited amount of time to ask questions before the sage says something mysterious and vanishes. What questions will have the greatest impact? You'll want to identify a handful of questions you really need answered—maybe a handful of questions you'd like to have answered, and then you'll have a mountain of questions you wish you had time to ask, but you'll just have to make do without them. The same is true with manual data collection. If the post-incident questionnaire asks too many questions or is too painful, people will lose interest quickly and the answers will end up being of poor quality—including the handful of questions you need answered. You must choose your questions wisely.

An Introduction to VERIS

When a security event is investigated, a narrative naturally emerges from the process. The investigator will typically try to answer the question, "Who did what to what (or whom) with what result?" That question presents a good core set of data points to collect. Therefore, as a starting point, you'll want to focus on those four points—"Who (threat actor) did what (action) to what or whom (asset) with what result (attribute)?"

But that's not all you may be interested in; you may also want to know how you discovered and responded to the incident and if possible the impact you experienced as a result. Finally, you'll have some housekeeping items (an identifier, summary, workflow status, and so on) and if you aggregate breaches or share the information, you'll want to record some victim demographics. Overall, you can break down the sections of data you want to gather like those in the VERIS framework, as shown in Table 7-1.

TABLE 7-1 *Sections within VERIS*

VERIS Section	Purpose
Incident Tracking	Metadata about the incident for management and tracking purposes
Threat Actor	One or more people who cause or contribute to an incident
Threat Actions	What the threat actor(s) did or used to cause or contribute to the incident
Information Assets	Information assets that were compromised or affected during the incident
Attributes	What happened to the asset during the incident
Discovery/Response	Timeline, discovery method, and lessons learned
Impact	What was the overall effect of the incident to the organization
Victim	Demographic information like industry and organizational size
Indicators	Optional indicators of compromise (IP addresses, malware hashes, domains, and so on)
Plus	Optional section for extending VERIS

Although it's tempting to dig into the data (and you will), it's important to understand the significance of these fields so you don't misapply them. Therefore, the following sections go through each part of VERIS in more detail and discuss these fields. Keep in mind that these sections are separated so analysts can think about the structure. There is nothing in the actual data denoting the `incident_id` field as helping with incident tracking, for example.

Warning

Although we are covering VERIS with some depth, we will not go into every field, and we don't cover every detail about the framework. For example, we won't call out all the places the framework specifies a "Notes" field (which is almost every section), and we don't cover the "Indicators" section in detail. Just keep in mind that the framework is actively maintained and evolving. This chapter discusses the 1.2.1 release, so be sure to refer to `http://veriscommunity.net/` for all the details and current specification of the VERIS framework.

Incident Tracking

Some of the fields within VERIS exist to simply describe or track the incident. These fields help you keep records straight by identifying each with a unique identifier and tracking the source of the incident and any related incidents. You use the `source_id` field to compare your unique "source" of incidents to something like the VCDB (which has `vcdb` in that field). If something has a value of `factor`, that means it is a restrictive list (we discussed creating those lists previously), and only those values are expected. See Table 7-2 to see the incident tracking fields.

TABLE 7-2 *Incident Tracking Fields*

Field	Value	Description
schema_version	string	VERIS version (currently 1.2.1)
incident_id	string	Unique identifier (VCDB uses GUID)
source_id	string	Origin of the data (VCDB data has vcdb)
reference	string	URL or internal ticketing system ID
security_incident	factor	Confirmed, Suspected, False Positive, Near Miss
confidence	factor	High, Medium, Low, None
summary	string	Free text summary of incident
related_incidents	string	Free text, other incident_ids
notes	string	Free text

There are only one or two fields you'll use during analysis and those are the two `factor` variables (again, this means they are restricted to a list of expected answers). The security incident is required and will help you split the analysis on whether the event was a confirmed security incident (an asset has a security attribute affected). The confidence rating is a rare subjective field. It enables the analysts to record their subjective assessments as to how confident they are in the accuracy of the data they entered. This optional field is not heavily used and won't appear much in the VCDB incidents that you'll look at.

Threat Actor

Earlier in this chapter you read about the challenge of conflation. This is something you want to be aware of, especially in these next three sections (actor, actions, and assets). You read about the framework DataLossDB used with a single conflated breach type, and you'll see the same thing with the framework used by Privacy Rights Clearinghouse (`http://www.privacyrights.org/data-breach`). Their framework also uses a singular "breach type" to define each event, and again it simplifies the actors and actions into the one label.

For example, they have an "insider (INSD)" type, which is defined as "someone with legitimate access intentionally breaches information—such as an employee or contractor." There is also the "physical loss (PHYS)" type, which is defined as "lost, discarded, or stolen non-electronic records, such as paper documents."

These simplified labels can quickly become confusing during data entry if, for example, an insider steals paper documents.

You may see insiders breach systems, drop malware, and social engineer, just as an external actor would and you want to separate the insiders from external actors clearly in the data. VERIS tackles that conflation by separating the who from what they did and what was affected. Note that the method that the Privacy Rights Clearinghouse uses isn't wrong. It just has a different focus and represents different priorities and goals. VERIS has the goal to inform and support security decisions, which benefits from more detail than a single "breach type" label. Table 7-3 shows the threat actor fields.

TABLE 7-3   *Threat Actor Fields*

Actor	Field	Value	Description
external	motive	factor	Helps understand intentions; same enumeration for the three actor types
	variety	factor	Defines resources and capabilities of external actor
	country	factor	ISO-3166-1 two-digit country field
internal	motive	factor	Helps understand intentions
	variety	factor	Defines resources and capabilities of internal actor
partner	motive	factor	Helps understand intentions
	industry	string	U.S. Census NAICS code
	country	factor	ISO-3166-1 two-digit country field

The threat actor section also introduces the nesting feature of VERIS. At the top level is the actor, so there is a section in the data for "actor," and then there are three classes of actors—external, internal, and partner—all of which are optional. Within each of those classes you'll want to add details about that type of actor. Looking down the values in this section, you can see all factors. That means you should be able to include any of these or use them as pivot points. In other words, if you want to support a threat-modeling exercise that compares different threat communities, you could extract the actions for financially motivated actors and compare them to disgruntled employees. See Figure 7-1.

Threat Actions

This section collects variables to describe what the threat actor(s) did or used during the event. Again, there are nest variables under the top-level categories:

- **Malware**—Malicious software, script, or code run on an asset that alters its state or function
- **Hacking**—Person (at a keyboard) attempting to access or harm an asset without authorization
- **Social**—Exploiting the human element (phishing, pretexting, and so on)
- **Misuse**—Abusing resources or privileges contrary to intended use

- **Physical**—Personal actions involving proximity, possession, or force
- **Error**—Anything done (or left undone) incorrectly or inadvertently
- **Environmental**—Natural events and hazards within the immediate environment or infrastructure of assets

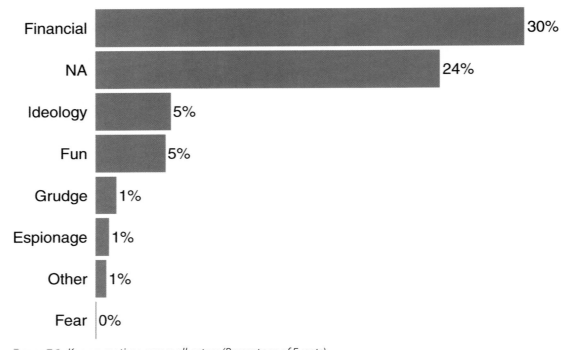

FIGURE 7-1 *Known motives across all actors (Percentage of Events)*

You have to be careful as you work with these categories. There are many opportunities for misinterpretation and misclassification across categories. These categories and the factors in each category are explained in detail along with use-case examples at the VERIS website (`http://veriscommunity.net/`). Once you spend some time and look at a few examples, these categories become more clear and eventually will become intuitive. See Table 7-4 to see the action fields.

TABLE 7-4 *Action Fields*

Action	Field	Value	Description
malware	variety	factor	Functionality of malware
	vector	factor	How the malware was installed/infected

Action	Field	Value	Description
hacking	variety	factor	Type(s) of hacking action
	vector	factor	Path of attack
social	variety	factor	Type(s) of social action
	vector	factor	Path or method of communication
	target	factor	Role of targeted person
misuse	variety	factor	Type(s) of misuse action
	vector	factor	Path or access method for misuse
physical	variety	factor	Type(s) of physical actions
	vector	factor	Method of physical access
	location	factor	Physical location of action
error	variety	factor	Type(s) of error actions
	vector	factor	Cause of error
environmental	variety	factor	Type(s) of environmental actions

Notice how `variety` and `vector` are repeated over and over? Every action category has a `variety` field with unique enumerations for each category. All but the environmental actions have a `vector` field, again with unique enumerations for each category. Finally, social actions also ask for the target of the social action, and physical actions ask for a location of the action. That explains the whole section! Notice how every field here is a factor, meaning you can split, pivot, and/or filter based on these fields. See Figure 7-2.

Multiple Events in the Attack Chain

Anyone who has been around information security knows that breaches tend not to be simple and single events. Oftentimes, the attacker will perform multiple actions, which complicates the recording process. Most of the factors in the VERIS framework support multiple answers. On one hand, this is very nice because you don't have to pick "the one best answer" for a complex security event, but on the flip side, this adds complexity for data management and analysis. As you'll see later in this chapter, this isn't as hard as it first seems.

(continues)

(continued)

As an example, suppose an attacker sends a phishing email to an executive's assistant and quickly follows that up with a phone call pretending to be a business partner who sent the email. These are two actions, and you should see both "pretexting" and "phishing" selected in the `social` `.variety` field. If the phishing email contained malware that is installed, you'd also see the malware action along the variety and vector of "email," since it was installed via the phishing attack. When you represent this data and count the actions, you'll have more individual actions than total events. This naturally precludes the use of pie charts, which ends up being beneficial for all parties involved.

There is also a common notion within information security of the "attack chain" or "kill chain." The concept is to establish the actions of the attacker in the order they happened. Although VERIS allows multiple actions, it does not record the order in which they occurred. This was a conscious trade-off of cost versus benefit. Attempting to put the events in order created substantial overhead for the analysts and was taking too long to enter. Most of the time the order of events in reports and tickets (definitely in media articles) are either vague or missing. As a result, VERIS simply records the presence of events within an attack to reduce the time and effort spent in data collection.

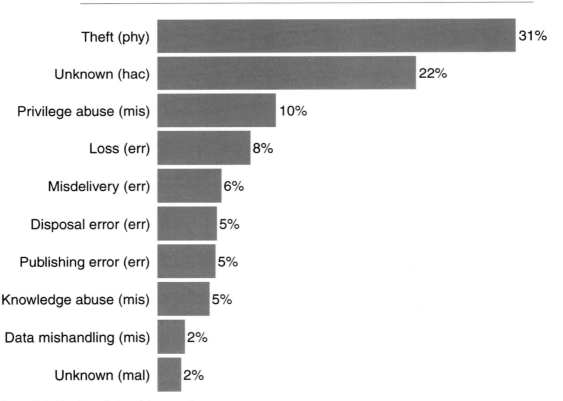

FIGURE 7-2 *Top 10 varieties of threat actions*

Information Assets

Assets are the information containers (servers or other devices) that you are trying to protect. Like the other sections we've covered so far, there are top-level categories, which are as follows:

- **Server (S)**—System providing service(s)
- **Network (N)**—Infrastructure device or appliance
- **User Device (U)**—End-user equipment (laptop or desktop)
- **Media (M)**—Data storage devices or physical documents
- **People (P)**—Since people can be affected
- **Kiosk/Public Terminal (K)**—Public-use devices

Within each category there are several varieties of assets, but the category and variety are stored in the same field. For example a mail server is stored as "S - Mail" and a desktop computer is a "U - Desktop." Associated with each asset is an optional `amount` field, which allows you to record multiple assets with the same variety as when they are involved in one event. Table 7-5 shows the asset fields.

TABLE 7-5 *Asset Fields*

Asset	Field	Value	Description
assets	variety	factor	Specific type of asset; prepended with letter for category
	amount	integer	Count of the above asset
asset	accessibility	factor	How accessible the assets are
	ownership	factor	Who owns the assets?
	management	factor	Who manages the assets?
	hosting	factor	Where (physically) is it hosted?
	country	factor	Location of assets (if different from victim)
	cloud	factor	Type of cloud service, if cloud

There is quite a bit packed into the assets, and these are relatively recent additions to the VERIS framework (version 1.2). There is a lot of focus on mobile devices and employees bringing their own devices into the corporate environment. Also, there may be unique exposures from cloud hosted applications and assets, so that is captured here as well. Note also that these are all factors, so there are only a handful of possible answers. You cannot write in "very" for accessibility of the asset as an example. See Figure 7-3.

Attributes

The attributes of the preceding assets are what you work hard in information security to not have affected. Attributes are based on the C.I.A. triad, which stands for confidentiality, integrity, and availability.

For a while VERIS extended these three with three more attributes to record the Parkerian Hexad (named after their originator, security pioneer, and long-time security researcher, Donn Parker). The extra three attributes included possession/control, authenticity, and utility. But the added fields just did not yield enough benefit for the added cost of separate categories, so they were combined with the three top categories. For simplicity, when a VERIS record is stored, the sections are labeled with the three primary categories (confidentiality, integrity, and availability). The three main sections of attributes are as follows:

- **Confidentiality, possession, and control**—Data was observed or disclosed to an unauthorized actor; owner may no longer have exclusive custody.

- **Integrity and authenticity**—Asset is incomplete or changed from authorized content and function; conforms to expected state.

- **Availability and utility**—Asset is not accessible, useful, or fit for use.

These categories can be quite helpful to the security team in determining the areas to focus on. The Verizon Data Breach Investigation report has exclusively focused only on breaches where the confidentiality attribute was affected and there was a confirmed data disclosure. See Table 7-6 for a look at the attribute fields.

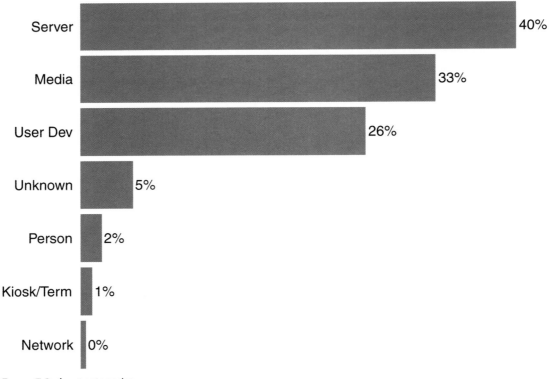

FIGURE 7-3 *Asset categories*

Table 7-6 *Attribute Fields*

Attribute	Field	Value	Description
confidentiality	data_disclosure	factor	Status of confidentiality breach
	data_total	integer	Number of records (see below)
	data.variety	factor	Type of data disclosed
	data.amount	integer	Number of records
	state	factor	State of data when disclosed
integrity	variety	factor	Nature of effect
availability	variety	factor	Nature of effect
	duration	time range	Duration of availability/utility loss

There is a new field type called `time range`, which is actually two fields, a "unit" of time and a "value" for that unit of time. The unit has basic measurements of time: seconds, minutes, hours, days, weeks, months, and years. The value represents how many of those, such as 3 weeks or 6 months. VERIS tried to support specific date/time fields instead of time ranges but found specific date/time was either time consuming or just impossible. However, VERIS analysts found knowing whether a range was days versus weeks was obvious even if a specific range was not known. For example, analysts might know that the server went offline during the DDoS attack, and that it was down for more than 60 minutes but not a full day. Tracking down the specific times may be difficult, but in that case, you would see "hours" in the unit, and if the specific number of hours is known, you'd see a value. Otherwise, it's blank if the precision is unknown.

Counting Records

One of the more common pieces of information disclosed in publicly disclosed breaches is the number of records affected. Perhaps reporters and the general public demand this, and the victims are forced to provide a number, even if it's all the records in a database. Records can be relatively easy to count when the data is obviously separated. Payment (credit) cards, identities, and medical records are all quite clear in their separation and lend themselves to being counted. But when you get into more complex types like classified information or trade secrets, the capability to count records becomes more difficult. Perhaps the number of physical documents could be used, or the number of files disclosed, but oftentimes it's difficult to count them. Overall, analysts struggle to record a precise number for the data varieties of classified or internal information and trade secrets. You will have to account for that in the analyses and visualizations.

Discovery/Response

You just saw your first time range in the availability attribute and you'll see that a lot more in this section for the timeline data. Some of these fields are not in a section as you saw in the previous four VERIS sections, but the timeline does have its own section. See Table 7-7.

TABLE 7-7 *Discovery and Response Fields*

Section	Field	Value	Description
	discovery_method	factor	How the event was discovered
	control_failure	string	Free text field to describe what, under the victim's control, failed
	corrective_action	string	Free text field describing what the victim should do
	targeted	factor	Targeted or opportunistic attack
timeline	incident_date	date	Date of incident
	compromise	time range	Time to initial compromise
	exfiltration	time range	Time from initial compromise to data exfiltration
	discovery	time range	Time from initial compromise to discovery
	containment	time range	Time from discovery to containment

Notice the new type of value called `date` here, which is not a standard date field. Because VERIS has to account for unknown values, the date fields are in separate variables. Too often than you'll like for your analyses, the precise date of the incident isn't known or isn't reported precisely. The framework assumes at least the year is known, but the month, day, and time fields are all optional in that date field. The other fields in the timeline are the same time range values you saw in the availability attribute.

Notice also that the control failure and corrective action suggestions are free text. This makes them difficult to include in the data analysis without more effort. Finally, the discovery method is one of the rare enumerations that cannot have multiple answers. The framework assumes that once the incident was discovered it could not be discovered again, so only one method of discovery is allowed.

Impact

The impact section (see Table 7-8) is perhaps one of the most, if not the most, sparsely populated section in the incidents. This has nothing to do with the framework, and everything to do with the lack of accurate data to collect and record about the impact. The result is that this section has some subjective measurements and estimates.

Notice the repeating rating and monetary estimations. There is a dedicated `overall` field here for those fields, but the loss section is defined in the data as an array. This means that the analyst can add multiple loss sections in the data for each variety of loss being recorded. The loss varieties are specific types of loss, for example "response and recovery" costs or "legal and regulatory" costs.

TABLE 7-8 *Impact Fields*

Section	Field	Value	Description
	currency	factor	ISO 4217 currencies for monetary estimations
overall	rating	factor	Qualitative rating of overall impact
	min_amount	number	Minimum estimated monetary amount
	amount	number	Most likely estimated monetary amount
	max_amount	number	Maximum estimated monetary amount
loss	variety	factor	Specific category of loss
	rating	factor	Qualitative rating of overall impact
	min_amount	number	Minimum estimated monetary amount
	amount	number	Most likely estimated monetary amount
	max_amount	number	Maximum estimated monetary amount

Victim

The last section to cover is the victim entry. If VERIS is being implemented inside a single organization and the victim is always the same, you can skip or hard-code the fields in this section. (This assumes that you aren't tracking incidents at partner organizations, suppliers, or customers.) For cases like the VCDB, which is aggregating across many victims, this section is vital. You want to capture data about the victim with the intention of contrasting and comparing breach data when you split these fields.

Chapter 5 discussed regression analysis, and you attempted to find independent variables that could help describe the outcomes you observed. The data you are collecting about the victim can go a long way to describe the types of threat actors and their actions. For example, in the 2013 DBIR, Verizon saw state-affiliated espionage in at least three out of every four cases within the manufacturing industry, yet none in the retail industry. Although industry alone is not a perfect predicting variable, it does help reduce the uncertainty, which is what you are after here. Table 7-9 shows the victim fields.

TABLE 7-9 *Victim Fields*

Victim	Field	Value	Description
victim	victim_id	string	Identifier or name of victim
	industry	string	U.S. Census NAICS code
	employee_count	factor	Label for number of employees

(continues)

TABLE 7-9 *Victim Fields (continued)*

Victim	Field	Value	Description
	country	factor	ISO 3166-1 two-digit country code
	state	string	State, province, or region in country
	locations_affected	integer	Number of locations affected
	revenue	integer	Annual revenue of the victim
secondary	victim_id	string	List of secondary victim_id or name(s)
	amount	integer	And/or count of secondary victims

The most recent change to the VERIS framework (version 1.2.1) changed how this section is stored. In version 1.2 and before, the entire victim section could be repeated for each victim involved in the incident. For example, if an organization is breached and was processing data on behalf of another organization, they would become a victim of the same breach. This was found to be confusing though, and the victim was reduced to just supporting one single victim. The fields in the "secondary" section were added in 1.2.1 to capture what was treated as a multiple victim breach. See Figure 7-4 to see the top five victimized industries according to the VCDB data set.

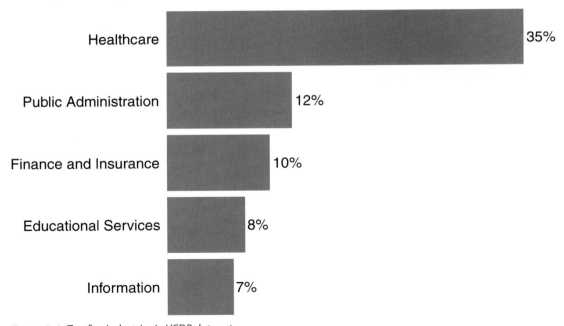

FIGURE 7-4 *Top five industries in VCDB data set*

Anywhere there is an industry (which is in this victim section and in the threat actor partner section), they are listed as a "string" but they should not be free text. Following one of the guidelines to leverage other resources wherever possible, VERIS leverages the U.S. Census Bureau's North American Industry Classification System (NAICS) mentioned earlier in this chapter. Doing so adds flexibility and a level of detail not possible with other industry classification systems. If analysts tried to create a list of industries, they'd probably come up with a dozen or so high-level categories and call it a day. NAICS started there (20 top-level categories actually), but then made it extendible and includes more detail for the industry specification. Industries within NAICS are represented by two- to six-digit integers, which is why VERIS stores them as a string and not a factor. The list is enormous (you can find it at `http://www.census.gov/eos/www/naics/`).

As an example, consider the pizza shop down the street. The NAICS code for such a place is 722511, which represents "pizza parlors, full service." Maybe in this case, however, the analyst just knows it's a restaurant, so she records 7225, or maybe she knows the place offers some type of food or beverage service, so she enters 722. If she is unsure as to what type of service establishment it is, she might just enter 72 for "accommodation and food services." When you analyze this field, you can drill down or up depending on the level of detail you want.

Indicators

We didn't want to go into detail about the indicators section, and that's because VERIS is set up to capture indicators from a security incident, which is often just a handful of IP address and malware hashes. If you're looking to capture indicators from multiple sources, we suggest you look at the Structured Threat Information Expression (STIX). It is a "collaborative community-driven effort to define and develop a standardized language to represent structured cyber threat information," and details about it can be found at `http://stix.mitre.org/`. If you'd like to see the details of the indicators section, they are covered on the VERIS community website at `http://veriscommunity.net/`.

Extending VERIS with Plus

Finally, VERIS has the catch-all section labeled "plus." Within the VERIS specifications there technically is nothing specified in this field, and the data schema simply allows anything to exist in this section. It exists to allow individual implementations to record additional fields not in the base VERIS schema. If you look at the VCDB repository, for example, each incident has a plus section with the analyst who recorded the incident and the time it was created along with a few other fields. Any implementation can apply the guidelines we presented earlier in this chapter (or not, at your own peril) and add their own fields here. If you have fields that are particularly useful, feel free to suggest the change to the core framework!

Seeing VERIS in Action

It's always helpful to take some time before jumping into the analysis to look directly at the data. It helps set the context and may help shape your approach to the analysis. Since the average incident is about 100 lines of JSON, we don't include the whole incident. Please take some time to surf around the VCDB repository and look at the data there for full records. As a good example, Listing 7-1 shows the actor and action sections from an incident from VCDB.

LISTING 7-1

```
"actor": {
    "external": {
        "country": [ "SY" ],
        "motive": [ "Ideology" ],
        "variety": [ "State-affiliated" ]
    }
},
"action": {
    "hacking": {
        "variety": [ "Use of stolen creds" ],
        "vector": [ "Web application" ]
    },
    "social": {
        "target": [ "End-user" ],
        "variety": [ "Phishing" ],
        "vector": [ "Email" ]
    }
}
```

If you have never seen JSON before, this is what it looks like. Rarely if ever would you want to edit the JSON by hand. It's not that JSON is terribly difficult, but it is terribly easy to mistype something. You could forget a comma or quote or something would prevent the data from loading properly. If you do attempt to create or modify a JSON file by hand, be sure you have a way to check your work, validate the JSON, and if possible, validate the values and factors within the data.

The best part about working with JSON is that it typically imports right into native objects in the languages you use. Within Python, an incident in JSON is imported directly into a Python dictionary. The Python code to load a JSON object and view the hacking variety is relatively simple (Listing 7-2).

LISTING 7-2

```
# python to load JSON and read hacking variety:
import os, json
# set working directory to chapter location
# (change for where you set up files in ch 2)
os.chdir("~/book/ch07")
# Open the JSON file and read the raw contents into jsondata
jsondata = open("data/vcdb/F58E9169-AC07-400E-AB0E-DB784C6CAE59.json")
# convert the contents into a python dictionary
incident = json.load(jsondata)
# now access the hacking variety (assuming it exists)
print(incident['action']['hacking']['variety'])
```

This code would print the Python list object for hacking variety and display [u'SQLi'] (an array of one Unicode string showing SQL injection was the only hacking variety used). In production code, you should wrap the json.load() command with try-except. If the file has any errors in the JSON syntax, they will be caught that way. Plus the hacking action is optional, and you'd want to test if the `hacking` key existed before you attempt to read it. But this example shows how easy JSON can be to load and work with.

Within R, JSON files are converted to a native list object. Before you run the R code in this chapter, you'll need to set your working directory and load the libraries used in this chapter (see Listing 7-3).

LISTING 7-3

```
# set working directory to chapter location
# (change for where you set up files in ch 2)
setwd("~/book/ch07")
# make sure the packages for this chapter
# are installed, install if necessary
pkg <- c("devtools", "ggplot2", "scales", "rjson")
new.pkg <- pkg[!(pkg %in% installed.packages())]
if (length(new.pkg)) {
  install.packages(new.pkg)
}
```

Now within R, in order to performing the same function we did in the python example in Listing 7-2, you need to load the `rjson` library in order to read in JSON data (Listing 7-4).

LISTING 7-4

```
library(rjson)
# fromJSON accepts a filename to read from
jsonfile <- "data/vcdb/F58E9169-AC07-400E-AB0E-DB784C6CAE59.json"
incident <- fromJSON(file=jsonfile)
# print the hacking variety
print(incident$action$hacking$variety)

## [1] "SQLi"
```

The R code returns a one-element vector with the value in the hacking variety. Again, in full-featured code, you'd want better error checking than this, but it does show how easy JSON data is to load into native objects and work with.

Working with VCDB Data

This section walks through some data from VCDB using R. While the data from the book website (at www.wiley.com/go/datadrivensecurity) has the VCDB data we use in this chapter, you may want to grab the current version of the VCDB data (there will be more incidents when you are reading this). Head on over to the VCDB GitHub repository at https://github.com/vz-risk/VCDB and either fork, copy, or download the VCSB-master.zip file of the repository (use the Download ZIP button on the right side of the window). The incidents themselves are quite small, but you can still learn quite a bit in spite of the data not being "big." Feel free to explore the incidents in the repository and get a feel for the files and the data. Keep in mind that all of these incidents are collected from publicly disclosed events, which makes many of the incidents rather light on the details.

For this analysis you'll leverage the `verisr` package, which was developed by our own Jay Jacobs and is in his GitHub repository (found at `https://github.com/jayjacobs/verisr/tree/master/R`). Note that the `verisr` package is actively in development, so be sure to refer to the latest documentation of the package for the most current description of its functions. By the time you are reading this, there may be all sorts of wonderful features in the package that aren't there at the time of this writing. Also, that means that some of the figures and output may be slightly different for you.

In order to install the `verisr` package from GitHub, you have to load the `devtools` package first (see Listing 7-5). This is one of many great packages from Hadley Wickham, and it allows you to install R packages directly from their GitHub repositories, which is what you'll do with `verisr`.

LISTING 7-5
```
# load up devtools
library(devtools)
# install the verisr package
install_github("verisr", "jayjacobs")
# load the verisr package
library(verisr)
```

You can now load up the VCDB data with the `verisr` package, if you downloaded current VCDB data, you must first modify the directory shown to be the location where you stored the VCDB JSON files (see Listing 7-6).

LISTING 7-6
```
# requires package : verisr
# set this to where VCDB incidents are stored
jsondir <- 'data/vcdb/'
# create a veris instance with the vcdb data
vcdb <- json2veris(jsondir)
```

This should load fairly quickly, but on slower machines it may take a moment or two. If you're on a computer with just a few gig of RAM or if VCDB grows exponentially, you might not be able to load all of them into memory. (We've loaded over 100,000 incidents into 8G of RAM with `verisr`, so you shouldn't hit that limit anytime soon.) After you load this data, it's time to get to know the data a little bit. Let's begin with the `summary()` command (see Listing 7-7). The `verisr` package implemented its own `summary()`, so the output is very specific to VERIS data.

LISTING 7-7
```
# requires package : verisr
# requires object: vcdb (7-6)
summary(vcdb)
## 1643 incidents in this object.
##
## Actor:
```

```
## external internal  partner  unknown
##      955      535      100       85
##
## Action:
##     error  hacking  malware  misuse physical    social
##       398      416       42     216      508        31
##
## Asset:
## Kiosk/Term   Media  Network   Person   Server  Unknown   User Dev
##         17     534        8       33      656       80        429
##
## Attribute:
##  confidentiality      availability  confidentiality      integrity
##                2               614             1604            165
```

If you've grabbed the latest data from VCDB, you'll undoubtedly see different numbers than these.

JSON Notation

It might take a while to get used to the naming structure in JSON and understand how the variables are accessed in different settings. If you load VERIS JSON data into a mongo database, you'd use JavaScript to query the data and leverage a dot-notation approach to the variables. That dot-notation is used in the `verisr` package since the fields are referenced and retrieved by passing in character strings. This means you can access the top-level action data by referencing `action`. If you want to access the social section within the action, you reference `action.social`, and the variety data under that is `action.social.variety`. Take some time and look at the JSON, and then try writing some code in R using `verisr`. With this hands-on experience, the dot-notation method will become second nature.

There are two high-level functions from the `verisr` package that you'll use to dig into the data. The first is a function to create a filter so you focus on certain aspects of the data. The second is a flexible function called `getenum()`, which will get the enumerated data from the data set with a variety of options and extensions. Let's start by looking at the actors. You can replicate the information in the previous summary with the following bit of code (Listing 7-8).

LISTING 7-8
```
# requires package : verisr
# requires object: vcdb (7-6)
actors <- getenum(vcdb, "actor")
# actors is a data frame
print(actors)
##        enum    x
```

(continues)

LISTING 7-8 *(continued)*

```
## 1 external 955
## 2 internal 535
## 3  partner 100
## 4  unknown  85
```

Within this data frame, you can see the raw numbers, but that isn't very helpful. Some incidents will contain multiple actors, so you can't simply add them and get a total number of incidents. Luckily, the `getenum` function can also return the total number of incidents where the field is defined. If you add `add.n=TRUE`, you get an additional column of the full sample. If you add `add.freq=TRUE`, you can get the percentage associated with each entry. Let's look at both of those options in one example (see Listing 7-9).

LISTING 7-9

```
# requires package : verisr
# requires object: vcdb (7-6)
actors <- getenum(vcdb, "actor", add.n=TRUE, add.freq=TRUE)
print(actors)
##        enum   x    n  freq
## 1 external 955 1643 0.581
## 2 internal 535 1643 0.326
## 3  partner 100 1643 0.061
## 4  unknown  85 1643 0.052
```

From this you can see that there were 1,643 incidents with something defined in the actor section, and external actors were present in 58 percent of them. Since this function returns a data frame, it's relatively straightforward to feed into the `ggplot2` library and produce any number of visuals (see the book's website, www.wiley.com/go/datadrivensecurity, for this chapter's R code to see how to create the figures in this chapter).

The `getenum()` function is quite versatile. You can pass in any of the variable names within the VERIS framework and get an object you can visualize right away. As an example, create a function that accepts a VERIS variable name, such as `action.hacking.vector`, and returns an image object that you can print or save or whatever (see Listing 7-10). This could be extendable to include in a report or dashboard.

LISTING 7-10

```
# requires package : verisr, ggplot2
# requires object: vcdb (7-6)
library(ggplot2)
# take in the vcdb object and the field to plot
verisplot <- function(vcdb, field) {
  # get the data.frame for the field with frequency
  localdf <- getenum(vcdb, field, add.freq=T)
  # now let's take first 5 fields in the data frame.
  localdf <- localdf[c(1:5), ]
  # add a label to the data.frame
  localdf$lab <- paste(round(localdf$freq*100, 0), "%", sep="")
  # now we can create a ggplot2 instance
```

(continues)

LISTING 7-10   *(continued)*

```
  gg <- ggplot(localdf, aes(x=enum, y=freq, label=lab))
  gg <- gg + geom_bar(stat="identity", fill="steelblue")
  # add in text, adjusted to the end of the bar
  gg <- gg + geom_text(hjust=-0.1, size=3)
  # flip the axes and add in a title
  gg <- gg + coord_flip() + ggtitle(field)
  # remove axes labels and add bw theme
  gg <- gg + xlab("") + ylab("") + theme_bw()
  # fix the y scale to remove padding and fit our label (add 7%)
  gg <- gg + scale_y_continuous(expand=c(0,0),
                                limits=c(0, max(localdf$freq)*1.1))
  # make it slightly prettier than the default
  gg <- gg + theme(panel.grid.major = element_blank(),
                   panel.border = element_blank(),
                   axis.text.x = element_blank(),
                   axis.ticks = element_blank())
}
```

What's a little funny about that function is that it will get all of the data ready in the first line of the function, trim to the top five entries in the second line, and spend the rest of the function making a pretty picture. But once this function is written and loaded, you can create any number of pictures from the data with a single line of code.

```
print(verisplot(vcdb, "action"))
```

Figure 7-5 shows a few of the possible values passed and printed.

Getting the Most Out of VERIS Data

One of our favorite images from the 2013 Verizon Data Breach Investigation Report was a heat map that compared the assets and actions overall and then separated the individual comparisons by the type of threat actors. You can create a similar image with the `verisr` package without too much effort (Listing 7-11).

LISTING 7-11

```
# requires package : verisr, ggplot2
# requires object: vcdb (7-6)
# get a data.frame comparing the actions to the assets
# this will add zero's in missing squares and include a frequency
a2 <- getenum(vcdb, enum="action", primary="asset.assets", add.freq=T)
# trim unknown asset and environment action for space
a2 <- a2[which(a2$enum!="environmental" & a2$primary!="Unknown"), ]
# so we should create a "slim" version without zeros to color it
slim.a2 <- a2[which(a2$x!=0), ]
# could sort these by converting to factors (we did in Fig 7-6)

# now make a nice plot
gg <- ggplot(a2, aes(x=enum, y=primary, fill=freq))
gg <- gg + geom_tile(fill="white", color="gray80")
```

(continues)

LISTING 7-11 *(continued)*

```
gg <- gg + geom_tile(data=slim.a2, color="gray80")
gg <- gg + scale_fill_gradient(low = "#F0F6FF",
                                high = "#4682B4", guide=F)
gg <- gg + xlab("") + ylab("") + theme_bw()
gg <- gg + scale_x_discrete(expand=c(0,0))
gg <- gg + scale_y_discrete(expand=c(0,0))
gg <- gg + theme(axis.ticks = element_blank())
# and view it
print(gg)
```

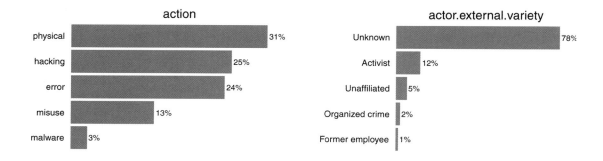

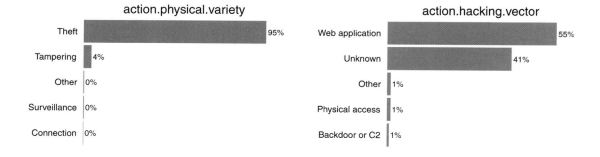

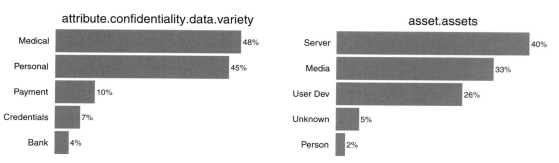

FIGURE 7-5 *Various top 5 views of VCDB data*

This code looks through all of the incidents and produces the simple colored heatmap shown in Figure 7-6. Keep in mind that the specifics vary depending on incidents in the VCDB.

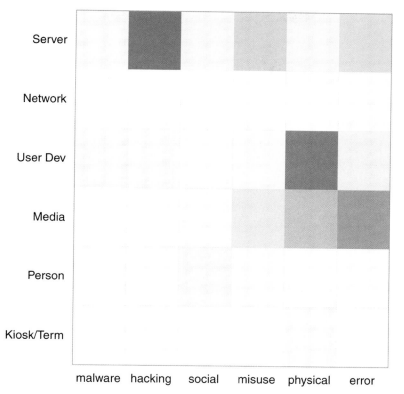

FIGURE 7-6 *A2 grid comparing assets and actions*

The real benefit of working with VERIS data is the ***ability to compare across disparate data sets***. If you were to collect your own internal incidents in the VERIS format, it would be a relatively trivial task to run comparisons on very specific slices of data across multiple data sets. Since one of us works for Verizon and has access to the DBIR data set, we decided to show this point by example. You should be able to quickly see differences across the two data sets. Remember, VCDB is collected from news articles and various public sources. Generally speaking, the details are far less prevalent than what you might want.

The Verizon data set is gathered from a variety of primary sources, but primarily from first-hand accounts of the forensic investigators that were brought in after the security event. This means this data has bias—it is generally limited to breaches that were complex or big enough for a victim to seek external help, either from law enforcement (many of the contributing partners are law enforcement) or from an incident response consulting company.

In this example, you could use the same code that generated Figure 7-6 and compare four differ-ent fields from the VCDB data and the Verizon DBIR data over the last 3 years. Start with all of the inci-dents in both data sets in the first row. Then filter out confirmed data loss events (where `attributes` `.confidentiliaty.data_disclosure = "Yes"`) in the second row. Then focus on financially motivated attackers with confirmed data loss events in the third row. Finally, look only at attackers motivated by ideology, curiosity, fun, or pride (which covers attackers labeled as activists), again with confirmed data loss. See Figure 7-7.

You can see a rather significant difference that's worth talking through. Because the VCDB data set includes only publicly disclosed events, there are a lot of daily "low hanging fruit" type things that would never make it into the DBIR data. Events like lost or stolen laptops, documents tossed in a dumpster without being shredded, or envelopes with personal information mailed to the wrong person appear quite often in the VCDB data set. That's why you see physical (theft/loss) and error (disposal error and bad delivery) in the row labeled "All Events" for VCDB, and those all but disappear when you filter for confirmed data loss in the second row for "Confirmed Data Loss." Keep in mind a lost or stolen laptop just has the potential for data loss.

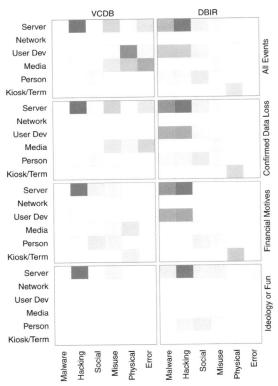

FIGURE 7-7 *The strength of VERIS: Comparing the same views from two very different sources of data*

Another interesting comparison is the malware category. The public disclosures rarely mention whether malware was used, but we know from the DBIR research that malware is often used, either to escalate privilege or to capture and exfiltrate data, yet the malware column is almost completely empty in the VCDB data. You will probably see the same type of effect for user devices. Even though user devices are often leveraged during a breach, a company that is publicly disclosing information will often neglect to mention which assets were involved and just say something vague like "the database was compromised." As a result, you'll see very little recorded events involving user devices.

We could go on and on about the subtle differences across these columns, but it's pretty clear that there is a lot to be learned by recording and comparing breach data.

Summary

You may never be able to shake the "blame the victim" mentality when it comes to data breaches. This means the victims will always try to be discrete and focus only on getting back to normal. You may always be fighting for more disclosures and more data when it comes to security breaches. That data is exactly what you need though, because these events produce a very rich set of data that has yet to be fully explored.

When you break the event down into its atomic components—"Who did what to what (or whom) with what result?"—you can do more research, develop better comparisons, and learn much more than if you apply a label or two on the whole chain of events. Identifying and recording the actors, their actions, the assets involved, and the attributes affected are a very good start. But remember—every data point comes with a cost and you will have to make some tough trade-offs between the time investment and the veracity of the results.

Using JSON has some direct advantages. You can quickly load it into a variety of languages and it feeds right into databases that can take JSON (like MongoDB). Within R you can use the `verisr` package to read in VERIS data and rapidly analyze fields and create visualizations. But the real strength of leveraging a framework like VERIS is when making comparisons. Are your problems unique? Or are others in your industry or across all industries seeing the same trends and attacks? Until recently, analysts struggled to answer those questions, but as more organizations take a data-driven approach to security, they'll be asking and answering those questions soon.

Recommended Reading

The following are some recommended readings that can further your understanding on some of the topics we touch on in this chapter.

Verizon RISK Team. "2013 data breach investigations report." Available at `http://www .verizonenterprise.com/DBIR`—This report is based on data collected using the VERIS framework. You might find it handy to look at some of the graphics in the report and then attempt to repeat them using the `verisr` package, discussed in this chapter, and the VCDB data.

`http://veriscommunity.net`—All of the documentation about VERIS and a mailing list is hosted at that website. If you are uncertain what a field is, or what one of the options represents, this is the place to check first.

`https://github.com/vz-risk/VCDB`—This is the location for the VCDB data (at the time of this writing). Be sure to check back often as new events are added regularly.

8

Breaking Up With Your Relational Database

"I call it the law of the instrument, and it may be formulated as follows: Give a small boy a hammer, and he will find that everything he encounters needs pounding."

Abraham Kaplan, *The Conduct of Inquiry: Methodology for Behavioral Science*

It's an all-too-familiar story. You've been faithful companions for years. You knew everything about your partner and came to depend and rely on it for many of your core needs. But, times have changed. Your needs are more nuanced and complex, and you're starting to have doubts about your relational structure. Your thoughts and queries begin to stray; you survey and index the field and find new, vibrant and exotic options that you never knew of before. And, then, you realize the hard truth: it's time to break up with your relational database.

Relational databases (RDBMS) have been around since the 1970s when Edgar Codd proposed "*a relational model of data for large shared data banks*" as an alternative to the network models—heavily inter-linked, on-disk structures—prevalent at that time.

> ### *Note*
>
> *Codd proposed this in 1970 in "A Relational Model of Data for Large Shared Data Banks,"* **Communications of the ACM,** *Vol. 13, No. 6, pp. 377-387. So much for big data being a 21st-century concept.*

Despite the hype surrounding newer database technologies, relational databases still have quite a bit to offer. However, they should not be the only tool you look to when trying to solve a problem, find "badness," or organize your security data. In this chapter, we'll explore these newer technologies through security use cases, but also show you how to breathe life into your existing RDBMS relationship.

You will need to run the code in Listings 8-0 and 8-1 to set up your R and Python environments (respectively) for the code examples in this chapter (which you can find online at www.wiley.com/go/datadrivensecurity).

LISTING 8-0

```
# This code sets up the R environemnt for the chapter
# set working directory to chapter location
# (change for where you set up files in ch 2)
setwd("~/book/ch08")
# make sure the packages for this chapter
# are installed, install if necessary
pkg <- c("RBerkeley")
new.pkg <- pkg[!(pkg %in% installed.packages())]
if (length(new.pkg)) {
  install.packages(new.pkg)
}
```

LISTING 8-1

```
# This code sets up the python environemnt for the chapter
# set working directory to chapter location
# (change for where you set up files in ch 2)
setwd("~/book/ch08")
# make sure the packages for this chapter are installed
```

For the Python examples, you will need to ensure the proper libraries are installed. First, if you did install Python with Canopy (see Chapter 2), you'll need to refer to this knowledge base article (`https://support.enthought.com/entries/23389761-Installing-packages-into-Canopy-User-Python-from-the-OS-command-line`) on the Enthought support site that will enable you to install Python packages from external sources. You will also need a working Redis server before installing the Python `redis` component. Refer to the Redis quickstart guide (`http://redis.io/topics/quickstart`) for information on how to get Redis up and running. The following code sets up the necessary environment from a typical Debain-style system shell prompt:

```
dds$ # install the Berkeley DB library
dds$ sudo apt-get install libdb-dev
dds$ # install Python package for Berkeley DB interface
dds$ # note that you may not need sudo depending on your environment
dds$ sudo pip install bsddb3
dds$ # install Python package for Redis interface
dds$ sudo pip install redis
```

A Primer on SQL/RDMBS Databases

Due to the regular attention given to InfoSec's "most wanted"—SQL Injection (SQLi) vulnerabilities—this chapter assumes the reader has some familiarity with traditional RDBMS systems such as MySQL (`http://www.mysql.com/downloads/`), MariaDB (`https://mariadb.org/`), Oracle (`http://www.oracle.com/technetwork/database/enterprise-edition/downloads/index.html`) or PostgreSQL (`http://www.postgresql.org/`).

If you are coming at this chapter without prior experience in relational databases you will have an edge up on many readers who have a predisposition toward them, but some of the topics and references could be a bit confusing. This short primer on RDBMS systems should help introduce you to the basic concepts.

Most RDBMS systems have the following core attributes:

Data is organized by *tables*, **with** *attributes* (*fields*) **in** *columns* **and individual** *records* **stored in** *rows*. For example, an RDBMS table to hold firewall log entries could have a structure that looks like Figure 8-1a with each log entry being a row and the individual data elements broken down into:

- A unique identifier for the firewall (***fw_id***)
- A timestamp (***ts***)
- Source IP address (***src_ip***)
- Source port (***src_port***)
- Destination IP address (***dst_ip***)
- Destination port (***dst_port***)
- Accept/Deny (***action***)
- Number of bytes transferred (***num_bytes***)

The complete structure of a table or set of tables is called a *schema*.

(continues)

(continued)

Data in tables is referenced by *rows* **and** *fields*. Individual fields or combinations of fields called *keys* ensure each record within a table can be uniquely identified and help distinguish the relationships between tables. The firewall (Figure 8-1a) and proxy (Figure 8-1b) tables are "linked" together by source IP address (*src_ip*) and both of them are "linked" to the asset database (Figure 8-1c) by their *id* fields.

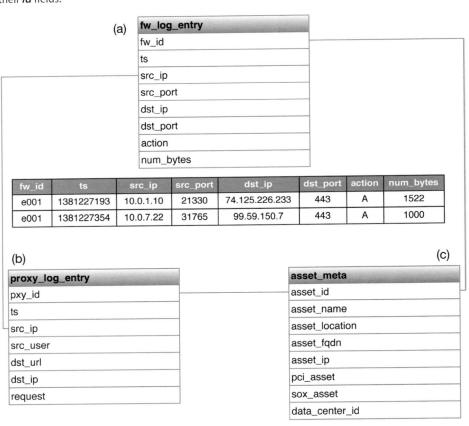

fw_id	ts	src_ip	src_port	dst_ip	dst_port	action	num_bytes
e001	1381227193	10.0.1.10	21330	74.125.226.233	443	A	1522
e001	1381227354	10.0.7.22	31765	99.59.150.7	443	A	1000

FIGURE 8-1 *Graphical representation of example firewall, proxy, and asset database tables*

Fields can also be part of one or more *indexes*, which are separate data structures that provide optimized ways to organize data in those fields and can dramatically speed up operations that look up data (*queries*).

Data is accessed and manipulated through a structured query language (*SQL*). SQL was designed to be both a human-readable and platform-independent way to perform insert, update and delete actions, plus run queries against the data. For the example database in Figure 8-1, you can query the destination information (timestamp and IP) for a source IP address in both the proxy and firewall tables with the following SQL statement:

```
SELECT ts, dst_ip
FROM proxy_log_entry
WHERE src_ip = "10.20.30.40"

UNION

SELECT ts, dst_ip
FROM fw_log_entry
WHERE src_ip = "10.20.30.40";
```

Application programs should not rely on the physical structure of the data. There are a host of options when it comes to deciding how to physically store data in a database and indicating how indexes are organized. All of these choices should be fully abstracted from the application or user who should be able to execute the same high-level query and have it work regardless of changes to physical representation.

The relational structure, mostly uniform query language, and physical abstraction properties were major contributors to the popularity of SQL databases, especially since mapping problems like customer records and sales orders into fields and rows is fairly straightforward and just "makes sense." Yet, as you'll see later in the chapter, the relational structure is not well suited for all types of data or problems.

Realizing the Container Has Constraints

Compared to Codd's era, we are awash in computing resources. Memory, storage, CPU, and network capacity are all relatively cheap and the need to accommodate the underlying architecture of physical storage when designing, building, and using databases is (for the most part) no longer present. Becoming an amateur DBA is now as simple as executing `sudo apt-get install mariadb-server` on any Debian-ish Linux box (with similar, easy installation options for Windows and MacOS). In some ways, this simplicity and ubiquity has contributed to the fallacy that traditional SQL/RDBMS databases are destined for extinction due to "lack of scalability and functionality."

The reality is that modern SQL databases are comparable to web servers, proxy servers, firewalls, and mail servers in that their out-of-the-box configuration is going to be in jack-of-all-trades mode. The default features and capabilities will be enough to get you off and running, and may even perform moderately well as your record counts and schema complexities increase. But, when the types or amounts of data begin to push the boundaries of the default configuration, you *will* run into problems. It's important to understand the most common types of constraints you will face as your SQL needs grow and where to turn when you begin to encounter them.

Constrained by Schema

It may not be obvious at first glance, but there are significant differences between the following two, simple SQL table structures:

```
CREATE TABLE fw1 (
  src varchar(15) NOT NULL,
  dst varchar(15) NOT NULL,
  dpt int NOT NULL,
  d int(11) NOT NULL)

CREATE TABLE fw2 (
  src int(10) unsigned NOT NULL,
  dst int(10) unsigned NOT NULL,
  dpt smallint(5) unsigned NOT NULL,
  d date NOT NULL)
```

For those who may be new to SQL, the statement in in the first code block creates a database table with IP address `src` and `dst` fields stored as a string of characters ("0" ... "9"), while the statement in the second block creates a table with those fields stored as an unsigned integer with a display width of 10 characters.

When you are creating a table to store "network" information, it's tempting to use character storage for IP addresses since that's how humans interact with them. It's also tempting to just handle a UNIX timestamp (as seen in the `ts` field in Figure 8-1) as a big integer value since, well, that's what it is. Also, destination TCP/UDP ports (`dpt`) **technically** are integers. There are, however, potentially significant issues at play with these choices.

If the `src` and `dst` fields are indexed you may not notice any issues at first if all you're doing is issuing queries for individual IP addresses, like this:

```
SELECT * FROM fw1 WHERE src = "10.35.14.16"
```

The index will speedily find the rows containing the value for `src` and the database engine will return the results as quickly as it can transfer data from disk to your query client. If you do not have an index on those fields, then the same query will have to perform *a full table sequential scan*, which could be a fairly long operation when you have millions of rows.

If you needed to find all matching rows for portions of a subnet, you may be faced with creating complex regular expressions (regex) or carving up the IP space into multiple slices to get the benefit of intelligent query prefix optimization for SQL's `LIKE` operator. Or you might have to split out the subnet into individual IP addresses to ensure you gain the benefit of full speed queries. Non-optimized wildcard searches—especially ones without a common prefix—will result in a full table scan, performing regex string comparisons for every field value.

By switching to the numeric representation of IP addresses (shown in the preceding code for table `fw2` and discussed in Chapter 4), you can gain disk space, memory size, and query time efficiency since many index types are optimized for numeric range selections. Converting to/from integers is usually as simple as using built-in INET_ATON or INET_NTOA functions. Similarly, moving from a straight integer timestamp to a `date` field brings with it more straightforward query composition and increased query execution speed. Finally, switching `dpt` from an `integer` to a `smallint` will save you two bytes per record which can be important if you plan on using in-memory tables or start racking up billions of records.

If you regularly work with specialized field types (for example, IP addresses and geolocation data), you could even consider using different database platforms—such as PostgreSQL—that have direct support for a diverse array of custom fields.

RDBMS schemas also tend to be somewhat fixed structures. Although it's possible to add or remove columns to/from existing tables, there are real penalties for doing so, both at creation time and beyond. You will immediately incur a space penalty as the new field is added to each row with that operation (whether necessary or not) also occupying a decent amount of time on large, established table structures. Some RDBMS systems can compensate for these issues, but you may need to leave your "amateur DBA" status at the door as you start to become a professional database administrator in order to solve these issues.

You've Got Some EXPLAINin' To Do!

To become a true database wizard requires delving into the dark arts of the subject matter. SQL queries are a bit like magic spells in that the wrong inflection can drastically change the results (usually for the worse). You can get an idea of how to tweak your schemas and optimize your queries with the EXPLAIN statement, available in most RDBMS systems.

EXPLAIN will, well, *explain* what the query engine will do with the SQL you've given it without executing it. For example, if you were to load the AlienVault database mentioned in Chapter 4 into a simple SQL database, it might look like this:

```
MariaDB> DESCRIBE avrep;
+--------+----------------------+------+-----+---------+-------+
| Field  | Type                 | Null | Key | Default | Extra |
+--------+----------------------+------+-----+---------+-------+
| ipn    | int(10)              | YES  | MUL | NULL    |       |
| bad    | tinyint(3) unsigned  | YES  |     | NULL    |       |
| con    | tinyint(3) unsigned  | YES  |     | NULL    |       |
| type   | varchar(50)          | YES  |     | NULL    |       |
| cc     | varchar(2)           | YES  |     | NULL    |       |
| city   | varchar(30)          | YES  |     | NULL    |       |
| latlon | varchar(30)          | YES  |     | NULL    |       |
+--------+----------------------+------+-----+---------+-------+
```

To get a count of all IP addresses coming from China (CN), you might issue the following query:

```
MariaDB> SELECT COUNT(ipn) FROM avrep WHERE cc="CN";
```

You can see how optimal that query is (or isn't) by prefixing it with EXPLAIN (we've added the EXTENDED and \G to make the output clearer for the book's printed format):

```
    EXPLAIN EXTENDED
 -> SELECT COUNT(ipn) FROM avrep WHERE cc="CN"\G
*************************** 1. row ***************************
           id: 1
  select_type: SIMPLE
        table: avrep
         type: ref
```

(continues)

(continued)

```
possible_keys: NULL
          key: NULL
      key_len: NULL
          ref: NULL
         rows: 265597
        Extra: Using where
```

For this query, no keys are being used, so this will require a table scan. You can optimize it by adding an index on the `cc` field:

```
CREATE INDEX cc_idx ON avrep (cc);
```

and rerun `EXPLAIN`:

```
EXPLAIN EXTENDED
-> SELECT COUNT(ipn) FROM avrep WHERE cc="CN"\G
*************************** 1. row ***************************
           id: 1
  select_type: SIMPLE
        table: avrep
         type: ref
possible_keys: cc_idx
          key: cc_idx
      key_len: 5
          ref: const
         rows: 132798
     filtered: 100.00
        Extra: Using where
```

to see if there are any changes. In this case, the `EXPLAIN` output shows that the SQL query engine identified the index for the `cc` field and that using it will reduce the number of rows scanned.

It's a good idea to use `EXPLAIN` on more complex queries, especially ones that may be run often. You may be able to identify bottlenecks that you are attributing to "those darn old school SQL databases" when it's really your schema or SQL composition that needs work.

Constrained by Storage

When this book hits the shelves in 2014, consumers will have access to 5TB hard drives. With that type of capacity being a general user commodity it's difficult to contemplate how a database could be constrained by storage given that enterprise-class disks have even more options through larger and faster disks and disk arrays. Open source SQL databases such as MySQL or MariaDB can have individual tables as large as 256TB, which will fit comfortably on, say, a BTRFS (`https://btrfs.wiki.kernel .org/index.php/Main_Page`) file system capable of holding 16EiB of data. What, then, are these storage "constraints"?

- **Speed**—If your analytics needs are modest, it's tempting to stick with consumer-grade equipment for both cost and ease of deployment. However, that 5400RPM USB 2.0 disk may be the bottleneck for even modestly sized projects, given the way consumer drives are designed (since they aren't designed to serve database workloads). You *could* use consumer disks in a consumer storage array, but this would only temporarily mask the problem. If your analytics workflow performance declines significantly when you increase the size of data sets, consider investing in faster disks with increased cache. Plus, if the impacts are severe enough, it may be time to switch to true commodity *server* hardware with faster enterprise-class storage—or even solid-state disks (SSD)—and a proper industrial-class storage array.

- **Caching**—Databases use both disk and RAM in concert when performing most of their operations. Delving into RAM and cache discussions can stir up as much debate in the DBA community as sparking a similar conversation about desktop signature antivirus in the defender community. Increasing the amount of RAM *will* help your database perform faster, especially when you need to issue the same query more than once (think a nested `SELECT` query used in multiple, but diverse main `SELECT` statements). RAM and disk caching will also help when inserting data into a database since write-caching can be employed to mask I/O bottlenecks.

- **Capability**—Just because you *can* store a huge quantity of data in a single table doesn't mean you *should*. For example, storing 3 years of enterprise firewall log data in a single RDBMS table *is* possible, but it's truly a bad idea because of all the performance problems this causes. By optimizing the underlying storage configuration and using table partitioning techniques available in most modern RDBMS systems, you can turn what may have been a marathon of a query into a sprint and probably still keep everything on one system.

Constrained by RAM

Lack of sufficient active RAM or using a traditional RDBMS with a configuration that cannot take advantage of large amounts of RAM is the harbinger of doom for any project that needs to scale. As indicated in the previous section, databases use RAM to (among other things) cache portions of tables that are on disk and also to cache query results. More advanced SQL databases can also use RAM for *in-memory tables*. If you know you're going to have regular use of referential data (for example, asset metadata, non-frequently changing IP lists), loading that information into an in-memory SQL table can reap huge rewards as you perform `JOIN`s, `UNION`s, and sub-`SELECT`s. It's usually as simple as identifying the query—which can be the full set of rows and fields from an existing table—you want to populate in an in-memory configuration. For example, if you wanted to store all the IP addresses contained in the AlienVault table in an in-memory table (to guarantee it stays there versus rely on the cache keeping it there) you could do the following:

```
CREATE TABLE avrep_mem ENGINE=MEMORY
    -> SELECT ipn AS ip
    -> FROM avrep;
```

It's also best to avoid consumer-grade RAM and opt for high quality ECC (error-correcting code) memory to avoid the perils of data corruption.

Constrained by Data

There are definitely examples of "security data" that fit well into the relational model including firewall logs, web server logs, anti-malware logs and asset information. Each of those example sources easily maps into interconnected rows and columns. But, what about the JSON structure of an incident recorded in VERIS format, as seen in Chapter 7? Although it's *possible* to develop a relational structure for this data, it's hardly an optimal solution.

To optimize database table structures and query efficiency, Codd came up with the notion of *normalization*, which is just a way of describing a method to organize fields and tables so as to eliminate as many redundancies as is feasible and make it easier to modify or extend the database schema with as little impact as possible. "Over-normalizing" a database can make working with the underlying data awkward and complex. "Under-normalizing" a database can increase the complexity of the application code or database stored procedures and will—most likely—needlessly expand the size of your data store.

Normalizing tabular data that is designed to fit into tables is generally a straightforward task. Mapping and normalizing hierarchical data (like the JSON VERIS data) means converting the hierarchies into graph adjacency lists, materialized paths, or nested sets that definitely increase query complexity. You could always go halfway and limit the nesting by storing large chunks of the JSON tree as BLOBs (binary large objects) in special fields, but that also makes queries complex *and* slow, since you'll likely be performing full text searches of those fields.

RDBMS systems are great for a wide variety of problem sets and data types, but they should not be the only tool in your toolbox since there are so many custom options available, as you'll see in the next section.

Who/What Is This 'Maria'?

Many readers may have used or come into contact with the MySQL RDBMS. For many years, it was a foundational element of the initial "LAMP" (Linux/Apache/MySQL/PHP) stack of components you would use to build websites. After Oracle acquired MySQL, there was a community-developed fork of the code created under the name "MariaDB." MariaDB is a drop-in replacement for MySQL. You can uninstall MySQL (preserving data, of course) and install MariaDB and everything will "just work."

MariaDB versioning and features have been on par with counterpart MySQL releases, but significant divergence is occurring with newer iterations, including support for cutting-edge storage engines, dynamic columns, and interfacing with NoSQL environments (Cassandra).

Choosing MariaDB over MySQL, PostgreSQL, or traditional commercial RDBMS offerings is a decision you and your security and analytics team members must make yourselves and may be highly dependent on corporate requirements, if you're constrained by them. Even if you "can't" use MariaDB, it's definitely a project that should be on your watch list.

Exploring Alternative Data Stores

There are many longstanding and new database storage and database management systems that have shunned the conventions and conformity of straight-laced SQL. These technologies are usually grouped under the term *NoSQL* (Not only SQL), which makes it easier to classify them, but also adds confusion since the features and functionality each provides can be radically different. By "not being SQL" they all offer alternate ways of designing solutions and storing information that can be of huge benefit when incorporating data analysis into your security strategy. This section takes a look at some of the more prominent ones and sneaks in a security use case or two along the way to give you an idea of when you might want to pick one over the other.

BerkeleyDB

Perl wonks will no doubt be familiar with Berkeley DB (BDB) (`http://www.oracle.com/technetwork/products/berkeleydb/overview/index.html`), and you can find support for it in R (`RBerkeley`), Python (`pybsddb`), and most other scripting/programming languages. BDB is a local (that is, embedded) *key/value* store that does what the description suggests: It lets you identify a *key* and store arbitrary data associated with it, and then perform highly efficient lookups with the *key*. By its own definition, it's not a relational database, an object-oriented database, a network database, or a database server. Unlike keys and fields in RDBMS systems, BDB is completely value-agnostic.

If you've ever worked with the default configuration of SpamAssassin (`http://spamassassin.apache.org/`) or postfix (`http://www.postfix.org/`) or dealt with open source LDAP servers such as OpenLDAP (`http://www.openldap.org/`), you've encountered BDB.

Key/value stores perform well in situations where data writes are infrequent but reads are potentially plentiful, for example, *caches*. Consider, once again, the IPv4 address space. If you needed to cache only certain attributes of an IP address (for example, geolocation data or reputation data) and needed only local resources, choosing BDB as your platform has some serious merit. It doesn't have the overhead that comes with traditional RDBMS databases (though modern versions of BDB "speak" SQL) and can be optimized for the key and value data structures. Plus, the keys and values can also be language-independent (that is, you can populate BDB stores with R and read them with Python, or vice versa). Listing 8-2 shows a very basic example of storing IP geolocation data with R:

LISTING 8-2
```
# requires packages: RBerkeley
# R code to interface with BDB
library(RBerkeley)

# create and open BDB database
dbh <- db_create()
db <- db_open(dbh, txnid = NULL, file = "av.db",
              type = "BTREE",
              flags = mkFlags(DB_CREATE, DB_EXCL))

# store geolocation data
db_put(dbh, key = charToRaw("24.62.253.107"),
```

LISTING 8-2 *(continued)*

```
        data = charToRaw("43.2555,-70.8829"))

# read it back to show it works
coords <- rawToChar(db_get(dbh,
                    key = charToRaw("24.62.253.107")))

db_close(dbh) # close BDB db

print(coords)
## [1] "43.2555,-70.8829"
```

> **Note**
>
> Note that R will return a warning message about the database handle being unusable after the db_close() function call. This is just an informative message and can be ignored.

Listing 8-3 shows a similar example of reading the same data back with Python:

LISTING 8-3

```
# Requires: bsddb3 and Berkeley DB library
# Python code to interface with BDB
from bsddb3 import db
import struct
import socket

# initialize and open BDB database
av_db = db.DB()
av_db.open('av.db',None,db.DB_BTREE, db.DB_DIRTY_READ)

# get first key/value pair
cursor = av_db.cursor()
av_rec = cursor.first()

# print it out to show it worked
print av_rec

## ('24.62.253.107', '43.2555,-70.8829')

av_db.close() # close BDB file
```

It would be very straightforward to expand this example to store the entire AlienVault database, indexed by IP address and with the other associated fields stored in the value component.

Berkeley DB also has solid thread support and scales as large as 256TB. If your workloads can deal with disk-seek times, you do not want the hassle of maintaining a server process or multi-node infrastructure for your caches, and if there's a chance you need multi-platform and multi-programming language support, it's definitely a good choice.

BDB Alternatives

Oracle is now the proprietor of Berkeley DB. Although it's still provided under a GNU AGPL v3 license, Oracle also offers a commercial version with fairly steep licensing options. If you are concerned that this may become fully commercial in the future, there are alternatives that provide the same feature set, including:

- Kyoto Cabinet (`http://fallabs.com/kyotocabinet/`)
- MapDB (`http://www.mapdb.org/faq-general.html`)

Redis

Redis is an open source, BSD licensed, advanced key-value store (`http://redis.io/`). It's tempting to think of Redis as just a server version of a key/value store since that's what it looks like on the surface. Its most basic commands are GET and SET, and its basic data type is a ***binary safe string*** (so you can store virtually any type of data in the key or value components). What Redis ***really*** is, however, is more of an in-memory ***data structure server*** that is also persisted on disk (that also has many other useful features). The in-RAM requirement should not be glossed over lightly since every data structure and element ***must*** fit into RAM for Redis to work. This constraint should help prevent you from trying to shoehorn large relational or hierarchical structures into Redis, since that's definitely not what it's designed for.

Redis operates as a data structure server by providing a framework of operations for four fundamental data storage types: *lists*, *hashes*, *sets*, and *sorted sets*.

- **Lists** store single binary safe strings that are pushed on to the front (LPUSH) or back (RPUSH) of the list. Lists make superb message queue structures and excel at keeping the "last *n*" number of items available.

- **Hashes** expand the key/value NoSQL model by providing a way to identify and manipulate fields within the value component in a very space-efficient manner. You could replicate the geolocation Berkeley DB geolocation example quite easily with Redis hashes, straight from the Redis command line interface:

```
redis> HMSET ip:24.62.253.107 lon 43.2555 lat -70.8829 zip 03878
redis> HMGET ip:24.62.253.107 lon lat
1) "43.2555"
2) "-70.8829"
```

The main differences here are that you can query this database server from any client on the network versus be constrained by just local file access and that everything is in memory, so lookups will be almost instantaneous.

- **Sets** store non-repeating collections of binary safe strings. This makes them ideal for associating elements together for quick membership determination. For example, creating a "workstations" set and populating the members with IP addresses makes it trivial to determine whether an IP address you've seen in a packet is coming from a workstation node:

```
redis> SADD workstations "10.23.34.45"
redis> SADD workstations "10.32.43.54"
redis> SADD workstations "10.45.34.32"
redis> SADD workstations "10.34.23.45"
redis> SISMEMBER workstations "10.10.10.10"
(integer) 0 // not in set
redis> SISMEMBER workstations "10.23.34.45"
(integer) 1 // in set
```

- **Sorted sets** provide a means to associate a ranked value with a member of a set. You could create risk or reliability sets for each of the malicious host types in the AlienVault database, using the values from those fields. You could also keep a running count of times you've seen those known-bad hosts attempt to access your resources (or when *your* resources have attempted to access those bad ones).

Advanced Redis Features

Redis supports *partitioning* which lets you use memory on other systems to hold portions of Redis data structures. This is similar to the way you can partition tables in MariaDB, MySQL, and Oracle and helps you get around single-system RAM constraints.

Redis also has a built-in *publish-subscribe* service. With it, you can create a number of clients that subscribe to a channel that is publishing log entries or just new, individual IP addresses that make their way on to your internal "suspicious" list. When any new value is pushed, each client will get the message and can take some type of action, like running a set of analytics routines or parsing and storing the information into multiple SQL and NoSQL data stores for later processing.

There is robust Redis support in Python (`redis-py`) and R (`rredis`), and the API is very straight-forward to work with. Say you want a centralized and efficient way to know whether you've seen an IP address in an indicator of compromise (IoC) that you've received from some external source. Rather than rely on a query to return from your clunky centralized log management system, set up a workload that takes IP addresses from the log streams and stores them in a centralized Redis simple key/value or hash data structure with as much metadata as you need. Listing 8-4 provides a Python example of how to "watch" a log file (in this case, a web server log) and store the data in Redis.

Note

Listings 8-4 (`ch08/python/watcher.py`) *and 8-5* (`ch08/python/lastseen.py`) *will work better as standalone shell scripts (each in their own file, as directed in the comments for each listing) versus within the Canopy environment. You will also need to have a web server running. To fully mimic the examples, you can install* `nginx` *(the one used in the 8-4 example) via* `sudo apt-get install nginx` *at a shell prompt and start it with* `sudo /etc/init.d/nginx start` *to generate output for the logs.*

LISTING 8-4

```python
# Web server log watcher/Redis importer
# Save this as "watcher.py"
# Start it in one shell window prompt with
#     python watcher.py
# Requires: Python redis package
import time
import re
import redis
import pickle

# setup regex to parse web log entries
logparts = r'(\S+) (\S+) (\S+) \[(.*?)\] \
    "(\S+) (\S+) (\S+)" (\S+) (\S+)'
logpart = re.compile(logparts)

# map field names to extracted regex values
def field_map(dictseq,name,func):
    for d in dictseq:
        d[name] = func(d[name])
        yield d

# extract data from weblog
def web_log(lines):
    groups = (logpart.match(line) for line in lines)
    tuples = (g.groups() for g in groups if g)
    colnames = ('host','referrer','user',
                'datetime','method', 'request',
                'proto','status','bytes')
    log = (dict(zip(colnames,t)) for t in tuples)
    log = field_map(log,"bytes",
            lambda s: int(s) if s != '-' else 0)
    log = field_map(log,"status",int)
    return log

# "tail" for python
def follow(thefile):
    thefile.seek(0,2)
    while True:
        line = thefile.readline()
        if not line:
            time.sleep(0.1)
            continue
        yield line

# setup log watching
# change this to an active, accessible web server log
```

(continues)

LISTING 8-4   *(continued)*

```
logfile = open("/var/log/nginx/access.log")
loglines = follow(logfile)
log = web_log(loglines)

# setup Redis connection
# for large environments, you will substitute
# localhost with a dedicated server host name
red = redis.StrictRedis(host='localhost',
                        port=6379, db=0)

# for each entry, store pythonic-data structure in
# associated with a key (could also use Redis hash
# for more language-independence)
for line in log:
    l = line['host']
    a = red.get("ip:%s" % l)
    if (a == None):
        a = {}
        a['ls'] = time.time()
        a['ct'] = 1
        red.set("ip:%s" % l,pickle.dumps(a))
    else:
        a = pickle.loads(a)
        a['ls'] = time.time()
        a['ct'] += 1
        red.set("ip:%s" % l,pickle.dumps(a))
```

Listing 8-5 shows the query component:

LISTING 8-5

```
# Listing 8-5
# Redis log watcher python query script
# Save this as "lastseen.py"
# Start it in one shell window prompt with
#    python query.py
# Requires: Python redis package
from datetime import datetime
import redis
import pickle
import sys

# setup Redis connection
red = redis.StrictRedis(host='localhost', port=6379, db=0)

# get IP address from the command line & query Redis
ipaddr = sys.argv[1]
```

```
ioc = red.get("ip:%s" % ipaddr)

# if found
if (ioc != None):
    b = pickle.loads(ioc)
    print("IP [%s] was last seen on [%s].\nTotal times seen ")
    print("since we started counting: [%d]." %
        (ipaddr, datetime.fromtimestamp(b['ls']),b['ct']))
else:
   print("%s has not been seen, yet." % ipaddr)
```

Now, it's quick work from the command line to know whether you've seen an IP address (substitute 24.62.253.107 with a known address to get a "found" result in your setup):

```
dds$ python lastseen.py 24.62.253.107
IP [24.62.253.107] was last seen on [2013-10-13 18:57:59.875430].
Total times seen since we started counting: [80787].
```

If you're thinking, "I could just use grep," remember that this is a constantly streaming, online activity from potentially hundreds or thousands of sources spanning weeks or months. If you architect it properly, Redis will always beat grep.

Hive

It's virtually impossible to write a book about data analysis without mentioning Hadoop (http://wiki.apache.org/hadoop), and if you're already investigating or using Hadoop, then you may have come across Hive (http://wiki.apache.org/hadoop/Hive/LanguageManual). Hive sits on top of the Hadoop Distributed file System http://hadoop.apache.org/docs/current/hadoop-project-dist/hadoop-hdfs/HdfsUserGuide.html) that partitions data across—potentially—*thousands* of nodes. Hadoop *MapReduce* jobs execute across these nodes using this data. The *map* component takes a set of data elements, breaks them into key/value pairs, and performs a comparison and/or computation on them. The *reduce* component takes these results and combines them to come up with a final result set (which may involve another comparison and/or computation).

MapReduce Redux

MapReduce is a Google creation (http://static.googleusercontent.com/external_content/untrusted_dlcp/research.google.com/en/us/archive/mapreduce-osdi04.pdf) and was designed to enable efficient computations across huge (for example, multi-thousand node) clusters. It does this by splitting the data across the entire cluster then instructing worker nodes to perform some operation on that local data set (the *map*). Those intermediary results are then collected and summarized by other worker nodes into a final operation (the *reduce*). Figure 8-2 illustrates the process.

(continues)

(continued)

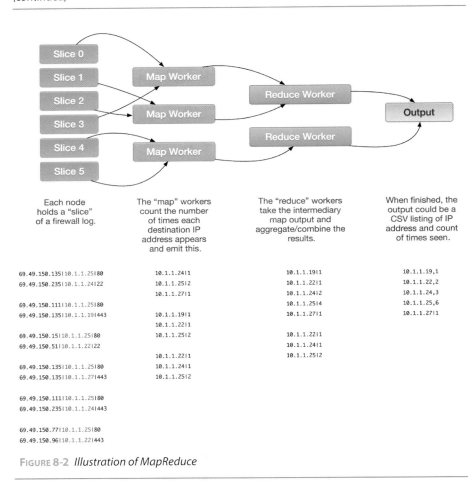

FIGURE 8-2 *Illustration of MapReduce*

Hive provides a SQL-like interface to this HDFS data. Rather than becoming an expert Java coder to compose and execute MapReduce jobs, Hive abstracts this complexity and converts SQL into MapReduce jobs for you. This is a very important point to remember: In the Hadoop ecosystem, ***everything*** boils down to a MapReduce job across very large amounts of data. The complexities of setting up a Hadoop environment and ***keeping*** it running are mixed into the cost/benefit analysis when choosing this as part of your analytics platform.

While Hive provides the comfort of SQL, some key features of SQL do not come along for the ride. For example, the Hive query language (HiveQL) provides only limited support for SQL `JOIN`s. If your needs go beyond combining tables on equality conditions, you cannot use Hive due to the limitations of the Hadoop MapReduce paradigm. You also need to use caution when ordering result sets with SQL's

ORDER BY, since Hive currently only uses a single reduce engine to perform that sorting task, creating potential bottlenecks. There are many other subtleties to Hive and HiveQL as well. While you may not need to become a Java expert, you will have to thoroughly understand how HiveQL queries translate to MapReduce jobs and learn how to optimize queries to take advantage of this platform.

Analyzing "At-Scale" NetFlow Data with Hadoop

If you ever enter a conversation about data and Hadoop, the concepts of *volume*, *velocity*, and *variety* will inevitably come up.

- **Volume** refers to how much data you have.
- **Velocity** refers to how fast that data is coming in or being analyzed.
- **Variety** speaks to the diversity of data types being ingested and processed.

Most security data falls somewhere on the lower end or middle section of each of those spectrums. However, even in a medium-sized network, NetFlow data can easily peg all the way to the upper bounds on the *velocity* and *volume* scales.

If you aren't familiar with NetFlow, here's the definition straight from RFC 3954 (`http://www .ietf.org/rfc/rfc3954.txt`):

> *A* flow *is defined as a unidirectional sequence of packets with some common properties that pass through a network device. These collected flows are exported to an external device, the* NetFlow *collector. Network flows are highly granular; for example, flow records include details such as IP addresses, packet and byte counts, timestamps, Type of Service (ToS), application ports, input and output interfaces, etc.*

NetFlow data is extremely useful for security analytics, but can be challenging to work with. For example, if you have a 10 Gbps link that is only 50 percent utilized, you can expect to churn out *2.3TB of NetFlow data per hour*. This is definitely a job for Hadoop since the input stream gathering and storage functions can be distributed across a large cluster (since it would overwhelm a single host) and converted on the fly to work with Hadoop native file formats. Then, you can begin to design MapReduce jobs such as performing anomaly detection or analyzing DDoS captures for patterns.

Tools such as PacketPig (`http://hortonworks.com/blog/big-data-security-part-one-introducing-packetpig/`) can help reduce some of the tedium involved in getting NetFlow data into an environment where analysis can be performed, but it cannot abstract the complexity of such an environment. You will need to thoroughly understand numerous NoSQL technologies if you wish to head down the path of analyzing NetFlow data at-scale.

If you have the time, space, personnel, budget, *and* use cases to set up Hadoop/HDFS/Hive, it may be well worth the investment. Imagine being able to keep a full year's online archive of every log file from every system, network device, firewall, and mail server in a massively efficient data warehouse and perform basic inquiries across all of those components. *That's* where the real power of Hive+Hadoop lies.

What about HBase, Cassandra, Pig ...?

The full Hadoop ecosystem continues to expand at a relentless pace. Advancements within the environment itself (for example, Hadoop 2.0) as well as integration with the environment (for example, Cassandra, MongoDB) and unique vendor-specific offerings are introducing nascent alternatives that have their own strengths, trade-offs, and idiosyncrasies.

You will need to spend some effort looking at all the options you have available and mapping them to your perceived needs. Then choose a direction and stick with it. A Hadoop analytics environment—much like Rome—cannot be built in a day. Despite the continuing advancements, this ecosystem is far from mature, and you will be forging new ground over a long period of time with each step you take.

MongoDB

MongoDB (http://www.mongodb.org/) could be called the "MySQL of NoSQL" databases as it has a large and active community, is easy to deploy in development, and scales fairly well in production. At its core, Mongo provides a way to do extremely quick prototyping given the schema-less nature of the platform. Unlike traditional SQL databases, where you need to define the fields you will be using up front, Mongo lets you start with a basic pseudo-schema and refine your needs along the way.

> ### Note
>
> To follow along with these examples, install MongoDB via `sudo apt-get install mongodb` at a shell prompt and then start it with `sudo /etc/init.d/mongodb start`.

For example, it's very straightforward to start storing IP geolocation info from the AlienVault Reputation database for an IP address with the following commands starting at a Linux shell prompt:

```
dds$ mongo
> db.av.insert ( { ip:"193.147.49.42",
                   geo:"40.4085,-3.6921" })
> db.av.find({ ip:"193.147.49.42" })
{ "_id" : ObjectId("525bfbe02074bfa7aaad8316"),
  "ip" : "193.147.49.42",
  "geo" : "40.4085,-3.6921" }
```

and then choose to add other information later, like the type of malicious activity the host is engaged in:

```
> db.av.update ( { ip:"193.147.49.42" },
                 { $set : { maltype:"Scanning Host" } } )
> db.av.find({ ip:"193.147.49.42" })
{ "_id" : ObjectId("525bfbe02074bfa7aaad8316"),
```

```
    "geo" : "40.4085,-3.6921",
    "ip" : "193.147.49.42",
    "maltype" : "Scanning Host" }
```

You do pay a price for these incremental field updates given the way Mongo stores the data and manages the on-the-fly schema changes, and you may need to dump and reload the database to regain storage and query efficiency if you perform these types of changes in production versus just experiment during development.

Mongo breathes JSON and uses binary JSON (BJSON) in API calls. This means you need to be comfortable with JavaScript notation and will definitely want to keep the JSONLint (http://jsonlint.com/) URL handy to assist you when errors crop up in your input data. The use of JSON provides the capability of storing deeply nested or hierarchical records and structures, which will require you to re-think any notions you may have on normalization. If you're used to performing RDBMS normalization, then you'll need to take a step back, ignore most of what you've been taught or have learned, and embrace the verbosity of this side of the NoSQL universe.

For example, malicious nodes in the AlienVault database can have multiple malicious activities associated with them. In traditional, normalized SQL, you would likely set up a separate table with host key and malicious node type field and have a row for each entry:

```
+-------------+-------------+
|193.147.49.42|Scanning Host|
|193.147.49.42|Spamming     |
+-------------+-------------+
```

then, perform a JOIN when retrieving results. With Mongo, you would store those components as a JSON array within the record:

```
> db.av.update ( { ip:"193.147.49.42" },
                 { $set : { maltype:[ "Scanning Host","Spamming" ] } } )
```

It may be difficult to see the value of this additional complexity with such a trivial example, but the power this holds starts to become much clearer if you look back at the VERIS JSON data in Chapter 7. Creating a normalized table structure to store all the fields in an incident is possible, but not necessary given Mongo's ability to efficiently store, process, and query complex field structures. If you have Mongo installed from the previous example, you can install the git tool via sudo apt-get install git, which will allow you to follow the steps in Listing 8-6 (found in other/ch08.sh) to download and import the complex incident data in the entire VERIS Community Database from their GitHub repository (https://github.com/vz-risk/) in about 5 minutes, without the need to create a database or table schema ahead of time.

LISTING 8-6

```
# Retrieve VCDB files, import into mongo and perform a query
# Requires mongodb and git
# clone the VCDB github repository
dds$ git clone https://github.com/vz-risk/VCDB.git
# import all the incdients
```

(continues)

LISTING 8-6   *(continued)*

```
dds$ cd VCDB/incidents
dds$ ls | head -5
0012CC25-9167-40D8-8FE3-3D0DFD8FB6BB.json
002599D4-A872-433B-9980-BD9F257B283F.json
005C42A3-3FE8-47B5-866B-AFBB5E3F5B95.json
0096EF99-D9CB-4869-9F3D-F4E0D84F419B.json
00CC39F6-D2E0-4FF4-9383-AE3E28922015.json
dds$ for f in *.json ; do \
       mongoimport -d veris -c public --jsonArray $f ;
    done
# find all financial firms with security incident in the VCDB
# 52 is NAICS code for financial firms
dds$ echo 'db.public.find({"victim.industry": { $regex : "^52" } },
           { "victim.victim_id" : 1, _id : 0 } )' | mongo veris
{ "victim" : [
{  "victim_id" : "Blue Cross & Blue Shield of Rhode Island" } ] }
{ "victim" : [
{  "victim_id" : "Group Health Incorporated" } ] }
{ "victim" : [
{  "victim_id" : "Delta Dental of Pennsylvania" },
{  "victim_id" : "ZDI" } ] }
{ "victim" : [
{  "victim_id" : "UK National Health Service" } ] }
{ "victim" : [
{  "victim_id" : "Mundo.com" },
{  "victim_id" : "Public Defender of Venezula" },
{  "victim_id" : "Caroni Seguros SA" } ] }
. . .
```

If your record count is large enough to span multiple Mongo nodes, these simple queries will work unaltered. Mongo can also perform data aggregation or even run MapReduce jobs across a whole cluster, mimicking some of the functionality of both Hadoop and more traditional SQL databases.

Mongo can also be used as a tool in your data acquisition and cleanup processes, where you may have traditionally used built-in structures in your programming or scripting languages. For example, log processing is one of the less glamorous activities of security data analysis. They come in all shapes and sizes and some, like Cisco's IronPort email logs, require extra processing to get into a form useful for analytics. Take a look at the following sample in Listing 8-7 (found in `ch08/other/ironport.log`):

LISTING 8-7

```
# Listing 8-7
# Example of an IronPort log file
Fri Oct 18 11:05:01 2011 Info: Start MID 346564 ICID 1042862
Fri Oct 18 11:05:01 2011 Info: MID 346564 ICID 1042862 From:
 <dave@example.com>
```

```
Fri Oct 18 11:05:01 2011 Info: MID 346564 ICID 1042862 RID 0 To:
 <steve@test.com>
Fri Oct 18 11:05:01 2011 Info: MID 346564 Message-ID
'<112067.438985349-em02@steel>'
Fri Oct 18 11:05:01 2011 Info: MID 346564 Subject 'TPS Reports Due'
Fri Oct 18 11:05:02 2011 Info: MID 346564 ready 864 bytes from
 <dave@example.com>
Fri Oct 18 11:05:02 2011 Info: MID 346564 matched all recipients for
 per-recipient policy local domains in the outbound table
Fri Oct 18 11:05:03 2011 Info: MID 346564 interim AV verdict using
 Sophos CLEAN
Fri Oct 18 11:05:03 2011 Info: MID 346564 antivirus negative
Fri Oct 18 11:05:03 2011 Info: MID 346564 DLP no violation
Fri Oct 18 11:05:03 2011 Info: MID 346564 queued for delivery
Fri Oct 18 11:05:03 2011 Info: Delivery start DCID 178987 MID 346564
 to RID [0]
Fri Oct 18 11:05:04 2011 Info: Message done DCID 178987 MID 346564
 to RID [0]
Fri Oct 18 11:05:04 2011 Info: MID 346564 RID [0] Response 'ok:
  Message 10569973 accepted'
Fri Oct 18 11:05:04 2011 Info: Message finished MID 346564 done
```

Because Mongo allows incremental schema build out, you can use that feature to create records for each message (MID) as you parse the log file. You can then add fields as you go, ending up with a final, complete database and an idea of how a complete per-record schema might look. The Mongo entry for the previous record could look like the one found in Listing 8-8 (found in ch08/other/ironport.json).

LISTING 8-8

```
// Example of an IronPort log file translated to JSON via MongoDB
{
    mid : "346564",
    icid : "1042862",
    from : "dave@example.com",
    to : "steve@test.com",
    messageID : "112067.438985349-em02@steel",
    subj: "TPS Reports Due",
    bytes: "864"
    matchStatus : 1,
    delivered : 1,
    av : { engine : "Sophos", verdict: "CLEAN" },
    dlp : { violation : "none" },
    start : "Fri Oct 18 11:05:01",
    finish : "Fri Oct 18 11:05:01"
}
```

Once all the records have been created, you can use Mongo and Python or R to perform time series analysis, z-scaled anomaly detection, clustering, or a host of other analyses.

Why Not Use Mongo for Everything?

It's possible to fall into the trap of trying to use Mongo for everything, especially since it allows you to be a bit lazy up front. Although it's great for some tasks, the platform still has some rough edges at the time this chapter was written. You might want to take into account when deciding on Mongo for a project:

- Record counting operations are improving but are still slower than other database platforms due to the way Mongo uses the underlying b-tree database file structures.

- Field names are not compressed and take up real space *per-record*. This leads to practices such as using `sip` instead of `src_ip` or `sourceIP` and `u` for `"username,"` making queries somewhat unreadable unless you're extremely familiar with the data.

- Maintenance operations are still required and can impair operations. You *will* need to compact the database regularly and this can be a time-consuming, blocking operation across a whole cluster. Although this is most likely not a problem for your analytics environment, be careful if you're using Mongo to present an interactive data interface to other users.

- By default, writes to a Mongo database work a bit like UDP packets in that it's "send, and pray it's received." You need to explicitly set options for enabling "write concern" to get more TCP-like behavior. This can have a serious impact on performance such as the need to guarantee writes of log entries you are aggregating into Mongo.

Special Purpose Databases

It's far too easy to get snarled on what truly constitutes a "database." For those still entrenched in the SQL world, NoSQL is a serious affront to their sensibilities. For those who've adjusted to the NoSQL paradigm, tools such as ElasticSearch (`http://www.elasticsearch.org/`) and Neo4j (`http://www.neo4j.org/`) may be equally as world jarring.

Databases will be an essential element in your analytics workflow, which might look like this:

1. Identify the data sources (for example, logs, traditional databases, alerts).

2. Collect, transform (if needed), and store the data.

3. Query the data store.

4. Provide analytics on the results.

If you choose to work with raw SQL or NoSQL databases, then you will need to perform most of the setup and cleanup tasks on your own, which requires DBA-like intimacy with the underlying database platforms.

ElasticSearch for Logs

If you're focused on the goal of analytics more than the journey of how to get your data there, you may be interested in tools like ElasticSearch that abstract the complexities of the back end and give you an input, query, and analytics interface to work with on the front end.

ElasticSearch consumes practically anything you give it and provides straightforward ways to ask it questions and get data out of it. You just need to feed it semi- or unstructured data and fold in some domain intelligence to enable smart indexing. It works its multi-node NoSQL magic in conjunction with a layer of full-text searching to give you almost instantaneous query results even for large amounts of data. It's **highly** geared toward log data and supports an aggregation framework similar to that of Mongo.

If you are analyzing a wide variety of logs in your security work, ElasticSearch may be something you should consider investigating.

Neo4j for "Connections"

As indicated in several previous chapters, many areas of information security analytics involve looking at connections between nodes. You've also seen how network graph structures can make working with these connections a bit easier. Although it's possible to model graph structures in SQL databases or Mongo, Redis, and so on, it's easier to use a something like Neo4j that provides direct support for network graph models and operations.

If the `igraph` operations in Chapter 4 intrigued you, then you'll be even more impressed with the feature set in Neo4j because it essentially scales similar computations and analytics across millions or billions of nodes. You can import high level vertex + edge connection data into Neo4j from NetFlow sources, firewall, proxy, email, and DNS logs, and augment the connection and node information with detail data from each of those sources.

You still need to have a graph model in mind when you're designing for Neo4j and will need to learn a new graph-specific query language—Cypher—to get work done. However, many fine-grained tasks will require that you either roll up your sleeves and code a bit in Java or Python or use the Neo4j REST interface to funnel query output into your analytics platform of choice.

Summary

Becoming truly effective as a security data scientist requires a shift in mindset from any monolithic relational database fidelity you may have. Solving real problems requires you to keep your options open, recognizing that each database technology has unique benefits for specific tasks.

This chapter has presented a survey of various technologies combined with small examples in many different types of SQL and NoSQL database environments. We've outlined strengths and weaknesses in the choices you have and even provided some counseling on how to enhance interactions with your traditional SQL stores.

We've focused on some core database offerings, but have not provided an exhaustive reference since that would be a book on its own. You will need to keep abreast of developments in the database space—both SQL and NoSQL—to see where you may need to make adjustments in the future. If you are working with larger and larger amounts of data, it may be time to wade a bit deeper into the Hadoop ecosystem, provided you understand the level of commitment required and the constraints you will be facing.

Finally, you've seen that databases can take many forms, that they can be used as a means to an end (for example, log parsing) as well as an end in and of themselves.

Recommended Reading

The following are some recommended readings that can further your understanding on some of the topics we touch on in this chapter. For full information on these recommendations and for the sources we cite in the chapter, please see Appendix B.

Relational Database Design Clearly Explained, Second Edition, **by Jan L. Harrington**—One of the most complete and accessible resources available; especially helpful to nascent arrivals to the world of RDBMS systems.

Professional Hadoop Solutions **by Boris Lublinsky, Kevin T. Smith, and Alexey Yakubovich**— An excellent and thorough introduction to the Hadoop ecosystem with modern, real-world examples and advice on how to secure your Hadoop analytics environments.

Professional NoSQL **by Shashank Tiwari**—Far more comprehensive reference on NoSQL database technologies that digs a bit deeper into many of the options described in this chapter.

9

Demystifying Machine Learning

"They know enough who know how to learn."

Henry Adams

There are two types of people in information security—those who are completely intimidated by machine learning and those who know machine learning largely solved the spam problem and are completely intimidated by machine learning. It's easy to be intimidated when machine learning is described as "a type of artificial intelligence that provides computers with the ability to learn without being explicitly programmed" by TechTarget. (`http://whatis.techtarget.com/definition/machine-learning`). How can a computer do anything without being explicitly programmed? Or better yet, consider this rather well known definition from Tom M. Mitchell in his 1997 book titled *Machine Learning*:

> *A computer program is said to learn from experience E with respect to some class of tasks T and performance measure P, if its performance at tasks in T, as measured by P, improves with experience E.*

Are you clear now on what machine learning is? This broad definition doesn't help much because it only describes the abstract results of machine learning, not what it is or how to use it. To help you understand machine learning at a practical and concrete level, we start this chapter with a learning task associated with realistic data. Prepare for the examples in this chapter by setting the directory to the working directory for this chapter and make sure the R libraries are installed (Listing 9-0).

LISTING 9-0

```
# set working directory to chapter location
# (change for where you set up files in ch 2)
setwd("~/book/ch09")
# make sure the packages for this chapter
# are installed, install if necessary
pkg <- c("ggplot2", "RColorBrewer")
new.pkg <- pkg[!(pkg %in% installed.packages())]
if (length(new.pkg)) {
  install.packages(new.pkg)
}
```

Detecting Malware

Assume that you have been able to record memory and processor usage on all of your systems. With some effort, you have been able to inspect almost 250 of the computers, discovering that some of the systems are infected with malware and some are operating normally (without malware). But you have 445 other systems that haven't been inspected, and you want to save time and use the data you have to determine if the other 445 systems you have are infected or not.

> ### Note
>
> *Please keep in mind that this is a contrived demonstration of a machine learning approach; for a much more complete application of machine learning to detect malware, see "Disclosure: Detecting Botnet Command and Control Servers Through Large-Scale NetFlow Analysis" from the **Proceedings of the 28th Annual Computer Security Applications Conference** by Leyla Bilge, et al. (Full reference is available in Appendix B.)*

This example will use R to build an algorithm that can be trained to perform the task of classifying systems as either infected or not. Start by loading the data on the hosts you know about and inspecting it (Listing 9-1).

LISTING 9-1

```
memproc <- read.csv("data/memproc.csv", header=T)
summary(memproc)
##         host         proc            mem           state
## crisnd0004:  1   Min.   :-3.1517   Min.   :-3.5939   Infected: 53
## crisnd0062:  1   1st Qu.:-1.2056   1st Qu.:-1.4202   Normal  :194
## crisnd0194:  1   Median :-0.4484   Median :-0.6212
## crisnd0203:  1   Mean   :-0.4287   Mean   :-0.5181
## crisnd0241:  1   3rd Qu.: 0.3689   3rd Qu.: 0.2413
## crisnd0269:  1   Max.   : 3.1428   Max.   : 3.2184
## (Other)   :241
```

Note

The `data/memproc.csv` *file is available as part of the Chapter 9 download materials for this book, which you can find at* `www.wiley.com/go/datadrivensecurity.`

You can see there are 53 hosts identified as "infected" and 194 identified as "normal." Also notice that both the processor data and the memory information have been normalized (see the discussion of z-score in Chapter 5). That will keep the numbers on the same scale. Scaling the variables like this is important in some machine learning approaches when you're comparing across variables. In order to explore this data a bit more, let's plot this data (Listing 9-2), comparing the processor data to the memory, and differentiate it based on the malware state (see Figure 9-1).

LISTING 9-2

```
# requires package : ggplot2
# requires object: memproc (9-1)
library(ggplot2)
gg <- ggplot(memproc, aes(proc, mem, color=state))
gg <- gg + scale_color_brewer(palette="Set2")
gg <- gg + geom_point(size=3) + theme_bw()
print(gg)
```

Notice how the infected systems appear to generally use more processor and memory? Perhaps you could develop an algorithm to classify this data just based on the relative location (on the scatterplot in Figure 9-1) of the known hosts. But before you get too far, you'll want to do a little planning. First you'll want to determine which machine learning algorithm you want to apply, and then you should figure out how to test if the algorithm is any good. In a real problem, you would try several different algorithms and features; you'll learn about model and feature selection later in this chapter.

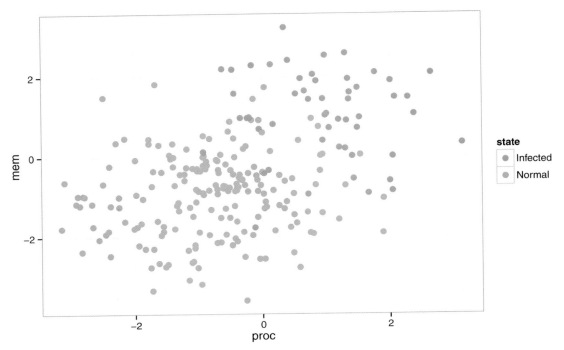

FIGURE 9-1 *Processor and memory across systems*

Developing a Machine Learning Algorithm

Does that title give you flashes of fear that we'll start talking about mathematical formulas and make you say things like "sub i of x"? Don't worry, we will keep this as light as we can, and we will start by demystifying the word *algorithm*. Anytime you see the word algorithm, try to mentally replace it with "a series of instructions" because that's all an algorithm is. You'll want to develop a series of instructions for the computer on how to inspect and understand the data (so it can learn about it). Then the computer can apply that learning to the systems you don't know about and classify them.

Do you see how you are not explicitly programming? Even though you are absolutely writing a program for the computer, you will not be explicitly writing the decision criteria the computer will use and that's the difference. Your series of instructions (the algorithm) will explicitly tell the computer how to inspect the data and how it should build its own decision criteria from the data. It will not tell the computer the decision criteria directly. Compare that to the traditional approach of programming firewall and intrusion-detection/prevention systems. With the traditional approach, humans try to think up what's best and then explicitly program the rules the machines should follow. There is a limit to that approach, and unfortunately, our security systems reached that limit years ago. In machine learning, you are asking the computer to learn from the data and then apply that learning to other data. The computer is far more capable of uncovering the differences and subtleties in the data than humans, and that is exactly what machine learning is doing.

Note

It may seem like this chapter uses the terms **model** *and* **algorithm** *somewhat interchangeably. The difference is subtle and may even be a bit confusing at first. The term* **model** *is more general and just defines how the elements fit together. An* **algorithm** *is a specific way of implementing a model, so there can be many alternative algorithms that fit the same model.*

Getting back to the data shown in Figure 9-1, you'll want to create a series of instructions to learn about the processor and memory usage on the normal hosts and then compare it to the processor and memory usage on the infected hosts. Once the computer has some notion of a difference between the two sets, you can give it some instructions on how to apply that information to the data collected from the unknown/unclassified systems. Remember the goal here is to have the computer guess whether or not a system is infected with malware. Consider this short algorithm, which is easy to understand and easy to follow:

1. Define and train an algorithm:

   a. Calculate the average (mean) processor and memory usage for known infected systems.

   b. Calculate the average (mean) processor and memory usage for known normal systems.

2. Make a prediction using processor and memory usage for an unknown host:

   a. If the processor and memory usage are closer to the average infected machine, label it as infected.

   b. If the processor and memory usage are closer to the average normal machine, label it as normal.

Congratulations! You have written your first machine learning algorithm and now the computers are one step closer to world domination with this extra bit of artificial intelligence! Notice the choice of wording in the first step, you'll want to *train* the algorithm. That's the term used to describe when the machine is learning from the data; it's being *trained* by the data just as an apprentice is trained by its master. The data used to train the algorithm is referred to as the *training data*. In this simple example, the "training" simply involved calculating the mean usage for infected and non-infected using the training data. This is a single-step training procedure. In contrast, most real machine learning algorithms use iterative or multi-step training procedures, as we'll describe later.

Validating the Algorithm

Before you rely on this algorithm for real decisions, you need to make sure it is valid. You'll want some way to test how accurate this algorithm is at predicting infected systems. Rather than using all of this data to train the algorithm, how about you hold back some of the data to test how accurate the algorithm can predict malware? The process of "making sure" you have a good approach is one of the strong suits of machine learning. It has evolved just as much (if not more so) in computer science as it has in statistics, and there is a strong element of pragmatism in the field. Many techniques have evolved to validate the decisions you'll make and they are so ingrained in the process, it becomes impossible not to perform those steps as part of the model selection.

For this example, you will keep it simple and split the original data into two data sets. In serious machine learning projects, you would probably create multiple data sets from the original data, and train and test the data over multiple iterations (and validations).

Once you split the data into two groups, as we mentioned, call the first group the training data, since you'll use it to train the algorithm, and call the second group the test data, since you'll use it to (yup, you guessed it) test your approach. To split the data randomly, make use of the sample() command. You will pull a random sample of the indexes (the index is the location in the vector data) of the original data and use that sample to split into the train and test data. There's no definitive rule as to where to make the split (different techniques split in different ways), so you will simply take one third for the test data and train the algorithm on the other two thirds. Since there is an element of randomness here we make the splitting repeatable by setting the seed for the random number generator (see Listing 9-3).

LISTING 9-3

```
# requires package : ggplot2
# requires object: memproc (9-1)
# make this repeatable
set.seed(1492)
# count how many in the overall sample
n <- nrow(memproc)
# set the test.size to be 1/3rd
test.size <- as.integer(n/3)
# randomly sample the rows for test set
testset <- sample(n, test.size)
# now split the data into test and train
test <- memproc[testset, ]
train <- memproc[-testset, ]
```

Now you can train the algorithm on the train data and verify how good it is with test data. Please keep in mind that there are much more robust methods for validation. Splitting the data once like this is better than just assuming the algorithm is good, but in the real world, you'd need something more robust like cross-validation, which we discuss later in this chapter.

Implementing the Algorithm

Recall that the first step in training this algorithm is to calculate the average (mean) for the infected processor and memory usage and the mean for the normal processor and memory usage. You do this by taking a subset of the rows based on the state field (so only infected or normal is returned) and then apply that to the columns of the proc and mem fields. That reduced data can be passed directly into colMeans(), which will compute the means on the two columns and return a named vector with two elements (see Listing 9-4).

LISTING 9-4

```
# requires object: train (9-3)
# pull out proc and mem columns for infected then normal
# then use colMeans() to means of the columns
inf <- colMeans(train[train$state=="Infected", c("proc", "mem")])
nrm <- colMeans(train[train$state=="Normal", c("proc", "mem")])
print(inf)
##      proc        mem
## 1.152025 1.201779
print(nrm)
##        proc         mem
## -0.8701412 -0.9386983
```

The differences between the means here is not exactly small, so this rather simple approach may do okay with your simple algorithm. With the algorithm now trained and ready to predict, the next step is to create a `predict.malware()` function (Listing 9-5). This will take in a single named vector called `data`, extract out the `proc` and `mem` values, than calculate how far those are from the means that you generated during the training. What is the best way to calculate distance? Think back to geometry class and the Pythagorean theorem—$a^2 + b^2 = c^2$, where a and b are the two sides of the triangle and c is the hypotenuse. This is called "Euclidean distance," since it is based on Euclidean geometry. In your case, *a* is the difference between the trained `proc` mean and the test `proc` value, and *b* is the difference between the trained `mem` mean and the test `mem` value. Once you get the two distances, you simply compare them. Whichever is smaller is the one you will predict.

LISTING 9-5

```
requires object: inf (9-4), nrm (9-4)
predict.malware <- function(data) {
  # get 'proc' and 'mem' as numeric values
  proc <- as.numeric(data[['proc']])
  mem <- as.numeric(data[['mem']])
  # set up infected comparison
  inf.a <- inf['proc'] - proc
  inf.b <- inf['mem'] - mem
  # pythagorean distance c = sqrt(a^2 + b^2)
  inf.dist <- sqrt(inf.a^2 + inf.b^2)
  # repeat for normal systems
  nrm.a <- nrm['proc'] - proc
  nrm.b <- nrm['mem'] - mem
  nrm.dist <- sqrt(nrm.a^2 + nrm.b^2)
  # assign a label of the closest (smallest)
  ifelse(inf.dist<nrm.dist,"Infected", "Normal")
}
```

Feel free to pass in a few values if you like and inspect the output. At this point, everything is ready to run against the test data. To pass in the test data you can use the `apply()` function with the first argument being the test data set and the second argument being a `1` to denote to apply it over the rows (instead of a `2` for columns). Then you'll pass in the function we just created called `predict.malware` (see Listing 9-6). The `apply` function will convert in each row to a named vector. We have to be careful here, because the `state` and `host` variables are characters, so the whole vector is converted to a character vector when `apply` passes it in. This is why you convert the `proc` and `mem` variables back to numeric variables with the `as.numeric()` function in the `predict.malware()` function.

LISTING 9-6

```
# requires object: test (9-3), predict.malware (9-5)
prediction <- apply(test, 1, predict.malware)
```

First, Do No Harm; Second, Do Better Than the Null Model

This is a great time to point out that this is a very basic algorithm and it's only for discussion purposes. There is a concept within statistics known as the *null model*, which is a very simple model that you'll always want to do better than (or at least no worse). For example, in the ZeroAccess infection data in Chapter 5, the null model could be the calculation of the average (mean) infection across all the states (5,253 infections). The null model (for prediction) would estimate 5,253 infections for any new state regardless of any data about that state. In this case you are omitting or "nullifying" the variables to simplify the model. Intuitively, you know that the average across the states will be a very poor predictor, but that's the purpose. You'll want to use this as a reference point and exceed it. And even though this seems like a "well duh" type of statement, we are not kidding about this. You could spend days preparing data and training an intricate support vector machine and do worse than a much simpler model. Just take the time to create a simple "must be this tall to ride" mark, and then make sure you surpass it.

Once the test data runs through that code, you'll have a set of predictions and the ability to compare them to the real values (see the power of this method?). To determine how well it did, you'll want to look at the proportion of correctly predicted results on the test data. You can calculate that by taking the number of correct predictions (where the real `test$state` and the predicted `prediction` match) and then dividing that by the total number of predictions (Listing 9-7).

LISTING 9-7

```
# requires object: test (9-3), prediction (9-6)
sum(test$state==prediction)/nrow(test)
## [1] 0.8780488
```

This very simple algorithm predicted almost 88 percent of the values correctly, which is probably more a statement about how segregated the data is than the strength of the algorithm. But overall, 88 percent is pretty good for your first machine learning algorithm; congratulations! The results are pictured in Figure 9-2.

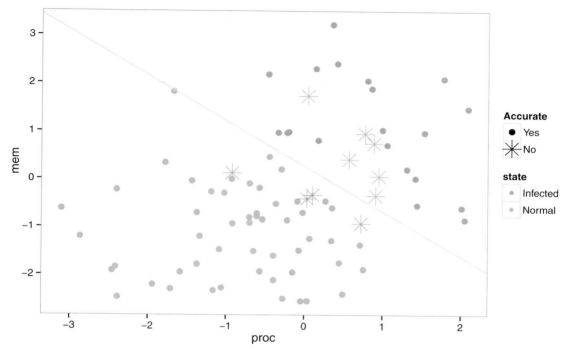

FIGURE 9-2 *Predictions from the algorithm*

This classifier creates a line halfway between the two means and perpendicular to an intersecting line. Anything above the line is predicted as infected; anything below is predicted to be normal. The misclassified values are clearly marked in Figure 9-2. You can see how any normal systems above the line are mislabeled as well as any infected systems below the line.

Spam, Spam, Spam

Open any non-InfoSec book on machine learning (which may be all of them) and you will probably see spam filtering mentioned, and perhaps even see an in-depth example. We've decided not to go into spam filtering, given that we've got a single chapter to cover everything and there are already some great examples out there. One of the better discussions of spam filtering (including a guided walkthrough) is in *Machine Learning for Hackers* by Drew Conway and John Myles White. Another good thing about playing with spam classification is that there is no end to the available data, right?

Benefiting from Machine Learning

Now that you've seen a rather simple example (perhaps too simple), you should have a basic understanding of the change in thinking that machine learning brings. Rather than focusing on rule sets and signatures, machine learning can shift the focus toward continual adaptation based on the computers learning directly from the data. Hopefully, the days of thresholds and regular expressions rules will soon be behind us.

Before you can read about the benefits of machine learning, you need to learn about the two types of machine learning algorithms—*supervised* and *unsupervised*. Which type you use is determined more by the type of data you have than by personal preference.

- **Supervised algorithms** require that the training set have known samples just like the opening example of this chapter. The data in that example was collected from hosts that were identified as infected with malware or not. Another example is the ZeroAccess data in Chapter 5, where you knew how many infections there were in each state and county and you could correlate that with other data about the states and counties. Supervised learning is possible only when you have labeled or known data.

- **Unsupervised algorithms** are usually applied to data when you don't know ahead of time what outcome you are seeking. Unsupervised learning "lets the data speak for itself," as much as possible. As an example, think of the recommendation systems at Amazon or Netflix. Those systems begin with data on the history of movie rentals or purchases and apply unsupervised learning techniques to group similar people (their habits actually) based on patterns in the data. This enables them to recommend products that other people like you have purchased. You don't decide ahead of time what the groups should be. Unsupervised methods enable you to discover groupings and relationships, and do other and typically deeper explorations like no other approach. Given the unsupervised nature of these approaches, it is difficult to definitively prove something with unsupervised methods, but that's not what these are designed to do. As you'll see, you can discover some interesting relationships with unsupervised learning methods.

To Parametric or Not to Parametric, That Is the Question

In addition to supervised and unsupervised, machine learning algorithms may also be separated into parametric methods and non-parametric methods. The term *parametric* refers to one or more parameters in the model or algorithm that must be estimated as a result of the training step. The linear regression performed in Chapter 5 is an example of a parametric model. Part of the output of the `lm()` command is the linear coefficients (parameters), which are then used in both prediction and inference within regression analysis. Compare this to the random forest algorithm (discussed later in this chapter). When you train a random forest algorithm, there are no parameters to estimate. Instead, you grow a series of decision trees that are then used for further classification.

Answering Questions with Machine Learning

What types of questions can machine learning answer? What sort of problems can it solve? Broadly speaking machine learning can help you with questions of:

- Classification
- Quantitative prediction

- Inference

- Exploration and discovery

The opening example in this chapter already introduced the concept of classification, where you tried to determine if the hosts were infected or not. **Classification** is the process of identifying the category something belongs in, or determining which label should be applied. Classification always begins with a list of possible categories and known data that describes those categories (so they are supervised algorithms). Many of the tactical challenges within information security revolve around a single classification problem, such as "Is this malicious or not?" Mechanisms exist to authenticate and authorize users, but do their actions match that of a normal user or a malicious user? Is this HTTP request valid or is the source attempting something they shouldn't be? These are all questions that classification algorithms are best at tackling.

What if you wanted to forecast a quantity instead? Machine learning (and classical statistics) offers methods to do **quantitative prediction**. The overall approach may make people with a strong engineering background a bit uneasy thinking that prediction is impossible. But relax—nobody is claiming that the precise future is hidden in the data. However you can use the data to make a pretty good estimate. Given a set of observations and the outcome that resulted (so again, these are supervised methods), you can build a predictive model that will provide estimates of future values.

Think back to the linear regression analysis performed in Chapter 5. If by some strange turn of events another state appears with 6 million people, the regression analysis using just population would predict just under 5,000 ZeroAccess infections in that state. Although that example isn't exactly practical, you could use techniques to estimate bandwidth usage next month, or even forecast the probable magnitudes for the next DDoS attack.

Sometimes the end result isn't a prediction of a quantity or category. Sometimes you just want to know about the variables you observe and determine how they contribute to and interact with the outcome. In these cases you'll want to apply methods for **inference**. Inferential methods allow you to describe your environment. How important are these variables? Are data around processor and memory usage the best predictors of an infected machine? For example, linear regression enables you to toss multiple variables into a single analysis and see how each of them contributes to the outcome and see the quantitative relationships around them. Both supervised and unsupervised methods support inference about the variables, and that inference is an important part of any model or algorithm.

The last application of machine learning is for **exploration and discovery**. This is an area where unsupervised algorithms truly excel, but supervised methods can also support exploration. Sometimes you may find yourself just sitting on a mound of data and you want to know what sort of relationships or patterns exist in the data. Using methods like multidimensional scaling and hierarchical clustering will help you explore and gain perspectives on the data that just aren't possible with simple descriptive statistics.

Measuring Good Performance

At the core of good learning is good feedback. If you're creating models and algorithms and never check if they are doing well, you're doomed to repeat the same mistakes and improvement is nigh impossible. This is such a fundamental concept that several techniques have been developed to measure performance within supervised algorithms. It's important to understand that unsupervised algorithms are generally not used to prove (or disprove) a theory. We don't have the space to go into the mathematical details for each method; instead this section explains a few basic approaches and some of the terms for further exploration.

Following common sense, the best way to measure the performance of any predictive algorithm is to simply see how well it predicts (or how poorly it predicts if you are a pessimist). There is no single, perfect approach, so you will want to choose an approach that performs better than all the available approaches (don't toss out a helpful approach simply because it's imperfect). All of the fancy math formulas that describe this process are just variations on a simple theme: If you are working with quantitative values, select the approach in which predictions are the closest to the observations. If you are working with a classification system, choose the model with the highest number of correct classifications.

Within classic regression analysis, the difference between the calculated prediction and the observed value is squared for each of the values and then added up. When the difference is squared, it amplifies the larger distances and rewards the smaller values and gives a better indication of quality. The fancy term for this is the **sum square of errors** (**SSE**). In the grand tradition of multiple ways to express the same thing, this is also called the error sum of squares, sum square of residuals (SS residual), or the residual sum of squares (RSS).

Since calculating SSE involves adding the squared differences, larger sample sizes have larger SSE values. That makes it impossible to compare between a training data set and the test data set when they don't have the same number of data points. To standardize the SSE, it is divided by the number of data points (sample size), and the result can be compared when the sample size is not the same. That result is called the **mean squared error** (**MSE**). Prior to the concept of a training data set and test data set, this was (and still is in default classic approaches) calculated on the data set used to train the model. The challenge with just relying on the MSE of the training data is that it is prone to **overfitting** (see the sidebar on overfitting). One approach to comparing quantitative models and algorithms is to calculate the MSE and compare it across multiple approaches and feature selections. You'll read more about this process in the section titled "Validating Your Model" later in this chapter.

Overfitting

Since learning algorithms "learn" what to do from the data, it's possible that they'll learn too much or put too much confidence in the data. When this happens, the algorithm may do very well on the training data, but fail miserably when run on real data. This is called **overfitting** and occurs when the training algorithm is too aggressive in fitting to the training data. Because it's a sample, the training data will have it's own quirks and characteristics that may not match the population. Ideally, you want the learning process to ignore the quirks of the training data and just focus on the characteristics that apply to the general population. It's a good thing to be aware of overfitting, but awareness alone doesn't help all that much. Several approaches exist to help detect and avoid overfitting, and you'll read about a few in the next section.

Selecting Features

Before you can train an algorithm and measure its performance, you need to have data to run on. One of the less talked about topics within machine learning is how you go about selecting the data to collect and include in your analysis. The variables that you collect and use within your algorithm are called **features**. Within classic statistics they are also called explanatory, independent, or predictor variables (and a few other things).

The processor and memory usage in the opening example of this chapter were the features you used to train your algorithm.

The tricky part with feature selection is that there are no guidelines in selecting the initial set of features, so this is where your domain expertise comes into play. You collect the data points that may be important and then (as discussed in the previous section) run them through the algorithm and check if they are actually contributing to the outcome. (By doing this relatively simple step that is supported in almost every statistical approach, you will have surpassed every risk analysis model within information security; congratulations.) Although it's tempting to grab everything and anything, remember that data collection and cleaning has a cost (at least in time and resources). And be aware that many approaches benefit from fewer variables and may perform quite poorly with a lot of variables.

As an example, if you were thinking of improving on the malware classifier, you could pull variables from network traffic logs, such as the ports and protocols used, how often, and how much, as a starting point. The first pass of variables doesn't really matter all that much because whatever you choose initially will undoubtedly be wrong-—and that's okay. Grab data that makes sense and then try to make sense of it. You may find that only some of the variables are helpful, or that none of the variables do well, or variables do well only when used in combination. But the point is that feature selection is an iterative process. In the end, you should not only look at how well the features contribute to the outcome, but also how well (or accurately) the whole algorithm performs and then try to improve on it.

Using the Best Subset

Given a bunch of features, how could you determine which ones to include or exclude? One approach is to try every possible combination of features and select the subset of features that performs the best. This technique is rather appropriately named the *best subset* approach. The benefit and drawback of this approach is the same—every possible combination is tested. On one hand, this approach may discover a combination of features that you wouldn't have found without this brute force method. On the other hand, you have to run through all the combinations of features and that may take considerable time. As a reference point, using the best subset selection method on 20 variables will require well over one million iterations through the algorithm and validation steps.

There is another caveat with the best subset approach. As the number of features increases, the probability of finding bogus relationships in the features also increases. The good news is that it will generally not happen silently. Overfitting with this method may look "best" on the training data, but perform very poorly on the test data. One way to tackle that problem is to apply several of the best subsets to the test data or move to another technique.

Using Stepwise Comparison

When the brute force method of the best subset is infeasible or undesirable, the stepwise approach may be a good compromise. Rather than tossing everything in, you build up the correct set of features by stepping over them. In a forward stepwise process, the method begins by training with each of the features individually. Whichever feature performs the best is kept and the process is repeated by adding one more feature to the previous results. The features are added in one by one based on their contribution. Once all of the features have been added, all of the best performing algorithms at each of the steps are compared. The overall best set of features is selected as the final set.

The benefit of this method is that it constitutes an enormous reduction in the number of iterations compared to the best subset method. But the drawback is that not all the combinations are tried and so the best combination may be hidden. In some cases, a feature that performs best alone may not perform best when other features are added. You can also perform a reverse stepwise comparison, where you start with all the features and then sequentially step backward, removing the least helpful feature until you're down to one feature again. Then, you look at all of the best combinations and select the best that way.

Validating Your Model

However you go about selecting the features to include, you still need to validate how well the approach performs. Each algorithm may have subtle differences in how it works and the test statistics it generates and focuses on. Still, there are a few general approaches for validating how you're doing, and they apply to almost all the methods. The most widely used method is *cross-validation*, and it's discussed here. As a second validation pass, you could look at any other resampling methods, such as bootstrapping or the jackknife method.

The opening example started with 247 observations and then was split into a training set to train the algorithm and a test set to test how the training set did. Recall that the data was arbitrarily split so that two thirds was training data and the remaining one third was test data. One drawback in doing that is that you can't train on the one third that you pulled out, and that introduces more variation in the outcome of the training process.

What if you were to repeat the splitting and testing process so all data could contribute to both the training and test of the algorithm? It is possible to increase the accuracy of the algorithm by generating multiple training and test data sets and comparing the results from all of the splits. This approach is called *cross-validation*, and it works better than when you just split the data once.

The common method of performing cross-validation is to split the data into some number of equal partitions (more than a few) and then iterate over the data using each partition as the test data once. This is known as *k-fold cross-validation*, because you *fold* the data *k times* (once for each partition). For example, you could go back to the data in the first example and divide it into 10 partitions and iterate through the process 10 times each, with a different test data set and a slightly different training data set. By combining (averaging) the estimation of the accuracy across each of the iterations, you can have more confidence in how that approach will perform on new data.

A variation on the k-fold cross-validation is to set the number of partitions equal to the number of samples in the data. The result is the *leave-one-out cross-validation*. Named because you can sequentially leave out one value from the training set and test against that one value across the whole data set. The results from this method are often more accurate in assessing the algorithm, but it comes at a computational cost.

Specific Learning Methods

There are a lot of learning methods, and it isn't possible to survey all of them in one chapter. We chose a handful of approaches and will briefly touch on what makes them unique, including their strengths, weaknesses, and so on. But the field of machine learning is as wide as it is deep, and there are many methods we don't touch on here. Do not take that to mean they are less important or not as good. On the contrary, a method such as neural networks or support vector machines may perform better in some circumstances. We have just picked a few to serve as an introduction and overview.

Supervised

Supervised methods require that you begin with known or labeled data. You will not be able to apply supervised methods for malware detection unless you have data from known infection and known normal systems. While this may present a challenge in some circumstances, the power of supervised learning may make the extra effort well worth it.

Linear Regression (and Transformation)

Linear regression is a very popular approach when it comes to quantitative prediction and inference about the independent variables, and for good reason. Linear regression has been around since the late 1800s and has evolved into a robust and flexible approach. One of the early "a-ha" moments with linear regression is that it can be used on data that is not actually linear. For example, look at the line in Figure 9-3. That line was fit to the data with linear regression.

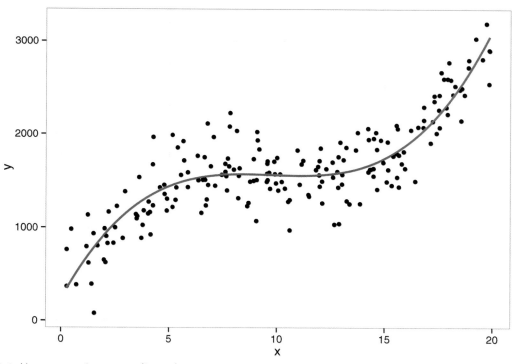

FIGURE 9-3 *Linear regression on non-linear data*

Can you see the linear relationship in Figure 9-3? Believe it or not, it's there. The *linear* part of linear regression is a reference to the *linear coefficients* estimated, not the data. In other words, you can use a linear model to describe non-linear data. The trick (although it's not really a trick) is to transform the data prior to running linear regression on it. Looking back at Figure 9-3, the relationship between x and y is a cubic polynomial, and some variation around $y = x^3$. Therefore, you would want to transform the x variable and include that in the model so you can estimate the (linear) coefficients for each of those variables. When transforming the variables like this, you must be careful not to overfit the data. It would be possible to add enough transformed variables to perfectly fit the training data, but such an approach would perform horribly on the test or real data.

Linear regression has many variations and nuances that make it powerful, especially when combined to some of the techniques mentioned earlier in this chapter. Classic linear regression relies on computing a p-value (see Chapter 5) to assess the strength of the model and variables. The recent trend is to also integrate validation methods such as cross-validation to support model selection and validation. See the `lm()` and `glm()` commands within R for the specifics on how to execute linear regression.

Logistic Regression

Although linear regression is designed for predicting quantitative variables, it isn't helpful when the problem isn't quantitative. For example, in the opening example, you needed to classify the hosts as infected or not; linear regression wouldn't be helpful in that circumstance. Instead, you can turn to logistic regression, which is an extension of linear regression. It models a yes/no output, that is, choosing between just two outcomes. Figure 9-4 shows logistic regression applied to that training data.

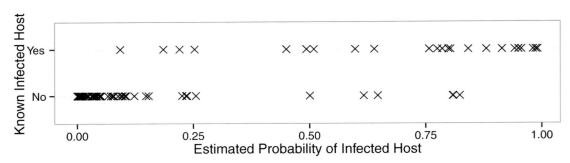

FIGURE 9-4 *Logistic regression on infection test data*

The output (on the x-axis) is an estimated probability of a host being infected based on the input variables. That output is plotted against the known value in the test data (on the y-axis, and remember the y-axis is not known in real life). It's clear that, given these input values, you would be able to estimate a large portion of the hosts correctly. No matter where the cutoff is set (for example, hosts above 0.4 are classified as "infected"), you will undoubtedly have some false positives (identifying hosts as infected when they are not) and false negatives (identifying hosts as not infected when they are). Traditionally, logistic regression is used to make a logical classification (this is or is not something). There are techniques for applying logistic regression to multiple categories, which we won't cover here.

Within R, there are several approaches to logistic regression; however, the `glm()` function can handle most situations.

K-Nearest Neighbors

The technique of k-nearest neighbors is best described using a generic sports analogy. Suppose you want to choose a person at random from anywhere in the world and predict his or her favorite sports teams. When you choose that person at random, you can ask his or her neighbors and friends ("k" of them, where k is any consistent number) which teams that person cheers for. Then, you determine which teams the majority of those neighbors cheer for and assume the person you plucked has similar taste as their neighbors.

The k-nearest neighbors algorithm does the same thing. Given a set of known (this is supervised algorithm) variables, for each new data point, this algorithm looks at the nearest k data points (you pick the value for k) and assumes that the new data point is like its neighbors. This gets away from the linear classification of the opening example. This approach increases in accuracy as the number of observations increases. One drawback is that it is sensitive to the selection of k. With very large values of k, this approach gets closer and closer to creating a linear boundary. Overall, the k-nearest neighbors can be a very effective classifier and outperform many other techniques. It's worth understanding.

Within R, the `class` package offers support for k-nearest neighbors (and other `knn` functions).

Random Forests

Random forests are built on the concept of the decision tree and excel at multidimensional data (data with a lot of features). The decision tree is what IT people think of as a flowchart. You start at the top of the tree and branch off in different directions, depending on the criteria within the tree compared to the observed features. Imagine the various types of decisions that could be built given data types—if the data is above average, fork here; if data fits into that category, go there. If you have complex data, you must use more than one decision tree. A technique called *boosting* was developed to create a whole lot of decision trees and then look at the aggregate result from all of them. Boosting provides a huge improvement. Although each individual tree performs poorly, they all performed poorly in a predictable spread around the best answer. Therefore, the best answer can be derived from looking at all the trees (see where this is going with the forest?).

Boosting decision trees works quite well, but it's influenced by noisy features. One or two bad eggs in the basket can bias the result by consistently pulling trees in a weird (and difficult to detect) direction. The random forest technique gets around that problem by growing the trees with only a small subset of the features. This makes each individual tree an even worse predictor, but the aggregate improves because the noisy variables are included only in a subset of the features selected for each tree, and not influenced by every tree in the forest.

Random forests bring a new way of thinking and are squarely in the non-parametric camp. They do not attempt to create a model of reality and then derive the parameters of the model (such as with regression techniques). Instead, random forests create a huge set of relatively weak predictors and then aggregate across them all. This is like going to a new town and asking only tourists for directions. Many of the answers will be way off, but if you look at the aggregation of all the answers, you'll probably get where you're going.

As you may be thinking, you would never attempt to apply the random forest technique with pencil and paper. This technique grows hundreds or even thousands of multi-branched decision trees based on random points in random features and can be done only with the aid of a computer. Within R, random forests are available from the appropriately named `randomForest` package. It's also worthwhile to explore parallel processing solutions, and the R package `doParallel` offers a good solution for spreading the processing across multiple cores and reducing the computational time needed for random forests.

Comprehension versus Performance

One of the challenges with machine learning is that some of the techniques are so complex and abstract that they push the boundaries of human comprehension. At some point, you'll reach a trade-off between the ability to comprehend an approach and the performance it brings. Neural networks are an example of this trade-off. In some cases, neural networks offer better performance, but they are rather complex and difficult to comprehend and difficult to tune properly without that comprehension. You may opt for an approach that is easier to comprehend, easier to explain to others, and easier to use at the expense of a slight deterioration in performance, and you should be comfortable with that. Given the complex nature of many decisions with information security, any approach with machine learning is better than any decision without machine learning.

Unsupervised

As we mentioned earlier in this chapter, unsupervised approaches are quite useful to find underlying patterns and relationships in the data. Given some pile of data, what kinds of trends exist in there?

K-Means Clustering

K-means, like k-nearest neighbor, uses the "k" to represent a variable that you will set as part of the approach. The k in this technique represents the number of clusters to be generated. The k-means approach follows the following algorithm:

1. Set k "center points" randomly among the data.
2. Assign all the data points to the nearest center point.
3. Calculate a new (mean) center of the data points assigned.
4. Move the center points to the new calculated (mean) center.
5. Repeat Steps 2-4 until all centers no longer move in Step 4.

Notice how Step 1 in the k-means technique uses randomness? This means that if you rerun a k-means clustering, you may get different clusters. Figure 9-5 shows the same data with multiple different k-values. The `kmeans()` function in base R will perform k-means clustering.

Hierarchical Clustering

The downside to k-means is that you have to specify the number of clusters. This is where hierarchical clustering can help by deriving all of the clusters within the data. The output of hierarchical clustering is called a ***dendrogram*** (see Figure 9-7 later in this chapter) and looks like a tree, starting at the top and branching off into two groups at a time until all of the objects are in their own cluster. Algorithmically, the approach actually starts at the bottom with everything in its own cluster. It then scans across all the pairs, comparing and looking for the most similar pairing. When it finds similar clusters, it will combine those two. This repeats until there is one cluster with everything at the top.

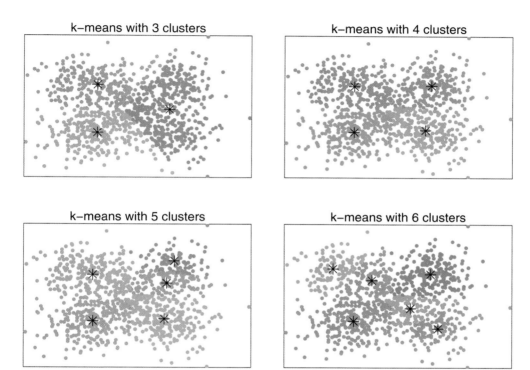

FIGURE 9-5 *K-means clustering with centers shown*

The advantage to hierarchical clustering is that it is possible to "cut" the tree down and inspect the clusters at any point in the tree, which is what you'll do later in this chapter when you use the `hclust()` function on breach data.

Principal Component Analysis

Principal component analysis (PCA) reduces the number of features you look at to those that really matter and is one of a few techniques to perform this ***dimension reduction***. PCA works best on data that is highly correlated because it can capture most of the variation in the data with a reduced number of variables. The outcome of PCA is a list of derived components ordered by how much variance they describe in the data. Once the data is reduced to that format, you can pull out the significant components and use those moving forward rather than the larger (and possibly noisy) number of dimensions. Running PCA in R requires the single command of `prcomp()`.

Multidimensional Scaling

Sometimes you'll just want to see the clusters. This can be problematic with multidimensional data because you cannot visualize in more than three dimensions (and even that third dimension is tough on a flat screen or paper). The solution is to use a technique called *multidimensional scaling* (MDS). Like PCA, MDS performs dimension reduction. It can squish the multidimensional data into two dimensions so you can visualize the relative similarities between objects. You'll run through an example of this technique later in this chapter, using the R command `cmdscale()` for classic multidimensional scaling. In the next section you will see the output of multidimensional scaling when applied to the industries of breach data.

Hands On: Clustering Breach Data

In this section, you revisit the VERIS community database (VCDB) data you used in Chapter 7 in order to see multidimensional scaling and hierarchical clustering in action.

The natural approach to breach data is to simply count the categories, see what occurs more often, and then draw some conclusions from that information. But the challenge with that approach is that any conclusions drawn may be applied too broadly if the conclusions don't apply across the board. After working with breach data for a while, it becomes clear that different industries have different problems. Each industry shares some common traits, like they all deal with the same type of information, causing some industries to be targeted more or less than others. Organizations in the same industry are more likely to copy others in the same industry, so the breach data may also show some type of pattern because of that.

The problem then is this:

Just how different (or similar) are the incidents across industries?

This is a rather interesting challenge because the only thing you start with is a hunch that industries are in fact, different. The best approach to this question is in some of the clustering algorithm. If you can isolate variables across the industries, you can calculate a "distance" between the industries in order to determine which are alike and which display some unique traits.

You'll begin this analysis by converting the VCDB data to a matrix (see Listing 9-8). You haven't read much about matrices in R, but they are similar to a data frame in that they have fixed row and column widths (think of spreadsheet cells, which are "rows" long and "columns" wide). The unique aspect of matrices is that they can contain only one type of variable (such as just characters or just numbers). For this work, you will convert the VCDB to a numeric matrix. Luckily, the `verisr` package has a function for just such an occasion, and it's appropriately called `veris2matrix()`. Begin by loading the `verisr` package (see Listing 7-5 in Chapter 7 if you haven't installed it yet).

LISTING 9-8

```
# requires package : verisr (7-5)
# requires VCDB data from chapter 7 (see comments)
library(verisr)
# if you have grabbed the incidents from the VCDB repository at
```

```
# https://github.com/vz-risk/VCDB you can set the directory to that
# Otherwise, this should reference the data from chapter 7
jsondir <- '../ch07/data/vcdb/'
# create a veris instance with the vcdb data
vcdb <- json2veris(jsondir)
# finally, you can convert veris object into a numeric matrix
vmat <- veris2matrix(vcdb)
# you may look at the size of
# the matrix with the dim() command
dim(vmat)
## [1] 1643   264
```

Looking at the output from the `dim()` command, the data from VCDB at this point is providing 1,643 rows (one row per incident in the data repository) and 264 columns. Each column is a single enumeration in the data, and you can see what the columns are by looking at the column names with the `colnames()` command. When `veris2matrix()` creates the matrix, it will create a unique column for every enumeration it sees within the VERIS data. For example, if the hacking variety of a SQL injection attack is present, one column in the matrix will be `action.hacking.variety.SQLi` and the column will be a 0 or a 1, depending on if that particular value was present in the incident, and will be set for all the incidents in the matrix. If none of the incidents is recorded with SQL injection, the whole column will not be present. The entire matrix is just a collection of ones and zeros at this point. This matrix isn't directly helpful as is, but it will serve as the base data from which you'll generate the training data.

Next, you'll identify the variables that you want to compare—the victim industries. In order to get that list, you can simply look at the column names, pull out columns with `victim.industry` in the title, and use them as the variables (see Listing 9-9). You will want to pass that into the function from `verisr` called `foldmatrix()`, which will take in the numeric matrix you just created and the list of variables you're going to fold this matrix on (the victim industries).

You will also pass in two other variables. The first variable is `min`, which enables you to set a minimum threshold for the number of incidents in each industry. If an industry has less than the minimum, it will not be included in the analysis. For this exercise, you'll set `10` as the minimum. The last variable to pass in is `clean`, which asks the function to clean up the final matrix by removing the rows less than the minimum and any columns that are all the same. You will need to clean it up since those variables will not contribute to the analysis. If you were using this approach to do PCA analysis, it would throw an error if you didn't first clean up the matrix.

LISTING 9-9

```
# requires package : verisr (7-5),
# requires object : vmat (9-8)
# now pull the column names and extract industries
vmat.names <- colnames(vmat)
industry <- vmat.names[grep('victim.industry', vmat.names)]
# "fold" the matrix on industries
# this pulls all the incidents for the industry
# and compresses so the proportions of the features are represented.
```

(continues)

LISTING 9-9   *(continued)*

```
imat <- foldmatrix(vmat, industry, min=10, clean=T)
dim(imat)
## [1]  17 251
```

There were 17 industries (actually 17 unique two-digit industry codes from the NAICS specification discussed in Chapter 7). It also looks like the function cleaned up 13 columns after folding the matrix. Now you have one row per industry; the columns represent a VERIS variable, and the value represents the proportion of incidents in the industry with the VERIS variable present.

For example, if you were looking at healthcare and SQL injection (again), and 40 of the 100 healthcare incidents involved SQL injection, you would see a 0.4 in the column of `action.hacking.variety.SQLi` in the healthcare row. This is where the comparison occurs. You compare the differences in all of these variables across the industries.

Multidimensional Scaling on Victim Industries

The purpose of all that prep work was to get the data ready to apply some multidimensional scaling to the industries. And finally, this is where the magic happens! As with many tasks within data analysis, you spent more time preparing the data than you spend actually running the analysis. The first command converts your matrix of industries and variables into a distance matrix. This matrix uses the Canberra metric of distance (it does better with values around the origin) to calculate a distance metric between each pair of industries. Then you can feed that distance matrix into the `cmdscale()` function, which projects it onto a two-dimensional plane for plotting (see Listing 9-10).

LISTING 9-10

```
# requires object : imat (9-9), vmat (9-8),
# convert the distance matrix
idist <- dist(imat, method='canberra')
# run it through classical MDS
cmd <- cmdscale(idist)
# and take a look at the first few rows returned
head(cmd)
##                              [,1]        [,2]
## victim.industry2.32 -75.080869 -50.662403
## victim.industry2.33 -29.457487  -2.942502
## victim.industry2.42 -24.727909  21.751872
## victim.industry2.44   3.692422   7.840992
## victim.industry2.45 -18.855236  93.787627
## victim.industry2.48 -54.382350  23.166301
```

Look at what is returned from `cmdscale()`. It looks ready to be visualized because those are x and y points. In fact, at this point you could run `plot(cmd)` and see where those points are. However, the points would be unlabeled, and it's worth it to spend some time to create a good-looking plot. In a final plot, it'd be nice if you gave some indication of size per industry, and since you still have that original `vmat` matrix, you should be able to pull out a count of incidents in each industry. Then you should fix those labels because the VERIS data deals with the NAICS industry codes. Although very helpful, the industry codes are not all that user friendly. You can get nicer labels by loading the `industry2` data in the `verisr` package and mapping the industry codes to the shorter labels (see Listing 9-11).

LISTING 9-11
```
# requires package : verisr (7-5),
# requires object : cmd (9-10), vmat (9-8),
# get the size of bubbles
ind.counts <- colSums(vmat[ , rownames(cmd)])
# extract the industry label
ind.label <- sapply(rownames(cmd), function(x) {
  tail(unlist(strsplit(x, "[.]")), 1)
})
# load up industry data, included with verisr package
data(industry2)
# create a new list of short tet
txt.label <- industry2$short[which(industry2$code %in% ind.label)]
```

And now you have variables called `ind.counts` and `txt.label` in the same order as the `cmd` object. Now you can create a data frame and create a plot with `ggplot2` (Listing 9-12).

LISTING 9-12
```
# requires package : ggplot2
# requires object : cmd (9-10), ind.counts, txt.label (9-11)
library(ggplot2)
indf <- data.frame(x=cmd[ ,1], y=cmd[, 2], label=txt.label,
                   size=ind.counts)
gg <- ggplot(indf, aes(x, y, label=label, size=size))
gg <- gg + scale_size(trans="log2", range=c(10,30), guide=F)
gg <- gg + geom_point(fill="lightsteelblue", color="white", shape=21)
gg <- gg + xlim(range(indf$x)*1.1) # expand x scale
gg <- gg + geom_text(size=4)
gg <- gg + theme(panel.grid = element_blank(),
                 panel.border = element_blank(),
                 panel.background = element_blank(),
                 axis.text = element_blank(),
                 axis.title = element_blank(),
                 axis.ticks = element_blank())
print(gg)
```

You use the ggplot `theme()` command to strip out everything because the scales and labels are irrelevant for viewing. You want to view the relative location of the industries in respect to other industries. In this plot the x- and y-axes are a distance measurement using the Canberra metric, and the numbers don't have any meaning or significance for a person viewing them.

Figure 9-6 is rather interesting. You can see that healthcare and government (public) victims appear to be similar (probably due to the large amount of lost devices and error that is reported within those demographics). The little cluster on the top of accommodation and retail is interesting. Those two industries see the bulk of the "point of sale smash and grab" attacks. The cluster of three in the lower-left corner might be worth more investigation. It's hard to say exactly why those three are grouped up there without looking further into the data.

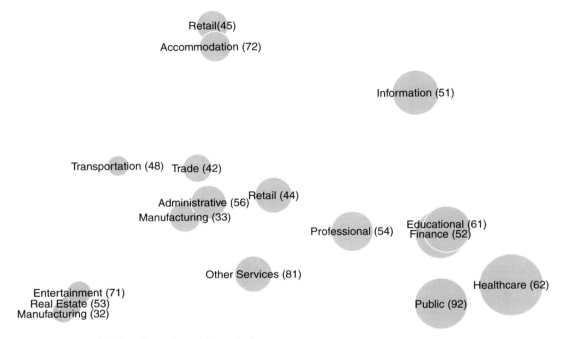

FIGURE 9-6 *Basic MDS plot of breaches within an industry*

Hierarchical Clustering on Victim Industries

Although it's possible to look at Figure 9-6 and make some clusters visually, you should be careful in doing so. MDS reduces (approximates) a multidimensional object into two dimensions so there will be some perspective and detail lost. Figure 9-6 can serve as a visual to some talking points or, better yet, a point from which to jump into more analysis.

So let's keep going with this data and apply some hierarchical clustering on this data to derive the clusters mathematically. You can simply feed the `idist` distance matrix right into the `hclust` command and plot it (Listing 9-13). To make the labels on the plot user friendly, you should relabel the rows of the original industry matrix and rerun the `dist()` command to recreate the `idist` object with readable labels:

LISTING 9-13
```
# requires object : imat (9-9), txt.label (9-11)
# go back and relabel imat
```

```
rownames(imat) <- txt.label
# rerun idist
idist <- dist(imat, 'canberra')
# hclust couldn't be easier
hc <- hclust(idist) # , method="complete")
plot(hc)
```

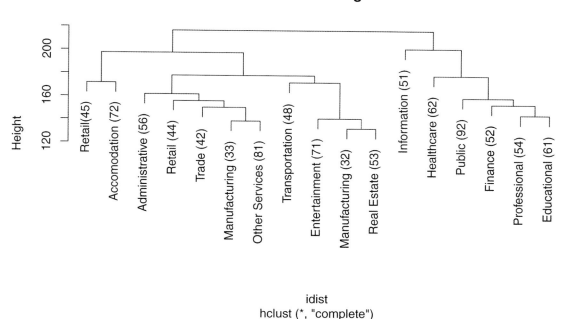

Cluster Dendrogram

idist
hclust (*, "complete")

FIGURE 9-7 *Hierarchical clustering on victim industries*

From Figure 9-7, you can see how and when things are split off into clusters. The end result is that they are all "clustered" into their own groups since each is unique. Now you can use the `cutree()` command to cut the hierarchical tree down into an appropriate number of clusters. You can try whatever number you like, but this example shows six clusters. Since you are subjectively choosing where to cut the tree, you cannot use this approach to prove there are six clusters here (or however many you choose). But what you can say is that, if the hierarchical cluster is cut at six, these are the clusters it produces. Of course, many people won't have a clue what you're talking about, but at least now you do.

When you run the `cutree()` command, it will take in the output from the `hclust()` command and the number of clusters to cut it off at. It will return a vector of the numbered clusters that each industry is assigned. You can then use that vector to assign a unique fill color per cluster so the plot will visually be clustered by color (Listing 9-14). You do this by converting the `cutree()` command to a factor and then adding it to the `indf` object created previously. Then plot it again with the colors, as shown in Figure 9-8.

```
LISTING 9-14
# requires package : ggplot2
# requires object : indf (9-12), hc (9-13)
# we can now cut off the heirarchical clustering at some level
# and use those levels to color the MDS plot
indf$cluster <- as.factor(cutree(hc, 6))
gg <- ggplot(indf, aes(x, y, label=label, size=size, fill=cluster))
gg <- gg + scale_size(trans="log2", range=c(10,30), guide=F)
gg <- gg + geom_point(color="gray80", shape=21)
gg <- gg + scale_fill_brewer(palette="Set2")
gg <- gg + xlim(range(indf$x)*1.06) # expand x scale
gg <- gg + geom_text(size=4)
gg <- gg + theme(panel.grid = element_blank(),
                 panel.border = element_blank(),
                 panel.background = element_blank(),
                 axis.text = element_blank(),
                 axis.title = element_blank(),
                 legend.position="none",
                 axis.ticks = element_blank())
print(gg)
```

Remember earlier we mentioned that this process converts multi-dimensional data into two dimensions? In looking at Figure 9-8, you can see how the transportation industry is clustered with the industries in the lower left, instead of the visually closer trade industry. Feel free to try changing experimenting with the number of clusters fed into the `cuttree` command. What you can take away from this particular visualization is that there are a lot more questions than answers from it. Why is healthcare in its own cluster? Why is the retail industry with NAICS code 44 so distant from the retail industry with NAICS code 45? What is going on in the Information industry that they are out on their own like that? The good news is that we've got the data, and the answers to these questions are just waiting to be discovered.

Summary

Open source applications like R and Python have made running machine learning algorithms accessible and relatively easy. However, there is a big difference between running a machine learning algorithm and running a machine learning algorithm *well*. Like it or not, machine learning has very deep roots in statistics and mathematics. Attempting to dive into these techniques without an understanding of the subtleties and nuances may create more problems than they solve. Having said that, the best way to learn is to jump in head first and splash around. Grab (or generate) data, read the blogs, books, and documentation, and try several approaches. I can guarantee there will be some frustration along the way, but the outcome will be better learning and an overall better understanding of the data and, thus, the world around you. Such knowledge can feed directly into the security decisions you and your organization are facing on a daily basis.

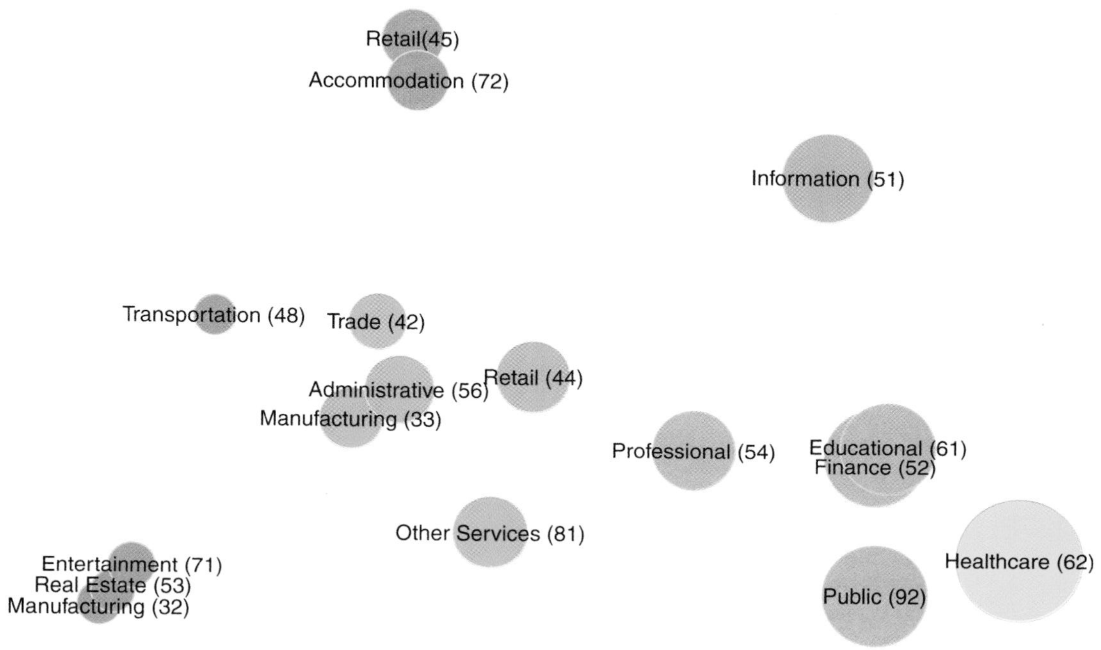

FIGURE 9-8 *Clustered MDS plot of victim industries*

Recommended Reading

The following are some recommended readings that can further your understanding on some of the topics we touch on in this chapter. For full information on these recommendations and for the sources we cite in the chapter, please see Appendix B.

Machine Learning for Hackers **by Drew Conway and John Myles White**—There aren't many machine learning books for beginners, but this book is one of them. It does a very good job at giving hands-on examples in both R and Python. They avoid most of the math but not the challenges with the approaches. Overall, this is a good first book to purchase.

An Introduction to Statistical Learning with Applications in R **by Gareth James, Daniela Witten, Trevor Hastie, and Robert Tibshirani**—As you progress beyond the basics and begin looking for that next step, this book is a fantastic next resource. It doesn't shy away from the math, but at the same time, it doesn't dive too deep into it and provides just enough explanation to make sense. The authors spend quite a bit of time on the algorithms, including covering resampling methods, model-selection techniques, and the foundations of all the algorithms.

10

Designing Effective Security Dashboards

"Perfection is achieved, not when there is nothing more to add, but when there is nothing left to take away."

Antoine de Saint-Exupéry, ***Airman's Odyssey***

Just when you thought it was safe to leave the comfort of your analytics lab to grab another caffeinated beverage you find yourself in a conversation with one of the security managers and are asked the inevitable and dreaded question, "Can you help us build a security dashboard?" If that sentence did not cause even a flicker of your own fight-or-flight response, you may not truly understand the difficulty of designing succinct, meaningful displays of quantitative information in order to drive some type of action. This chapter presents techniques and advice that will enable you to design dashboards to help measure, monitor, and mobilize every layer of security in your organization.

What Is a Dashboard, Anyway?

It's nigh impossible to discuss the subject of dashboards without quoting the definition of *dashboard* coined by the "Godfather" of dashboards, Stephen Few:

> *"A dashboard is a visual display of the most important information needed to achieve one or more objectives that has been consolidated in a single computer screen [or printed page] so it can be monitored at a glance."*
>
> —**Stephen Few**, *Information Dashboard Design*

We've added "or printed page" since organizations are still quite fond of paper, and there are special design considerations when including printed output.

We can make Few's definition a bit more real by phrasing it another way: A dashboard provides a single screen/page opportunity to provide the most critical/relevant information in the most concise and effective ways possible to enable the viewer to quickly understand the elements being described and, if necessary, make the most appropriate decision(s).

If you present data that is irrelevant, your dashboard will not be used. If you have too many or too complex encodings, your dashboard will be ignored. If it's ugly . . . well, at least you won't be asked to make dashboards anymore! Dashboard creation truly is a daunting endeavor. To fully grasp the nuances of what a dashboard *is* we'll start by chipping away at the marble block of what a dashboard *is not* to reveal the underlying true nature.

A Dashboard Is Not an Automobile

The term *dashboard* originally referred to a board in a horse-drawn carriage that helped prevent mud from splashing on occupants. When the automobile was invented, the term morphed into something that we all recognize today as the crucial set of performance indicators available to drivers. It was this familiarity (almost everyone knows what an automobile dashboard is) that caused the computer industry to associate the term with the summary displays in executive information systems.

The automobile dashboard has the elements it does because they make sense in context. Gauges react to the point-in-time changes we make when accelerating or decelerating; we get an accurate—but not necessarily precise—understanding of fuel supply and battery condition; and, we know how far we've gone—all at a quick glance. Somewhere along the way, designers of executive information systems forgot the concept of "makes sense in context" and brought these (and other) real-world elements into the digital world.

Gauges, dials, thermometers, stoplights, and other skeuomorphic elements consume valuable space and rarely communicate information better than other visual elements, but they **can** hold useful information, including:

- Current value of key measure(s)

- Comparison to target measure(s)

- A range of possible values of the measure(s) with a qualitative association

Consider Splunk's dashboard example for "Notable Events by Security Domain" gauges in Figure 10-1. The gauges are **huge** and the information displayed in each—47, 81, 8, 2, 31, 30—is repeated in the top-level labels, making them also redundant. It's also hard to mentally correlate the gauge needle position to any type of urgency, since each one has a giant red arrow above it, but not all needles are in the red zone on the gauge.

FIGURE 10-1 *Sample Splunk dashboard*

If you apply the knowledge gained from Chapter 6, you can combine a few basic plots to make what's known as a **bullet graph** and replace the skeuomorphic gauges (see Figure 10-2), although you have to invent some of the comparative measures and guess at the quantitative scale since the original did not encode those well (or at all). This new view makes it much easier to see where you are exceeding event thresholds in various areas than you could in the figure using the gauges.

The value change is also important to display, but the giant red, upward-pointing arrows in Figure 10-1 do not help to tell an accurate story. You can augment the bullet graph with paired sparklines—"data-intense, design-simple, word-sized graphics" (from Tufte and Graves-Morris, 1983, which you can find in the references in Appendix B of this book)—of each 24-hour measure to provide a quick picture of what happened in the various event streams. See Figure 10-4.

The file `ch10/R/bullet.R` on the book's website (`www.wiley.com/go/data drivensecurity`) shows how to create bullet graphs in R, but you can easily create basic bullet graphs in Google Charts by building a simple URL such as (enter the following as one, contiguous line in your browser or look at the example in `ch10/docs/bullet.html`):

```
http://chart.apis.google.com/chart?cht=bhs&chs=250x30&chd=t:93
&chm=r,DDDDDD,0,0.0,0.57|r,999999,0,0.57,0.85|r,888888,0,0.85,
1.0|r,FF0000,0,0.85,0.86&chco=000000&chbh=15
```

You can even use Excel to make enhanced visualization elements. The source for the sparklines used in Figure 10-4 can be found in `ch10/docs/ch10-sparklines.xlsx`, and Excel offers both sparkline and sparkbar chart options with many options for customization.

Ironically, Splunk has a rich visualization library that includes bullet graphs and sparklines, so if you're building your dashboards in that tool, ditch the gauges and switch to the more informative options.

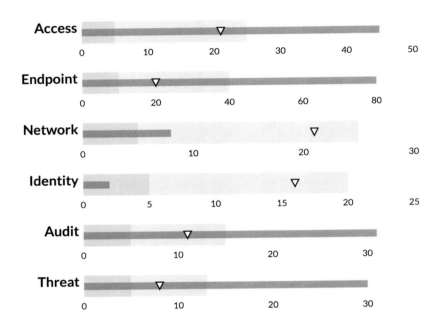

FIGURE 10-2 *Bullet graph makeover*

A Dashboard Is Not a Report

IT and information security professionals tend to be very detail-oriented people. They are the type of people who get excited at the "show your work" directive on school assignments and love to dig into the details to show folks how they arrived at their conclusions. It's absolutely necessary to have multiple levels of detail behind the dashboards you create to enable verification/validation and to support drilling into specific areas as needed. However, the top-level view should be designed solely to give the viewer situational awareness of the desired task. Just because the onboard diagnostic system in an automobile *can* tell you the value of the "Bank 2, Sensor 3: Oxygen sensor voltage, Short term fuel trim" does not mean that we need another gauge in our cars that displays this value while we're driving. The "check engine" light is enough for us to know that something requires more deliberate attention and detailed examination.

Bullet Graph Basics

The bullet graph is a fairly new chart type, especially when compared to more traditional visualizations, such as bar charts and line graphs. It was invented in 2005 by Stephen Few as a way to incorporate the positive attributes of gauges into a more utilitarian graphic. As such, there is a bit of a learning curve both in creating them (encoding) and understanding (decoding) them.

As seen in Figure 10-3, there are five core components of a bullet graph:

- A bar that encodes the **performance measure** of the actual item you are measuring and trying to communicate the value of
- The overall **scale** of measures
- At least one marker with a **comparison measure**
- Background shades or colors that represent qualitative ranges for values
- A label for the bullet graph

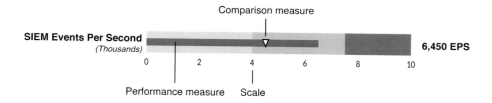

FIGURE 10-3 *Elements of a bullet graph*

The sixth component shown in Figure 10-3—the actual value of the number of events per second being processed by the security information and event management (SIEM) system on the right side—is optional, but useful if your viewers need more precision.

Although these examples are sized a bit larger for the purposes of explanation, bullet graphs resize/shrink quite well without losing their ability to communicate effectively and efficiently.

Do not take this caution to mean that you shouldn't use text, lists, and tables in a dashboard. Those elements are valid to include where you need precision, provided they support quick perception, comprehension, and a call to action. If you wanted to communicate number of events per second being processed by the SIEM from Figure 10-3 with just straight text, there are multiple possibilities to choose from, as shown in Figure 10-5, including plain text or colored text (if highlighting the value as "interesting"), or even a simple textual table. If you really just need to drive action without presenting underlying detail, the simple "Variance +43%" statement should be enough to motivate someone to find out why the system is suddenly seeing 43 percent more events than usual.

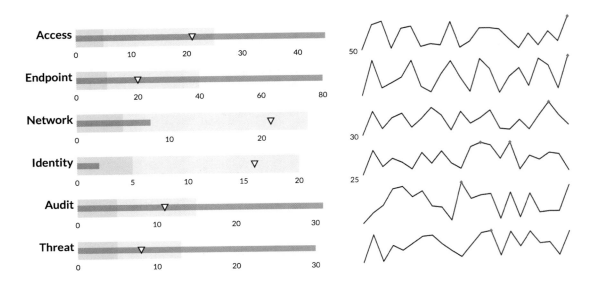

FIGURE 10-4 *Sparklines*

SIEM EPS 6,450

SIEM EPS 6,450

	Current	Normal	Variance %
SIEM EPS	6,450	4,500	+43%

SIEM EPS Variance +43%

FIGURE 10-5 *Encoding measures with text*

As indicated in Chapter 6, it's usually best to display a graphic instead of large amounts of tabular data. Numbers and text always require attention whereas shapes and colors can draw attention preattentively. Just be ready to call up specific values or provide a data table if there is a call to action that requires a detailed review before making a decision. This can be easily done online, since most dashboard-creation tools provide some sort of drill-down capability. For printed or non-interactive dashboards, you can provide a standalone, supplemental report or a link to an online resource that supports further investigation.

When Dashboards Fail

Dashboards establish a partnership between the viewers and producers. Viewers need to trust that the summarized views they are interpreting represent a good-faith attempt on the part of the producers to provide the most accurate data in the most effective way possible. Similarly, producers must have some assurance that the "messenger won't be shot" for providing honest, accurate information.

This seems obvious, but how many times have you been in a dashboard review meeting where you cringed at some measure being reported as acceptable when you *knew* that there was cause for concern (especially as it relates to the status of highly visible projects). This is a situation even the most elegantly crafted dashboard cannot resolve. Chapter 6 presented the concept of "truth" as it relates to data, and it's vital that a dashboard always display truthful measures if an organization is serious about managing operations with them.

Dashboards also fail when they regularly miscommunicate or overcommunicate the performance measures. It's a far easier task to make a lazy guess and put a green stoplight in a PowerPoint document than it is to admit you don't have enough real data to back the analysis and quantification of an important measure. Similarly, if the viewers always review the supporting material for every performance measure, they probably don't trust the producers and should trade their dashboards in for reports.

A Dashboard Is Not a Moving Van

Boxes are great for shipping items, but they are detrimental to the effective display of information on a dashboard, as seen in Figure 10-6.

Most of the elements contained in those boxes are themselves boxes, making the extra framing redundant. Excessive framing is often an issue with online dashboards. This is because many interfaces tend to align items in singular cells in a fixed grid and provide options for "on-the-fly" modification.

Figure 10-7 shows a transformation of Figure 10-6 using Microsoft Excel. You start by removing superfluous markings, borders, and annotations. We also take the opportunity to change the encoding of some of the measures to enhance the readability.

Whitespace now frames each element and there is a more cohesive feel to the entire dashboard. We've removed the map, since a color-coded table is a better choice for the type of information displayed. We've also replaced the "funnel" with a normalized, grouped bullet graph. We significantly reduced the "chartjunk" and used a more subdued but deliberate color. You can find an Excel version of most of the components for this example in `ch10/docs/ch10-overhaul.xlsx` on the book's website at `www.wiley.com/go/datadrivensecurity`, which should be a good starting point for your own dashboard makeovers.

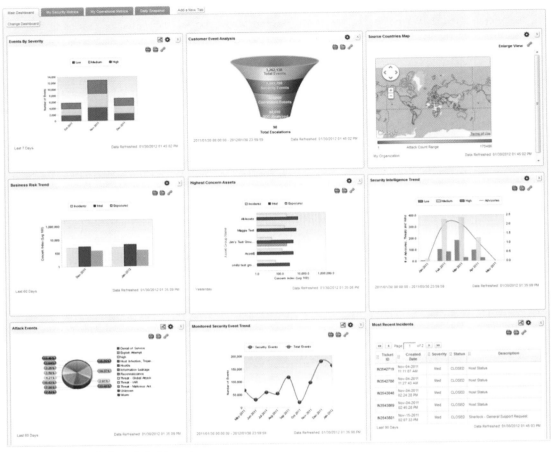

FIGURE 10-6 *Sample "boxy" dashboard*

There are still some core issues with this dashboard. The individual elements seem haphazardly chosen and put together with almost no opportunity for logical groupings. The foremost issue is that there are no indicators of what is good or bad (we had to fabricate thresholds for the bullet graphs in order to use them). Without those indicators, a dashboard like this more appropriately belongs in the "report" category, although it falls short of those requirements as well.

Dashboard Excel-lence

We chose to model the dashboard in Figure 10-7 in Excel, as this will likely be the only tool available to most readers. Books dedicated to dashboards often provide examples of perfect dashboards that require specialized tools or post-processing by hand in applications like Adobe Illustrator to generate. With a *little* extra effort, it *is* possible to make well-designed charts, graphs, and dashboards in Excel.

It's important to note that the single-cell, fixed-grid is not your only option. Different layouts can layer on top of a virtual landscape grid to provide more room for larger or more prominent chart types or to allow for logical groupings of elements that naturally fit together. You must take your output medium into consideration when planning your dashboard elements and layout. Your dashboard may look wonderful on the 27-inch "retina" display where you designed it, but it may be unintelligible on a standard resolution, 15-inch laptop screen. There may also be times when a vertical (portrait) layout works better with your data, so you should not box yourself into a corner by having only one layout system handy.

FIGURE 10-7 *Dashboard makeover*

Be sure to follow the advice on eye movements in Chapter 6 and reserve the upper-left area for the most critical information that needs attention by your viewers.

A Dashboard Is Not an Art Show

Given the graphical nature of dashboards, it's easy to fall into the trap of making them look like pieces of modern (or fringe) art when they are far more akin to architectural/industrial diagrams that require more controlled, deliberate, and constrained design. To put it simply: Just because you *can* do some-thing in the context of a dashboard does not mean you *should*. Take Figure 10-8 (from `http://www`
`.securitywizardry.com/radar.htm`), for example.

This is an example of a situational awareness dashboard from Security Wizardry. It uses the "modern" light-on-black design with quite a diversity of colors and tries to pull in data from multiple sources. It's "glitzy" but it is not informative.

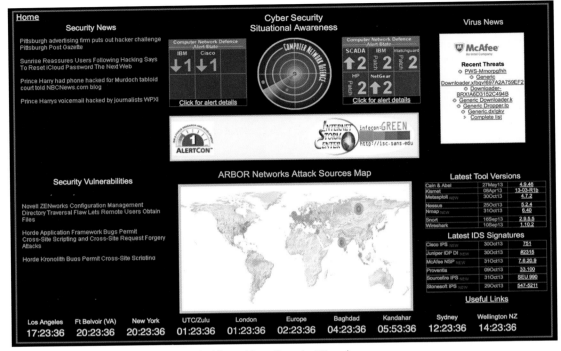

Figure 10-8 *Example of a monitoring dashboard from Security Wizardry*

The system dashboard in Figure 10-9 pushes the artistic envelope even further with considerable use of various 3D charts. If you can overlook the redundancy between the "Recently Completed Scans" and "Current Threat Level" panels (even with the discrepancy between where the gauge reports the value versus the marked, segmented bar), you are faced with having to spend real mental cycles processing 3D shapes for "Current License Usage" and "Total Vulnerabilities Last 12 Months" when a simple numeric value would have sufficed. The pyramid in the "Vulnerability Severities" forces you to perform even more cognitive processing to decode and inverts the usual "most critical on top" rule that is usually associated with triangular charts. In other words, you spend far more time deciphering and decoding these panels than understanding what information they are trying to convey and reacting to those messages.

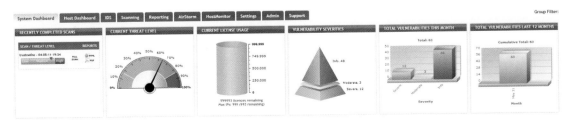

Figure 10-9 *-3D dashboard*

To be effective, dashboards must be pleasant to view, so there must be *some* amount of artistic choice going into the creation. However, it's necessary to design within constraints. It's similar to the difference between free verse poetry and more formal types—such as a haiku or a Shakespearean sonnet—where constraints provide context for creativity without muting it in any way. Likewise, there are some design guidelines that can help channel your creative side when building dashboards.

Limit Chart Types

When encoding information into a chart, stick with the ones that are easiest for viewers to decode. Some good choices are:

- Bar graphs/bullet graphs
- Dot plots/scatterplots
- Line graphs/sparklines
- Boxplots
- Spatial maps/heatmaps/treemaps

Limit the diversity of chart types used in any single dashboard and ensure that the chart you've chosen is the most appropriate one for the type of information you are encoding. Tools such as Chart Chooser (`http://labs.juiceanalytics.com/chartchooser/index.html`) by Juice Analytics and Chart Suggestions (`http://extremepresentation.typepad.com/files/choosing-a-good-chart-09.pdf`) can help refresh your memory if that book isn't handy and you are unsure which chart to use.

Remember Space Constraints

You have one page or screen. That's it. Choose the best encoding element for the medium you are using. This may mean re-thinking the types of elements you choose if you learn that your viewers prefer viewing information on their phones or mini-tablet-sized screens.

You should also be wary of cramming elements into that single screen and use whitespace whenever possible to group and separate elements. If the information density of the dashboard is too high to enable the use of whitespace, subtle placement of very light lines and borders can facilitate the same grouping and separation.

Take Care with Colors

Choose a focused color palette and stick with it throughout the dashboard. Color has a strong ability to tie elements together, even when they are separated onscreen. Your viewers may draw erroneous correlations if your dashboard lacks color consistency. Take a look back at Figure 10-7. We deliberately used consistent colors for categorical measures—(High, Medium, Low) and (Incidents, Intel, Exposures)—to logically tie elements with similar attributes together even though they were not physically grouped together.

Remember the lessons of Chapter 6 and also consider that your digital creations may find their way to black-and-white laser printers more often than you would like to admit. The charts in the dashboard in Figure 10-7 lose much of their meaning when they become black and white (Figure 10-10). In this case, we knew our graphics were destined for a four-color press. Make sure *your* creations can withstand such a transformation without completely losing their meaning.

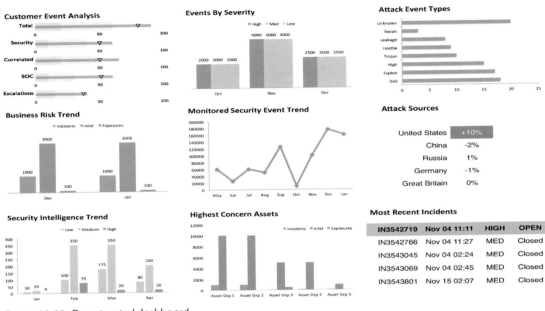

FIGURE 10-10 *De-saturated dashboard*

Use Fonts Wisely

Stick to a single font if at all possible. Choose serif (such as Palatino or Times New Roman) or sans-serif (such as Verdana or Arial) and be consistent where and how you apply the font. If you look to more modern or esoteric font choices, be sure to select one that scales consistently, supports variable width text, and has fixed-width numbers. Finally, use **bold**, *italics*, and color sparingly with fonts to highlight only the most important qualitative elements.

No One Dashboard to Rule Them All

DASHBOARD EVOLUTION

From their first physical incarnations, dashboards have been living, evolving organisms. For example, the dashboard on the Ford Model T—produced in 1908—contained a single element: an *ammeter* (an instrument used to measure the electric current) that helped show the health of ignition system. It was one of the only components that could not be visually inspected without a specialized instrument. To know the status of gas reserves, you just checked the dipstick. To see whether the car was overheating, you just looked for the signs of smoke and steam coming out of the engine compartment!

(continues)

(continued)

Drivers who were concerned about violating the speed limit (8 mph city/20 mph highway at that time) *could* purchase an optional speedometer, which eventually joined the ammeter as standard equipment years later. It was also possible to replace the radiator cap with a *motometer*, a very fancy and expensive temperature gauge that was more ornamental than operational (perhaps a sign of things to come in modern dashboards?). As drivers became more dependent on the automobile, other elements were added to the dashboard out of both need and convenience.

Dashboards in many modern vehicles retain most of the same elements as the updated Model T instrument panel, but some require new and customized elements to, say, monitor the performance of their electric, natural gas, or hybrid systems. Similarly, vehicles that can switch between two-wheel and four-wheel drive require a special indicator letting the driver know which mode they are operating in.

An Iterative Process

This same process of evolution and customization should occur in the digital realm where each dashboard must be tailored to:

- The specific process(es) being monitored
- The viewers of the information
- The display medium
- The data available for encoding
- The expected update frequency

For example, when creating a dashboard for the chief information security office (CISO), it's unlikely that executive will care about the number of events per second being processed by the SIEM. However, this is a performance measure that the Security Operations Manager may be keenly interested in, especially when if there have been performance issues with the SIEM.

Indeed, if SIEM issues are emerging, you should consider adding salient performance measures to the interactive, daily or weekly operations dashboard until the situation is resolved. Once stable, the measure can be replaced with other important items requiring evaluation and response. Thoughtful, regular updates to dashboard's core content will help keep it fresh and—more importantly—reviewed and processed by your viewers. *If a dashboard developed 2 years ago has never changed a single element, chances are good that your organization is not using dashboards effectively.*

The only way to know what truly belongs on a dashboard is to have regular dialogue with the various viewers/process owners to understand what *they* care about and inform them as to *what data is available*. Ask them to identify what they view as the model for the processes or objectives they find most important. Ask them how they mentally assess the efficacy of those models now and then ask them what data would help support a more quantitative view of this model. This will help you make the dashboard a success while also identifying and resolving gaps in your ability to provide situational awareness for a given process.

Communicating and Managing "Security" through Dashboards

There is an inherent "call to action" nature to dashboards, with each element being either quantitative (has a value) or categorical (a list of items). Most of us have a great deal of readily available quantitative data related to information security ranging from lost assets, to security incidents, to SIEM events-per-second, to firewall/IPS operational data. In order for this data to be useful in the context of a dashboard, these quantitative measures must be able to answer two questions:

- What's going on?
- So what?

For the categorical measures, you are usually identifying a set of elements that:

- **Provide useful information**—such as "which incident handlers are primary for the day?";
- **Require the most attention**—such as "which Payment Card Industry Data Security Standard (PCI DSS) controls are slipping?"; or
- **Need follow up**—such as "what are the top expedited firewall port open requests?"

Let's take a look at these measures through some examples.

Lending a Hand to Handlers

The incident response team has asked for help in creating an incident response dashboard and—among other items—would like a view of "bad port" activity. You decide, without probing any further, that the problem is the number of denied firewall transactions for a port for the month-to-date, so you whip up the graphic shown in Figure 10-11.

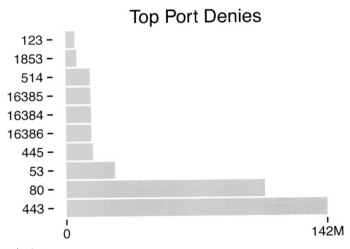

FIGURE 10-11 *Top port denies*

Although the chart answers *a* "what's going on?" question, it may not fully answer *the* "what's going on?" question for the incident response team. It definitely lacks an answer to the "so what?" question. It's back to the drawing board and back to the incident response team to see if you can glean more about what they are looking for and whether you have the data to support it.

Through your investigation, you learn that the team really wants a view of the top five ports with *anomalous* activity. This is quite a different measure than just a raw port count and requires answering both questions—"what's going on" and "so what?"—in order to provide the view they are looking for.

In general, "what's going on?" will be a count of some kind (it's a quantitative value, after all). For the anomalous port measure, what will you count? Session attempts and/or bytes transferred? What time frame will you count over? The past hour, intra-day to now, or the past week/month? Will you focus on denies and accepts or just denies (which will shape the answers to some of the previous questions)?

After further consultation with the team, you agree that "what's going on" is answered by counting denied attempts over the past 24 hours. But...so what? This measure alone has little value. It requires context or comparison to be useful and comparisons are trickier than you might expect at first glance. For the port activity, for example, do you compare the measure against:

- The same port's position in SANS trending port list (`https://isc.sans.edu/trends.html`) for that time period (that is, the same measure but from a different source)?
- The same value against the same 24-hour period (that is, the same day of the week) at one or more points in the past?
- The same value against a different 24-hour period (that is, a different day of the week)?
- The same value as it relates to daily activity across the previous week or month?

If you choose to compare the port activity against the same value for the same day the previous week (in this case, percentage change from previous week), you get a much different view/list (Figure 10-12).

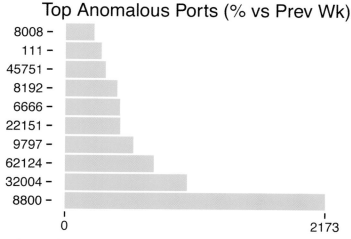

FIGURE 10-12 *Top anomalous ports*

Knowing there was a 2,000+ percent change in volume for this port is definitely more actionable that a raw session count. That's a significant change that should trigger an investigation into *why*. For example, you might examine which nodes were involved in the communication, and check to see if external Information Sharing and Analysis Centers (ISACs) identified malicious activity on this port. Although it's not perfect, it's a good starting place for this new dashboard element. As the team uses this data and as you perform additional exploratory data analyses using the other comparative conditions, you may find that one or more of the other measures works better for the team.

Raising Dashboard Awareness

Your dashboard prowess is garnering quite a bit of attention with your latest request coming from the CISO. She wants a new measure added to the CISO dashboard that shows how well the new security awareness initiatives are working. You can't say "no" to the CISO, but this request lies far outside your comfort zone of bytes, sessions, and IP addresses. How are you going to measure the effectiveness of an awareness program?

Consider the advice offered on the website of the SANS "Securing the Human" project (`http://www.securingthehuman.org/resources/metrics`). There, you will find some seemingly "easy" measures such as "percent completion of annual security awareness training," but these you should quickly dismiss. That example may be good for a compliance dashboard, but it's not what the CISO is looking for. Instead, there are some good candidates that you can hone in on:

- Tracking the number of people who fall victim to a phishing attack
- Tracking the number of people who detect and report a phishing attack
- Tracking the results from a comprehensive security awareness survey

You might offer these to your CISO to see which one(s) meet her objectives. After your discussion, she chooses to go the security awareness survey route. For you, this means working with the appropriate internal groups to regularly set up the survey; select the recipients; distribute the survey; and collect, analyze, and publish the results. However, dealing with the mechanics of the survey is the easy part.

This dashboard request is going a bit more smoothly than the last one, but still poses some challenges. Which part of the organization is going to get the survey, and when will they receive it? How frequently will you run the survey? What supplemental data will be required if the CISO asks for more information?

Although it may seem intuitive to decide who will receive the survey, you actually need to step back and define whom you want to describe with the survey. In statistics, this is known as defining the *population* from which you want to sample. For example, if you want to measure all employees, you should survey a random sample of employees. If you limit these surveys to one or two departments, you could be introducing bias and might not be able to apply these results to all employees. You may also want to think about how and if this survey will be repeated. If you know the survey will be repeated and you want the results to be comparable (conducting a *benchmark study*), you need to focus on standardizing the questions and the long-term goals. Conducting a survey like this has some challenges and pitfalls, but with a little preparation you can get some interesting and informative data from surveys.

After significant collaboration, you decide to focus on new hires as the population, so the samples are defined as the monthly new hires as the survey recipients. Most of these individuals are completely unfamiliar with the security awareness program. There is a full multi-month training program that interleaves security awareness messages throughout this introduction period. By waiting 3 months after the hire date, you can see how much each new hire class retains. You can also get a feel for how tweaks to the awareness program impact new groups.

You get only one measure for the CISO dashboard, so let's opt for the summary effectiveness metric recommended by SANS (the calculation is documented in their survey materials). See Table 10-1.

TABLE 10-1   *Security Program Effectiveness Measures*

SECURITY AWARENESS RISK LEVEL	DESCRIPTION
Low (25–39)	Users are aware of good security principles and threats, have been properly trained, and comply with all organizational security standards and policies.
Elevated (40–60)	Users have already been trained on organizational security standards and policies; they are aware of threats, but may not follow good security principles and controls.
Moderate (61–81)	Users are aware of threats and know they should follow good security principles and controls, but need training on organizational security standards and policies. They also may not know how to identify or report a security event.
Significant (82–96)	Users are not aware of good security principles or threats, nor are they aware of or compliant with organizational security standards and policies.
High (97–120)	Users are not aware of threats and disregard known security standards and policies or do not comply. They engage in activities or practices that are easily attacked and exploited.

Source: http://www.securingthehuman.org/resources/metrics

The benefit of the SANS approach is that you get standardized questions and a defined and open source method for computing the metric. This should provide a good measure for the CISO and you can refer to the individual responses to the survey questions when you're asked for more details. This new process also tracks the number of new hires per survey, the primary "handlers" responsible for the new hires during their introductory period, and the date the survey was held along with the survey results. None of this detail should or will make it to the dashboard chart, but may be invaluable when seeking to make changes based upon the dashboard element.

As this new process runs, data is accumulated and the awareness performance measure becomes populated. As you can see in Figure 10-13, the measure begins to trend in the wrong direction but never gets to the point where it needs immediate action; instead, it seems to level off. Rather than bombard the CISO with colored bands, this method uses subtle, colored level markers that delineate when an individual month measure moves into a different zone. It also shows, at a glance, how well the awareness program is performing.

The CISO becomes curious and asks someone to look at the supplementary data you collected to see what happened in June and July. It turns out that there is usually a single "handler" for the new hires and she was out on maternity leave in June and July, leaving a substitute to take her place. The new individual was not as familiar with the security elements of the new hire program and did not follow up in the same ways the primary handler typically does. Because of this knowledge, the CISO was able to ensure that all potential handlers were familiar with the elements of the security awareness program.

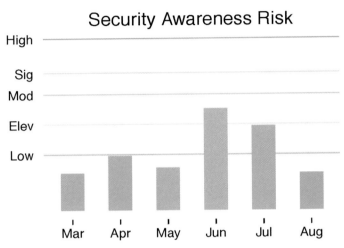

FIGURE 10-13 *Security awareness risk*

This measure will no doubt change yearly. Once there is a comfort level that the awareness program is reaching new employees, you might want to consider running the survey against other areas of the organization or switch to one or both of the phishing measures to get a different view of program effectiveness.

The Devil (and Incident Response Delays) Is in the Details

Just as you are about to dive into a new data set, you get an instant message from the incident response manager stating that her dashboard is "broken." Since you take a great deal of pride in your professional work, you head down to her office to see what the problem is and (hopefully) find a quick resolution.

It seems that she received a call from one of the application teams complaining about how long it took to resolve an incident last week. She was surprised, given that there were no indications on the weekly dashboard that anything was amiss. The performance measure showed that Tier 4 incidents (the level of the incident that was flagged by the application team) were handled within the standard one-day timeframe. You immediately suspect what's causing the issue and you head to the data to validate your assumptions. Sure enough, the culprit lies in the name of the performance measure itself: "*Mean* Time to Incident Resolution."

The *mean* is often used as a singular, descriptive statistic for a data set, and it *can* be used as a quick comparative measure of performance (such as batting average in baseball), but it isn't perfect. Consider the resolution times (in days) for the incidents on the "broken" dashboard:

```
0.50 1.10 1.10 1.10 0.10 0.30 0.20
0.10 0.60 0.10 0.10 0.10 0.60 7.00
```

The mean works out to be `0.9286`, which falls within normal parameters. Now, look at the last value (`7.00`). This incident took substantially longer than normal, but did not generate a call to action on the dashboard. There are a few ways to fix this. If there is room, you could add a new performance measure that lists all incidents that fall within a certain percentage outside of an expected range. However, the incident manager really likes the single line encoding you've provided for the measure:

```
MTT Incident Resolution: 0.93
```

You need to come up with a way to programmatically identify problematic conditions and fit the encoding in the same space without losing any detail. The ultimate solution comes from three data analysis and visualization allies: the five number summary from Chapter 3, boxplots from Chapter 6, and sparklines (introduced in this chapter).

As a refresher, the five number summary consists of:

- The **minimum** (smallest observation)
- The **lower quartile** or **first quartile**
- The **median** (middle value)
- The **upper quartile** or **third quartile**
- The **maximum** (largest observation)

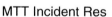 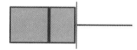

MTT Incident Res

FIGURE 10-14 *Boxplot sparkline*

These values are important for encoding many types of performance measures and can be used to succinctly summarize data without losing as much detail as you currently do with the mean alone. A boxplot provides a visual representation of these values that you can augment with a line for the performance measure threshold, as shown in Figure 10-14.

The incident manager now has an at-a-glance view that encodes valuable details without sacrificing space. If necessary, the boxplot can be color-coded to more overtly call attention to measures outside normal parameters. The mean value can be displayed next to the boxplot if that measure still provides value.

Projecting "Security"

The word "security" is in quotes here and in the section title because the definition of security is up to individual interpretation. A penetration tester might think of security in a completely different way than a CISO, just as an application developer will likely have a different view of it than a firewall engineer. From a big picture perspective, these interpretations are complementary because they are all parts of a whole. Each activity is necessary to ensure the protection of an organization's information assets.

Perhaps one of the least "security-like" elements that readily lends itself to a dashboard is the venerable project or task "status view." This could involve tracking projects for remediation of internal audit issues or monitoring full-scale, enterprise-wide security programs. Security, IT, and business executives need some way to get a quick overview of all these moving parts so they know where resources and attention should potentially be redirected. It might not be sexy, but there would be little happening in "security" without this governance layer.

If you become known as the "dashboard person" in your organization, you must face the inevitable request to build a set of measures to track program, project, and remediation status. These initiatives will have their own set of detailed measures and reports, which project and program managers will gladly provide. The challenge lies in how to communicate the status of 35-50 (or more) measures at a glance as one component of an executive-level dashboard.

The first step is to identify the components that your viewers want to track. For our make-believe organization, the components will be:

- Internal audit issues remediation items

- Enterprise-wide security program initiatives

- Customer audit-remediation process (these are the items your customers are requesting that your organization remediate)

- PCI DSS compliance controls remediation progress

From your discussions with the CISO you know that you are constrained to one quadrant of the executive dashboard, and that the items of most importance to her are PCI controls and customer audits. You've verified that the data for the performance measures are readily available and accurate, and you set off to meet this challenge head on.

The prioritization and list of measures provided by the CISO gives you logical groupings for the measures you need to encode. For each group, you must decide how to prioritize the elements within the group. Given that all of these elements will themselves be grouped together, the individual encoding for each measure you choose should be common across all four groups. Finding a way to satisfy all these constraints will create a seamless message for the "Security Program, Project, & Remediation Status" dashboard component.

After reviewing the data, you settle on four sections and draw a rough sketch showing how you want to present the information. This sketch eventually turns into the wireframe concept, as shown in Figure 10-15 (the phrases "Lorem ipsum" are placeholders for real text labels).

This will become a common process for your dashboard development:

1. Stakeholder/viewer identifies a need.

2. You work to understand the need and determine if you have the data to support the dashboard or dashboard element.

3. You sketch a set of rough concepts for the dashboard, and then wireframe and model the ones that seem to work best.

4. You choose a final model and find the most efficient process to encode the measures in support of the frequency requirements.

For encoding each list of items, the proper order becomes apparent after examining the project and program artifacts:

- The PCI program has been laid out according to the 12 requirements.

- The customer audits make the most sense in reverse date order (so the ones that should be closing soon are at the top).

- The enterprise-wide security program initiatives are displayed in the order they appear in the budget documents.
- The internal audit items are ordered like the customer audits.

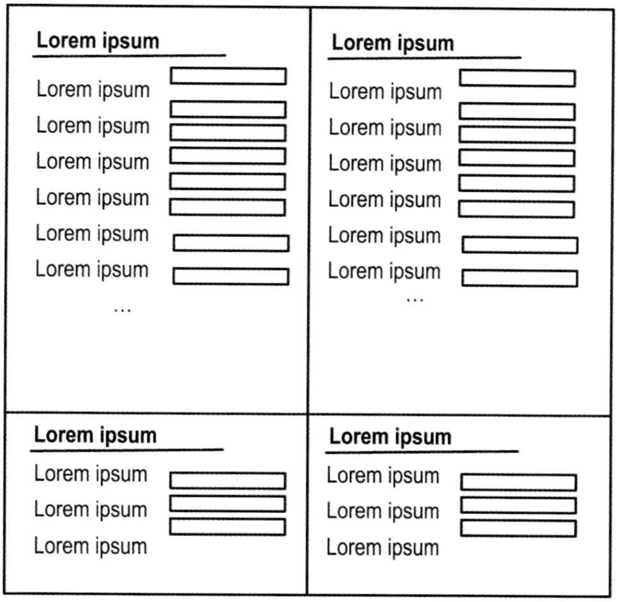

Figure 10-15 *Dashboard wireframe*

This ordering is part of the dashboard contract with the CISO and other viewers. Once established, the expectation will be that it does not change without informing involved parties.

Given that projects track completion to 100 percent, bars are good choices for the overall encoding. However, shorter does not necessarily mean "bad" in this case. You could use a variation on a bullet graph to provide more details, but that level of encoding is not necessary for this scenario. The viewers can always head to the supporting data (which includes detailed Gantt charts, project risks, and status history) for more detail. A subtle color highlight for the projects or program elements that are truly in danger of missing their dates is all that is needed to identify areas of concern, projects or elements that may need help from senior management to get back on track. Management will need to dig into the details of each wayward issue, so make sure the project and program managers have armed the CISO with all the necessary details.

The finished product can be seen in Figure 10-16, and the Excel template can be found in `ch10/docs/ch10-project-security.xlsx` on the book's website (`www.wiley.com/go/datadrivensecurity`).

Note

Excel's built-in ability to make sparkline-like "data bars" can drastically reduce the time it takes to produce an effective dashboard component. These elements implement user-defined rules to apply color and size from cell values.

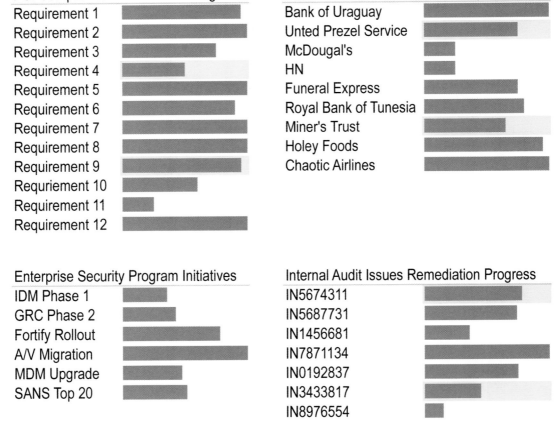

FIGURE 10-16 *Project and program status dashboard*

Summary

Designing, building, and delivering dashboards is not for the casual practitioner. It takes skill, practice, and a great deal of trial and error to create minimal, optimal encodings for critical measures and present them in a logical and visually appealing manner.

This chapter presented core dashboard concepts through both real-world scenarios and critiques/makeovers of actual dashboards found in the wild. You also learned about innovative encodings (such as bullet graphs and sparklines) along with design techniques that you can replicate in Excel and R using materials provided on the companion website.

Recommended Reading

The following are some recommended readings that can further your understanding on some of the topics we touch on in this chapter. For full information on these recommendations and for the sources we cite in the chapter, please see Appendix B.

Information Dashboard Design: The Effective Visual Communication of Data by Stephen Few—If you can acquire only one other resource for designing dashboards, pick this one. It provides detail on every level of element creation with numerous examples.

Security Metrics: Replacing Fear, Uncertainty, and Doubt by Andrew Jaquith—Dashboards are about displaying the most important information and driving action. Jaquith's book is your gateway drug into finding the right *security* information to present and how best to present it.

The Visual Display of Quantitative Information by Edward R. Tufte and P. R. Graves-Morris—This book is required reading for anyone who wishes to fully understand how information should be presented. While not a "dashboards" book, it emphasizes how best to *communicate* with visualizations with numerous examples.

Design, Evaluation, and Analysis of Questionnaires for Survey Research by Willem E. Saris and Irmtraud N. Gallhofer—This book will help you see that designing surveys is no trivial task. Even researchers in fields that are reliant upon surveys have trouble building ones that are effective at getting to the information that they truly want captured. If you dare to delve into this area for your security program, you'll absolutely need this book as a guide.

Modern Analysis of Customer Surveys: with Applications Using R by Ron Kenett and Silvia Salini—If you're still adamant on using surveys, you'll need to know how to analyze them. This text will provide you with the proper statistical foundations along with a good set of reusable R code that should make you more confident in presenting your results.

## 11

Building Interactive Security
Visualizations

"Many in the design community understand that design must convey the essence
of a device's operation; the way it works; the possible actions that can be taken;
and, through feedback, just what it is doing at any particular moment. Design is
really an act of communication, which means having a deep understanding of the
person with whom the designer is communicating."

Donald A. Norman, *The Design of Everyday Things*

The main purpose behind any of your data visualization efforts should be to help consumers understand and learn from the data. In other words, effective communication is the primary goal of your visual creations.

As you've seen in previous chapters, developing simple and successful fixed tables and charts requires knowledge, skill, and practice, but can provide substantive illumination of a topic, issue, or problem if executed correctly. In most cases—probably 95 percent of the time—these fixed views are all that is needed to achieve the goal of communication. There are situations, however, when static views of data are either insufficient or just not practical, requiring the move to a more dynamic medium to help consumers explore the messages the data has to offer. This chapter helps you understand when the move to interactive visualizations makes sense and introduces you to some of the resources and techniques that will help you craft effective messages, dashboards, and exploration tools.

> ### Note
>
> *The skills, art, and science surrounding interactive visualizations span a multitude of disciplines across many decades. As a result, this single chapter serves more as a survey and reference for further study for the topic as a whole. It provides practical guidance for where to apply interactivity within the scope of information security.*

Moving from Static to Interactive

Assuming the "95 percent" premise holds true, your first instinct when planning visualizations should be to "go static." It will generally take much less time to construct fixed visualizations even with the tweaking and polishing necessary to produce an audience-worthy graphic. You should also consider sticking with stationary images if the project you're working on is fairly discrete with a data set having a minimal number of dimensions (that is, rows, variables/columns/fields). As Scott Murray put it in his book *Interactive Data Visualization for the Web*, "A fixed image is ideal when alternate views are neither needed nor desired, and required when publishing to a static medium, such as print."

If you're still feeling the "interactive itch," there are three primary goals to consider when contemplating a new visualization:

- **Augmentation**—If adding interactive capabilities helps speed up or automate tasks consumers would normally perform manually, going interactive is definitely the right thing to do.

- **Exploration**—If the number of dimensions and size/diversity of the data set grow sufficiently large, it may be better to enable consumers to explore the relationships and outcomes on their own rather than trying to guess which set of static graphics will be most useful.

- **Illumination**—If a topic is complex enough, it may help to provide a well-executed, interactive visualization that provides a user-friendly interface for directed/constrained navigation around the data you've chosen to present.

Let's delve a bit further into each of these areas with a focus on information security examples.

Interaction for Augmentation

There are many repetitive, time-consuming, data-driven tasks in information security. Logs must be collected and correlated, alerts must be received and attended to, and anomalies must be investigated. These actions often involve running a variety of utilities over individual pieces of data or sets of data elements to determine whether there truly is an issue on your network. Any tool that helps alleviate this tedium and speeds up reliable detection of malicious activity is a welcome addition to any security engineer's toolbox.

Recognizing this fact, a research team led by Robert Erbacher worked to understand both the problem domain—situational awareness of malicious network activity—and how incident responders think and process information. This resulted in the creation of VisAlert (`http://digital.cs.usu.edu/~erbacher/publications/VisAlertCGA2006.pdf`), a visual correlation tool that facilitates situational awareness in complex network environments. Figure 11-1 shows an example screen from the VisAlert tool that we'll be focusing on in the remainder of this section. This single image places a logical network layout at the center so there is immediate, practical context for the viewer. The concentric circles represent delta time intervals for when security events happened (that is now, 5 minutes ago, 15 minutes ago, etc.). The lines from those events to the resources provide quick context for what type of attacks were happening to what systems and when, all without having to stare at multiple lines in multiple log files.

With tools such as Circos (`http://circos.ca/`), it's fairly straightforward to build a radial diagram similar to the VisAlert model in Figure 11-1 and add some interactive features. However, it takes more than eye-candy appeal for any visualization—fixed or interactive—to be truly useful. VisAlert's detailed focus on the following areas makes it notable.

Define the Problem

This is merely an extension of the "start with a question" mantra you've seen in many of the preceding chapters. Although there is merit in building visualizations in a vacuum to learn how to work with a new language or framework, it is imperative that you understand what problem you're trying to solve with a consumer-oriented interactive visualization and who the users will be before you attempt to deliver a finished product. Even if you're an established practitioner, your personal experiences may give you insight into only one aspect of a problem domain, and collaboration with others—especially those who you believe to be the natural consumers of your interactive visualization work—can make or break a project.

For the VisAlert team, this ultimately meant their goal was to aid analysts' decision-making processes by providing a robust visual correlation mechanism. Rather than try to build a new intrusion-detection system or deliver a "toy model" solution that works only with perfect and limited data sets, they chose to design a system that works at-scale with real-world data volumes and types that security analysts already use in their daily workflows. Although the problem scope is narrowly defined, it has sufficient breadth and scope to be useful as well as visually appealing.

Seek Domain Expertise

The VisAlert team started with real-world information security analysts to understand their ***mental models*** of how they go about identifying badness. Mental models are conceptual models of the way things work or people's understanding of how to interact with the world or systems around them. Security analysts develop domain-specific mental models through their training and practical work experiences. These models evolve with each successful (or failed) identification and eradication of malicious activity. With each investigation, analysts learn which processes provided the most value, and these are automatically added to their existing mental framework. By working with these individuals throughout the design process, the team was able to identify what parts of the analysts' workflows would benefit from enhanced visualizations (for example, inclusion of salient parts of network diagrams and automatically highlighting specific protocols and paths) and automation (for example, DNS lookups and targeted correlations).

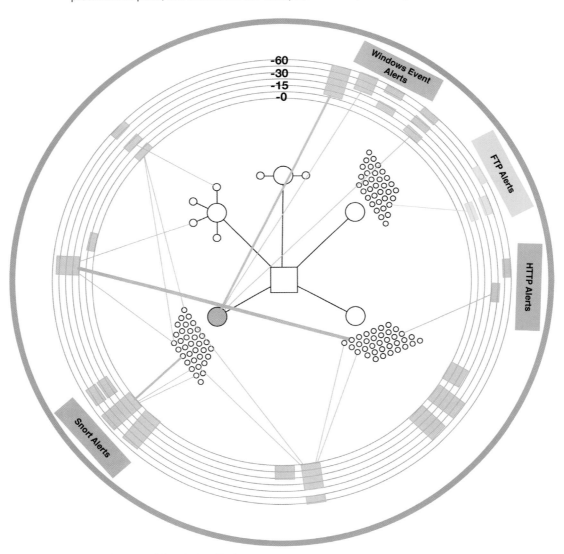

FIGURE 11-1 *The VisAlert Visual Correlation Tool*

Figures based on Foresti, Stefano, James Agutter, Yarden Livnat, Shaun Moon, and Robert Erbacher. "Visual correlation of network alerts." Computer Graphics and Applications, IEEE 26, no. 2 (2006): 48–59.

Take an Interdisciplinary Approach

The team drew on the talents and works of experts in the fields of information architecture, cognitive psychology, application development, and computer science—along with the domain experts—to build and refine the tool. They called this process a "modified hermeneutic circle"—the movement back and forth between the parts and the whole. It's shown in Figure 11-2.

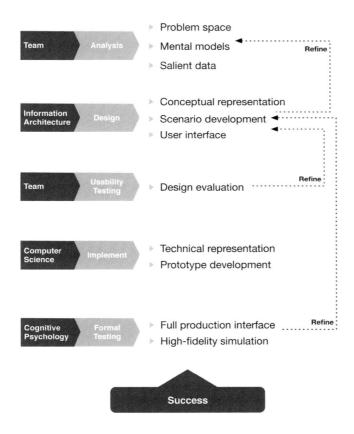

FIGURE 11-2 *The VisAlert Visual Correlation Tool design methodology*

Figures based on Foresti, Stefano, James Agutter, Yarden Livnat, Shaun Moon, and Robert Erbacher. "Visual correlation of network alerts." Computer Graphics and Applications, IEEE 26, no. 2 (2006): 48–59.

Their methodology has a strong resemblance to the Agile development process (http://agilemanifesto.org/principles.html), where all those involved are equal partners, each working together to yield a successful finished product. If your organization has an application development team and you're not familiar with Agile, you would do well to invite a member to lunch to understand how Agile works in the real world. (Plus, you'll have made a friend in the development community and can hopefully help them understand application security a bit better as well.)

Fundamentally, both concepts employ highly effective and efficient feedback loops to help ensure your project stays on the rails and arrives at the desired destination as quickly as possible. You may be the one building the finished product and you may be a savvy practitioner, but you should also regularly seek input and feedback from others in and outside your domain to ensure you're constructing the right elements.

The VisAlert tool has been featured in papers and security-oriented conferences since 2006 but has not been developed as a commercial or open source product as of this book's publication.

Interaction for Exploration

Most networks contain their fair share of vulnerabilities. The Nessus (http://www.tenable.com/products/nessus) vulnerability scanner (by Tenable) is one of the most commonly used tools that can help you find them. If you've ever seen the output from a detailed Nessus report (Figure 11-3), you know that each host will have a listing of vulnerable components and each component will have many attributes, including basic and detailed descriptions, overall rating, and Common Vulnerability Scoring System (CVSS) (http://www.first.org/cvss) score. A full report can be hundreds of pages long and makes for excellent nighttime reading if you're having trouble sleeping.

Even a small network, such as the one created for the VAST 2011 visualization challenge (http://hcil.cs.umd.edu/localphp/hcil/vast11/), can have thousands of vulnerability findings. (The VAST network data—included as ch11/data/vast_2011.nbe on this book's website at www.wiley.com/go/datadrivensecurity—has over 2,000.) Although it's possible to spin the data multiple ways and produce reams of static visualizations, this is definitely a perfect example of how an interactive tool can help security analysts explore and prioritize how they will attack the problem of which vulnerabilities to remediate first.

Tenable does provide interactive reporting tools, but this chapter focuses on an innovative open source tool released in 2013 by John Goodall called the Nessus Vulnerability Explorer (NV) (http://ornl-sava.github.io/nv/#). NV allows you to take an export from your Nessus scans, drag the file right into your browser, and begin exploring the vulnerabilities contained within. See Figure 11-4.

The interface is based on a treemap, which is a visualization that enables presentation of hierarchical data in a very compact way through nested rectangles, with the size and color of each rectangle being mapped to categorical or quantitative variables within the data set. Treemaps take a bit of getting used to, but once you learn how to decode them they can become valuable allies in targeted visualizations.

Goodall's interactive treemap lets the consumer rearrange the structure of the hierarchy through a simple drag-and-drop action, so you can present a traditional IP address-centric view of the vulnerabilities or switch to a view based on Nessus vulnerability (plug-in) ID or even by port. Through a single click, nodes can be sized by volume or potential impact and vulnerability details are revealed through single clicks on individual rectangles.

56860 (1) - USN-1263-1 : icedtea-web, openjdk-6, openjdk-6b18 vulnerabilities

Synopsis

The remote Ubuntu host is missing one or more security-related patches.

Description

Deepak Bhole discovered a flaw in the Same Origin Policy (SOP) implementation in the IcedTea web browser plugin. This could allow a remote attacker to open connections to certain hosts that should not be permitted. (CVE-2011-3377)

Juliano Rizzo and Thai Duong discovered that the block-wise AES encryption algorithm block-wise as used in TLS/SSL was vulnerable to a chosen-plaintext attack. This could allow a remote attacker to view confidential data. (CVE-2011-3389)

It was discovered that a type confusion flaw existed in the in the Internet Inter-Orb Protocol (IIOP) deserialization code. A remote attacker could use this to cause an untrusted application or applet to execute arbitrary code by deserializing malicious input. (CVE-2011-3521)

It was discovered that the Java scripting engine did not perform SecurityManager checks. This could allow a remote attacker to cause an untrusted application or applet to execute arbitrary code with the full privileges of the JVM. (CVE-2011-3544)

It was discovered that the InputStream class used a global buffer to store input bytes skipped. An attacker could possibly use this to gain access to sensitive information. (CVE-2011-3547)

It was discovered that a vulnerability existed in the AWTKeyStroke class. A remote attacker could cause an untrusted application or applet to execute arbitrary code. (CVE-2011-3548)

It was discovered that an integer overflow vulnerability existed in the TransformHelper class in the Java2D implementation. A remote attacker could use this cause a denial of service via an application or applet crash or possibly execute arbitrary code. (CVE-2011-3551)

It was discovered that the default number of available UDP sockets for applications running under SecurityManager restrictions was set too high. A remote attacker could use this with a malicious application or applet exhaust the number of available UDP sockets to cause a denial of service for other applets or applications running within the same JVM. (CVE-2011-3552)

It was discovered that Java API for XML Web Services (JAX-WS) could incorrectly expose a stack trace. A remote attacker could potentially use this to gain access to sensitive information. (CVE-2011-3553)

It was discovered that the unpacker for pack200 JAR files did not sufficiently check for errors. An attacker could cause a denial of service or possibly execute arbitrary code through a specially crafted pack200 JAR file. (CVE-2011-3554)

It was discovered that the RMI registration implementation did not properly restrict privileges of remotely executed code. A remote attacker could use this to execute code with elevated privileges. (CVE-2011-3556, CVE-2011-3557)

It was discovered that the HotSpot VM could be made to crash, allowing an attacker to cause a denial of service or possibly leak sensitive information. (CVE-2011-3558)

It was discovered that the HttpsURLConnection class did not properly perform SecurityManager checks in certain situations. This could allow a remote attacker to bypass restrictions on HTTPS connections. (CVE-2011-3560)

See Also

http://www.ubuntu.com/usn/usn-1263-1/

Solution

Update the affected package(s).

Risk Factor

Critical

CVSS Base Score

10.0 (CVSS2#AV:N/AC:L/Au:N/C:C/I:C/A:C)

FIGURE 11-3 *Sample Nessus detailed vulnerability report*

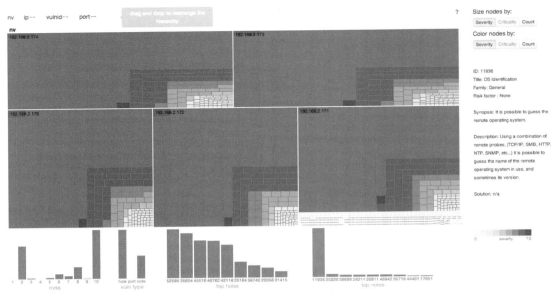

FIGURE 11-4 *Nessus Vulnerability Explorer interactive treemap interface*

The view in Figure 11-4 has over 240 nodes, yet it's very straightforward (and quick) to see all nodes with similar vulnerability profiles. All necessary information is kept onscreen and the bar charts at the bottom of the display provide a useful high-level overview to help guide exploration. A traditional summarized report view would no doubt require much scrolling and panning to provide the same type of information and it would be almost impossible to discern patterns in the environment.

However, all exploratory interfaces do not need to be this elaborate. Figure 11-5 shows a simple Excel workbook of a firewall log extract that includes filtering controls at the top of the log entry data table. It also has two pivot tables showing views by firewall and port (respectively), with matching bar charts that dynamically change as you manipulate the pivot table values. More modern versions of Excel do not have the workbook size limitations of previous offerings and can comfortably fit over a million rows and 16,000 columns, provided you have a robust enough system to support such a large workbook. You might be surprised just how useful it can be to simply provide intelligently summarized tabular views of data sets—paired with basic visualizations—that can be easily sorted on demand by the consumer. It may sound simple, but remember: You still need to do the hard work of finding, cataloging, acquiring, cleaning, augmenting, and processing the data (ah, the glamorous life of a security data scientist).

Interaction for Illumination

Although everyone may seem to be carrying an i-device of some sort and is constantly plugged in to everything, the truth is that most individuals still have only a surface-level understanding of the digital world they live in. For instance, they know that their Instagram app requires an account with a username and password before they can post pictures for their friends to see, but the details of the binary world below that process—where hue, saturation, and brightness are digitized; network packets are exchanged; and information is transported and stored potentially thousands of miles away—remains as much a mystery as does most of the inner workings of a modern automobile engine.

Time	Msg	Action	Firewall	Protoc	Source	Dest	Source.Po	Dest.Po	Service	Directio
4/6/12 17:20	Info	Built	ASA-6-302013	TCP	172.23.27.50	10.32.0.100	4348	80	http	outbound
4/6/12 17:20	Info	Teardown	ASA-6-302014	TCP	172.23.27.50	10.32.0.100	4348	80	http	outbound
4/6/12 17:20	Info	Built	ASA-6-302013	TCP	172.23.238.76	10.32.5.54	48494	80	http	outbound
4/6/12 17:20	Info	Teardown	ASA-6-302014	TCP	172.23.238.76	10.32.5.54	48494	80	http	outbound
4/6/12 17:20	Info	Built	ASA-6-302013	TCP	172.23.24.85	10.32.0.100	4349	80	http	outbound
4/6/12 17:20	Info	Teardown	ASA-6-302014	TCP	172.23.24.85	10.32.0.100	4349	80	http	outbound
4/6/12 17:20	Info	Built	ASA-6-302013	TCP	172.23.36.140	10.32.0.100	4319	80	http	outbound
4/6/12 17:20	Info	Teardown	ASA-6-302014	TCP	172.23.36.140	10.32.0.100	4319	80	http	outbound
4/6/12 17:20	Info	Built	ASA-6-302013	TCP	172.23.19.146	10.32.0.100	4391	80	http	outbound
4/6/12 17:20	Info	Teardown	ASA-6-302014	TCP	172.23.19.146	10.32.0.100	4391	80	http	outbound
4/6/12 17:20	Info	Built	ASA-6-302013	TCP	172.23.12.46	10.32.0.100	4295	80	http	outbound
4/6/12 17:20	Info	Teardown	ASA-6-302014	TCP	172.23.12.46	10.32.0.100	4295	80	http	outbound
4/6/12 17:20	Info	Built	ASA-6-302013	TCP	172.23.33.72	10.32.0.100	4361	80	http	outbound
4/6/12 17:20	Info	Teardown	ASA-6-302014	TCP	172.23.33.72	10.32.0.100	4361	80	http	outbound
4/6/12 17:20	Info	Built	ASA-6-302013	TCP	172.23.234.150	10.32.5.57	22958	80	http	outbound
4/6/12 17:20	Info	Built	ASA-6-302013	TCP	172.23.17.199	10.32.0.100	4316	80	http	outbound
4/6/12 17:20	Info	Teardown	ASA-6-302014	TCP	172.23.17.199	10.32.0.100	4316	80	http	outbound
4/6/12 17:20	Info	Teardown	ASA-6-302014	TCP	172.23.234.150	10.32.5.57	22958	80	http	outbound
4/6/12 17:20	Info	Built	ASA-6-302013	TCP	172.23.34.136	10.32.0.100	4344	80	http	outbound
4/6/12 17:20	Info	Teardown	ASA-6-302014	TCP	172.23.34.136	10.32.0.100	4344	80	http	outbound
4/6/12 17:20	Info	Built	ASA-6-302013	TCP	172.23.42.68	10.32.0.100	4317	80	http	outbound
4/6/12 17:20	Info	Teardown	ASA-6-302014	TCP	172.23.42.68	10.32.0.100	4317	80	http	outbound
4/6/12 17:20	Info	Built	ASA-6-302013	TCP	172.23.36.67	10.32.0.100	4320	80	http	outbound
4/6/12 17:20	Info	Teardown	ASA-6-302014	TCP	172.23.36.67	10.32.0.100	4320	80	http	outbound
4/6/12 17:20	Info	Built	ASA-6-302013	TCP	172.23.33.71	10.32.0.100	4362	80	http	outbound
4/6/12 17:20	Info	Teardown	ASA-6-302014	TCP	172.23.33.71	10.32.0.100	4362	80	http	outbound
4/6/12 17:20	Info	Built	ASA-6-302013	TCP	172.23.27.106	10.32.0.100	4349	80	http	outbound
4/6/12 17:20	Info	Teardown	ASA-6-302014	TCP	172.23.27.106	10.32.0.100	4349	80	http	outbound
4/6/12 17:20	Info	Built	ASA-6-302013	TCP	172.23.10.114	10.32.0.100	4295	80	http	outbound
4/6/12 17:20	Info	Teardown	ASA-6-302014	TCP	172.23.10.114	10.32.0.100	4295	80	http	outbound
4/6/12 17:20	Info	Built	ASA-6-302013	TCP	172.23.233.157	10.32.5.57	23549	80	http	outbound
4/6/12 17:20	Info	Teardown	ASA-6-302014	TCP	172.23.233.157	10.32.5.57	23549	80	http	outbound
4/6/12 17:20	Info	Built	ASA-6-302013	TCP	172.23.6.27	10.32.0.100	4342	80	http	outbound
4/6/12 17:20	Info	Teardown	ASA-6-302014	TCP	172.23.6.27	10.32.0.100	4342	80	http	outbound
4/6/12 17:20	Info	Built	ASA-6-302013	TCP	172.23.21.180	10.32.0.100	4341	80	http	outbound
4/6/12 17:20	Info	Teardown	ASA-6-302014	TCP	172.23.21.180	10.32.0.100	4341	80	http	outbound
4/6/12 17:20	Info	Built	ASA-6-302013	TCP	172.23.26.79	10.32.0.100	4329	80	http	outbound
4/6/12 17:20	Info	Teardown	ASA-6-302014	TCP	172.23.26.79	10.32.0.100	4329	80	http	outbound
4/6/12 17:20	Info	Built	ASA-6-302013	TCP	172.23.20.36	10.32.0.100	4288	80	http	outbound
4/6/12 17:20	Info	Teardown	ASA-6-302014	TCP	172.23.20.36	10.32.0.100	4288	80	http	outbound

% of Connections by Destination by Firewall

Service (All)

Count of Dest Firewall	Total
ASA-2-106001	1.43%
ASA-6-106015	3.69%
ASA-6-302013	47.47%
ASA-6-302014	47.40%
Grand Total	100.00%

Firewall (All)

Count of Service Service	Total
13713_tcp	1
19654_tcp	1
2189_tcp	1
26267_tcp	1
28607_tcp	1
30450_tcp	1
3205_tcp	1
33772_tcp	1
36211_tcp	1
38160_tcp	1
3852_tcp	1
43670_tcp	1
46334_tcp	1
47732_tcp	1
48289_tcp	1
52272_tcp	1
52326_tcp	1
56400_tcp	1
58738_tcp	1
61293_tcp	1
6658_tcp	1
6667_tcp	716
http	727
Grand Total	1464

FIGURE 11-5 *Excel pivot table with linked charts*

Even in our workplaces, where business processes are more often understood, the complexity of the information technology components that make those processes possible can be somewhat overwhelming to IT specialists, let alone business professionals.

Consider that a modest application has code that might be touched by over 30 developers, supported by over 15 operations administrators, span 3 firewall zones, and have components that reside on 16 disparate systems. It's incredible we have as much security as we do in such diverse and complex environments and a bit more understandable why all of those individuals involved in the process don't fully grasp all the nuances of how to ensure that security is a primary emergent property of the system as a whole.

Understanding how complexity is masked, hidden, or ignored should make it easier to see why topics we security-folk are passionate about—such as encryption, system/data integrity, and data privacy—are faint blips on the radars of most individuals. However, our cause and profession have merit, and we *can* help raise awareness of these important topics. One good way to do this is through the use of interactive visualizations.

A great example of *how* to do this is the "World's Biggest Data Breaches" visualization (http://www.informationisbeautiful.net/visualizations/worlds-biggest-data-breaches-hacks/), created by David McCandless and Tom Evans of Information is Beautiful (http://www.informationisbeautiful.net/). See Figure 11-6.

Data breaches, as discussed in Chapter 7, are a reality, yet are not well understood outside of the security domain (perhaps not even fully *within* the security domain). When the technical and general news media report almost one breach per week, it can be difficult for people to keep up, let alone digest the diversity of the attacks. David and Tom—who are visualization and development experts, not information security professionals—set out to build an easy-to-use tool that would help consumers gain a better understanding of the quantity, variety, and magnitude of breaches that have made headlines over the past few years.

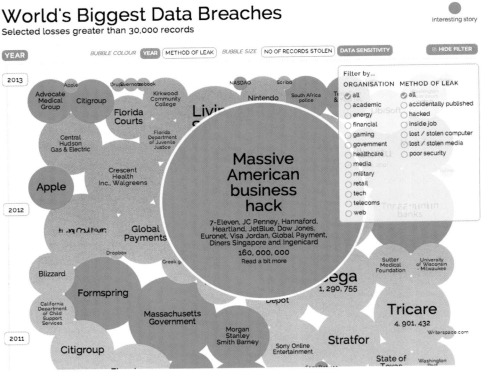

FIGURE 11-6 *World's Biggest Data Breaches interactive visualization*

By following a paradigm of "overview first, zoom and filter, then details-on-demand" put forth by Ben Shneiderman back in 1996 in his "Visual Information Seeking Mantra," they created an interactive bubble chart (see Figure 11-6) organized vertically by year. Consumers can filter the display to show breaches by organization type or method of leak and can also change the factors that make up bubble size and color.

Publications such as the Verizon Data Breach Investigations Report (http://www.verizonenterprise.com/DBIR/2013/) and Trustwave Global Security Report (http://www2.trustwave.com/rs/trustwave/images/2013-Global-Security-Report.pdf), plus online databases such as DataLoss DB (http://datalossdb.org/) and the Privacy Rights Clearinghouse (http://www.privacyrights.org/data-breach), have covered breaches for many years, yet tend to be read and mined mostly by information security professionals. What has made David and Tom's interactive tool more appealing and useful to a much broader audience than these established resources?

Make Interfaces Accessible

There's nothing quite like a never-ending, scrolling table filled with security jargon and wrapped in cold, official language to make the average person head for the nearest cat picture. Even a well-crafted, comprehensive report can be daunting to pick up and look through when the topic is so far removed from the daily experience of even the most tech-savvy business executive.

The World's Biggest Data Breaches visualization succeeds because it presents the data within a familiar and friendly setting—a web page—and makes excellent use of color, style, and design to present a tool that has an intuitive look and feel with no fear of "breaking" anything. The "buttons" look and behave as expected. The filtering interface has plenty of whitespace and steers clear from too much jargon or too little context. Mouse movements and actions provide instant, game-like feedback; and, even without instruction, the interface is almost instantly usable.

Imagine if this had been released as a Microsoft Excel file (yes, you can make clickable bubble charts with Excel) with macro warnings popping up on open, and the ribbon and column headers consuming prime display space, and with your operating system switching between Excel and your default browser whenever you clicked to see the news story behind the detail. The basic functionality would have been the same, but the user experience would have been radically different.

Your consumers live in the browser and that's where most (if not all) your creations should be targeted for deployment. Latter sections of this chapter introduce some of the technologies that make these visualizations possible, but they do not include phrases like "Java applet" or "Adobe Flash." Relying on the native capabilities of modern browsers and web frameworks will help you reach the largest possible audience in the most compatible and accessible ways possible. It will have the added benefit of making you sympathize a bit more with the complexities faced by user-interface developers (whom you should also take to lunch on occasion to trade security knowledge for useful front-end coding tips and techniques).

Facilitate Directed Exploration

Donald Norman coined the phrase "the tyranny of the blank screen" in his book *The Design of Everyday Things*. The perfect, illuminating, interactive visualization lies somewhere between this fully open, onscreen world and a fixed graphic. Which design choices made the World's Biggest Data Breaches visualization easy to explore?

- **Critical exploration elements and operations are prominent and visible.** Through consistent colors, shapes, and prominent placement, the controls for the visualization are immediately discernible. By having the filter controls come up right after the visualization loads, there is the immediate reaction of "Oh, I can click this!" on the part of the consumer. Color also draws attention to what the creators feel are especially compelling stories.

- **All components and actions are consistent and deliberate.** Mouse movements highlight elements and mouse clicks select options and provide detail. There is no jumping between mouse and keyboard or switching between dragging and clicking. The interface becomes immediately predictable with no surprises, apart from interesting and engaging stories.

- **Feedback is instant and all operations are safe.** Although the site loads fairly quickly given all the data and resources it uses behind the scenes, there is a slight delay and this is where the helpful feedback starts. A familiar "loading" message appears but quickly fades directly to the core visualization. Every click produces instant feedback that is 100 percent undoable, either via the controls on the visualization or with a quick click of the browser reload button. This feeling of safety puts consumers at ease and encourages them to explore.

The (Slow) Demise of Flash and Java

There was a time when Java and Flash applets were the only way to add "decent" visual interactivity to a website. Java was (and is) a formal language taught in many schools, which had made it an especially easy choice for academic visualizations. Flash was (and is) easy to learn with friendly development tools that have made it highly popular among the general web development community.

Although Flash still commands a presence on around 17 percent of websites (Figure 11-7), the use of it as a visualization medium is in a slow, steady decline. In contrast, Java applets hold on to a razor-thin 0.1 percent share of the web.

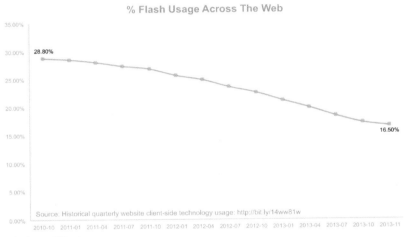

FIGURE 11-7 *The decline of Flash*

The fading of each technology can be attributed to many factors, including:

- The never-ending vulnerability, breach, and security update cycle
- The rise in popularity of platforms such as the iPad, iPhone, and other touch environments that do not provide support for website elements built with these tools
- The increased native platform capabilities due to widespread adoption of HTML5, CSS, and JavaScript across the most used browsers

To reach the broadest audience, it's best to avoid proprietary technologies or visualization toolkits that require browser extensions.

- **Actions are limited.** The interface provides options to change color and size of bubbles and highlight certain organization and breach types. However, you cannot group elements together and generate a bar chart or select individual organizations out from a list of thousands. These constraints make the interface much less daunting—a condition referred to as the *paradox of choice*—since some argue that people want more freedom and more tools and ways to explore. Limiting actions also enables you to shape or guide the exploration in a particular direction. Considering how fixed graphics represent the extreme in limiting actions, you should be able to think back to what made the data interesting to you as you explored it and come up with a set of constrained, exploratory actions that lie somewhere between the freedom of an RStudio window and the constraints of a static graphic.

Note

Barry Schwartz writes about **The Paradox of Choice: Why Less Is More** *(Ecco, 2004) in more detail in his book.*

Include Appropriate Detail

Breaches are complex entities, as illustrated by the breadth and depth of the VERIS taxonomy explained in Chapter 7. This level of technical detail is completely inappropriate for the mass-consumer audience of the World's Biggest Data Breaches visualization. Rather than bombard the consumer with multi-level taxonomy details, McCandless and Evans opt for simple summaries and succinct descriptions available upon clicking, while making detailed news stories also available on demand.

The level of detail you choose to provide in this type of visualization is highly dependent on the target consumer. Including VERIS-level taxonomy details within a similar tool released at a conference of security professionals focused on metrics (Metricon, `http://securitymetrics.org/`) is both appropriate and expected by the audience. You must have a solid grasp of who will be using your creations and what their level of expertise and expectations are in order to build a truly successful interactive visualization.

Developing Interactive Visualizations

Even with the elimination of Flash and Java as options, you are still faced with the aforementioned paradox of choice when it comes to deciding on how you want to develop interactive visualizations. Most often, you'll have to roll up your sleeves and write code, especially since you will usually be dealing with sensitive data that cannot be published on the public Internet. The vast majority of Internet-accessible "point-and-click" tools store data in the "cloud" and use public websites for the presentation layer, but there are desktop tools that can be of great assistance when fixed visualizations are not sufficient.

Building Interactive Dashboards with Tableau

One standalone, Office-like tool that excels at building assisted/directed interactive visualizations and dashboards is Tableau (`http://tableausoftware.com/`). Tableau is a Windows-only application that was heavily influenced by research conducted by Jock Mackinlay in automating the design of graphical presentations of relational information (http://cs171.org/2008/papers/mackinlay86.pdf). A foundational premise of Tableau, therefore, is to have the system analyze your data and provide suggestions for the best way to visualize it. If your goal is to build interactive, user-friendly dashboards or quickly provide an interactive exploratory interface for a complex data set, Tableau should be your "go to" tool of choice.

If you look back at the security awareness use case in Chapter 10, one way to build such a survey is to use an in-house tool such as Microsoft SharePoint or look to a commercial solution such as SurveyMonkey to present the desired survey questions. The raw survey results will look something like the almost endless series of data points shown in Figure 11-8. Slicing and dicing that data into generate static views *is* possible, but it is neither practical nor useful for communicating the messages contained within the data set.

Level	Business Unit	Campus Identifier	Years Employed	Does our company have a security team?	Does our company have a security team?	Do you know who to contact in case you are hacked, lost customer data, or if your	Do you know who to contact in case you are hacked, lost customer data, or if your	Have you ever found a virus or Trojan on your computer at work?	Have you ever found a virus or Trojan on your computer at work?	Do you know how to tell if your computer is hacked or infected?	Do you know how to tell if your computer is hacked or infected?	Have you ever given out your work password to anyone?	Have you ever given out your work password to anyone?	If you delete files from your computer or even format your hard drive, all the information	If you delete files from your computer or even format your hard drive, all the information	How secure do you feel your computer is?
Individual Contributor	Capital	Canada	2	Yes	1	Yes	1	No	2	Yes	1	No	1	FALSE	1	Secure
Individual Contributor	Energy	Canada	15	Yes	1	Yes	1	No	2	Yes	1	No	1	FALSE	1	Secure
Individual Contributor	Energy	Canada	26	Yes	1	Yes	1	No	2	Yes	1	No	1	FALSE	1	Secure
Individual Contributor	Energy	Canada	7	Yes	1	Yes	1	No	2	Yes	1	No	1	FALSE	1	Secure
Individual Contributor	Energy	Southwest	22	Yes	1	Yes	1	No	2	Yes	1	No	1	FALSE	1	Secure
Individual Contributor	Energy	Canada	8	Yes	1	Yes	1	No	2	Yes	1	No	1	FALSE	1	Secure
Individual Contributor	Energy	Canada	14	Yes	1	Yes	1	No	2	Yes	1	No	1	FALSE	1	Secure
Individual Contributor	Infrastructure	Midwest	13	Yes	1	Yes	1	No	2	Yes	1	No	1	FALSE	1	Secure
Individual Contributor	Infrastructure	Northeast	2	Yes	1	Yes	1	No	2	Yes	1	No	1	FALSE	1	Secure
Individual Contributor	Capital	Southwest	21	Yes	1	Yes	1	No	2	Yes	1	No	1	FALSE	1	Secure
Individual Contributor	Energy	Canada	26	Yes	1	Yes	1	No	2	Yes	1	No	1	FALSE	1	Secure / Very Secure
Individual Contributor	Home	Midwest	20	Yes	1	Yes	1	No	2	Yes	1	No	1	FALSE	1	Secure
Individual Contributor	Capital	Southwest	23	Yes	1	Yes	1	No	2	Yes	1	No	1	FALSE	1	Secure / Very Secure
Individual Contributor	Capital	Southwest	1	Yes	1	Yes	1	No	2	Yes	1	No	1	FALSE	1	Secure / Very Secure
Individual Contributor	Energy	Southwest	16	Yes	1	Yes	1	No	2	Yes	1	No	1	FALSE	1	Secure
Management	Capital	Southwest	16	Yes	1	Yes	1	No	2	Yes	1	No	1	FALSE	1	Secure
Individual Contributor	Home	Canada	13	Yes	1	Yes	1	No	2	Yes	1	No	1	FALSE	1	Secure / Very Secure
Individual Contributor	Energy	Southwest	2	Yes	1	Yes	1	No	2	Yes	1	No	1	FALSE	1	Secure
Individual Contributor	Energy	Midwest	15	Yes	1	Yes	1	No	2	Yes	1	No	1	FALSE	1	Secure / Very Secure
Individual Contributor	Home	Northeast	13	Yes	1	Yes	1	No	2	Yes	1	No	1	FALSE	1	Secure
Individual Contributor	Infrastructure															

FIGURE 11-8 *Raw data from the security awareness survey*

Tableau can easily digest this data, analyze the types of variables it contains, and guide you through selecting the most appropriate visualizations to encode the individual elements or relationships between elements. That's great for producing fixed graphics, but Tableau can also be used to quickly generate interactive visualizations that can be distributed to other Tableau Desktop users or be presented to web browsers via Tableau Server.

After looking at the data (`ch11/data/awareness-survey.csv`, which is available on the book's website, `www.wiley.com/go/datadrivensecurity`, as part of Chapter 11 download materials), we decided it would be most helpful to provide views of each survey answer by business unit, years employed, and employee level (management or individual contributor), since we could then attempt to discern if any of those factors stood out (which will help us tailor messages in future awareness initiatives). With this goal in mind, we used Tableau to create the interactive dashboard shown in Figure 11-9. It's viewable at `http://public.tableausoftware.com/views/UserAwareness/UserAwareness`. The whole process—from data import to finished dashboard—took about 20 minutes.

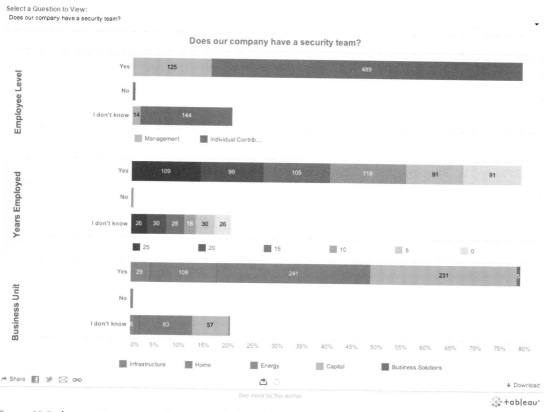

FIGURE 11-9 *Awareness survey results presented with Tableau*

Rather than build a giant, scrolling web page, we chose to let consumers explore individual survey questions and had Tableau automatically pivot the compact detail views on demand. Each visual component in each section is also selectable and provides further levels of detail when inspected (Figure 11-10).

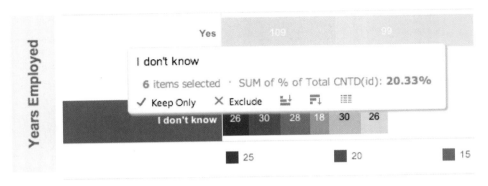

FIGURE 11-10 *Tableau details on demand*

This all required nothing more than a few mouse clicks and drags. We never entered even one line of code, yet produced an interactive tool that can be used by anyone with a web browser. Plus, we can give the entire workbook (also available at www.wiley.com/go/datadrivensecurity at ch11/data/user-awareness.twbx) to other analysts to produce other customized views—provided they also have the Tableau Desktop software.

Tableau is great for producing straightforward fixed and interactive visualizations using standard charting components. However, if you want to create more specialized interactive visualizations or prefer not to be locked into a proprietary desktop tool, you'll need to head to your favorite text editor and start coding.

Building Browser-Based Visualizations with D3

There is a vast landscape of tools, languages, and techniques available to help you craft engaging, web-based, fixed, and interactive data visualizations. It would be impossible to cover them all in one book, let alone part of one chapter, so we'll highlight one of the most flexible and popular visualization libraries available today—D3—and show you a fully working example using a meta-language built on top of D3—Vega.

D3 (http://d3js.org/) is a powerful JavaScript library created by Mike Bostock that makes it possible to dynamically transform and manipulate the contents of web pages based on data. To fully bend D3 to your will, you'll need to:

- Become proficient in the web trifecta¾HTML5, Cascading Style Sheets (CSS), and JavaScript

- Be familiar with the structure of Scalable Vector Graphics (SVG)

- Have a solid understanding of the Document Object Model (DOM); see http://www.w3.org/TR/1998/WD-DOM-19980720/introduction.html

However, you can begin to learn D3 without deep knowledge in those areas, just by viewing and exploring the plethora of examples found on the "official" D3 GitHub site (`https://github.com/mbostock/d3/wiki/Gallery`) and by gathering expertise along the way.

Unlike most proprietary technologies, you can dissect and inspect all D3 visualizations just by choosing "view source" from your web browser. Since D3 visualizations are fully driven by the data being visualized, the data itself is also available for download and should be in a recognizable format—usually CSV, TSV, JSON, or hardcoded HTML tables and JavaScript arrays.

Getting started with D3 requires only three things—a text editor, the D3 JavaScript library, and a web server. To prove this, read through this annotated, basic example of a static bar chart (Figure 11-11) to see what it's like to code in D3. You can find the source for Listing 11-1 in `ch11/support/ch11-figure11.html`.

LISTING 11-1

```html
<!--
    -- Listing 11-1
    -- Example of D3 visualization
    -->
<!DOCTYPE html>
<html>
<head>
<meta charset="utf-8">
<style>
rect.bar {
  fill: #8DA0CB; /* fill color for the bars */
}
.axis text {
  font: 10px sans-serif; /* 10-pt text for axis labels */
}
.axis path, .axis line { /* line style for the axes */
  fill: none;
  stroke: #000;
  shape-rendering: crispEdges;
}
</style>
// Load the D3 js library
<script src="http://d3js.org/d3.v3.min.js"
        charset="utf-8"></script>
</head>
<body>
<script>
// set up the data that will generate the bar chart
var data = [3, 3, 5, 9, 15, 18];

// define that margins for the plot and document
var margin = {top: 40, right: 40, bottom: 40, left: 40},
```

(continues)

Listing 11-1   *(continued)*

```
    width = 960,
    height = 500;

// we can use many scales with D3, but we'll stick with a basic
// linear scale for the X axis that is based on the values
// contained in our data set. in ggplot parlance this would
// be akin to using scale_x_continuous()
var x = d3.scale.linear()
    .domain([0, d3.max(data)])
    .range([0, width - margin.left - margin.right]);

// for the Y axis, we'll use an ordinal scale since these are really
// just individual factors being displayed. in ggplot parlance, this
// would be akin to scale_y_discrete()
var y = d3.scale.ordinal()
    .domain(d3.range(data.length))
    .rangeRoundBands([height - margin.top - margin.bottom, 0], .2);

// apply the scales to each axis, setting attributed for text
// text alignment and tick marks
var xAxis = d3.svg.axis()
    .scale(x)
    .orient("bottom")
    .tickPadding(8);

var yAxis = d3.svg.axis()
    .scale(y)
    .orient("left")
    .tickSize(0)
    .tickPadding(8);

// create an SVG element at the top of the the document body
// that will hold the bar chart visualiztion, setting basic
// layout parameters
var svg = d3.select("body").append("svg")
    .attr("width", width) // 'attr' sets DOM element attributes
    .attr("height", height)
    .attr("class", "bar chart")
  .append("g")
    .attr("transform",
          "translate(" + margin.left + "," + margin.top + ")");

// this creates all the bars in the chart using SVG 'rects'.
// try chaning the number of entries and values in the 'data' array
// above to see how it affects the display
svg.selectAll(".bar")
    .data(data)
```

```
    .enter().append("rect") // 'enter+append' creates new elements
      .attr("class", "bar") // each 'rect' will use the CSS 'bar' format
      .attr("y", function(d, i) { return y(i); }) // scaled y coordinate
      .attr("width", x) // width based on the x value
      .attr("height", y.rangeBand()); // bar widths dynamically scaled to
fit

// display the axes we set up earlier
svg.append("g")
    .attr("class", "x axis")
    .attr("transform", "translate(0," + y.rangeExtent()[1] + ")")
    .call(xAxis);

// we could have embedded labels in array, but this just assigns
// A-Z+ character codes, which helps show how to make almost any
// D3 element dynamic
svg.append("g")
    .attr("class", "y axis")
    .call(yAxis)
  .selectAll("text")
    .text(function(d) { return String.fromCharCode(d + 65); });
</script>
</body>
</html>
```

You can test the visualization in your browser by using the built-in HTTP server found in Python standard library and executing:

```
python -m SimpleHTTPServer 8888 &
```

Execute this in the directory containing the example D3 HTML file (ch11/support) and point your browser to http://localhost:8888/ch11-figure11.html.

If the syntax looks a bit daunting, remember that it's just a web page with formatting and JavaScript. You can start to get more comfortable with this code (or any D3 example) by experimenting with changing small things like the bar color and axis fonts. Then add, remove, and modify elements in the data array. If you use Google Chrome or Mozilla Firefox, you can bring up the Developer Tools JavaScript console and interact directly with the document elements. For instance, you can see all of the objects that were created by D3 when you told it to make the bars by typing svg.selectAll(".bar") in the console (once the visualization displays). You can inspect the results (Figure 11-12).

More complex and interactive D3 code can take a bit of getting used to, but there are ways of using D3 without always having to interact with code on this level.

Going Meta with Vega

If the ggplot library is the R incarnation of the "grammar of graphics," then Vega (http://trifacta .github.io/vega/) is D3's counterpart.

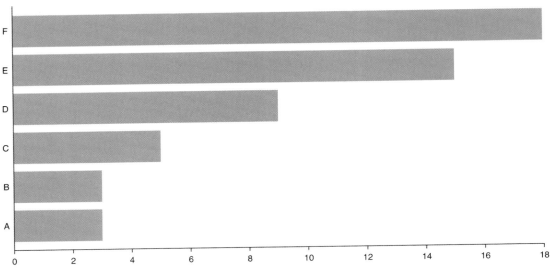

FIGURE 11-11 *Basic D3 bar chart*

FIGURE 11-12 *Viewing D3-created elements in the JavaScript Console*

Note

For more on the grammar of graphics, read Leland Wilkinson's **The Grammar of Graphics, Second Edition** *(Springer, 2005).*

With Vega, you describe a visualization using very readable JSON and simply use Vega's `parse()` function to read the file and display the visualization. The Vega library takes care of translating the specification into the appropriate D3 code. To see the difference, compare the raw D3 bar chart example given previously with this Vega version described in Listing 11-2 and shown in Figure 11-13.

LISTING 11-2

```
// Listing 11-2
// Vega chart description
{
  "width": 500,
  "height": 960,
  "padding": {"top": 40, "left": 40, "bottom": 40, "right": 40},
  "data": [
    {
      "name": "table",
      "values": [
        {"x": "A",  "y": 3}, {"x": "B",  "y": 3},
        {"x": "C",  "y": 5}, {"x": "D",  "y": 9},
        {"x": "E",  "y": 15}, {"x": "F",  "y": 18}
      ]
    }
  ],
  "scales": [
    {
      "name": "x",
      "type": "ordinal",
      "range": "width",
      "domain": {"data": "table", "field": "data.x"}
    },
    {
      "name": "y",
      "range": "height",
      "nice": true,
      "domain": {"data": "table", "field": "data.y"}
    }
  ],
  "axes": [
    {"type": "x", "scale": "x"},
    {"type": "y", "scale": "y"}
  ],
```

(continues)

LISTING 11-2 *(continued)*

```
"marks": [
  {
    "type": "rect",
    "from": {"data": "table"},
    "properties": {
      "enter": {
        "x": {"scale": "x", "field": "data.x"},
        "width": {"scale": "x", "band": true, "offset": -1},
        "y": {"scale": "y", "field": "data.y"},
        "y2": {"scale": "y", "value": 0}
      },
      "update": {
        "fill": {"value": "#8DA0CB"}
      }
    }
  }
]
}
```

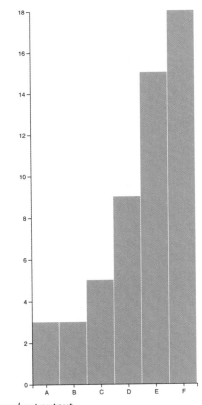

FIGURE 11-13 *Basic Vega bar chart output*

This syntax is much more readable than straight D3 code and the JSON format makes it easy to build graphics based on templates that are populated with computed data and customized styles. You can also use this flexibility—combined with some extra JavaScript code—to build fully interactive visualizations.

Creating an Interactive "Threat Explorer"

Imagine that you've been asked to visualize which internal hosts are talking to external hosts on a port-by-port basis using the same visualization technique as the network graphs highlighting malicious traffic that you saw in Chapter 4. This will require adapting the graph code a bit to work with firewall data, but that should be a simple exercise at this point.

You find this request intriguing and sit down with the SOC analysts to get more requirements. After delving into the details with them, you come up with the following objectives:

- The interface must let an analyst choose which port to explore.

- The visualization should—if the metadata is available—identify internal nodes by type (server or workstation) and IP address and also by which data center egress connection attempts were made from.

- External nodes should be easy to identify, with the default direction for graph edges being internal to external.

- The analysts would like to be able to view at least a month's data at a time.

During your interaction with the analysts, you notice that when they are looking for malicious traffic, they often check IP address reputation using external resources. This gives you an idea to have your code perform this lookup ahead of time and color-code external nodes that are found in the AlienVault Reputation database. You want to also provide a way for analysts to quickly check all external nodes against other external resources. With the problem domain fairly well defined, you set off to create the tool.

You decide to use Vega for the visualization components and the jQuery (http://jquery.com/) and Opentip (http://www.opentip.org/) JavaScript libraries to add the interactive layer to the core, static Vega visualizations. "Interaction" is just a fancy way of saying "listening and responding to mouse and keyboard events," something that browser-based JavaScript is very good at. By targeting the browser environment, you can take advantage of all the other open web development resources to help simplify and accelerate the development process. You can also work directly with these events in low-level D3 code.

The result is an interactive "threat viewer" shown in Figure 11-14. The entirety of the code for this visualization is in the Chapter 11 download materials at www.wiley.com/go/datadriven security, with the main component of the visualization contained in the index.html file in the ch11/support/ch11-threat-view/ directory.

Rather than go line-by-line through the file, we'll highlight some of the core components that make up the interactive visualization. The following jQuery routine starts the whole visualization:

```
// The $(document).ready(…) pattern lets us excude a block of code
// once all of the HTML in the document has been read and parsed by
// the browser. This means we can rely on all the base objects being
// ready when we want to start our visualization display
$(document).ready(function() {
  // Opentip is a very flexible tooltip library that we'll use
```

```
// to pop-up details of individual nodes on demand
Opentip.defaultStyle = "dark" // dark-styled tooltips
// This tells Opentip to look for mouse events on the vis div
// element which can be found in the <body> of the HTML file
tip = new Opentip(document.getElementById("vis"));
tip.deactivate(); // hide tooltip for now
doParse("22"); // start visualization with port 22
});
```

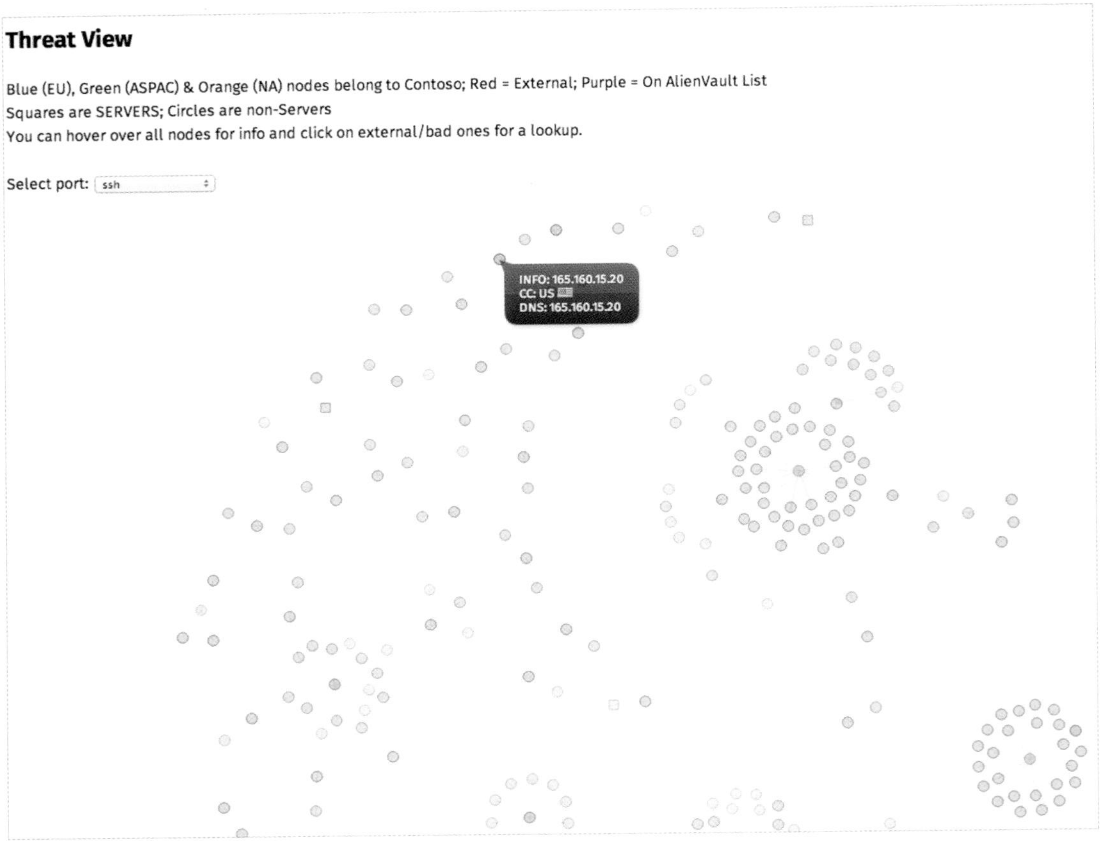

Threat View

Blue (EU), Green (ASPAC) & Orange (NA) nodes belong to Contoso; Red = External; Purple = On AlienVault List
Squares are SERVERS; Circles are non-Servers
You can hover over all nodes for info and click on external/bad ones for a lookup.

Select port: [ssh ⌄]

INFO: 165.160.15.20
CC: US
DNS: 165.160.15.20

FIGURE 11-14 *The "Threat View" interactive visualization*

Each "port" visualization has its own pair of files, one for the JSON visualization graph specification (##-vega.json) and one for the actual graph data (##-data.json). This naming convention makes it very straightforward to programmatically change the display—via doParse()—when the port popup registers a new selection.

```
<div>Select port: <select name="port" onchange="doParse(this.value)">
<option value="22">ssh</option>
<option value="23">telnet</option>
<option value="prt">Printers</option>
<option value="161">SNMP</option>
<option value="554">Streaming (554)</option>
<option value="7070">Streaming (7070)</option>
<option value="16464">Port 16464</option>
</select></div>
```

The doParse() routine does some minor error checking and then calls Vega's parse() function to do all the work:

```
function parse(spec) {

  // load the visualization specficication (spec) which,
  // in turn, loads the data file and lets us create the graph
  // and attach mouse events to the graphic
  vg.parse.spec(spec, function(chart) {

    // render the chart in the vis div and give us a handy
    // reference to it in the graph object
    graph = chart({el:"#vis"})
    graph.renderer("svg").update()

    // when the user mouses over one of the shapes,
    // build the tooltip on the fly and display it.
    // tooltips can contain any type of HTML formatting.
    // here we add whatever metadata we have, including
    // country flag if available.
    graph.on("mouseover", function(event, item) {
      if (item.shape == "circle" || item.shape == "square") {
        tip.setContent("<div>INFO: " + item.datum.info + " <br/>CC: " +
          item.datum.cc + " <img src=\"images/flags/png/" +
          item.datum.cc.toLowerCase() + ".png\"/><br/>DNS: " +
          item.datum.dns + " <br/></div>");
        tip.activate();
        tip._storeAndLockDimensions();
        tip.reposition();
        tip.show();
      } else {
        tip.deactivate();
        tip.hide();
      }
    })

    // turn off tooltips when the mouse moves out of an element
    graph.on("mouseout", function(event, item) {
```

```
      tip.hide();
      tip.deactivate();
    })

    // if the user clicks on an external node, look up the selected IP
    // address on the tcpiputils.com site
    graph.on("click", function(event, item) {
      a = item
      if ((item.datum.group == 4) || (item.datum.group == 5)) {
        window.open("http://www.tcpiputils.com/browse/ip-address/" +
          item.datum.name,"_blank")
      }
      graph.update("click", item);
    });
  });

}
```

There are many additions you could make to enhance this basic interactive tool, including:

- Sizing nodes based on the number of connections

- Incorporating other IP reputation resources

- Performing additional metadata queries on internal hosts that have suspicious activity and display-ing other layers of information

This should be a good starting point to help you explore both D3 and JavaScript further.

> **Note**
>
> You can find the complete working "threat-view" example on the book's website (www.wiley.com/go/datadrivensecurity) *and interact with it by starting the Python web server in the* ch11/support/ch11-threat-view/ *directory in the Chapter 11 download materials.*

Summary

Creating interactive dashboards and visualizations is a multi-disciplinary endeavor. You must understand both the problem domain and mental models of your consumers, know which goals—augmentation, exploration and illumination—must be accounted for in the finished product, and be certain that interaction is truly necessary for effective communication.

Avoid proprietary solutions whenever possible to ensure your creations can be viewed by the largest audience. Make note of characteristics in other visualizations that you find to be effective so you can duplicate their best parts in your own work.

Although there are ways of building useful interactive visuals without coding, you will need to learn the intricacies of modern web frameworks to build highly customized and tailored interactive tools. As you work to fine-tune your finished product, you should endeavor to create a regular feedback loop with those who will end up using your work. This will ensure that you are delivering the most effective tool possible with just the right amount of functionality to make it a success.

Recommended Reading

The following are some recommended readings that can further your understanding on some of the topics we touch on in this chapter. For full information on the book included in these recommendations and for any sources we mention in the chapter, please see Appendix B.

The Design of Everyday Things by Donald A. Norman—This book will change your perspective of everything around you and how you approach building things for others, whether it be a user interface or a static visualization. You will learn how to approach design in very practical ways and will come away with a much better perspective on how individuals work in and perceive the world.

Interactive Data Visualization for the Web by Scott Murray—If you endeavor to build D3-based interfaces, this is the seminal text on the subject. It is a very hands-on and extremely practical text. *The Functional Art* by Alberto Cairo—This book is ***beautiful***. You will learn the core elements of design and come away with a solid understanding of how to approach visualization projects of all scopes and sizes.

"VisAlert: From Idea to Product" by Stefano Foresti and James Agutter—This paper is one of the few domain-specific "soup to nuts" explanations of how to apply data science concepts to solve real world information security problems. It will teach you how to avoid designing in a vacuum and provide invaluable insight into the development process.

D3 Tips and Tricks: *Interactive Data Visualization in a Web Browser* by Malcolm Maclean—See `http://leanpub.com/D3-Tips-and-Tricks`. This book is one of the most comprehensive D3 reference and "cookbook" texts. With this book and Scott Murray's book, you will have at your fingertips almost everything you need to understand and implement D3-based visualizations.

12

Moving Toward Data-Driven Security

...y job was to find questions about baseball that have objective answers; that's all that I do; that's all that I've done."

—Bill James, sabermetrician

If you've been following along up to this point, you have covered a lot of ground, and you've hopefully realized that there is knowledge buried in the data. As you begin to move your security practice into a data-driven mindset, we suggest that you take a "panning for gold" approach instead of a "drilling for oil" stance—meaning that you shouldn't get bogged down with a single focus (or a single source of data) out of the gate. Instead, roll your pants up, step into the stream of data, and just explore and learn what you can about it. Once you understand what's in the data, you can start to ask (and answer) the interesting questions that will begin to make a difference.

This last chapter is dedicated to that difference. The first half is about moving yourself (or those you work with) toward a data-driven approach at a personal level. The second half is about moving your organization toward a data-driven security program.

Moving Yourself toward Data-Driven Security

Figure 12-1 is a slight modification of Drew Conway's "Data Science Venn Diagram" (`http://drewconway.com/zia/2013/3/26/the-data-science-venn-diagram`), which is a simple visualization that can help you quickly evaluate where you currently are on your journey toward data-driven security. This chapter looks at each major component, along with the interactions between some components. The idea is to help you identify areas that aren't currently your strengths. You don't have to be strong in all the major areas discussed here, but you want to be sure that weakness in any one area doesn't silently pull you off course.

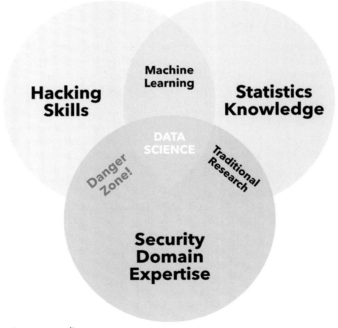

FIGURE 12-1 *The Data science venn diagram*

The Hacker

The term *hacker* has a great deal of confusion surrounding it, as it has been usurped by news media and manipulated by marketing firms. In the context of a security data scientist, we are updating the classic use of "hacker" to describe someone with a passion for using (and perhaps abusing) technology for a benevolent goal, including skills such as:

- Being able to command computers through code, either via scripting in a language like Python or full on programming in something like C

- Knowing a wide variety of data formats and understanding how to slice, dice, and bend them to your will

- Having the ability to think critically, logically, scientifically (essentially, not jumping to conclusions) as well as algorithmically (break apart a problem into its composite parts)

- Being able to communicate your work through visualizations, charts, tables, or even a good old-fashioned collection of words

The Coder

If you are an information security professional who isn't a coder, Chapters 2, 3, and 4 have been designed to help you bootstrap into that skill. If you are a coder, those same chapters cover a language that is most likely new to you (R) and place coding in the context of data analysis versus application building or systems administration, which may be more familiar problem domains for you. Whether you're at the top of your game as a programmer or just getting started, there is always more to learn. There is no shortage of resources available, including:

- **Codecademy** (`http://www.codecademy.com/`)—This is an especially good resource for those new to programming in general or those unfamiliar with a particular language. It's worthwhile to take a look at the JavaScript and jQuery offerings given the emphasis on JSON in Chapter 8 and D3.js in Chapter 11. If you don't know Python well (or at all), their Python course can definitely help.

- **Code School** (`https://www.codeschool.com/courses`)—The offerings at Code School can be a bit overwhelming and not all are free. However, their R course is freely available at the time of this writing and will help you navigate the syntax and nuances of the language.

- **W3Schools** (`http://www.w3schools.com/`)—If you haven't had the opportunity to shore up your HTML/CSS/JavaScript skills, W3Schools provides an extremely friendly environment to learn and experiment. You'll need at least a basic understanding of these client-side components if you want your analyses and results to reach the widest audience.

- **StackExchange** (`http://stackexchange.com/`)—Although you won't necessarily learn how to code at the StackExchange family of websites, you will have a place to look for answers or ask questions when you're stumped. Whether it's trying to understand some esoteric option in `ggplot2` or doing something a bit more complex with a pandas data frame, there's a very good chance the answer will be in StackExchange.

The Data Munger

When it comes to data formats, security professionals are in the unenviable position of having to be able to manipulate everything from NetFlow captures, to full packet capture (PCAP) dumps, and almost every log format known to humankind. The IronPort log file snippet in the "MongoDB" section of Chapter 8 is an example of how "imperfect" your data world is. Although that log file contains highly useful data, it's in a format that you must parse and convert to make useful. The only way to get good at that is to do it over and over again, building up reusable bits of code and techniques along the way to save time later.

> ### Note
>
> *We can tell you from experience, while data analysis is absolutely about the analysis, that's not where you will spend most of your time. Most of your time will be spent transforming, cleaning, and preparing data. That task is at its core a combination of the previous section on coding and the next section on thinking, as both of those skills will be used to extract the useful data and prepare it for analysis. Though the skills of security domain expertise and statistics will also help to identify what you want to keep and how you want to clean it to be helpful in the analysis. For a list of helpful tools for this task, see Appendix A, the section on "Data Cleansing."*

The Thinker

Learning how to think critically, logically, scientifically, and algorithmically requires time, effort, and practice. Formal, in-person, instructor-led education may work best for some students, especially those who have shied away from programming. However, introductory sites like Project Euler (`http://projecteuler.net/problems`) can get you started down this path; more advanced and diverse problem sets can be found at Kaggle (`http://www.kaggle.com/competitions`); and you can delve into wide and deep security domain problems at the VAST Challenge (`http://vacommunity.org/VAST+Challenge+2013`) site (look in both the current and previous years' sections).

These resources will supply data in various states. One of the criticisms of competitions like Kaggle though, is that they offer the data in a ready-to-be-analyzed format. As we mentioned in the last section, this is very much unlike the real world and so just focusing on things like the Kaggle competitions may give you a skewed perspective of the real world. As a stark contrast, the VAST Challenge has constructed real-world logs and device outputs that must be cleaned and prepared prior to analysis, thus giving you a better idea of what real-world data is like.

The Visualizer

The skill to communicate to outsiders was never part of the original use of the term *hacker*, though it certainly is evolving into that. It's not enough to make the technology bend to your will and make a discovery. You must also be able to communicate that in a language that the audience can not only understand, but also relate to and appreciate. While this skill may mostly be about data visualization skill (and all of Chapter 6), that shouldn't be the only tool in your toolbox. Realizing when to scrap those glossy color pictures and produce a simple table or even just describe the results in an email or in person is more valuable sometimes than the data visualization skill itself. Many resources are freely available and doing a quick search over the Internet will lead you to far more resources than we can list here. However, here are a few to get you started:

- **Flowing Data** (`http://flowingdata.com`)—Not only does the maintainer Nathan Yau provide some incredibly inspirational data visualizations, but he will also include a few comments and insights into the data. Having written two books on the subject of data visualization, Yau knows good data visualizations!

- **Junk Charts** (`http://junkcharts.typepad.com`)—Because sometimes knowing how *not* to create a visualization is more helpful than knowing how to create one.

- **Storytelling with Data** (`http://www.storytellingwithdata.com`)—One of the great things about this site is that Cole Nussbaumer has a very pragmatic approach to visualizations and will talk about visualization makeover and the processes used so almost anyone can follow along and learn.

There are other sites that aggregate visualizations and are good to keep an eye on such as `http://visualizing.org`, `http://visual.ly`, or `http://eagereyes.org`, and there are plenty of other tools and resources in Appendix A.

Overarching these traits is the need to develop and hone a sense of curiosity. In fact, curiosity may be the single most important trait of a *hacker*. The need to know why or how something works the way it does from start to finish is an invaluable driving force when faced with a complex data science problem. When combined with the other main security data science skills (statistics knowledge and security domain expertise), you'll eventually get to a place where developing a successful NetFlow-based malware traffic clustering algorithm is as rewarding as beating the other team in a capture-the-flag competition.

Developing Developer Skills

Although the resources in this section can help you pick up the skills necessary to write code, there are skills *around* writing code that come in handy as a code warrior. Two of the not-so-secret skills you should develop are unit testing and source code control.

- Becoming comfortable with writing and executing unit tests tightens up not just your code, but how you think about your code. Yes—you are a brilliant person with amazing skills—but you will still make mistakes and logic errors in your code despite that fact. Unit testing helps you catch those inevitable oversights that creep into your code.

- Along the same lines, source code control helps track multiple developers' code efforts, and enables more advanced features such as version control and code branching. More than that, source code repositories also help you avoid that awful question, "Now where did we put that source code?"

The Statistician

Given some of the "rookie mistakes" seen in many security industry reports and the prevalence of raw counts in security dashboards, there's a high probability that statistics is the weakest area for information security professionals. You learned about some statistical concepts in depth and read a whirlwind overview of others in Chapters 4, 5, 7, and 9. Okay, you don't need a PhD in statistics to be an effective security data scientist. However, it's important to have an understanding of the fundamentals of statistical analysis and machine learning, even when you're part of a multidisciplinary team.

Although you can head over to your local college or university and dive into a traditional classroom program, there are two other options to consider when you want a better understanding of statistics:

- Massively Open Online Courses (MOOCs) like Coursera's Introduction to Data Science course (`https://www.coursera.org/course/datasci`), edX's Learning From Data course (`https://www.edx.org/course/caltechx/cs1156x/learning-data/1120`), and Syracuse University's Data Science Open Online course (`http://ischool.syr.edu/future/cas/introtodatasciencemooc.aspx`) provide a low-risk way to plug into a formal statistics curriculum, but aren't right for everyone. Lectures, handouts, and assignments are available at your convenience (within a course's overall schedule), and discussion forums provide a way to interact with professors, teaching assistants, and fellow students. It can be bit overwhelming or even distracting to be in a setting with 2,000 to 4,000 individuals. Individual attention can also be difficult to obtain if you're struggling. Employers and professional organizations may also not yet accept the certifications from MOOCs, making the time investment more for personal benefit than professional credential gains.

- Online certificate or master's courses such as UC Berkeley's MIDS program (`http://www.ischool.berkeley.edu/programs/mids`), University of Washington's certificate in data science (`http://www.pce.uw.edu/certificates/data-science.html`), and Penn State's Applied Statistics online curriculum (`http://www.worldcampus.psu.edu/degrees-and-certificates/applied-statistics-certificate/overview`) offer the structure and size of a traditional classroom with the convenience being online.

Understanding and applying statistics correctly is more complex than you might imagine, and individuals in disciplines with a rich history of using statistics to solve complex problems oftentimes fall into common traps. Resources such as Alex Reinhart's Statistics Done Wrong (`http://www.refsmmat.com/statistics/`) and DZone's misnamed "Big Data" Machine Learning reference (`http://refcardz.dzone.com/refcardz/machine-learning-predictive`) are good to have on hand to keep your analyses on track.

The Security Domain Expert

When focusing on the topic of security domain expertise as it relates to data science, "thought leaders," "gurus," and "rock stars" need not apply. What I'm talking about here are practitioners with solid, in the trenches, real-world experience. Depending on your area of focus (information security covers a broad range of topics), you may be applying your combined hacking skills, statistics knowledge, and expertise to:

- Develop smarter endpoint-protection system algorithms.

- Discover new ways to detect anomalous behavior in network data.

- Uncover patterns from vulnerability assessments to help determine why some systems fall out of compliance more than others.

- Provide meaningful and useful metrics for various components of your overall security program.

Or a host of other areas.

Your insight is, perhaps, the most valuable component to this data science triad, as it will move computations sans context into the realm of analyses driving action. There is virtually no way for an organization or individual to effectively crunch "security data" without this domain expertise. Your assistance and knowledge is vital in crafting clever questions and confirming results. Your insight into the networks and systems of your organization, the behaviors and characteristics of malware, and the classification and qualification incidents is the critical factor in corresponding analyses.

The Danger Zone

A little knowledge is a dangerous thing, and having the basic ability to gather and programmatically crunch data, along with a bit of industry knowledge is tricky. Don't fall into the trap of thinking you're doing data science when all you're doing is reputational damage to all three component areas (and, potentially, yourself). How do you steer clear of the danger zone? Try these approaches:

- **Embrace (versus dabble in) statistics**. Statistics and machine learning have enabled advancements in everything from a deeper understanding of the microscopic workings of human genes, to telling you how many steps and flights of stairs you've taken, to building spacecraft that eventually break past the limits of the solar system. They can absolutely help enhance your knowledge of security issues and even help solve some of them. Just don't think you can dip your toe in. Not everyone can become a genius with statistics, but make sure your team (physical or virtual) has at least one strong stats person.

- **Dig deep, but stay wide.** You need to know certain aspects of information security just as thoroughly as individual biologists know the deep vertical segments of their discipline. But, because so many areas outside security (for example, economics, politics, and human rights) have an impact on security, you'll need to factor those in as you move from asking what and how, to why and who. Finally, there's a reason the CISSP certification has 10 domains. You can't be an expert in each, but you should know enough about each of them to bring in expert help when needed.

- **Challenge assumptions and validate results.** Keep an open mind, because data has a way of changing your mind for you. Hold yourself and ask others to hold you accountable all the way through your analyses. Whether you're working on internal organizational data or performing research you intend to publish and/or speak about, pair up with practitioners who can help you keep on the straight and narrow path. When you've released your findings, take an example from the reproducible research movement (`http://www.foastat.org/resources.html`) and ensure there is sufficient documentation and data available for others to test your findings.

Moving Your Organization toward Data-Driven Security

By now you realize that becoming data-driven doesn't just mean firing up R or Python and tossing in the data. Becoming data-driven is an evolutionary process that will slowly shift how you and those in your organization view the world. The value will not be immediate. Instead, the value will develop over time with punctuated flashes of brilliance. The components of a good data-driven program within any organization have some combination of the following:

- Ask questions that have objective answers.
- Find and collect relevant data.
- Learn through iteration.
- Find statistics (again).

The most difficult part of the transformation is getting started because the first two components present a chicken and egg problem. You want to ask questions that you have data for, yet you only want to gather data that answer your questions. But don't worry; through iteration, you can build up both.

Ask Questions That Have Objective Answers

The opening quote in this chapter was from sabermetrician Bill James. You may know him and his work portrayed in the book *Moneyball* by Michael Lewis. He challenged much of the conventional wisdom within baseball by leveraging data. Recall that he said, "My job was to find questions about baseball that have objective answers, that's all that I do, that's all that I've done." His focus was not on simply exploring and describing the data that is available, nor did he focus on creating colorful visualizations from the data. His focus was on finding good questions that have answers in the data.

Chapter 1 discussed creating a good question. Remember that a good question has two qualities—it can be objectively answered with data, and somebody wants to know the answer. Although Bill James could have asked about the effect of stealing bases on player sponsorships, nobody (except maybe the players stealing bases) wanted to know that. He focused on relationships with runs scored or players on base because those are the questions people wanted answered. The same is true in your work. Although you can count blocked spam or create maps covered with botnet infections, if it's not answering a practical question that someone wants answered, it might be a waste of time.

Knowing that someone cares about the answer can also help shape the question and make the analysis easier. Remember back in Chapter 1, we changed the question from asking how much spam was blocked to asking how much time employees spent dealing with unblocked spam. If, for example, you identified that nothing would change if employees spent less than an hour a week on unfiltered spam, the question then becomes "do employees spend more than an hour a week dealing with spam?" With that threshold in mind, you should be able to simplify the analysis. Rather than calculating how much time, you just need to know if it's over an hour a week. Context and purpose of the question can only clarify the work you do.

Find and Collect Relevant Data

As mentioned at the beginning of this section, data collection and asking good questions have a natural interdependency. The questions you ask depend on having data to answer them, yet you don't want to collect data you'll never use. Which comes first? Just from being in your environment you should have some concept of available data—proxy and firewall logs, server authentication logs, and even data within the company ticketing system are all good candidates to start. Start there and form a few practical questions that data can answer. As you get the data to answer your questions, you may need to refine your questions and then learn more about the data and refine again.

Be prepared to work with others on getting data. Chances are very good you won't be the custodian of all of the data you'll want. This is why having executive sponsorship is important. If you're a practitioner, seek executive sponsorship. If you're in executive leadership, make data sharing happen internally. This will have very limited success as a grassroots effort. You need to involve others and probably even reach out across corporate silos in order to get data. You will undoubtedly encounter several objections in some combination of real and imaginary. Keep your eye on the goal, though; the effort will pay off in the long run.

Information Sharing Takes a Lot More Than Information

There is a subtle push across the information security industry that we should all be sharing data, which is a good thing. The initial objection (and a big objection you may run into internally) is a lack of trust and/or a concern about the privacy and confidentiality of the data being shared, even internally within an organization. This is a valid concern and it's something that you have to address. But that's actually the easy part of information sharing. Sharing information often turns out to be a much larger effort than people imagine. There is an eye-opening moment when the people sharing the information realize that they have underestimated the amount of time and energy it takes to prepare and share data. There may be some fields that do not or should not be shared and those must be removed. Then there is a validation step to ensure they are sharing only what they intend to share. Finally, storage and transfer of the data may present a challenge in logistics, as the data may be too large to simply email or even to set up for downloading. The best course is to be open about these challenges and communicate the reality to potential partners. The silver lining is that the amount of learning you can do when you share data often more than makes up for the effort to share it.

Learn through Iteration

When you're building a data-driven security program, you won't follow a typical waterfall project plan where the tasks are defined up front and executed one after another. It's a much more iterative process like the one shown in Figure 12-2, and the path from question to resolution can easily turn into a twisty maze. Each source of data offers its own challenges and opportunities. Iteration becomes the name of the game, and setbacks and challenges become just as much a part of the project as success. But do not get discouraged; the setbacks will occur less and less frequently, and each one is a learning opportunity.

One of the big lessons you will undoubtedly learn early on is the importance of data quality and the benefit of building in repeatability. It won't take long before you pull a data extract and realize a date variable was corrupted, a field was clipped, or some other act of nature requires that the whole process be repeated. So not only will the extract, transformation, and loading tools need to be automated, data validation processes should be introduced often. You'll want to realize that the integrity of the data was compromised long before you're generating the final report.

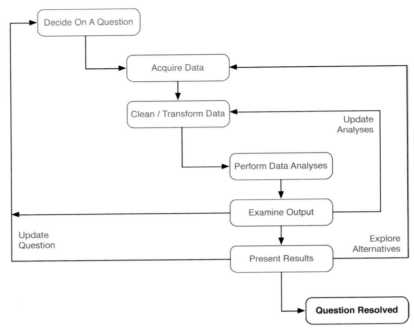

FIGURE 12-2 *The data science workflow*

Finally, with the iteration and constant discovery that comes from working with data, you will be forced to check your ego at the door. There is very little room for estimations and guesswork. If things go well, you'll have this lesson forced upon you over and over. Once the data has proven you wrong a few times, you'll realize that the data works without motive or agenda and may produce unpopular results. Assumptions should be replaced by questions and data analysis. When things start to come together, you'll be impressed about the types of questions you can answer.

Find Statistics

We debated on putting this at the top of the list, but hopefully we've pounded this point home by now. Proceeding down a data-driven path may head right into the danger zone we talked about in the previous section without some element of statistics involved. The entire point of moving to a data-driven security program is to learn from data. The wide field of statistics (encompassing classic, data mining, and machine learning) has already learned how to learn from data. Not taking advantage of all that history may doom you to repeat the failures others have already overcome.

There are two options here: Hire someone with a background in statistics or start enhancing current employees (or yourself!) with training and education we mentioned in the first part of this chapter.

Unfortunately, candidates with both good domain expertise and good statistics experience are few and far between. So hiring externally may mean bringing in someone with less experience with information security, which is fine if you are prepared for it. On the other hand, becoming a professional statistician isn't possible through a simple weeklong training session. If you are seeking educational programs in statistics, keep in mind the two cultures Leo Breiman wrote about. Some universities focus on the classic statistics with less (or no) focus on programming and data management, whereas others focus heavily on programming at the expense of teaching a strong foundation in classical statistics.

Building a Real-Life Security Data Science Team

When Bob had his internal team start their move into security data science, it was difficult to resist the urge to spin up a giant, shiny Hadoop cluster and start importing every log from every system into a massive data store. In truth, his team did start down the Hadoop path and found it fraught with peril (and screens full of warning messages).

Rather than focus on the technology, they stopped and focused on defining what single question they would like answered if they had the data. Not five. Not three. One. That single question was "Have we seen this IP before?" That question set them up for a clear goal: Given an IP address (or IP/Port combination), search across **all** our perimeter devices in less than five minutes. For most organizations—including Bob's—the total volume of such data would fit well within the category of "medium-sized" (that is, not "big") data.

His team focused on using traditional SQL (MariaDB), NoSQL (MongoDB & Redis), R, Python, and JavaScript. For 6 long months, they iterated through tasks, adjusting as they learned, trying different ways to acquire, clean, and store data (they call that *data curating*); structure schemas; and formulate queries. Along the way, they suffered setbacks when log file formats changed without warning, when data access issues cropped up, and when the absolute need for referential metadata reared its ugly head.

Three core principles focused the team.

- First, explore the open source versions of tools before engaging vendors. If you don't know how the sausage is being made, you really have no idea what's being done, and this is vital when working with real data.

- Second, follow the mantra of "no single tool; no single database; and, no single approach to solving a problem." Do not put blinders on because you are either comfortable with certain technologies or have an affinity for a certain tool.

- Third, failure is expected, but you must learn from each journey down the wrong path. Continuous adaptation and adjustment is the name of the game.

Ultimately, Bob's team met the 5-minute challenge and is moving on to other questions. Your team—and it is a team effort—will also be successful if they start with a question, are iterative and methodical in their approach, and never stop learning from their mistakes.

Summary

You have learned a lot through the pages of this book, and you should realize that you don't have to do all of this right out of the gate. Through the mixture of hacking skills, domain expertise, and statistics, you can move toward a data-driven lifestyle. Combine that with the art of asking the right questions and getting the data to answer those questions, and you'll start to move your organization toward a data-driven security program. You don't have to implement everything right away to see value. An iterative approach should provide more value over time and help you adapt to the inevitable challenges that arise. Start slow, try everything, try everything again, and let us know how you're doing.

Recommended Reading

The following are some recommended readings that can further your understanding on some of the topics we touch on in this chapter. For full information on these recommendations and for the sources we cite in the chapter, please see Appendix B.

"The Data Science Venn Diagram" by Drew Conway (`http://drewconway.com/zia/2013/3/26/the-data-science-venn-diagram`)—We discussed this in the chapter but it's worth reading the original post.

Building Data Science Teams **by D. J. Patil**—This book was written by folks who have real-world experience recruiting, managing, and retaining data science teams. They include a special section specifically on fraud, abuse, risk, and security teams and also cover topics on tooling, hiring, and team/department organization. It's definitely a "must-read" for those who are looking to delve into data science.

A

Resources and Tools

Though we've provided contextual links and resources throughout the book, there were a few that didn't fit properly in the chapters, but are still important go-to resources and part of our daily workflows. We've compiled them—along with a "best of the best" of links from selected chapters—into an organized and annotated list for quick reference.

Data Cleansing

- *OpenRefine* (`http://openrefine.org/`)—An open source, locally installed, cross-platform toolkit that makes it extremely easy to import, explore, clean, transform, and enrich messy data into something usable for analysis.

- *DataWrangler* (`http://vis.stanford.edu/wrangler/`)—A browser-based, JavaScript tool created by Stanford University's Visualization Group that lets you explore and transform small data sets in-browser, and then export a custom Python or JavaScript source file, suitable for running locally on both small and large data sets.

- *WebPlotDigitizer* (`http://arohatgi.info/WebPlotDigitizer/app/`)—This online tool makes it possible to quickly "reverse engineer" charts and graphs that have no associated open data files.

- *Google CRUSH Tools* (`https://code.google.com/p/crush-tools/`)—A command-line processing engine and data transformation tool that makes it possible to work efficiently with large data sets from a shell prompt.

- *csvkit* (`https://github.com/onyxfish/csvkit`)—A suite of open source Python utilities that are similar to the *CRUSH* tools, but usable from both the command line and from within Python scripts.

- *DataCleaner* (`http://datacleaner.org/`)—This product is similar to OpenRefine, but with both commercial and open source offerings.

- *Mr. Data Converter* (`http://shancarter.github.io/mr-data-converter/`)—In-browser and locally installable open source tool created by Shan Carter to improve data cleansing workflows at **The New York Times**.

- *Miso Dataset* (`http://misoproject.com/dataset/`)—Client-side JavaScript data transformation and management library.

- *Your favorite scripting language*—Never underestimate the power of a Python, R, Perl, or awk script when it comes to cleaning data. You'll have to do more up-front work, but you may be able to build a far more reusable and customized cleanup and transformation workflow with your own tools.

Data Analytics and Visualization: Core Tools

- **R** (`http://www.r-project.org/`) + **RStudio** (`http://www.rstudio.com/`)—*The* language of data science. Commercial offering available via *Revolution Analytics* (`http://www.revolutionanalytics.com/`).

- **Python** (`http://www.python.org/`) + **pandas** (`http://pandas.pydata.org/`)—The *other* language of data science. Additional open source and commercial offerings available via *Enthought* Canopy (`https://www.enthought.com/products/canopy/`) and *Continuum Analytics Anaconda* (`http://docs.continuum.io/anaconda/install.html`).

- *Tableau* (`http://www.tableausoftware.com/`)—Commercial tool with an emphasis on producing interactive dashboards and visualizations.

Data Analytics and Visualization: JavaScript Tools

- *D3.js* (`http://d3js.org/`)—Enables the creation of "data-driven documents" and provides templates and examples for creating almost every type of modern static and interactive visualization.

- *JavaScript InfoVis Toolkit* (`http://philogb.github.io/jit/`)—Similar to D3, but may be more accessible to those new to JavaScript.

- *Highcharts JS* (`http://www.highcharts.com/`)—Provides robust charting and graphing functions, especially well-suited for dashboards.

Data Analytics and Visualization: Mapping Tools

- *OpenHeatMap* (`http://www.openheatmap.com/`)—Produce high-quality heatmaps from CSV data right in your browser. No coding required.

- *Leaflet* (`http://leafletjs.com/`)—A very robust and mobile-friendly JavaScript mapping library.

Data Analytics and Visualization: Specialized Tools

- *TimeFlow* (`https://github.com/FlowingMedia/TimeFlow/wiki`)—An open source tool specifically designed for analysis and visualization of temporal/time series data.

- *Gephi* (`https://gephi.org/`)—Open source network graph analysis and visualization tool.

- *Quadrigram* (`http://www.quadrigram.com/`)—Provides a visual programming interface for working with data and designing highly customized, interactive visualizations.

Aggregation Sites, Q&A Sites, and Blogs to Follow

- *R-Bloggers* (`http://www.r-bloggers.com/`)—Rather than follow a plethora of individual blogs, you can follow the R-Bloggers RSS feed to see only R-related posts that deal with all aspects of data analysis and visualization.

- *Stats Blogs* (`http://www.statsblogs.com/`)—An aggregation of sites, similar to R-Bloggers, but with a focus on statistics.

- *StackExchange* (`http://stackexchange.com/`)—The perfect place to go if you have R, Python, or pandas questions, can't remember a `ggplot` option, or need some help with a gnarly statistics problem.

- *Junk Charts* (`http://junkcharts.typepad.com/`)—Learn from the visualization mistakes of others.

- *FlowingData* (`http://flowingdata.com/`)—Resources, news, and tutorials that will improve the way you think and design visualizations.

- *DataVisualization.ch* (`http://selection.datavisualization.ch/`)—Aggregation and index of the most popular and useful visualization tools currently available.

- *Data Analysis* & *Visualization Bit.ly Bundle* (`http://bitly.com/bundles/hrbrm-str/1`)—An aggregation of links maintained by us, the authors of this book, along with David Severski.

Color

- *ColorBrewer* (`http://colorbrewer2.org/`)—Designed by Cynthia Brewer, this is *the* color resource that should be the first tool you head for when designing visualizations. It provides a wide range of palettes with options for creating print-safe and colorblind-friendly images.

- *HCL Picker* (`http://tristen.ca/hcl-picker/`)—An open source, D3-based color picker that lets you select colors based on hue, chroma, and lightness.

- *Adobe Kuler* (`https://kuler.adobe.com/`)—An online tool provided by Adobe that allows you to design compelling color palettes or choose from a wide assortment of pre-made palettes.

- *OS X Color Picker Palettes* (`https://github.com/sathomas/colors`)—Use *ColorBrewer* palettes in Excel, Photoshop, and any other application on your Mac.

B

References

Chapter 1

Barnard, G. A. 1990. "Fisher: A Retrospective." *Chance: New Directions For Statistics and Computing* 3(1): 22-28.

Bingham, P., N. Q. Verlander, and M. J. Cheal. 2004. "John Snow, William Farr and the 1849 Outbreak of Cholera that Affected London: a Reworking of the Data Highlights the Importance of the Water Supply." *Public Health* 118(6): 387-394.

Box, Joan Fisher. 1987. "Guinness, Gosset, Fisher, and Small Samples." *Statistical Science* 2(1): 45-52.

Breiman, Leo. 2001. "Statistical Modeling: The Two Cultures (with Comments and a Rejoinder by the Author)." *Statistical Science* 16(3): 199-231.

Cook, Richard. I. 1998. "How Complex Systems Fail." Cognitive Technologies Laboratory, University of Chicago. Chicago, IL.

Farr, W. 1852. "Report on the Mortality from Cholera in England, 1848–1849." London: HMSO. (Also published as Farr, W. 1852. "Registrar General's Report on Cholera in England 1849–1850." London: W. Clowes & Son.)

Fisher, Ronald A. 1925. "The Influence of Rainfall on the Yield of Wheat at Rothamsted." *Philosophical Transactions of the Royal Society of London. Series B, Containing Papers of a Biological Character* 213: 89-142.

General Board of Health (UK). 1855. "Report of the Committee for Scientific Inquiries in Relation to the Cholera-Epidemic of 1854." London: HMSO.

Hubbard, Douglas W. 2010. *How to Measure Anything: Finding the Value of Intangibles in Business*. John Wiley & Sons, Inc.

Kahneman, Daniel, and Gary Klein. 2009. "Conditions for Intuitive Expertise: a Failure to Disagree." *American Psychologist* 64(6): 515.

Lipowski, Earlene E. 2008. "Developing Great Research Questions." *American Journal of Health-System Pharmacy* Vol 65(17): 1667-1670.

Morris, Robert, and Ken Thompson. 1979. "Password Security: A Case History." *Communications of the ACM* 22(11): 594-597.

"Report of JPMorgan Chase & Co. Management Task Force Regarding 2012 CIO Losses." 2013. Retrieved from `http://files.shareholder.com/downloads/ONE/2532388207x0x628656/4cb574a0-0bf5-4728-9582-625e4519b5ab/Task_Force_Report.pdf`

Tukey, John W. 1962. "The Future of Data Analysis." *The Annals of Mathematical Statistics* 33(1): 1-67. Retrieved from `http://projecteuclid.org/DPubS?service=UI&version=1.0&verb=Display&handle=euclid.aoms/1177704711`

Tukey and the Prim-9 video. Available from `http://flowingdata.com/2008/01/01/john-tukey-and-the-beginning-of-interactive-graphics/`

Watts, Duncan. "The Myth of Common Sense: Why Everything that Seems Obvious Isn't." Speaking to the Santa Fe institute; viewed on 7/14/2013 from `http://www.youtube.com/watch?v=EF8tdXwa-AE`

Wheelan, Charles. 2013. *Naked Statistics: Stripping the Dread from the Data*. W.W. Norton & Co.

Chapter 2

Cotton, Richard. 2013. *Learning R*. O'Reilly Media, Inc.

Crawley, Michael J. 2012. *The R Book, Second Edition*. John Wiley & Sons, Inc.

Lutz, Mark. 2013. *Learning Python*. O'Reilly Media, Inc.

Shaw, Zed A. 2010. *Learn Python the Hard Way*. Retrieved from `http://learnpythonthehardway.org/`

Chapter 3

Cohen, Yosef, and Jeremiah Y. Cohen. 2008. *Statistics and Data with R: An Applied Approach Through Examples*. John Wiley & Sons, Inc.

McKinney, Wes. 2012. *Python for Data Analysis*. O'Reilly Media, Inc.

Chapter 4

Cook, Diane J., and Lawrence B. Holder, eds. 2006. *Mining Graph Data*. John Wiley & Sons, Inc.

Højsgaard, Søren, David Edwards, and Steffen Lauritzen. 2012. *Graphical Models with R*. Springer Media.

Chapter 5

Chang, Winston. *R Graphics Cookbook*. O'Reilly Media, Inc. 2012.

Goodman, Steven. 2008. "A Dirty Dozen: Twelve P-Value Misconceptions." *Seminars in Hematology* 45(3): 135-140.

Neter, John, William Wasserman, and Michael H. Kutner. 1996. *Applied Linear Statistical Models*. Vol. 4. Chicago. Irwin.

Wheelan, Charles. 2013. *Naked Statistics: Stripping the Dread from the Data*. W.W. Norton & Co.

Yau, Nathan. 2013. *Data Points: Visualization that Means Something*. John Wiley & Sons.

Chapter 6

Cairo, Alberto. 2012. *The Functional Art: An Introduction to Information Graphics and Visualization*. New Riders.

Card, Stuart K., and Jock D. Mackinlay. 1997. "The Structure of the Information Visualization Design Space." *Information Visualization*, 1997. Proceedings, IEEE Symposium on.

Cleveland, William S., and Robert McGill. 1984. "Graphical Perception: Theory, Experimentation, and Application to the Development of Graphical Methods." *Journal of the American Statistical Association* 79(387): 531-554.

Cleveland, William S., and Robert McGill. 1985. "Graphical Perception and Graphical Methods for Analyzing Scientific Data." *Science* 229(4716): 828-833.

Few, Stephen. 2004. *Show Me the Numbers: Designing Tables and Graphs to Enlighten*. Analytics Press.

Healey, Christopher G., Kellogg S. Booth, and James T. Enns. 1996. "High-Speed Visual Estimation Using Preattentive Processing." *ACM Transactions on Computer-Human Interaction (TOCHI)* 3(2): 107-135.

Kosara, Robert. "In Defense of Pie Charts." 2011. Retrieved 8/27/2013 from `http://eagereyes.org/criticism/in-defense-of-pie-charts`

Simkin, David, and Reid Hastie. 1987. "An Information-Processing Analysis of Graph Perception." *Journal of the American Statistical Association* 82(398): 454-465.

Stone, Maureen. 2006. "Choosing Colors for Data Visualization." *Business Intelligence Network*. Retrieved 9/2013 from `http://www.perceptualedge.com/articles/b-eye/choosing_colors.pdf`

Tufte, Edward R. 1990. *Envisioning Information*. Graphics Press.

Ware, Colin. 2013. *Information Visualization, Third Edition*. Morgan Kaufmann.

Yau, Nathan. 2013. *Data Points: Visualization that Means Something*. John Wiley & Sons.

Chapter 7

Open Security Foundation. "Data Loss DB." Available from `http://datalossdb.org`

Privacy Rights Clearinghouse. "Chronology of Data Breaches." Available from `http://www.privacyrights.org/data-breach`

Verizon RISK Team. "2013 Data Breach Investigations Report." Available from `http://www.verizonenterprise.com/DBIR`

Verizon RISK Team. "VERIS Community." Available from `http://veriscommunity.net`

Verizon RISK Team. "VERIS Community Database." Available from `https://github.com/vz-risk/VCDB`

Chapter 8

Codd, Edgar Frank. 1970. "A relational model of data for large shared data banks." **Communications of the ACM 13**(6): 377-387.

Harrington, Jan L. 2009. **Relational Database Design and Implementation**: **Clearly Explained**, **Third Edition**. Morgan Kaufmann.

Lublinsky, Boris, Kevin T. Smith, and Alexey Yakubovich. 2013. **Professional Hadoop Solutions**. John Wiley & Sons.

Tiwari, Shashank. 2011. **Professional NoSQL**. John Wiley & Sons.

Chapter 9

Bilge, Leyla, et al. 2012. "Disclosure: Detecting Botnet Command and Control Servers Through Large-Scale NetFlow Analysis." **Proceedings of the 28th Annual Computer Security Applications Conference**. ACM: 129-138.

Cherkassky, Vladimir, and Filip M. Mulier. 2007. **Learning from Data**: **Concepts**, **Theory**, **and Methods**. John Wiley & Sons.

Conway, Drew, and John Myles White. **Machine Learning for Hackers**. 2012. O'Reilly Media, Inc.

Emran, Syed Masum, and Nong Ye. 2001. "Robustness of Canberra Metric in Computer Intrusion Detection." **Proc. IEEE Workshop on Information Assurance and Security**. West Point, NY.

Genuer, Robin, Jean-Michel Poggi, and Christine Tuleau-Malot. 2010. "Variable Selection Using Random Forests." **Pattern Recognition Letters** 31(14-15): 2225-2236.

James, Gareth, et al. 2013. **An Introduction to Statistical Learning with Applications in R**. Springer.

Mitchell, Tom M. 1997. **Machine Learning**. McGraw-Hill.

Weston, Steven, and Rich Calaway. 2013. "Getting Started with doParallel and foreach." Retrieved 10/2013 from `http://cran.r-project.org/web/packages/doParallel/vignettes/gettingstartedParallel.pdf`

Chapter 10

Few, Stephen. 2013. **Information Dashboard Design**: **Displaying Data for At-a-Glance Monitoring**, **Second Edition**. Analytics Press. 2013.

Jaquith, Andrew. 2007. **Security Metrics**: **Replacing Fear**, **Uncertainty**, **and Doubt**. Addison-Wesley.

Index